HISTORY

OF

THE SABBATH

AND

FIRST DAY OF THE WEEK.

BY J. N. ANDREWS.

THIRD EDITION, REVISED

BATTLE CREEK, MICH.:
REVIEW & HERALD PUBLISHING ASSOCIATION.
OAKLAND, CAL.: PACIFIC PRESS.

1887.

2007   08   09   10   11   12   ·   5   4   3   2   1

Copyright © 1998 TEACH Services, Inc.
ISBN-13: 978-1-57258-107-4
ISBN-10: 1-57258-107-7
Library of Congress Control Number: 98-85408

Published by

TEACH Services, Inc.
www.TEACHServices.com

PREFACE.

THE history of the Sabbath embraces a period of 6,000 years. The seventh day is the Sabbath of the Lord. The acts which constituted it such were, first, the example of the Creator; secondly, his placing his blessing upon the day; and thirdly, the sanctification or divine appointment of the day to a holy use. The Sabbath, therefore, dates from the beginning of our world's history. The first who Sabbatized on the seventh day was God, the Creator; and the first seventh day of time was the day which he thus honored. The highest of all possible honors does, therefore, pertain to the seventh day. Nor is this honor confined to the first seventh day of time; for so soon as God had rested upon that day, he appointed the seventh day to a holy use, that man might hallow it in memory of his Creator.

This divine appointment grows out of the nature and fitness of things, and must have been made directly to Adam, for himself and wife were then the only beings who had the days of the week to use. As it was addressed to Adam while yet in his uprightness, it must have been given to him as the head of the human family. The fourth commandment bases all its authority upon this original mandate of the Creator, and must, therefore, be in substance what God commanded to Adam and Eve as the representatives of mankind.

The patriarchs could not possibly have been ignorant of the facts and the obligation which the fourth commandment shows to have originated in the beginning, for Adam was present with them for a period equal to nearly half the Christian dispensation. Those, therefore, who walked with God in the observance of his commandments, did certainly hallow his Sabbath.

The observers of the seventh day must therefore include the ancient godly patriarchs, and none will deny that they include also the prophets and the apostles. Indeed, the entire church of God embraced within the records of inspiration were

Sabbath-keepers. To this number must be added the Son of God.

What a history, therefore, has the Sabbath of the Lord! It was instituted in Paradise, honored by several miracles each week for the space of forty years, proclaimed by the great Lawgiver from Sinai, observed by the Creator, the patriarchs, the prophets, the apostles, and the Son of God! It constitutes the very heart of the law of God, and so long as that law endures, so long shall the authority of this sacred institution stand fast.

Such being the record of the seventh day, it may well be asked, How came it to pass that this day has been abased to the dust, and another day elevated to its sacred honors ? The Scriptures nowhere attribute this work to the Son of God. They do, however, predict the great apostasy in the Christian church, and that the little horn, or man of sin, the lawless one, should think to change times and laws.

It is the object of the present volume to show, 1. The Bible record of the Sabbath ; 2. The record of the Sabbath in secular history ; 3. The record of the Sunday festival, and of the several steps by which it has usurped the place of the ancient Sabbath.

The writer has attempted to ascertain the exact truth in the case by consulting the original authorities as far as it has been possible to gain access to them. The margin will show to whom he is mainly indebted for the facts presented in this work, though it indicates only a very small part of the works consulted. He has given the exact words of the historians, and has endeavored conscientiously to present them in such a light as to do justice to the authors quoted.

It is not the fault of the writer that the history of the Sunday festival presents such an array of frauds and of iniquities in its support. These are, in the nature of the case, essential to its very existence, for the claim of a usurper is necessarily based in fraud. The responsibility for these rests with those who dare commit or uphold such acts. The ancient Sabbath of the Lord has never needed help of this kind, and never has its record been stained by fraud or falsehood.

J. N. A.

Battle Creek, Mich., *Nov. 14, 1873.*

CONTENTS.

PART I — BIBLE HISTORY.

CHAPTER XV.

CHAPTER XVI.

CHAPTER XVII.

CHAPTER XVIII.

CHAPTER XIX.

CHAPTER XX.

CHAPTER XXI.

CHAPTER XXII.

CHAPTER XXIII.

CHAPTER XXIV.

CHAPTER XXV.

CHAPTER XXVI.

CHAPTER XXVII.

HISTORY OF THE SABBATH.

PART I—BIBLE HISTORY.

CHAPTER I.

IN THE BEGINNING—THE CREATION.

Time and eternity—The Creator and his work—Events of the first day
of time—Of the second—Of the third—Of the fourth—Of the fifth—
Of the sixth.

IME, as distinguished from eternity, may be
defined as that part of duration which is
measured by the Bible. From the earliest
date in the book of Genesis to the resurrection of the
unjust at the end of the millennium, a period of about
7000 years is measured off.[1] Before the commencement
of this great week of time, duration without beginning
fills the past; and at the expiration of this period, un-
ending duration opens before the people of God. Eternity is that word which embraces duration without beginning and without end; and that Being whose existence comprehends eternity is he who only hath immor-

---

[1] For the scriptural and traditional evidence on this point, see Shimeall's Bible
Chronology, part 1, chap. 6 ; Taylor's Voice of the Church, pp. 25-30 ; and Bliss's
Sacred Chronology, pp. 199-203.

tality, the King eternal, immortal, invisible, the only wise God.[2]

When it pleased this infinite Being, he gave existence to our earth. Out of nothing, God created all things;[3] "so that things which are seen were not made of things which do appear." This act of creation is that event which marks the commencement of the first week of time. He who could accomplish the whole work with one word chose rather to employ six days, and to

---

[2] Isa. 57: 15; 1 Sam. 15: 29, margin; Jer. 10: 10, margin; Micah 5: 2, margin; 1 Tim. 6: 16; 1: 17; Ps. 90: 2.

[3] Dr. Adam Clarke, in his Commentary on Gen. 1: 1, uses the following language: "Created] Caused that to exist which previously to this moment had no being. The rabbins, who are legitimate judges in a case of verbal criticism on their own language, are unanimous in asserting that the word *bara* expresses the commencement of the existence of a thing, or its egression from nonentity to entity. . . . These words snould be translated, 'God in the beginning created the *substance* of the heavens and the *substance* of the earth; *i. e.*, the *prima materia*, or first elements, out of which the heavens and the earth were successively formed.'"

Purchase's Pilgrimage, b. 1, chap. 2, speaks thus of the creation: "Nothing but nothing had the Lord Almighty, whereof, wherewith, whereby, to build this city" [that is, the world].

Dr. Gill says: "These are said to be *created*, that is, to be made out of nothing; for what pre-existent matter to this chaos [of verse 2] could there be out of which they could be formed?"

"Creation must be the work of God; for none but an almighty power could produce something out of nothing."—*Commentary on Gen. 1: 1.*

John Calvin, in his Commentary on this chapter, thus expounds the creative act: "His meaning is, that the world was made out of nothing. Hence the folly of those is refuted who imagine that unformed matter existed from eternity."

The work of creation is thus defined in 2 Maccabees 7: 28: "Look upon the heaven and the earth, and all that is therein, and consider that God made them of things that were not; and so was mankind made likewise."

That this creative act marked the commencement of the first day instead of preceding it by almost infinite ages, is thus stated in 2 Esdras 6: 38: "And I said, O Lord, thou spakest from the beginning of the creation, even the first day, and saidst thus: Let heaven and earth be made; and thy word was a perfect work."

Wycliffe's translation, the earliest of the English versions, renders Gen. 1: 1 thus: "In the first, made God of naught heaven and earth."

accomplish the result by successive steps. Let us trace the footsteps of the Creator from the time when he laid the foundation of the earth until the close of the sixth day, when the heavens and the earth were finished, "and God saw everything that he had made, and, behold, it was very good." [4]

On the first day of time, God created the heaven and the earth. The earth thus called into existence was without form, and void; and total darkness covered the Creator's work. Then "God said, Let there be light; and there was light." "And God divided the light from the darkness," and called the one day and the other night. [5]

On the second day of time, "God said, Let there be a firmament [margin, Heb., expansion] in the midst of the waters, and let it divide the waters from the waters." The dry land had not yet appeared; consequently the earth was covered with water. As no atmosphere existed, thick vapors rested upon the face of the water; but the atmosphere being now called into existence by the word of the Creator, causing those elements to unite which compose the air we breathe, the fogs and vapors that had rested upon the bosom of the water were borne aloft by it. This atmosphere, or expansion, is called heaven. [6]

On the third day of time, God gathered the waters together, and caused the dry land to appear. The gathering together of the waters God called seas; the dry land, thus rescued from the waters, he called earth. "And God said, Let the earth bring forth grass, the

---

[4] Heb. 11:3; Gen. 1:31.   [5] Gen. 1:1–5; Heb. 1:10.   [6] Gen. 1:6–8; Job 37:18.

herb yielding seed, and the fruit-tree yielding fruit after his kind, whose seed is in itself, upon the earth; and it was so." "And God saw that it was good."[7]

On the fourth day of time, "God said, Let there be lights in the firmament of the heaven, to divide the day from the night; and let them be for signs, and for seasons, and for days, and years." "And God made two great lights; the greater light to rule the day, and the lesser light to rule the night; he made the stars also." Light had been created on the first day of the week; and now, on the fourth day, he causes the sun and moon to appear as light-bearers, and places the light under their rule. And they continue unto this day, according to his ordinances; for all are his servants. Such was the work of the fourth day. And the Great Architect, surveying what he had wrought, pronounced it good.[8]

On the fifth day of time, "God created great whales, and every living creature that moveth, which the waters brought forth abundantly, after their kind, and every winged fowl after his kind; and God saw that it was good."[9]

On the sixth day of time, "God made the beast of the earth after his kind, and cattle after their kind, and everything that creepeth upon the earth after his kind; and God saw that it was good." Thus the earth, having been fitted for the purpose, was filled with every order of living creature, while the air and waters teemed with animal existence. To complete this noble work of creation, God next provides a ruler, the representative of himself, and places all in subjection under him.

---

[7] Gen. 1:9–13; Ps. 136:6; 2 Pet. 3:5.   [8] Gen. 1:14–19; Ps. 119:91; Jer. 33:25.   [9] Gen. 1:20–23.

"And God said, Let us make man in our image, after our likeness; and let them have dominion over the fish of the sea, and over the fowl of the air, and over the cattle, and over all the earth, and over every creeping thing that creepeth upon the earth." "And the Lord God formed man of the dust of the ground, and breathed into his nostrils the breath of life; and man became a living soul. And the Lord God planted a garden eastward in Eden; and there he put the man whom he had formed. And out of the ground made the Lord God to grow every tree that is pleasant to the sight, and good for food; the tree of life also in the midst of the garden, and the tree of knowledge of good and evil." Last of all, God created Eve, the mother of all living. The work of the Creator was now complete. "The heavens and the earth were finished, and all the host of them." "And God saw everything that he had made, and, behold, it was very good." Adam and Eve were in paradise; the tree of life bloomed on earth; sin had not entered our world, and death was not here, for there was no sin. "The morning stars sang together, and all the sons of God shouted for joy." Thus ended the sixth day. [10]

---

[10] Gen. 1:24–31; 2:7–9, 18–22; 3:20; Job 38:7.

CHAPTER II.

THE INSTITUTION OF THE SABBATH.

Event of the seventh day—Why the Creator rested—Acts by which the Sabbath was made—Time and order of their occurrence—Meaning of the word *sanctified*—The fourth commandment refers the origin of the Sabbath to creation—The second mention of the Sabbath confirms this fact—The Saviour's testimony—When did God sanctify the seventh day?—Object of the Author of the Sabbath—Testimony of Josephus and of Philo—Negative argument from the book of Genesis considered—Adam's knowledge of the Sabbath not difficult to be known by the patriarchs.

LTHOUGH the work of the Creator was finished, the first week of time was not yet completed. Each of the six days had been distinguished by the Creator's work upon it; but the seventh was rendered memorable in a very different manner. "And on the seventh [1] day, God ended his work which he had made; and he rested on the seventh day from all his work which he had made." In yet stronger language it is written: "On the seventh day he rested, and was REFRESHED." [2]

Thus the seventh day of the week became the rest-day of the Lord. How remarkable is this fact! "The everlasting God, the Lord, the Creator of the ends of

---

[1] "On the sixth day, God ended his work which he had made; and he rested on the seventh day," etc., is the reading of the Septuagint, the Syriac, and the Samaritan; "and this should be considered the genuine reading," says Dr. A. Clarke.—*Commentary on Gen. 2.*

[2] Gen. 2: 2; Ex. 31: 17.

the earth, fainteth not, neither is weary."[3] He needed no rest; yet it is written, "On the seventh day he rested, and was refreshed." Why does not the record simply state the cessation of the Creator's work? Why did he at the close of that work employ a day in rest? The answer will be learned from the next verse. He was laying the foundation of a divine institution, the memorial of his own great work.

"And God blessed the seventh day, and sanctified it; *because* that in it he had rested from all his work which God created and made." The fourth commandment states the same fact: He "rested the seventh day; *wherefore* the Lord blessed the Sabbath-day, and hallowed it."[4]

The blessing and sanctification of the seventh day were because that God had rested upon it. His resting upon it, then, was to lay the foundation for blessing and sanctifying the day. His being refreshed with this rest implies that he delighted in the act which laid the foundation for the memorial of his great work.

The second act of the Creator in instituting this memorial was to place his blessing upon the day of his rest. Thenceforward it was the blessed rest-day of the Lord. A third act completes the sacred institution: the day

---

[3] Isa. 40:28.

[4] Gen. 2:3; Ex. 20:11. In an anonymous work, entitled, "Morality of the Fourth Commandment," London, 1652, but not the same with that of Dr. Twisse of the same title, is the following striking passage:—

"The Hebrew root for seven signifies *fullness, perfection,* and the Jews held many mysteries to be in the number seven: so John in his Apocalypse useth much that number; as, seven churches, seven stars, seven spirits, seven candlesticks, seven angels, seven seals, seven trumpets: and we no sooner meet with a seventh day, but it is blessed; no sooner with a seventh man [Gen. 5:24; Jude 14], but he is translated." Page 7.

already blessed of God is now, last of all, sanctified, or hallowed, by him. To sanctify is "to make sacred or holy; to set apart to a holy or religious use; to consecrate by appropriate rites; to hallow." To hallow is "to make holy; to set apart for holy or religious use; to consecrate." [5]

The time when these three acts were performed is worthy of special notice. The first act was that of rest. This took place on the seventh day; for the day was employed in rest. The second and third acts took place when the seventh day was past. "God blessed the seventh day, and sanctified it; because that in it he *had* rested from all his work." Hence it was on the first day of the second week of time that God blessed the seventh day, and set it apart to a holy use. The blessing and sanctification of the seventh day, therefore, relate, not to the first seventh day of time, but to the seventh day of the week for time to come, in memory of God's rest on that day from the work of creation.

With the beginning of time, God began to count days, giving to each an ordinal number for its *name*. Seven *different* days received as many different *names*. In memory of that which he did on the last of these days, he set that day apart by *name* to a holy use. This act gave existence to weeks, or periods of seven days; for with the seventh day he ceased to count, and by the divine appointment of that day to a holy use in memory

---

[5] Webster's Unabridged Dictionary on the words *sanctify* and *hallow*. Ed. 1882.

"God blessed the seventh day, and *sanctified* it. Gen. 2: 3. Moses . . . sanctified Aaron and his garments. Lev. 8: 30."

Worcester defines it thus: " *To ordain or set apart to sacred ends;* to consecrate; to hallow. God blessed the seventh day, and *sanctified* it. Gen. 2: 3."

of his rest thereon, he caused man to begin the count of a new week as soon as the first seventh day had ceased. And as God has been pleased to give man *in all* but *seven* different days, and has given to each one of these days a name which indicates its exact place in the week, his act of setting apart one of these by name, which act created weeks and gave man the Sabbath, can never— except by sophistry—be made to relate to an indefinite or uncertain day.

The days of the week are measured off by the revolution of *our earth* on its axis; and hence our seventh day, as such, can come only to dwellers on this globe. To Adam and Eve, therefore, as inhabitants of this earth, and not to the inhabitants of some other world, were the days of the week given to use. Hence, when God set apart one of these days to a holy use in memory of his own rest on that day of the week, the very essence of the act consisted in his telling Adam that this day should be used only for sacred purposes. Adam was then in the Garden of God, placed there by the Creator to dress it and to keep it. He was also commissioned of God to subdue the earth. [6] When, therefore, the rest-day of the Lord should return from week to week, all this secular employment, however proper in itself, must be laid aside, and the day be observed in memory of the Creator's rest.

Dr. Twisse quotes Martin Luther as follows :—

"And Martin Luther professeth as much (tome 6, in Gen. 2 : 3). 'It follows from hence,' saith he, 'that if Adam had stood in his innocency, yet he should have kept the seventh day holy; that is, on that day he should have taught his children and

---

[6] Gen. 2: 15; 1: 28.

children's children what was the will of God, and wherein his worship did consist; he should have praised God, given thanks, and offered. On other days he should have tilled his ground, looked to his cattle.' " [7]

The Hebrew verb *qädäsh*, here rendered *sanctified*, and in the fourth commandment rendered *hallowed*, is defined by Gesenius, " To pronounce holy, to sanctify; to institute any holy thing, to appoint." [8] It is repeatedly used in the Old Testament for a public appointment, or proclamation. Thus, when the cities of refuge were set apart in Israel, it is written: " They appointed [margin, Heb., sanctified] Kedesh in Galilee in Mount Naphtali, and Shechem in Mount Ephraim," etc. This sanctification, or appointment, of the cities of refuge was by a public announcement to Israel that these cities were set apart for that purpose. This verb is also used for the appointment of a public fast, and for the gathering of a solemn assembly, as in the following instances: " Sanctify [*i. e.*, appoint] ye a fast, call a solemn assembly, gather the elders and all the inhabitants of the land into the house of the Lord your God." " Blow the trumpet in Zion, sanctify [*i. e.*, appoint] a fast, call a solemn assembly." " And Jehu said, Proclaim [margin, Heb., sanctify] a solemn assembly for Baal." [9] This appointment for Baal was so public that all the worshipers of Baal in all Israel were gathered together. These fasts and solemn assemblies were sanctified or set apart by a public appointment or proclamation of the fact. When, therefore, God set apart the seventh day to a holy

---

[7] Morality of the Fourth Commandment, pp. 56, 57, London, 1641.

[8] Hebrew Lexicon, p. 914. Ed. 1854.

[9] Josh. 20: 7; Joel 1: 14; 2: 15; 2 Kings 10: 20, 21; Zeph. 1: 7, margin.

use, it was necessary that he should state that fact to those who had the days of the week to use. Without such announcement, the day could not be set apart from the others.

But the most striking illustration of the meaning of this word may be found in the record of the sanctification of Mount Sinai. [10] When God was about to speak the ten commandments in the hearing of all Israel, he sent Moses down from the top of Mount Sinai to restrain the people from touching the mount. " And Moses said unto the Lord, The people cannot come up to Mount Sinai; for thou chargedst us, saying, Set bounds about the mount, and *sanctify it*." Turning back to the verse where God gave this charge to Moses, we read: " And thou shalt set bounds unto the people round about, *saying*, Take heed to yourselves, that ye go not up into the mount, or touch the border of it." Hence to sanctify the mount was to command the people not to touch even the border of it; for God was about to descend in majesty upon it. In other words, to sanctify, or set apart to a holy use, Mount Sinai, was to tell the people that God would have them treat the mountain as sacred to himself. And thus also to sanctify the rest-day of the Lord was to tell Adam that he should treat the day as holy to the Lord.

The declaration, " God blessed the seventh day, and sanctified it," is not indeed a commandment for the observance of that day; but it is the record that such a precept was given to Adam. [11] For how could the Crea-

---

[10] Ex. 19: 12, 23.

[11] Dr. Lange's Commentary speaks on this point thus, in vol. 1, p. 197: " If we had no other passage than this of Gen. 2: 3, there would be no difficulty in deducing from it a precept for the universal observance of a Sabbath, or seventh

tor " set apart to a holy use " the day of his rest, when those who were to use the day knew nothing of his will in the case? Let those answer who are able.

This view of the record in Genesis we shall find to be sustained by all the testimony in the Bible relative to the rest-day of the Lord. The facts which we have examined are the basis of the fourth commandment. Thus spake the great Lawgiver from the summit of the flaming mount: "Remember the Sabbath-day, to keep it holy." "The seventh day is the Sabbath of the Lord thy God." "For in six days the Lord made heaven and earth, the sea, and all that in them is, and rested the seventh day; wherefore the Lord blessed the Sabbath-day, and hallowed it." [12]

The term Sabbath is transferred from the Hebrew language, and signifies rest.[13] The command, " Remember the Sabbath-day to keep it holy," is therefore

---

day, to be devoted to God as holy time by all of that race for whom the earth and its nature were specially prepared. The first men must have known it. The words, 'He hallowed it,' can have no meaning otherwise. They would be a blank unless in reference to some who were required to keep it holy."

Dr. Nicholas Bound, in his " True Doctrine of the Sabbath," London, 1606, page 7, thus states the antiquity of the Sabbath precept:—

" This first commandment of the Sabbath was no more then first given when it was pronounced from heaven by the Lord, than any other one of the moral precepts, nay, that it hath so much antiquity as the seventh day hath being; for, so soon as the day was, so soon was it sanctified, that we might know that, as it came in with the first man, so it must not go out but with the last man; and as it was in the beginning of the world, so it must continue to the end of the same; and as the first seventh day was sanctified, so must the last be. And this is that which one saith, that the Sabbath was commanded by God, and the seventh day was sanctified of him even from the beginning of the world; where (the latter words expounding the former) he showeth that, when God did sanctify it, then also he commanded it to be kept holy: and therefore look how ancient the sanctification of the day is, the same antiquity also as the commandment of keeping it holy; for they two are all one."

[12] Ex. 20:8–11.

[13] Buck's Theological Dictionary, article, Sabbath; Calmet's Dictionary, article, Sabbath.

exactly equivalent to saying, "Remember the rest-day, to keep it holy." The explanation which follows sustains this statement: "The seventh day is the Sabbath [or rest-day] of the Lord thy God." The origin of this rest-day is given in these words: "For in six days the Lord made heaven and earth, the sea, and all that in them is, and rested the seventh day; wherefore the Lord blessed the Sabbath-day, and hallowed it." That which is enjoined in the fourth commandment is to keep holy the rest-day of the Lord. And this is defined to be the day on which he rested from the work of creation. Moreover, the fourth commandment calls the seventh day the Sabbath-day at the time when God blessed and hallowed that day; therefore the Sabbath is an institution dating from the foundation of the world. The fourth commandment points back to the creation for the origin of its obligation; and when we go back to that point, we find the substance of the fourth commandment given to Adam: "God blessed the seventh day, and sanctified it;" *i. e.*, set it apart to a holy use. And in the commandment itself, the same fact is stated: "The Lord blessed the Sabbath-day, and hallowed it;" *i. e.*, appointed it to a holy use. The one statement affirms that "God blessed the seventh day, and sanctified it;" the other, that "the Lord blessed the Sabbath-day, and hallowed it." These two statements refer to the same acts. Because the word Sabbath does not occur in the first statement, it has been contended that the Sabbath did not originate at creation, it being the seventh day merely which was hallowed. From the second statement it has been contended that God did not bless the seventh day at all, but simply the Sabbath institution.

But both statements embody all the truth. God blessed the seventh day, and sanctified it; and this day thus blessed and hallowed was his holy Sabbath, or rest-day. Thus the fourth commandment establishes the origin of the Sabbath at creation.

The second mention of the Sabbath in the Bible furnishes a decisive confirmation of the testimonies already adduced. On the sixth day of the week, while in the wilderness of Sin, Moses said to Israel, " To-morrow is the rest of the holy Sabbath unto the Lord. [14] What had been done to the seventh day since God blessed and sanctified it as his rest-day in paradise ?—Nothing. What did Moses do to the seventh day to make it the rest of the holy Sabbath unto the Lord ?—Nothing. On the sixth day, Moses simply states the fact that the morrow is the rest of the holy Sabbath unto the Lord. The seventh day had been such ever since God blessed and hallowed the day of his rest.

The testimony of our divine Lord relative to the origin and design of the Sabbath is of peculiar importance. He is competent to testify; for he was with the Father in the beginning of the creation. [15] " The Sabbath was made for man," said he, "not man for the Sabbath." [16] The following grammatical rule is worthy of notice : " A noun without an adjective is invariably taken in its broadest extension; as, Man is accountable." [17] The following texts will illustrate this rule, and also this statement of our Lord's : " Man lieth down and riseth not; till the heavens be no more, they shall not awake, nor be raised out of their sleep." " There hath

---

[14] Ex. 16 : 22, 23.   [15] John 1 : 1–3; Gen. 1 : 1, 26; Col. 1 : 13–16.   [16] Mark 2 : 27.   [17] Barrett's Principles of English Grammar, p. 29.

no temptation taken you but such as is common to man." "It is appointed unto men once to die." [18]   In these texts, "man" is used without restriction, hence all mankind are necessarily intended. The Sabbath was therefore made for the whole human family, and consequently originated with mankind. But the Saviour's language is yet more emphatic in the original: "The Sabbath was made for THE man, not THE man for the Sabbath." This language fixes the mind on the man Adam, who was formed of the dust of the ground just before the Sabbath was made for him, of the seventh day.

This is a striking confirmation of the fact already pointed out,—that the Sabbath was given to Adam, the head of the human family.

"The seventh day is the Sabbath of the Lord thy God;" yet he made the Sabbath for man. "God made the Sabbath his by solemn appropriation, that he might convey it back to us under the guarantee of a divine charter, that none might rob us of it with impunity."

But is it not possible that God's act of blessing and sanctifying the seventh day did not occur at the close of the creation week? May it not be mentioned then, because God designed that the day of his rest should be afterward observed? Or rather, as Moses wrote the book of Genesis long after the creation, might he not insert this account of the sanctification of the seventh day with the record of the first week, though the day itself was sanctified in his own time?

It is very certain that such an interpretation of the record cannot be admitted, unless the facts in the case demand it; for it is, to say the least, a forced explana-

---

[18] Job 14:12; 1 Cor. 10:13; Heb. 9:27.

tion of the language. The record in Genesis, unless this be an exception, is a plain narrative of events. What God did on each day is recorded in its order down to the seventh. It is certainly doing violence to the narrative to affirm that the record respecting the seventh day is of a different character from that respecting the other six. He rested the seventh day; he sanctified the seventh day, because he had rested upon it. The reason why he should sanctify the seventh day existed when his rest was closed. To say, therefore, that God did not sanctify the day at that time, but did it in the days of Moses, is not only to distort the narrative, but to affirm that he neglected for twenty-five hundred years to do that for which the reason existed at creation. [19]

But we ask that the facts be brought forward which prove that the Sabbath was sanctified in the wilderness of Sin, and not at creation. And what are the facts that show this? It is confessed that such facts are not upon record. Their existence is assumed in order to sustain the theory that the Sabbath originated at the fall of the manna, and not in paradise.

Did God sanctify the Sabbath in the wilderness of Sin?—There is no intimation of such a fact. On the contrary, it is mentioned at that time as something already set apart of God. On the sixth day, Moses said,

---

[19] Dr. Twisse illustrates the absurdity of that view which makes the first observance of the Sabbath in memory of creation to have begun some 2500 years after that event: "We read that when the Ilienses, inhabitants of Ilium, called anciently by the name of Troy, sent an embassage to Tiberius, to condole the death of his father Augustus, he, considering the unreasonableness thereof, it being a long time after his death, requited them accordingly, saying that he was sorry for their heaviness also, having lost so renowned a knight as Hector was, to wit, above a thousand years before, in the wars of Troy."—*Morality of the Fourth Commandment*, p. 198.

" To-morrow is the rest of the holy Sabbath unto the Lord." [20]   Surely this is not the act of instituting the Sabbath, but the familiar mention of an existing fact. We pass on to Mount Sinai.   Did God sanctify the Sabbath when he spoke the ten commandments ?—No one claims that he did.   It is admitted by all that Moses spoke of it familiarly the previous month. [21]   Does the Lord at Sinai speak of the sanctification of the Sabbath ? —He does ; but in the very language of Genesis he goes back for the sanctification of the Sabbath, not to the wilderness of Sin, but to the creation of the world. [22]   We ask those who hold the theory under examination, this question : If the Sabbath was not sanctified at creation, but was sanctified in the wilderness of Sin, why does the narrative in each instance [23] record the sanctification of the Sabbath at creation, and omit all mention of that fact in the wilderness of Sin ?   Nay, why does the record of events in the wilderness of Sin show that the holy Sabbath was at that time already in existence ?   In a word, How can a theory which is subversive of all the facts in the record, be maintained as the truth of God ?

We have seen the Sabbath ordained of God at the close of the creation week.   The object of its Author is worthy of special attention.   Why did the Creator set up this memorial in paradise ?   Why did he set apart from the other days of the week that day which he had employed in rest ?—" Because that in it," says the record, " he had rested from all his work which God created and made."   A *rest* necessarily implies a *work performed ;* and hence the Sabbath was ordained of God as a memo-

---

[20] Ex. 16: 23.   [21] Ex. 16.   [22] Ex. 20: 8-11.
[23] Compare Gen. 2: 1-3 and Ex. 20: 8-11.

rial of the work of creation.   Therefore that precept of
the moral law which relates to this memorial, unlike
every other precept of that law, begins with the word,
"Remember."   The importance of this memorial will be
appreciated when we learn from the Scriptures that it is
the work of creation which is claimed by its Author as
the great evidence of his eternal power and Godhead, and
as that great fact which distinguishes him from all false
gods.   Thus it is written :—

"He that built all things is God."   "The gods that have
not made the heavens and the earth, even they shall perish from
the earth, and from under these heavens."   "But the Lord is
the true God, he is the living God, and an everlasting King."
"He hath made the earth by his power, he hath established the
world by his wisdom, and hath stretched out the heavens by his
discretion."   "For the invisible things of him from the creation
of the world are clearly seen, being understood by the things that
are made, even his eternal power and Godhead."   "For he spake,
and it was done; he commanded, and it stood fast."   Thus "the
worlds were framed by the word of God, so that things which are
seen were not made of things which do appear." [24]

Such is the estimate which the Scriptures place upon
the work of creation as evincing the eternal power and
Godhead of the Creator.   The Sabbath stands as the
memorial of this great work.   Its observance is an act
of grateful acknowledgment on the part of his intelligent
creatures that he is their Creator, and that they owe all
to him ; and that for his pleasure they are and were created.   How appropriate this observance for Adam!   And
when man had fallen, how important for his well-being
that he should "remember the Sabbath-day, to keep it
holy."   He would thus have been preserved from athe-

_____

[24] Heb. 3:4; Jer. 10:10–12; Rom. 1:20; Ps. 33:9; Heb. 11:3.

ism and from idolatry; for he could never forget that there was a God from whom all things derived their being; nor could he worship as God any other being than the Creator.

The seventh day, as hallowed by God in Eden, was not Jewish, but divine; it was not the memorial of the flight of Israel from Egypt, but of the Creator's rest. Nor is it true that the most distinguished Jewish writers deny the primeval origin of the Sabbath, or claim it as a Jewish memorial. We cite the historian Josephus and his learned contemporary, Philo Judæus. Josephus, whose "Antiquities of the Jews" run parallel with the Bible from the beginning, when treating of the wilderness of Sin, makes no allusion whatever to the Sabbath, —a clear proof that he had no idea that it originated in that wilderness. But when giving the account of creation, he bears the following testimony :—

"Moses says that in just six days the world and all that is therein was made. And that the seventh day was a rest and a release from the labor of such operations; WHENCE it is that we celebrate a rest from our labor on that day, and call it the Sabbath, which word denotes rest in the Hebrew tongue." [25]

And Philo bears an emphatic testimony relative to the character of the Sabbath as a memorial. He says :—

"But after the whole world had been completed according to the perfect nature of the number six, the Father hallowed the day following, the seventh, praising it, and calling it holy. For that day is the festival, not of one city or one country, but of all the earth; a day which alone it is right to call the day of festival for all people, and the birth-day of the world." [26]

---

[25] Antiquities of the Jews, b. 1, chap. 1, sec. 1.
[26] Works, vol. 1, The Creation of the World, sec. 30.

Nor was the rest-day of the Lord a shadow of man's rest after his recovery from the fall. God will ever be worshiped in an understanding manner by his intelligent creatures. When, therefore, he set apart his rest-day to a holy use, if it was not as a memorial of his work, but as a shadow of man's redemption from the fall, the real design of the institution must have been stated; and as a consequence, man in his unfallen state could never observe the Sabbath as a delight, but ever with deep distress, as reminding him that he was soon to apostatize from God. Nor was the holy of the Lord and honorable, one of the "carnal ordinances imposed on them until the time of reformation;"[27] for there could be no reformation with unfallen beings.

But man did not continue in his uprightness. Paradise was lost, and Adam was excluded from the tree of life. The curse of God fell upon the earth, and death entered by sin, and passed upon all men.[28] After this sad apostasy, no further mention of the Sabbath occurs until Moses, on the sixth day, said, "To-morrow is the rest of the holy Sabbath unto the Lord."

It is objected that there is no precept in the book of Genesis for the observance of the Sabbath, and consequently no obligation on the part of the patriarchs to observe it. There is a defect in this argument not noticed by those who use it. The book of Genesis was not a rule given to the patriarchs to walk by. On the contrary, it was written by Moses 2500 years after creation, and long after the patriarchs were dead. Consequently, the fact that certain precepts were not found in Genesis is no evidence that they were not obligatory

---

[27] Isa. 58: 13, 14; Heb. 9: 10.   [28] Gen. 3; Rom. 5: 12.

upon the patriarchs. Thus the book does not command men to love God with all their hearts, and their neighbors as themselves; nor does it prohibit idolatry, blasphemy, disobedience to parents, adultery, theft, false witness, or covetousness. Who will affirm from this that the patriarchs were under no restraint in these things? As a mere record of events, written long after their occurrence, it was not necessary that the book should contain a moral code. But had the book been given to the patriarchs as a rule of life, it must of necessity have contained such a code. It is a fact worthy of special notice that as soon as Moses reaches his own time in the book of Exodus, the whole moral law is given. The record and the people were then contemporary, and ever afterward the written law is in the hands of God's people as a rule of life, and a complete code of moral precepts.

The argument under consideration is unsound, 1. Because based upon the supposition that the book of Genesis was the rule of life for the patriarchs; 2. Because if carried out, it would release the patriarchs from every precept of the moral law except the sixth; [29] 3. Because the act of God in setting apart his rest-day to a holy use, as we have seen, necessarily involves the fact that he gave a precept concerning it to Adam, in whose time it was thus set apart. And hence, though the book of Genesis contains no precept concerning the Sabbath, it does contain direct evidence that such a precept was given to the head and representative of the human family.

After giving the institution of the Sabbath, the book

---

[29] Gen. 9 : 5, 6.

of Genesis, in its brief record of 2370 years, does not again mention it. This has been urged as ample proof that those holy men, who, during this period, were perfect, and walked with God in the observance of his commandments, statutes, and laws,[30] all lived in open profanation of that day which God had blessed and set apart to a holy use. But the book of Genesis also omits any distinct reference to the doctrine of future punishment, the resurrection of the body, the revelation of the Lord in flaming fire, and the judgment of the great day. Does this silence prove that the patriarchs did not believe these great doctrines? Does it make them any the less sacred?

But the Sabbath is not mentioned from Moses to David, a period of five hundred years, during which it was enforced by the penalty of death. Does this prove that it was not observed during this period?[31] The jubilee occupied a very prominent place in the typical system, yet in the whole Bible a single instance of its observance is not recorded. What is still more remarkable, there is not on record a single instance of the observance of the great day of atonement, notwithstanding the work in the holiest on that day was the most important service connected with the worldly sanctuary. And yet the observance of the other and less important festivals of the seventh month, which are so intimately connected with the day of atonement, the one preceding it by ten days, the other following it in five, is repeatedly and particularly recorded.[32] It would be sophistry to

---

[30] Gen. 5:24; 6:9; 26:5.   [31] See the beginning of chap. 8 of this work.
[32] Ezra 3:1–6; Neh. 8:2, 9–12, 14–18; 1 Kings 8:2, 65; 2 Chron. 5:3; 7:8,9; John 7:2–14, 37.

argue from this silence respecting the day of atonement, when there were so many instances in which its mention was almost demanded, that that day was never observed; and yet it is actually a better argument than the similar one urged against the Sabbath from the book of Genesis.

The reckoning of time by weeks is derived from nothing in nature, but owes its existence to the divine appointment of the seventh day to a holy use, in memory of the Lord's rest from the six days' work of creation. [33] This period of time is marked only by the recurrence of the sanctified rest-day of the Creator. That the patriarchs reckoned time by weeks and by seven of days, is evident from several texts. [34] That they should retain the week, and forget the Sabbath by which alone the week is marked, is not a probable conclusion. That the reckoning of the week was rightly kept, is evident from the fact that in the wilderness of Sin the people of their own accord gathered a double portion of manna on the sixth day. And Moses said to them, " To-morrow is the rest of the holy Sabbath unto the Lord." [35]

The brevity of the record in Genesis causes us to overlook many facts of the deepest interest. Adam

[33] " The week, another primeval measure, is not a natural measure of time, as some astronomers and chronologers have supposed, indicated by the phases or quarters of the moon. It was originated by divine appointment at the creation, six days of labor and one of rest being wisely appointed for man's physical and spiritual well-being."—*Bliss's Sacred Chronology*, p. 6; *Hale's Chronology*, vol. 1, p. 19.

" Seven has been the ancient and honored number among the nations of the earth. They have measured their time by weeks from the beginning. The original of this was the Sabbath of God, as Moses has given the reasons of it in his writings."—*Brief Dissertation on the First Three Chapters of Genesis, by Dr. Coleman*, p. 26.

[34] Gen. 29: 27, 28; 8: 10, 12; 7: 4, 10; 50: 10; Ex. 7: 25; Job 2: 13.

[35] Ex. 16: 22, 23.

lived 930 years. How deep and absorbing the interest that must have existed in the human family to see the first man! to converse with one who had himself talked with God! to hear from his lips a description of that paradise in which he had lived! to learn from one created on the sixth day the wondrous events of the creation week! to hear from his lips the very words of the Creator when he set apart his rest-day to a holy use! and to learn, alas! the sad story of the loss of paradise and the tree of life! [36]

It was, therefore, not difficult for the facts respecting the six days of creation and the sanctification of the rest-day to be diffused among mankind in the patriarchal age. Nay, it was impossible that it should be otherwise, especially among the godly. From Adam to Abraham, a succession of men—probably inspired of God—preserved the knowledge of God upon the earth; for Adam lived till Lamech, the father Noah, was 56 years of age; Lamech lived till Shem, the son of Noah, was 93; Shem lived till Abraham was 150 years of age. Thus are we brought down to Abraham, the father of the faithful. Of him it is recorded that he obeyed God's voice, and kept his charge, his commandments, his statutes, and his laws. And of him the Most High bears the following testimony: " I know him, that he will command his children and his household after him, and they shall keep the way of the Lord, to do justice and judgment." [37] The knowledge of God was preserved in the family of Abraham; and we shall next find the Sabbath familiarly mentioned among his posterity as an existing institution.

---

[36] The interest to see the first man is thus stated: " Sem and Seth were in great honor among men, and so was Adam, above every living thing in the creation." Ecclesiasticus 49: 16.   [37] Gen. 26: 5; 18: 19.

CHAPTER III.

THE SABBATH COMMITTED TO THE HEBREWS.

Object of this chapter—Total apostasy of the human family in the antediluvian age—Destruction of mankind—The family of Noah spared—
Second apostasy of mankind in the patriarchal age—The apostate
nations left to their own ways—The family of Abraham chosen—
Separated from the rest of mankind—Their history—Their relation
to God—The Sabbath in existence when they came forth from Egypt
—Analysis of Ex. 16—The Sabbath committed to the Hebrews.

E are now to trace the history of divine truth
for many ages in almost exclusive connection
with the family of Abraham. That we may
vindicate the truth from the reproach of pertaining only
to the Hebrews,—a reproach often urged against the
Sabbath,—and justify the dealings of God with mankind
in leaving to their own ways the apostate nations, let us
carefully examine the Bible for the reasons which
directed divine Providence in the choice of Abraham's
family as the depositaries of divine truth.

The antediluvian world had been highly favored of
God. The period of life extended to each generation
was twelvefold that of the present age of man. For almost one thousand years, Adam, who had conversed
with God in paradise, had been with them. Before the
death of Adam, Enoch began his holy walk of three
hundred years, and then he was translated that he
should not see death. This testimony to the piety of
Enoch was a powerful evidence to the antediluvians in

3

behalf of truth and righteousness. Moreover, the Spirit of God strove with mankind; but the perversity of man triumphed over all the gracious restraints of the Holy Spirit. "And God saw that the wickedness of man was great in the earth, and that every imagination of the thoughts of his heart was only evil continually." Even the sons of God joined in the general departure from him. At last, a single family was all that remained of the worshipers of the Most High.[1]

Then came the deluge, sweeping the world of its guilty inhabitants with the besom of destruction.[2] So terrible a display of divine justice might well be thought sufficient to restrain impiety for ages. Surely the family of Noah could not soon forget this awful lesson. But alas! revolt and apostasy speedily followed, and men turned from God to the worship of idols. Against the divine mandate, separating the human family into nations,[3] mankind united in one great act of rebellion in the plain of Shinar. "And they said, Go to, let us build us a city, and a tower whose top may reach unto heaven; and let us make us a name, lest we be scattered abroad upon the face of the whole earth." Then God confounded them in their impiety, and scattered them abroad from thence upon the face of all the earth.[4] Men did not like to retain God in their knowledge; wherefore God gave them over to a reprobate mind, and suffered them to change the truth of God into a lie, and

---

[1] Gen. 2 to 6; Heb. 11: 4–7; 1 Pet. 3: 20; 2 Pet. 2: 5.

[2] Gen. 7; Matt. 24: 37–39; Luke 17: 26, 27; 2 Pet. 3: 5, 6.

[3] Deut. 32: 7, 8; Acts 17: 26.

[4] Gen. 11: 1–9; Josephus's Ant., b. 1, chap. 4. This took place in the days of Peleg, who was born about one hundred years after the flood. Gen. 10: 25 compared with 11: 10–16; Ant., b. 1, chap. 6, sec. 4.

to worship and serve the creature rather than the Creator. Such was the origin of idolatry and the consequent heathenism.[5]

In the midst of this wide-spread apostasy, one man was found whose heart was faithful to God. Abraham was chosen from an idolatrous family, as the depositary of divine truth, the father of the faithful, the heir of the world, and the friend of God.[6] When the worshipers of God were found only in the family of Noah, God gave up the rest of mankind to perish in the flood; and now that they were again reduced almost to a single family, God gave up the idolatrous nations to their own ways, and took the family of Abraham as his peculiar heritage. "For I know him," said God, "that he will command his children and his household after him, and they shall keep the way of the Lord, to do justice and judgment."[7] That they might preserve in the earth the knowledge of divine truth and the memory and worship of the Most High, they were to be a people walled in from all mankind, and dwelling in a land of their own. That they might thus be separated from the heathen around, God gave to Abraham the rite of circumcision, and afterward to his posterity the whole ceremonial law.[8] But they could not possess the land designed for them until the iniquity of the Amorites, its inhabitants, was full, that they should be thrust out before them. The horror of great darkness, and the smoking furnace seen by Abra-

---

[5] Rom. 1: 18–32; Acts 14: 16, 17; 17: 29, 30.

[6] Gen. 12: 1–3; Josh. 24: 2, 3, 14; Neh. 9: 7, 8; Rom. 4: 13–17; 2 Chron. 20: 7; Isa. 41: 8; James 2: 23.

[7] Gen. 18: 19.

[8] Gen. 17: 9–14; 34: 14; Acts 10: 28; 11: 2, 3; Eph. 2: 12–19; Num. 23: 9. Deut. 33: 27, 28.

ham in vision, foreshadowed the iron furnace and the bitter servitude in Egypt. The family of Abraham must go down thither. Brief prosperity and long and terrible oppression follow.[9]

At length the power of the oppressor is broken, and the people of God are delivered. The expiration of four hundred and thirty years from the promise to Abraham marks the hour of deliverance to his posterity.[10] The nation of Israel is brought forth from Egypt as God's peculiar treasure, that he may give them his Sabbath, and his law, and himself. The psalmist testifies that God " brought forth his people with joy, and his chosen with gladness, and gave them the lands of the heathen, and they inherited the labor of the people; that they might observe his statutes, and keep his laws." And the Most High says, " I am the Lord which hallow you, that brought you out of the land of Egypt, *to be your God.*" [11] Not that the commandments of God, his Sabbath, and himself had no prior existence, nor that the people were ignorant of the true God and his law; for the Sabbath was appointed to a holy use before the fall of man; and the commandments of God, his statutes, and his laws were kept by Abraham; and the Israelites themselves, when some of them had violated the Sabbath, were reproved by the question, " How long refuse ye to keep my commandments and my laws?"[12] And as to the Most High, the psalmist exclaims, " Before the mountains were brought forth, or ever thou hadst formed the earth and the world, even from everlasting to everlast-

---

[9] Gen. 15; Ex. 1 to 5; Deut. 4 : 20.   [10] Ex. 12 : 29–42; Gal. 3 : 17.
[11] Ps. 105 : 43–45 ; Lev. 22 : 32, 33; Num. 15 : 41.   [12] Gen. 2 : 2, 3; 26 : 5; Ex. 16 : 4, 27, 28; 18 : 16.

ing, thou art God."[13] But there must be a formal public espousal of the people by God, and of his law and Sabbath and himself by the people.[14] But neither the Sabbath, nor the law, nor the great Lawgiver, by their connection with the Hebrews, became Jewish. The Lawgiver, indeed, became the God of Israel,[15] (and what Gentile shall refuse him adoration for that reason?) but the Sabbath still remained the Sabbath of the Lord,[16] and the law continued to be the law of the Most High.

In the month following their passage through the Red Sea, the Hebrews came into the wilderness of Sin. It is at this point in his narrative that Moses for the second time mentions the sanctified rest-day of the Creator. The people murmured for bread :—

" Then said the Lord unto Moses, Behold, I will rain bread from heaven for you ; and the people shall go out and gather a certain rate every day, that I may prove them, whether they will walk in my law, or no. And it shall come to pass, that on the sixth day they shall prepare that which they bring in; and it shall be twice as much as they gather daily. . . . I have heard the murmurings of the children of Israel : speak unto them, saying, At even ye shall eat flesh, and in the morning ye shall be filled with bread; and ye shall know that I am the Lord your God. And it came to pass, that at even the quails came up, and covered the camp ; and in the morning the dew lay round about the host. And when the dew that lay was gone up, behold, upon the face of the wilderness there lay a small round thing, as small as the hoar frost on the ground. And when the children of Israel saw it, they said one to another, It is manna ; for they wist not what it was. And Moses said unto them, This is the bread

---

[13] Ps. 90: 2.

[14] Ex. 19: 3–8; 24: 3–8; Jer. 3:14 compared with last clause of Jer. 31: 32.

[15] Ex 20: 2; 24: 10.   [16] Ex. 20: 10; Deut. 5: 14; Neh. 9: 14.

which the Lord hath given you to eat.   This is the thing which
the Lord hath commanded, Gather of it every man according to
his eating, an omer for every man, according to the number of
your persons ; take ye every man for them which are in his tents.
And the children of Israel did so, and gathered some more, some
less.   And when they did mete it with an omer, he that gathered
much had nothing over, and he that gathered little had no lack ;
they gathered every man according to his eating.   And Moses
said, Let no man leave of it till the morning.   Notwithstanding,
they hearkened not unto Moses ; but some of them left of it until
the morning, and it bred worms, and stank ; and Moses was
wroth with them.   And they gathered it every morning, every
man according to his eating ; and when the sun waxed hot, it
melted.   And it came to pass, that on the sixth day they
gathered twice as much bread, [17] two omers for one man ; and all
the rulers of the congregation came and told Moses.   And he
said unto them, This is that which the Lord hath said, [18] To-mor-

[17] On this verse, Dr. A. Clarke thus comments : *On the sixth day they gathered
twice as much.*   This they did that they might have a provision for the Sabbath."

[18] The Douay Bible reads : " To-morrow is the rest of the Sabbath sanctified
unto the Lord."   Dr. Clarke comments as follows upon this text : " *To-morrow
is the rest of the holy Sabbath*] There is nothing either in the text or context that
seems to intimate that the Sabbath was now *first* given to the Israelites, as some
have supposed; on the contrary, it is here spoken of as being perfectly well known,
from its having been generally observed.   The commandment, it is true, may be
considered as being now *renewed ;* because they might have supposed that in
their unsettled state in the wilderness they might have been exempted from the
observance of it.   Thus we find, 1. That when God finished his creation, he instituted the Sabbath; 2. When he brought the people out of Egypt, he insisted on
the strict observance of it; 3. When he gave the LAW, he made it a tenth part of
the whole: such importance has this institution in the eyes of the Supreme
Being ! "

Richard Baxter, a famous divine of the seventeenth century, and a decided
advocate of the abrogation of the fourth commandment, in his " Divine appointment of the Lord's Day," thus clearly states the origin of the Sabbath: " Why
should God begin two thousand years after [the creation of the world] to
give men a Sabbath upon the reason of his rest from the creation of it, if he had
never called man to that commemoration before ?   And it is certain that the Sabbath was observed at the falling of the manna before the giving of the law; and
let any considering Christian judge . . . 1. Whether the not falling of the manna,
or the rest of God after the creation, was like to be the original reason of the

row is the rest of the holy Sabbath unto the Lord : bake that which ye will bake to-day, and seethe that ye will seethe ; and that which remaineth over lay up to be kept until the morning. And they laid it up until the morning, as Moses bade ; and it did not stink, neither was there any worm therein. And Moses said, Eat that to-day ; for to-day is a Sabbath unto the Lord : [19] to-day ye shall not find it in the field. Six days ye shall gather it ; but on the seventh day, which is the Sabbath, in it there shall be none. And it came to pass, that there went out some of the people on the seventh day for to gather, and they found none. And the Lord said unto Moses, how long refuse ye to keep my commandments and my laws ? See, for that the Lord hath given you the Sabbath, therefore he giveth you on the sixth day the bread of two days ; abide ye every man in his place, let no man go out of his place on the seventh day. So the people rested on the seventh day." [20]

This narrative shows, 1. That God had a law and commandments prior to the giving of the manna. 2. That God, in giving his people bread from heaven, designed to prove them respecting his law. 3. That in this law was the holy Sabbath; for the test relative to walking in the law pertained directly to the Sabbath; and when God said, " How long refuse ye to keep my commandments and my laws ? " it was the Sabbath which they had violated. 4. That in proving the people respecting this existing law, Moses gave no new

---

Sabbath. 2. And whether, if it had been the first, it would not have been said, Remember to keep holy the Sabbath-day; for on six days the manna fell, and not on the seventh; rather than ' for in six days God created heaven and earth, etc., and rested the seventh day.' And it is casually added, ' Wherefore the Lord blessed the Sabbath-day, and hallowed it.' Nay, consider whether this annexed reason intimates not that the day on this ground being hallowed before, therefore it was that God sent not down the manna on that day, and that he prohibited the people from seeking it."—*Practical Works*, vol. 3, p. 784. Ed. 1707.

[19] The Douay Bible reads: " Because it is the Sabbath of the Lord."

[20] Ex. 16.

precept respecting the Sabbath, but remained silent relative to the preparation for the Sabbath until after the people of their own accord had gathered a double portion on the sixth day. 5. That by this act the people proved, not only that they were not ignorant of the Sabbath, but that they were disposed to observe it.[21] 6. That the reckoning of the week, traces of which appear through the patriarchal age,[22] had been rightly kept; for the people knew when the sixth day had arrived. 7. That had there been any doubt existing on that point, the fall of the manna on the six days, the withholding of it on the seventh, and the preservation of that needed for the Sabbath over that day, must have settled that point incontrovertibly.[23] 8. That there was no act of instituting the Sabbath in the wilderness of Sin; for God did not then make it his rest-day, nor did he then bless and sanctify the day. On the contrary, the record shows that the seventh day was already the sanctified rest-day of the Lord.[24] 9. That the obligation

---

[21] It has indeed been asserted that God by a miracle equalized the portion of every one on five days, and doubled the portion of each on the sixth, so that no act of the people had any bearing on the Sabbath. But the equal portion of each on the five days was not thus understood by Paul. He says: "But by an equality, that now at this time your abundance may be a supply for their want, that their abundance also may be a supply for your want; that there may be equality; as it is written, He that had gathered much had nothing over; and he that had gathered little had no lack." 2 Cor. 8: 14, 15. And that the double portion on the sixth day was the act of the people, is affirmed by Moses. He says that "on the sixth day they gathered twice as much bread." Verse 22.

[22] Gen. 7: 4, 10; 8: 10, 12; 29: 27, 28; 50: 10; Ex. 7: 25; Job 2: 13.

[23] By this threefold miracle, occurring every week for forty years, the great Lawgiver distinguished his hallowed day. The people were therefore admirably prepared to listen to the fourth commandment, enjoining the observance of the very day on which he had rested. Ex. 16: 35: Josh. 5: 12; Ex. 20: 8–11.

[24] The twelfth chapter of Exodus relates the origin of the Passover. It is in striking contrast with Exodus 16, which is supposed to give the origin of the

to observe the Sabbath existed and was known before the fall of the manna; for the language used implies the existence of such an obligation, but does not contain a new enactment until after some of the people had violated the Sabbath. God says to Moses, " On the sixth day they shall prepare that which they bring in," but he does not speak of the seventh. And on the sixth day, Moses said, " To-morrow is the rest of the holy Sabbath unto the Lord," but he does not command them to observe it. On the seventh day he says that it is the Sabbath, and that they would find no manna in the field. " Six days ye shall gather it; but on the seventh day, which is the Sabbath, in it there shall be none." But in all this there is no precept given, yet the existence of such a precept is plainly implied. 10. That when some of the people violated the Sabbath, they were reproved in language which clearly indicated a previous transgression of this precept. " How long refuse ye to keep my commandments and my laws ? " 11. And that this rebuke of the Lawgiver restrained for the time the transgression of the people.

" See, for that the Lord hath given you the Sabbath, therefore he giveth you on the sixth day the bread of two days : [25] abide ye every man in his place, let no man go out of his place on the seventh day." [26]   As a special

Sabbath. If the reader will compare the two chapters, he will see the difference between the origin of an institution as given in Exodus 12, and a familiar reference to an existing institution as in Exodus 16. If he will also compare Genesis 2 with Exodus 12, he will see that the one gives the origin of the Sabbath in the same manner that the other gives the origin of the Passover.

[25] This implies, first the fall of a larger quantity on that day, and second, its preservation for the wants of the Sabbath.

[26] This must refer to going out for manna, as the connection implies; for religious assemblies on the Sabbath were commanded and observed. Lev. 23 : 3; Mark 1 : 21; Luke 4 : 16; Acts 1 : 12; 15 : 21.

trust, God committed the Sabbath to the Hebrews. It was now given them, not now made for them. It was made for man at the close of the first week of time; but all other nations having turned from the Creator to the worship of idols, it was given to the Hebrew people. Nor does this prove that all the Hebrews had hitherto disregarded it; for Christ uses the same language respecting circumcision. Thus he says, "Moses therefore gave unto you circumcision; not because it is of Moses, but of the fathers." [27] Yet God had enjoined that ordinance upon Abraham and his family four hundred years previous to this gift of it by Moses, and it had been retained by them.[28]

The language, "The Lord hath given you the Sabbath," implies a solemn act of committing a treasure to their trust. How was this done? No act of instituting the Sabbath here took place. No precept enjoining its observance was given until some of the people violated it, when it was given in the form of a reproof; which evinced a previous obligation, and that they were transgressing an existing law. And this view is certainly strengthened by the fact that no explanation of the institution was given to the people,—a fact which indicates that some knowledge of the Sabbath was already in their possession.

---

[27] John 7: 22.

[28] Gen. 17: 34; Ex. 4. Moses is said to have given circumcision to the Hebrews; yet it is a singular fact that his first mention of that ordinance is purely incidental, and plainly implies an existing knowledge of it on their part. Thus it is written: "This is the ordinance of the Passover: There shall no stranger eat thereof; but every man's servant that is bought for money, when thou hast circumcised him, then shall he eat thereof." Ex. 12: 43, 44. And in like manner, when the Sabbath was given to Israel, that people were not ignorant of the sacred institution.

But how, then, did God give them the Sabbath?
He did this, first, by delivering them from the abject
bondage of Egypt, where they were a nation of slaves;
and secondly, by providing them with food in such a
manner as to impose the strongest obligation to keep the
Sabbath. Forty years did he give them bread from
heaven, sending it for six days, and withholding it on
the seventh, and preserving food for them over the
Sabbath. Thus was the Sabbath specially intrusted to
them.

As a gift to the Hebrews, the Creator's great memorial became a sign between God and themselves. "I
gave them my Sabbaths, to be a sign between me and
them, that they might know that I am the Lord that
sanctify them." As a sign, its object is stated to be, to
make known the true God; and we are told why it was
such a sign. "It is a sign between me and the children
of Israel forever; for in six days the Lord made heaven
and earth, and on the seventh day he rested, and was
refreshed." [29] The institution itself signified that God
created the heavens and the earth in six days, and
rested on the seventh. Its observance by the people
signified that the Creator was their God.

The Sabbath was a sign between God and the children of Israel, because they alone were the worshipers
of the Creator. All other nations had turned from him
to " the gods that have not made the heavens and the
earth." [30] For this reason the memorial of the great
Creator was committed to the Hebrews. Thus was the
Sabbath a golden link uniting the Creator and his worshipers.

---

[29] Eze. 20: 12; Ex. 31: 17.　　　　　[30] Jer. 10: 10–12.

CHAPTER IV.

THE FOURTH COMMANDMENT.

The Holy One upon Mount Sinai—Three great gifts bestowed upon the
Hebrews—The Sabbath proclaimed by the voice of God—Position
assigned it in the moral law—Origin of the Sabbath—Definite character of the commandment—Revolution of the earth upon its axis—
Name of the Sabbatic institution—Seventh day of the commandment
identical with the seventh day of the New-Testament week—Testimony of Nehemiah—Moral obligation of the fourth commandment.

OW we approach the record of that sublime
event, the personal descent of the Lord upon
Mount Sinai.[1]   The sixteenth chapter of Exodus, as we have seen, is remarkable for its record of
the fact that God gave to Israel the Sabbath; the nineteenth chapter, that God gave himself to that people in
solemnly espousing them as a holy nation unto himself;
while the twentieth chapter will be found remarkable
for recording the act of the Most High in giving to Israel his law.

It is customary to speak against the Sabbath and
the law as being Jewish, because they were given to
Israel.   As well might the Creator be spoken against,
who brought them out of Egypt to be *their* God, and
who styles himself the God of Israel.[2]   The Hebrews

---

[1] That the Lord was there in person with his angels, see, in addition to the
narrative in Exodus, chapters 19, 20, and 32 to 34, the following testimonies:
Deut. 33:2; Judges 5:5; Nehemiah 9:6–13; Ps. 68:17.

[2] Ex. 24:10; Lev. 22:32, 33; Num. 15:41; Isa. 41:17.

were honored by being thus intrusted with the Sabbath
and the law, not the Sabbath and the law and the Creator rendered Jewish by this connection. The sacred
writers speak of the high exaltation of Israel in being
thus intrusted with the law of God.

" He showeth his word unto Jacob, his statutes and his judgments unto Israel. He hath not dealt so with any nation; and
as for his judgments, they have not known them. Praise ye the
Lord!" " What advantage then hath the Jew ? or what profit
is there of circumcision ? Much every way: chiefly, because
that unto them were committed the oracles of God." " Who are
Israelites; to whom pertaineth the adoption, and the glory, and the
covenants, and the giving of the law, and the service of God, and
the promises ; whose are the fathers, and of whom, as concerning
the flesh, Christ came, who is over all, God blessed forever.
Amen." [3]

After the Most High had solemnly espoused the people unto himself as his peculiar treasure in the earth, [4]
they were brought forth out of the camp to meet with
God. "And Mount Sinai was altogether on a smoke,
because the Lord descended upon it in fire : and the
smoke thereof ascended as the smoke of a furnace, and
the whole mount quaked greatly." Out of the midst of
this fire did God proclaim the ten words of his law. [5]
The fourth of these precepts is the grand law of the Sabbath. Thus spake the great Lawgiver :—

---

[3] Ps. 147: 19, 20; Rom. 3: 1, 2; 9: 4, 5. The following from the pen of Wm.
Miller presents the subject in a clear light: " I say, and believe I am supported
by the Bible, that the moral law was never given to the Jews as a people exclusively; but they were for a season the keepers of it in charge. And through
them the law, oracles, and testimony have been handed down to us. See Paul's
clear reasoning in Romans, chapters 2, 3, and 4, on that point."—*Miller's Life
and Views,* p. 161.

[4] Ex. 19; Deut. 7: 6; 14: 2; 2 Sam. 7: 23; 1 Kings 8: 53; Amos 3: 1, 2.

[5] Ex. 20: 1–17; 34: 28, margin; Deut. 5: 4–22; 10: 4, margin.

" Remember the Sabbath-day, to keep it holy. Six days shalt thou labor, and do all thy work; but the seventh day is the Sabbath of the Lord thy God : in it thou shalt not do any work, thou, nor thy son, nor thy daughter, thy man-servant, nor thy maid-servant, nor thy cattle, nor thy stranger that is within thy gates; for in six days the Lord made heaven and earth, the sea, and all that in them is, and rested the seventh day; wherefore the Lord blessed the Sabbath-day, and hallowed it."

The estimate which the Lawgiver placed upon his Sabbath is seen in that he deemed it worthy of a place in his code of ten commandments, thus causing it to stand in the midst of nine immutable moral precepts. Nor is it to be thought a small honor that the Most High, naming one by one the great principles of morality until all are given, and he adds no more,[6] should include in their number the observance of his hallowed rest-day. This precept is expressly given to enforce the observance of the Creator's great memorial; and unlike all the others, this one traces its obligation back to the creation, where that memorial was ordained.

The Sabbath is to be remembered and kept holy, because God hallowed it, *i. e.*, appointed it to a holy use, at the close of the first week. And this sanctification, or hallowing, of the rest-day, when the first seventh day of time was past, was the solemn act of setting apart the seventh day for time to come, in memory of the Creator's rest. Thus the fourth commandment reaches back, and embraces the institution of the Sabbath in paradise; while the sanctification of the Sabbath in paradise extends forward to all coming time. The narrative respecting the wilderness of Sin admirably cements the union of the two; for there, before the fourth command-

---

[6] Deut. 5 ; 22.

ment was given, stands the Sabbath, holy to the Lord, with an existing obligation to observe it, though no commandment in that narrative creates the obligation. This obligation is derived from the same source as the fourth commandment, namely, the sanctification of the Sabbath in paradise, showing that it was an existing duty, and not a new precept. It should never be forgotten that the fourth commandment does not trace its obligation to the wilderness of Sin, but to the creation,— a decisive proof that the Sabbath did not originate in the wilderness of Sin.

The fourth commandment is remarkably definite. It embraces, first, a precept: "Remember the Sabbath-day, to keep it holy;" secondly, an explanation of this precept: "Six days shalt thou labor, and do all thy work; but the seventh day is the Sabbath of the Lord thy God: in it thou shalt not do any work, thou, nor thy son, nor thy daughter, thy man-servant, nor thy maid-servant, nor thy cattle, nor thy stranger that is within thy gates;" thirdly, the reasons on which the precept is based, embracing the origin of the institution, and the very acts by which it was made, and enforcing all by the example [7] of the Lawgiver himself; "for in six days the Lord made heaven and earth, the sea, and all that in them is, and rested the seventh day; wherefore the Lord blessed the Sabbath-day, and hallowed it."

The rest-day of the Lord is thus distinguished from the six days on which he labored. The blessing and sanctification pertain to the day of the Creator's rest. There

[7] He who created the world on the first day of the week, and completed its organization in six days, rested on the seventh day, and was refreshed. Gen. 1 and 2; Ex. 31: 17.

can be, therefore, no indefiniteness in the precept. It is not merely one day in seven, but that day in the seven on which the Creator rested, and upon which he placed his blessing, namely, the seventh day.[8]   And this day is definitely pointed out in the name given it by God: "The seventh day is the Sabbath [*i. e.*, the rest-day] of the Lord thy God."

That the seventh day in the fourth commandment is the seventh day of the New-Testament week may be plainly proved. In the record of our Lord's burial, Luke writes thus :—

"And that day was the preparation, and the Sabbath drew on. And the women also which came with him from Galilee, followed after, and beheld the sepulcher, and how his body was laid. And they returned, and prepared spices and ointments; and rested the Sabbath-day according to the commandment. Now upon the first day of the week, very early in the morning, they came unto the sepulcher, bringing the spices which they had prepared, and certain others with them."[9]

Luke testifies that these women kept "the Sabbath-day according to the commandment." The commandment says, "The seventh day is the Sabbath of the Lord thy God." This day thus observed was the last or

---

[8] To this, however, it is objected that in consequence of the revolution of the earth on its axis, the day begins earlier in the east than with us; and hence that there is no definite seventh day to the world of mankind. To suit such objectors, the earth ought not to revolve. But in that case, so far from removing the difficulty, there would be no seventh day at all; for one side of the globe would have perpetual day, and the other side perpetual night. The truth is, everything depends upon the revolution of the earth. God made the Sabbath for man [Mark 2:27]; he made man to dwell on the face of the earth [Acts 17: 26]; he caused the earth to revolve on its axis that it might measure off the days of the week; causing that the sun should shine on the earth, as it revolves from west to east, thus causing the day to go round the world from east to west. Seven of these revolutions constitute a week; the seventh one brings the Sabbath to all the world.

[9] Luke 23: 54–56; 24: 1.

seventh day of the week, for the following [10] day was the first day of the week. Hence the seventh day of the commandment is the seventh day of the New-Testament week.

The testimony of Nehemiah is deeply interesting. "Thou camest down also upon Mount Sinai, and spakest with them from heaven, and gavest them right judgments, and true laws, good statutes and commandments: and madest known unto them thy holy Sabbath, and commandedst them precepts, statutes, and laws, by the hand of Moses thy servant." [11] It is remarkable that God is said to have made known the Sabbath when he thus came down upon the mount; for the children of Israel had the Sabbath in possession when they came to Sinai. This language must therefore refer to that complete unfolding of the Sabbatic institution which is given in the fourth commandment. And mark the expression, "Madest known [12] unto them thy holy Sabbath," not madest the Sabbath for them,—language which plainly implies its previous existence, and cites the mind back to the Creator's rest for the origin of the institution. [13]

The moral obligation of the fourth commandment,

---

[10] See also Matt. 28: 1; Mark 16: 1, 2.   [11] Neh. 9: 13, 14.

[12] This expression is strikingly illustrated in the statement of Eze. 20: 5, where God is said to have made himself known unto Israel in Egypt. This language cannot mean that the people were ignorant of the true God, however wicked some of them might be, for they had been God's peculiar people from the days of Abraham. Ex. 2: 23–25; 3: 6, 7; 4: 31. The language implies the prior existence both of the Lawgiver and of his Sabbath, when it is said that they were "made known" to his people.

[13] It should never be forgotten that the term Sabbath-day signifies rest-day; that the Sabbath of the Lord is the rest-day of the Lord; and hence that the expression, "Thy holy Sabbath," refers the mind to the Creator's rest-day, and to his act of blessing and hallowing it.

which is so often denied, may be clearly shown by reference to the origin of all things. God created the world, and gave existence to man upon it. To him he gave life, and breath, and all things. Man therefore owes everything to God. Every faculty of his mind, every power of his being, all his strength, and all his time, belong of right to the Creator; hence it was the benevolence of the Creator that gave to man six days for his own wants. And in setting apart the seventh day to a holy use, in memory of his own rest, the Most High was reserving unto himself one of the seven days, when he could rightly claim all as his. The six days are the gift of God to man, to be rightly employed in secular affairs, not the seventh day the gift of man to God. The fourth commandment, therefore, does not require man to give something of his own to God; but it does require that man should not appropriate to himself that which God has reserved for his own worship. To observe this day, then, is to render to God of the things that are his; to appropriate it to ourselves is simply to rob God.

CHAPTER V.

THE SABBATH WRITTEN BY THE FINGER OF GOD.

Classification of the precepts given through Moses—The Sabbath renewed—Solemn ratification of the covenant between God and Israel—Moses called up to receive the law which God had written upon stone—The ten commandments probably proclaimed upon the Sabbath—Events of the forty days—The Sabbath becomes a sign between God and Israel—The penalty of death—The tables of testimony given to Moses, and broken when he saw the idolatry of the people—The idolaters punished—Moses goes up to renew the tables—The Sabbath again enjoined—The tables given again—The ten commandments were the testimony of God—Who wrote them?—Three distinguished honors which pertain to the Sabbath—The ten commandments a complete code—Relation of the fourth commandment to the atonement—Valid reason why God himself should write that law which was placed beneath the mercy-seat.

HEN the voice of the Holy One had ceased, "the people stood afar off, and Moses drew near unto the thick darkness where God was." A brief interview followed,[1] when God gave to Moses a series of precepts, which, as a sample of the statutes given through him, may be classified thus: Ceremonial precepts, pointing to the good things to come; judicial precepts, intended for the civil government of the nation; and moral precepts, stating anew in other forms the ten commandments. In this brief interview the Sabbath is not forgotten:—

"Six days thou shalt do thy work, and on the seventh day

---

[1] Ex. 20 to 24.

thou shalt rest; that thine ox and thine ass may rest, and the son of thy handmaid, and the stranger, may be refreshed." [2]

This scripture furnishes incidental proof that the Sabbath was made for mankind, and for those creatures that share the labors of man. The stranger and the foreigner must keep it, and it was for their refreshment.[3] But the same persons could not partake of the Passover until they were made members of the Hebrew church by circumcision.[4]

When Moses had returned unto the people, he repeated all the words of the Lord. With one voice all the people exclaimed, "All the words which the Lord hath said will we do." Then Moses wrote all the words of the Lord. "And he took the book of the covenant, and read in the audience of the people; and they said, All that the Lord hath said will we do, and be obedient." Then Moses "sprinkled both the book and all the people, saying, This is the blood of the testament which God hath enjoined unto you."[5]

The way was thus prepared for God to bestow a second signal honor upon his law.

"And the Lord said unto Moses, Come up to me into the mount, and be there; and I will give thee tables of stone, and a law, and commandments which I have written, that thou mayest teach them. . . . And Moses went up into the mount, and a cloud covered the mount. And the glory of the Lord abode upon Mount Sinai, and the cloud covered it six days; and the seventh day he called unto Moses out of the midst of the cloud. [6]

---

[2] Ex. 23 : 12.   [3] See also Ex. 20: 10; Deut. 5: 14; Isa. 56.
[4] Ex. 12: 43–48.   [5] Ex. 24: 3–8; Heb. 9: 18–20.

[6] Dr. Clarke has the following note on this verse : "It is very likely that Moses went up into the mount on the first day of the week ; and having with Joshua remained in the region of the cloud during six days, on the seventh, which was

And the sight of the glory of the Lord was like devouring fire on the top of the mount in the eyes of the children of Israel. And Moses went into the midst of the cloud, and gat him up into the mount; and Moses was in the mount forty days and forty nights." [7]

During this forty days, God gave to Moses a pattern of the ark in which to place the law that he had written upon stone, and of the mercy-seat to place over that law, and of the sanctuary in which to deposit the ark. He also ordained the priesthood, which was to minister in the sanctuary before the ark. [8] These things being ordained, and the Lawgiver about to commit his law as written by himself into the hands of Moses, he again enjoins the Sabbath:—

"And the Lord spake unto Moses, saying, Speak thou also unto the children of Israel, saying, Verily my Sabbaths ye shall keep; for it is a sign between me and you throughout your generations; that ye may know that I am the Lord that doth sanctify you. Ye shall keep the Sabbath, therefore; for it is holy unto you: every one that defileth it shall surely be put to death; for whosoever doeth any work therein, that soul shall be cut off from among his people. Six days may work be done; but in the seventh is the Sabbath of rest, holy to the Lord: whosoever doeth any work in the Sabbath-day, he shall surely be put to death. Wherefore the children of Israel shall keep the Sabbath, to ob-

---

the Sabbath, God spake to him."—*Commentary on Ex. 24: 16.* The marking off of a week from the forty days in this remarkable manner goes far toward establishing the view of Dr. Clarke. And if this be correct, it would strongly indicate that the ten commandments were given upon the Sabbath; for there seems to be good evidence that they were given the day before Moses went up to receive the tables of stone; for the interview in which chapters 21–23 were given would require but a brief space, and certainly followed immediately upon the giving of the ten commandments. Ex. 20: 18–21. When the interview closed, Moses came down to the people, and wrote all the words of the Lord. In the morning he rose up early, and, having ratified the covenant, went up to receive the law which God had written. Ex. 24: 3–13.

[7] Ex. 24: 12–18.   [8] Ex. 25 to 31.

serve the Sabbath throughout their generations, for a perpetual covenant. It is a sign between me and the children of Israel forever; for in six days the Lord made heaven and earth, and on the seventh day he rested, and was refreshed. And he gave unto Moses, when he had made an end of communing with him upon two tables of testimony, tables of stone, written with the finger of God." [9]

This should be compared with the testimony of Ezekiel, speaking in the name of God,—

"I gave them my statutes, and showed them my judgments, which, if a man do, he shall even live in them. Moreover, also, I gave them my Sabbaths, to be a sign between me and them, that they might know that I am the Lord that sanctify them. . . . I am the Lord your God: walk in my statutes, and keep my judgments, and do them; and hallow my Sabbaths; and they shall be a sign between me and you, that ye may know that I am the Lord your God." [10]

It will be observed that neither of these scriptures teaches that the Sabbath was made *for* Israel, nor yet do they teach that it was made *after* the Hebrews came out of Egypt. In neither of these particulars do they even *seem* to contradict those texts that place the institution of the Sabbath at creation. But we do learn, 1. That it was God's act of giving to the Hebrews his Sabbath that made it a sign between himself and *them.* "I gave them my Sabbaths, TO BE a sign between me and them." This act of committing to them the Sabbath has been already noticed.[11] 2. That it was to be a sign between God and the Hebrews, "that they might know that I am the Lord that sanctify them." Wherever the word LORD in the Old Testament is in small capitals, as in the texts under

---

[9] Ex. 31: 12–18.   [10] Eze. 20: 11, 12, 19, 20.
[11] See chapter 3 of this work.

consideration, it is Jehovah in the Hebrew. The Sabbath, then, as a sign, signified that it was Jehovah, *i. e.*, the infinite, self-existent God, who had sanctified them. To *sanctify* is to separate, set apart, or appoint to a holy, sacred, or religious use.[12] That the Hebrew nation had thus been set apart in the most remarkable manner from all mankind, was sufficiently evident. But who was it that had thus separated them from all other people? As a gracious answer to this important question, God gave to the Hebrews his own hallowed rest-day. But how could the great memorial of the Creator determine such a question? Listen to the words of the Most High: "Verily my Sabbaths," *i. e.*, my rest-days, "ye shall keep; for it is a sign between me and you. . . . It is a sign between me and the children of Israel forever; for in six days the Lord made heaven and earth, and on the seventh day he rested, and was refreshed." The Sabbath, as a sign between God and Israel, was a perpetual testimony that he who had separated them from all mankind as his peculiar treasure in the earth, was that Being who had created the heavens and the earth in six days, and rested on the seventh. It was, therefore, the strongest possible assurance that he who sanctified them was indeed Jehovah.

From the days of Abraham, God had set the Hebrews apart. He who had previously borne no local, national, or family name, did from that time until the end of his covenant-relation with the Hebrew race, take to himself

---

[12] To sanctify, *kadash*, signifies to consecrate, separate, and set apart a thing or person from all secular purposes to some religious use."—*Clarke's Commentary on Ex. 13: 2.* The same writer says, on Ex. 19: 23, "Here the word *kadash* is taken in its proper, literal sense, signifying the separating of a thing, person, or place from all profane or common uses, and devoting it to sacred purposes.

such titles as seemed to show him to be their God alone. From his choice of Abraham and his family forward, he designates himself as the God of Abraham, of Isaac, and of Jacob; the God of the Hebrews and the God of Israel:[13]   He brought Israel out of Egypt to be *their God,*[14] and at Sinai he joined himself to them in solemn espousal. In this way did he set apart or sanctify unto himself the Hebrews, because all other nations had given themselves to idolatry.   Thus the God of heaven and earth condescended to give himself to a single race, and to set them apart from all mankind.   It should be observed that it was not the Sabbath which had set Israel apart from all other nations, but it was the idolatry of all other nations that had caused God to set the Hebrews apart for himself; and that God gave to Israel the Sabbath which he had hallowed for mankind at creation as the most expressive sign that he who thus sanctified them was indeed the living God.

It was the act of God in giving his Sabbath to the Israelites that rendered it a sign *between himself and them.* But the Sabbath did not derive its existence from being given to the Hebrews as it was; for it was the ancient Sabbath of the Lord when given to them, and we have seen [15] that it was not given by a new commandment. On the contrary, it rested at that time upon existing obligation.   But it was the providence of God in behalf of the Hebrews, first, in rescuing them from abject servitude, and second, in sending them bread from heaven for six days, and preserving food for the Sabbath, that constituted the Sabbath a gift to that people.   And mark

---

[13] Gen. 17: 7, 8; 26: 24; 28: 13; Ex. 3: 6, 13–16, 18; 5: 3; Isa. 45: 3.

[14] Lev. 11: 45.   [15] See chapter three.

the significance of the *manner* in which this gift was bestowed, as showing who it was that sanctified them. It
became a gift to the Hebrews by the wonderful providence of the manna,—a miracle that ceased not openly
to declare the Sabbath every week for the space of forty
years, thus showing incontrovertibly that He who led
them was the author of the Sabbath, and therefore the
Creator of heaven and earth. That the Sabbath, which
was made for man, should be given to the Hebrews in
such a manner, is certainly not more remarkable than
that the God of the whole earth should give his oracles
and himself to that people. The Most High and his law
and Sabbath did not become Jewish; but the Hebrews
were made the honored depositaries of divine truth, and
the knowledge of God and of his commandments was
preserved in the earth.

The reason on which this sign is based, points unmis-
takably to the true origin of the Sabbath. It did not
originate from the fall of the manna for six days, and its
cessation on the seventh; for the manna was given in
this way because the Sabbath was in existence; but
because that "in six days the Lord made heaven and
earth, and on the seventh day he rested, and was refreshed." Thus the Sabbath is shown to have originated
with the rest and refreshment of the Creator, and not at
the fall of the manna. As an INSTITUTION, the Sabbath
declared its author to be the Creator of heaven and earth;
as a *sign* [16] *between God and Israel*, it is declared that he
who had set them apart was indeed Jehovah.

---

[16] As a sign, it did not thereby become a shadow and a ceremony; for the Lord
of the Sabbath was himself a sign. "Behold, I and the children whom the Lord
hath given me are for signs and wonders in Israel from the Lord of hosts, which

The last act of the Lawgiver in this memorable interview was to place in the hands of Moses the "two
tables of testimony, tables of stone, written with the
finger of God." Then he revealed to Moses the sad
apostasy of Israel, and urged him to hasten down to them.

"And Moses turned, and went down from the mount, and
the two tables of the testimony were in his hand; the tables
were written on both their sides; on the one side and on the
other were they written. And the tables were the work of God,
and the writing was the writing of God, graven upon the tables.
. . . And it came to pass, as soon as he came nigh unto the
camp, that he saw the calf and the dancing; and Moses' anger
waxed hot, and he cast the tables out of his hands, and brake
them beneath the mount."

---

dwelleth in Mount Zion." Isa. 8:18. In Heb. 2:13 this language is referred
to Christ. "And Simeon blessed them, and said unto Mary his mother, Behold,
this child is set for the fall and rising again of many in Israel; and for a sign
which shall be spoken against." Luke 2:34. That the Sabbath was a sign between God and Israel throughout their generations, that is, for the time that they
were his peculiar people, no more proves that it is now abolished than the fact
that Jesus is now a sign that is spoken against proves that he will cease to exist
when he shall no longer be such a sign. Nor does this language argue that the
Sabbath was made for them, or that its obligation ceased when they ceased to be
the people of God; for the prohibition against eating blood was a perpetual statute for their generations; yet it was given to Noah when God first permitted the
use of animal food, and was still obligatory upon the Gentiles when the apostles
turned to them. Lev. 3:17; Gen. 9:1-4; Acts 15.

The penalty of death at the hand of the civil magistrate is affixed to the violation of the Sabbath. The same penalty is affixed to most of the precepts of
the moral law. Lev. 20:9, 10; 24:15-17; Deut. 13:6-18; 17:2-7. It should
be remembered that the moral law embracing the Sabbath formed a part of the
CIVIL code of the Hebrew nation. As such, the great Lawgiver annexed penalties to be inflicted by the magistrate, thus doubtless shadowing forth the final
retribution of the ungodly. Such penalties were suspended by that remarkable
decision of the Saviour that those who were without sin should cast the first
stone. But such a Being will arise to punish men, when the hailstones of his
wrath shall desolate the earth. Our Lord did not, however, set aside the real
penalty of the law, the wages of sin, nor did he weaken that precept which had
been violated. John 8:1-9; Job 38:22, 23; Isa. 28:17; Rev. 16:17-21; Rom.
6:23.

Then Moses inflicted retribution upon the idolaters, "and there fell of the people that day about three thousand men." Moses returned unto God, and interceded in behalf of the people; and God promised that his angel should go with them, but that he himself would not go up in their midst, lest he should consume them.[17] Then Moses presented an earnest supplication to the Most High that he might see his glory. This petition was granted, saving that the face of God should not be seen.[18]

But before Moses ascended, that he might behold the majesty of the infinite Lawgiver, the Lord said unto him,—

"Hew thee two tables of stone like unto the first; and I will write upon these tables the words that were in the first tables, which thou breakest. . . . And he hewed two tables of stone like unto the first; and Moses rose up early in the morning, and went up unto Mount Sinai, as the Lord had commanded him, and took in his hand the two tables of stone. And the Lord descended in the cloud, and stood with him there, and proclaimed the name of the Lord. And the Lord passed by before him."[19]

Then Moses beheld the glory of the Lord, and he "made haste, and bowed his head toward the earth, and worshiped." This interview lasted forty days and forty nights, as did the first, and seems to have been spent by Moses in interceding with God that he would not destroy the people for their sin. The record of this period is very brief, but in this record the Sabbath is mentioned. "Six days thou shalt work, but on the seventh day thou shalt rest: in earing time and in harvest thou shalt

---

[17] This fact will shed light upon these texts which introduce the agency of angels in the giving of the law. Acts 7: 38, 53; Gal. 3: 19; Heb. 2: 2.

[18] Ex. 32 and 33.   [19] Ex. 34; Deut. 9; 10: 1, 2.

rest," [20] thus admonishing them not to forget in their busiest season the Sabbath of the Lord.

This second period of forty days ends, like the first, with the act of God in placing the tables of stone in the hands of Moses. "And he was there with the Lord forty days and forty nights; he did neither eat bread nor drink water. And he [21] wrote upon the tables the words of the covenant, the ten commandments." From this it appears that the tables of testimony were two tables of stone with the ten commandments written upon them by the finger of God, which proves that the testimony of God is, in truth, the ten commandments. The writing on the second tables was an exact copy of that on the first. "Hew thee two tables of stone like unto the first: and I will write," said God, "upon these tables the words that were in the first tables, which thou breakest." And of the first tables, Moses says: "He declared

---

[20] Ex. 34: 21.

[21] The idea has been suggested by some from this verse that it was Moses, and not God, who wrote the second tables. This view is thought to be strengthened by the previous verse: "Write thou these words; for after the tenor of these words I have made a covenant with thee and with Israel." But it is to be observed that the words upon the tables of stone were the ten commandments; while the words here referred to were those which God spoke to Moses during this interview of forty days, beginning with verse 10 and extending to verse 27. That the pronoun *he* in verse 28 might properly enough refer to Moses, if positive testimony did not forbid such reference, is readily admitted. That it is necessary to attend to the connection in deciding the antecedents of pronouns is strikingly illustrated in 2 Sam. 24: 1, where the pronoun *he* would naturally refer to the Lord, thus making God the one who moved David to number Israel. Yet the connection shows that this was not the case; for the anger of the Lord was kindled by the act; and 1 Chron. 21: 1 positively declares that *he* who thus moved David was Satan. For positive testimony that it was God and not Moses who wrote upon the second tables, see Ex. 34: 1; Deut. 10: 1-5. These texts carefully discriminate between the work of Moses and the work of God, assigning the preparation of the tables, the carrying of them up to the mount, and the bringing of them down from the mount, to Moses, but expressly assigning the writing on the tables to God himself.

unto you his covenant, which he commanded you to perform, even ten commandments; and he wrote them upon two tables of stone." [22]

Thus did God commit to his people the ten commandments. Without human or angelic agency, he proclaimed them himself; and not trusting his most honored servant, Moses, nor even an angel of his presence, himself wrote them with his own finger. "Remember the Sabbath-day, to keep it holy," is one of the ten words thus honored by the Most High. Nor are these two high honors the only ones conferred upon this precept. While it shares them in common with the other nine commandments, it stands in advance of them in that it is established by the EXAMPLE of the Lawgiver himself. These precepts were given upon two tables with evident reference to the twofold division of the law of God; supreme love to God, and the love of our neighbor as ourselves. The Sabbath commandment, placed at the close of the first table, forms the golden clasp that binds together both divisions of the moral law. It guards and enforces that day which God claims as his; it follows man through the six days which God has given him to be properly spent in the various relations of life, extending over the whole of human life, and embracing in its loan of six days to man all the duties of the second table, while itself belonging to the first.

That these ten commandments form a complete code of moral law, is proved by the language of the Lawgiver, when he called Moses up to receive them. "Come up to me into the mount, and be there; and I will give thee tables of stone, and a law, and commandments which I

---

[22] Ex. 34: 1, 28; Deut. 4: 12, 13; 5: 22.

have written." [23]   This law and commandments was the
testimony of God engraved upon stone.   The same great
fact is presented by Moses in his blessing pronounced
upon Israel: "And he said, The Lord came from Sinai,
and rose up from Seir unto them; he shined forth from
Mount Paran, and he came with ten thousands of saints;
from his right hand went a fiery law for them." [24]   There
can be no dispute that in this language the Most High
is represented as personally present with ten thousands
of his holy ones, or angels.   And that which he wrote
with his own right hand is called by Moses "a fiery
law," or as the margin has it, "a fire of law."   And now
the man of God completes his sacred trust. He rehearses
what God did in committing his law to him, and what he
himself did in its final disposition: "And he wrote on
the tables, according to the first writing, the ten commandments, which the Lord spake unto you in the
mount out of the midst of the fire in the day of the
assembly; and the Lord gave them unto me.   And I
turned myself, and came down from the mount, and put
the tables in the ark which I had made; and there they
be, as the Lord commanded me."   Thus was the law of
God deposited in the ark beneath the mercy-seat.[25]

The top of the ark was called the mercy-seat, because
all those who had broken the law contained in the ark
beneath the mercy-seat could find pardon by the sprinkling of the blood of atonement upon it.

The law within the ark was that which demanded an

---

[23] Ex. 24: 12.

[24] Deut. 33: 2. That angels are sometimes called saints or holy ones, see Dan.
8: 13-16.   That angels were present with God at Sinai, see Ps. 68: 17.

[25] Deut. 10: 4, 5; Ex. 25: 10-22.

atonement; the ceremonial law, which ordained the Levitical priesthood and the sacrifices for sin, was that which taught men how the atonement could be made. The broken law was beneath the mercy-seat, the blood of sin-offering was sprinkled upon its top, and pardon was extended to the penitent sinner. There was actual sin, and hence a real law which man had broken; but there was not a real atonement, and hence the need of the great Antitype to the Levitical sacrifices. The real atonement, when it is made, must relate to that law respecting which an atonement had been shadowed forth. In other words, the shadowy atonement related to that law which was shut up in the ark, indicating that a real atonement was demanded by that law. It is necessary that the law which demands atonement in order that its transgressor may be spared, should itself be perfect, else the fault would, in part at least, rest with the Lawgiver, and not wholly with the sinner. Hence, the atonement, when made, does not take away the broken law, for that is perfect, but is expressly designed to take away the guilt of the transgressor.[26] Let it be remembered, then, that the fourth commandment is one of the ten precepts of God's broken law, one of the immutable, holy principles that made the death of God's only Son necessary before pardon could be extended to guilty man. These facts being borne in mind, it will not be thought strange that the Lawgiver should reserve the proclamation of such a law to himself; and that he should intrust to no created being the writing of that law which should demand as its atonement the death of the Son of God.

---

[26] 1 John 3 : 4, 5.

CHAPTER VI.

THE SABBATH DURING THE DAY OF TEMPTATION.

General history of the Sabbath in the wilderness—Its violation one cause of excluding that generation from the promised land—Its violation by their children in the wilderness one of the causes of their final dispersion from their own land—The statute respecting fires upon the Sabbath—Various precepts relative to the Sabbath—The Sabbath not a Jewish feast—The man who gathered sticks upon the Sabbath— Appeal of Moses in behalf of the decalogue—The Sabbath not derived from the covenant at Horeb—Final appeal of Moses in behalf of the Sabbath—The original fourth commandment—The Sabbath not a memorial of the flight from Egypt—What words were engraved upon stone?—General summary from the books of Moses.

HE history of the Sabbath during the provocation in the day of temptation in the wilderness, when God was grieved for forty years with his people, may be stated in few words. Even under the eye of Moses, and with the most stupendous miracles in their memory and before their eyes, they were idolaters,[1] neglecters of sacrifices, neglecters of circumcision,[2] murmurers against God, despisers of his law,[3] and violators of his Sabbath.   Of their treatment of the Sabbath while in the wilderness, Ezekiel gives us the following graphic description :—

"But the house of Israel rebelled against me in the wilderness : they walked not in my statutes, and they despised my

---

[1] Ex. 32; Josh. 24:2, 14, 23; Eze. 20:7, 8, 16, 18, 24.

[2] Amos 5:25–27; Acts 7: 41–43; Josh. 5:2–8.

[3] Num. 14; Ps. 95; Eze. 20:13.

judgments, which if a man do, he shall even live in them; and my Sabbaths they greatly polluted: then I said I would pour out my fury upon them in the wilderness, to consume them. But I wrought for my name's sake, that it should not be polluted before the heathen, in whose sight I brought them out." [4]

This language shows a general violation of the Sabbath, and evidently refers to the apostasy of Israel during the first forty days that Moses was absent from them. God did then purpose their destruction; but at the intercession of Moses he spared them for the very reason assigned by the prophet.[5] A further probation being granted them, they signally failed a second time, so that God lifted up his hand to them, that they should not enter the promised land. The prophet continues,—

"Yet also I lifted up my hand unto them in the wilderness, that I should not bring them into the land which I had given them, flowing with milk and honey, which is the glory of all lands; BECAUSE they despised my judgments, and walked not in my statutes, but polluted my Sabbaths; for their heart went after their idols. Nevertheless, mine eye spared them from destroying them, neither did I make an end of them in the wilderness." [6]

The above has undoubted reference to the act of God in excluding all that were over twenty years of age from entering the promised land.[7] It is to be noticed that the violation of the Sabbath is distinctly stated as one of the reasons for which that generation was excluded from the land of promise. God spared the people so that the nation was not utterly cut off; for he extended to the younger part a further probation. Continuing in verses 18–24, he says :—

---

[4] Eze. 20: 13, 14. [5] Ex. 32. [6] Eze. 20: 15–17. [7] Num. 14.

" But I said unto their children in the wilderness, walk ye not in the statutes of your fathers, neither observe their judgments, nor defile yourselves with their idols : I am the Lord your God ; walk in my statutes, and keep my judgments, and do them ; and hallow my Sabbaths ; and they shall be a sign between me and you, that ye may know that I am the Lord your God. Notwithstanding, the children rebelled against me ; they walked not in my statutes, neither kept my judgments to do them, which if a man do, he shall even live in them ; they polluted my Sabbaths : then I said I would pour out my fury upon them, to accomplish my anger against them in the wilderness. Nevertheless, I withdrew my hand, and wrought for my name's sake, that it should not be polluted in the sight of the heathen, in whose sight I brought them forth. I lifted up mine hand unto them also in the wilderness, that I would scatter them among the heathen, and disperse them through the countries ; because they had not executed my judgments, but had despised my statutes, and had polluted my Sabbaths, and their eyes were after their fathers' idols."

Thus it appears that the younger generation, which God spared when he excluded their fathers from the land of promise, did, like their fathers, transgress God's law, pollute his Sabbath, and cleave to idolatry. God did not see fit to exclude them from the land of Canaan, but he did lift up his hand to them in the wilderness, that he would give them up to dispersion among their enemies after they had entered the land of promise. By this it is seen that the Hebrews, while in the wilderness, laid the foundation for their subsequent dispersion from their own land ; and that one of the acts which led to their final ruin as a nation was the violation of the Sabbath before they had entered the promised land. Well might Moses say to them in the last month of his life : " Ye have been rebellious against the Lord from the day that I knew you." [8]   In Caleb and Joshua was another spirit, for they followed the Lord fully. [9]

Such is the general history of Sabbatic observance in the wilderness. Even the miracle of the manna, which every week for forty years bore public testimony to the Sabbath, [10] became to the body of the Hebrews merely an ordinary event, so that they dared to murmur against the bread thus sent from heaven; [11] and we may well believe that those who were thus hardened through the deceitfulness of sin, had little regard for the testimony of the manna in behalf of the Sabbath. [12] In the Mosaic record we next read of the Sabbath as follows :—

" And Moses gathered all the congregation of the children of Israel together, and said unto them, These are the words which the Lord hath commanded, that ye should do them. Six days shall work be done, but on the seventh day there shall be to you an holy day, a Sabbath of rest to the Lord; whosoever doeth work therein shall be put to death. [13] Ye shall kindle no fire throughout your habitations upon the Sabbath-day." [14]

The chief feature of interest in this text relates to the prohibition of fires on the Sabbath. As this is the only prohibition of the kind in the Bible, and as it is often urged as a reason why the Sabbath should not be kept, a brief examination of the difficulty will not be out of place. It should be observed, 1. That this language does not form a part of the fourth commandment, the grand law of the Sabbath; 2. That as there were laws

---

[8] Deut. 9:24.

[9] Num. 14; Heb. 3:16.

[10] Ex. 16; Josh. 5:12.

[11] Num. 11 and 21.

[12] A comparison of Ex. 19; 20:18–21; 24:3–8, with chapter 32, will show the astonishing transitions of the Hebrews from faith and obedience to rebellion and idolatry. See a general history of these acts in Ps. 78 and 106.

[13] For a notice of this penalty, see chapter 5 of this work.

[14] Ex. 35:1–3.

pertaining to the Sabbath which were no part of the Sabbatic institution, but grew out of its being intrusted to the Hebrews,—such as the law respecting the presentation of the shew-bread on the Sabbath, and that respecting the burnt-offering for the Sabbath,—[15] so it is at least possible that this is a precept pertaining only to that nation, and not a part of the original institution; 3. That as there were laws peculiar only to the Hebrews, so there were many that pertained to them only while they were in the wilderness (such were all those precepts that related to the manna, the building and setting up of the tabernacle, the manner of encamping about it, etc.); 4. That of this class were all the statutes given from the time that Moses brought down the second tables of stone until the events narrated in the close of the book of Exodus, unless the words under consideration form an exception; 5. That the prohibition of fires was a law of this class, *i. e.*, a law designed only for the wilderness; and this is evident from several decisive facts :—

1. That the land of Palestine, during a part of the year, is so cold that fires are necessary to prevent suffering.[16]

---

[15] Lev. 24: 5–9; Num. 28: 9, 10.

[16] The Bible abounds in facts which establish this proposition. The psalmist, in an address to Jerusalem, uses the following language: "He giveth snow like wool; he scattereth the hoar-frost like ashes. He casteth forth his ice like morsels; who can stand before his cold? He sendeth out his word, and melteth them; he causeth his wind to blow, and the waters flow. He showeth his word unto Jacob, his statutes and his judgments unto Israel." Ps. 147: 16–19. Dr. Clarke has the following note on this text: "At particular times the cold in the East is so very intense as to kill man and beast. Jacobus de Vitriaco, one of the writers in the *Gesta Dei per Francos*, says that in an expedition in which he was engaged against Mount Tabor, on the 24th of December, the cold was so intense that many of the poor people and the beasts of burden died by it. And Albertus Aquensis,

2. That the Sabbath was not designed to be a cause of distress and suffering, but of refreshment, of delight, and of blessing.[17]

3. That in the wilderness of Sinai, where this precept respecting fires on the Sabbath was given, it was not a cause of suffering, as they were two hundred miles south of Jerusalem, in the warm climate of Arabia.

4. That this precept was of a temporary character is further implied in that while other laws are said to be perpetual statutes and precepts to be kept after they should enter the land,[18] no hint of this kind appears here. On the contrary, this seems to be similar in character to

---

another of these writers, speaking of the cold in Judea, says that *thirty* of the people who attended Baldwin I. in the mountainous districts near the Dead Sea, were killed by it; and that in that expedition they had to contend with horrible hail and ice, with unheard-of snow and rain. From this we find that the winters are often very severe in Judea; and that in such cases as the above we may well call out, ' Who can stand against his cold?' " See his commentary on Ps. 147. See also Jer. 36: 22; John 18: 18; Matt. 24: 20; Mark 13: 18. 1 Maccabees 13: 22 mentions a very great snow-storm in Palestine, so that horsemen could not march.

[17] The testimony of the Bible on this point is very explicit. Thus we read: " Six days thou shalt do thy work, and on the seventh day thou shalt rest; that thine ox and thine ass may rest, and the son of thy handmaid, and the stranger may be refreshed." Ex. 23: 12. To be without fire in the severity of winter would cause the Sabbath to be a curse and not a refreshment. It would ruin the health of those who should thus expose themselves, and render the Sabbath anything but a source of refreshment. The prophet uses the following language: "If thou turn away thy foot from the Sabbath, from doing thy pleasure on my holy day; and call the Sabbath a delight, the holy of the Lord, honorable," etc. The Sabbath, then, was designed by God to be a source of delight to his people, and not a cause of suffering. The merciful and beneficent character of the Sabbath is seen in the following texts: Matt. 12: 10–13; Mark 2: 27, 28; Luke 14: 3–6. From them we learn that God regards the sufferings of the brute creation, and would have them alleviated upon the Sabbath; how much more the distress and the needs of his people, for whose refreshment and delight the Sabbath was made.

[18] Ex. 29: 9; 31: 16; Lev. 3: 17; 24: 9; Num. 19: 21; Deut. 5: 31; 6: 1; 7. The number and variety of these allusions will surprise the inquirer.

the precept respecting the manna,[19] and to be co-existent with, and adapted to it.

5. If the prohibition respecting fires did indeed pertain to the promised land, and not merely to the wilderness, it would every few years conflict directly with the law of the Passover; for the Passover was to be roasted by each family of the children of Israel on the evening following the fourteenth day of the first month,[20] which would fall occasionally upon the Sabbath. The prohibition of fires upon the Sabbath would not conflict with the Passover while the Hebrews were in the wilderness; for the Passover was not to be observed until they reached that land.[21] But if that prohibition did extend forward to the promised land, where the Passover was to be regularly observed, these two statutes would often come in direct conflict. This is certainly a strong confirmation of the view that the prohibition of fires upon the Sabbath was a temporary statute, relating only to the wilderness.[22]

---

[19] Ex. 16: 23.   [20] Ex. 12; Deut. 16.

[21] The law of the Passover certainly contemplated the arrival of the Hebrews in the promised land before its regular observance. Ex. 12: 25. Indeed, it was only once observed in the wilderness; namely, in the year following their departure from Egypt; and after that, was omitted until they entered the land of Canaan. Num. 9; Josh. 5. This is proved, not merely from the fact that no other instances are recorded, but because circumcision was omitted during the whole period of their sojourn in the wilderness; and without this ordinance the children would have been excluded from the Passover. Ex. 12; Josh. 5.

[22] Dr. Gill, who considered the seventh-day Sabbath as a Jewish institution, beginning with Moses and ending with Christ, and one with which Gentiles have no concern, has given his judgment concerning this question of fire on the Sabbath. He certainly had no motive in answering this popular objection, only that of stating the truth. He says:—

"This law seems to be a temporary one, and not to be continued, nor is it said to be throughout their generations, as elsewhere, where the law of the Sabbath is given or repeated; it is to be restrained to the building of the tabernacle, and

From these facts it follows that the favorite argument drawn from the prohibition of fires, that the Sabbath was a local institution, and adapted only to the land of Canaan, must be abandoned; for it is evident that that prohibition was a temporary statute, not even adapted to the land of promise, and not designed for that land. We next read of the Sabbath as follows :—

"And the Lord spake unto Moses, saying, Speak unto all the congregation of the children of Israel, and say unto them, Ye shall be holy; for I the Lord your God am holy. Ye shall fear every man his mother, and his father, and keep my Sabbaths; I am the Lord your God." "Ye shall keep my Sabbaths, and reverence my sanctuary; I am the Lord." [23]

These constant references to the Sabbath contrast strikingly with the general disobedience of the people. Again God says :—

"Six days shall work be done; but the seventh day is the Sabbath of rest, an holy convocation; ye shall do no work therein; it is the Sabbath of the Lord in all your dwellings." [24]

---

while that was about to which it is prefaced; and it is designed to prevent all public or private working on the Sabbath-day in anything belonging to that;" etc.—*Commentary on Ex. 35 : 3.*

Dr. Bound gives us St. Augustine's idea of this precept: "He doth not ad monish them of it without cause; for that he speaketh in making the tabernacle, and all things belonging to it, and showeth that, notwithstanding that, they must rest upon the Sabbath-day, and not under the color of that (as it is said in the text) so much as kindle a fire."—*True Doctrine of the Sabbath,* p. 140.

[23] Lev. 19: 1–3, 30.

[24] Lev. 23: 3. It has been asserted from verse 2 that the Sabbath was one of the feasts of the Lord. But a comparison of verses 2 and 4 shows that there is a break in the narrative, for the purpose of introducing the Sabbath as a holy convocation, and that verse 4 begins the theme anew in the very language of verse 2; and it is to be observed that the remainder of the chapter sets forth the actual Jewish feasts; viz., that of unleavened bread, the Pentecost, and the Feast of Tabernacles. What further clears this point of all obscurity is the fact that verses 37 and 38 carefully discriminate between the feasts of the Lord and the

Thus did God solemnly designate his rest-day as a season of holy worship, and as the day of weekly religious assemblies. Again the great Lawgiver sets forth his Sabbath :—

"Ye shall make you no idols nor graven image, neither rear you up a standing image, neither shall ye set up any image of stone in your land, to bow down unto it; for I am the Lord your God. Ye shall keep my Sabbaths, and reverence my sanctuary; I am the Lord." [25]

Happy would it have been for the people of God had they thus refrained from idolatry, and sacredly regarded the rest-day of the Creator. Yet idolatry and Sabbath-breaking were so general in the wilderness that the generation which came forth from Egypt were excluded from the promised land.[26] After God had thus cut off from inheriting the land the men who had rebelled against him,[27] we next read of the Sabbath as follows :—

"And while the children of Israel were in the wilderness, they found a man that gathered sticks upon the Sabbath-day. And they that found him gathering sticks brought him unto Moses and Aaron, and unto all the congregation. And they put him in ward, because it was not declared what should be done to him. And the Lord said unto Moses, The man shall be surely put to death; all the congregation shall stone him with stones without the camp. And all the congregation brought him without the camp, and stoned him with stones, and he died; as the Lord commanded Moses." [28]

The following facts should be considered in explain-

Sabbaths of the Lord. But Ex. 23:14 settles the point beyond controversy: "Three times thou shalt keep a feast unto me in the year." And then verses 15–17 enumerate these feasts as in Lev. 23:4–44. See also 2 Chron. 8:13.

[25] Lev. 26:1, 2.   [26] Eze. 20:15, 16.   [27] Num. 13 and 14.

[28] Num. 15:32–36.

ing this text: 1. That this was a case of peculiar guilt; for the whole congregation before whom this man stood in judgment, and by whom he was put to death, were themselves guilty of violating the Sabbath, and had just been excluded from the promised land for this and other sins.[29] 2. That this was not a case which came under the existing penalty of death for work upon the Sabbath; for the man was put in confinement that the mind of the Lord respecting his guilt might be obtained. The peculiarity of his transgression may be learned from the context. The verses which next precede the case in question read thus :—

" But the soul that doeth aught presumptuously, whether he be born in the land, or a stranger, the same reproacheth the Lord; and that soul shall be cut off from among his people. Because he hath despised the word of the Lord, and hath broken his commandment, that soul shall utterly be cut off; his iniquity shall be upon him." [30]

These words, being followed by this remarkable case, were evidently designed to be illustrated by it. It is manifest, therefore, that this was an instance of presumptuous sin, in which the transgressor intended despite to the Spirit of grace and to the statutes of the Most High; hence this case cannot be quoted as evidence of extraordinary strictness on the part of the Hebrews in observing the Sabbath; for we have direct evidence that they did greatly pollute it during the whole forty years of their sojourn in the wilderness.[31] It stands as an instance of transgression in which the sinner intended to show

---

[29] Eze. 20: 15, 16 comp. with Num. 14: 35.

[30] Num. 15: 30.   [31] Eze. 20.

his contempt for the Lawgiver, and in this consisted his peculiar guilt.[32]

In the last month of his long and eventful life, Moses rehearsed all the great acts of God in behalf of his people, with the statutes and precepts that he had given them. This rehearsal is contained in the book of Deuteronomy, a name which signifies *second law*, and is applied to that book, because it is a second writing of the law. It is the farewell of Moses to a disobedient and rebellious people ; and he endeavors to fasten upon them the strongest possible sense of personal obligation to obey. When he is about to rehearse the ten commandments, he uses language evidently designed to impress upon the minds of the Hebrews a sense of their individual obligation to do what God had commanded. He says :—

"Hear, O Israel, the statutes and judgments which I speak in your ears this day, that ye may learn them, and keep and do them. The Lord our God made a covenant with us in Horeb. The Lord made not this covenant with our fathers, but with us, even us, who are all of us here alive this day." [33]

It was not the act of your fathers that placed this

---

[32] Hengstenberg, a distinguished German anti-Sabbatarian, thus candidly treats this text: "A man who had gathered wood on the Sabbath is brought forth at the command of the Lord, and stoned by the whole congregation before the camp. Calvin says rightly, 'The guilty man did not fall through error, but through gross contempt of the law, so that he treated it as a light matter to overthrow and destroy all that is holy.' It is evident from the manner of its introduction that the account is not given with any reference to its chronological position ; it reads, 'And while the children of Israel were *in the wilderness*, they found a man that gathered sticks upon the Sabbath-day.' It stands simply as an example of the presumptuous breach of the law, of which the preceding verses speak. He was one who despised the word of the Lord, and broke his commandments [verse 31]; one who with a high hand sinned and reproached the Lord. Verse 30."—*The Lord's Day*, pp. 31, 32.

[33] Deut. 5: 1–3.

responsibility upon you, but your own individual acts that brought you into the bond of this covenant. You have personally pledged yourselves to the Most High to keep these precepts.[34] Such is the obvious import of this language; yet it has been gravely adduced as proof that the Sabbath of the Lord was made for the Hebrews, and was not obligatory upon the patriarchs. The singularity of this deduction appears in that it is brought to bear against the fourth commandment alone; whereas, if it were a just and logical argument, it would show that the ancient patriarchs were under no obligation in respect to any precept of the moral law. But it is certain that the covenant at Horeb was simply an embodiment of the precepts of the moral law, with mutual pledges respecting them between God and the people, and that that covenant did not give existence to any of the ten commandments. At all events, we find the Sabbath ordained of God at the close of creation,[35] and obligatory upon the Hebrews in the wilderness before God had given them a new precept on the subject.[36] As this was before the covenant at Horeb, it is conclusive proof that the Sabbath did no more originate from that covenant than did the prohibition of idolatry, theft, or murder.

The man of God then repeated the ten commandments, giving the fourth as follows :—

"Keep the Sabbath-day, to sanctify it, as the Lord thy God hath commanded thee. Six days thou shalt labor, and do all thy work; but the seventh day is the Sabbath of the Lord thy God: in it thou shalt not do any work, thou, nor thy son, nor thy

---

[34] See the pledges of this people in Ex. 19 and 24.

[35] See chapter 2 of this work. [36] See chapter 3.

daughter, nor thy man-servant, nor thy maid-servant, nor thine ox, nor thine ass, nor any of thy cattle, nor thy stranger that is within thy gates; that thy man-servant and thy maid-servant may rest as well as thou. And remember that thou wast a servant in the land of Egypt, and that the Lord thy God brought thee out thence through a mighty hand and by a stretched-out arm; therefore the Lord thy God commanded thee to keep the Sabbath-day." [37]

It is a singular fact that this scripture is uniformly quoted as the original fourth commandment by those who write against the Sabbath, while the original precept itself is carefully left out. Yet there is the strongest evidence that this is not the original precept; for Moses rehearsed these words at the end of the forty years' sojourn, whereas the original commandment was given in the third month after the departure from Egypt.[38] The commandment itself, as here given, contains direct proof on the point. It reads: "Keep the Sabbath-day, to sanctify it, AS the Lord thy God HATH COMMANDED thee," citing elsewhere for the original statute. Moreover, the precept as here given is evidently incomplete. It contains no clue to the origin of the Sabbath of the Lord, nor does it show the acts by which the Sabbath came into existence. This is why those who represent the Sabbath as made in the wilderness and not at creation quote this as the fourth commandment, and omit the original precept which God himself proclaimed, where all these facts are distinctly stated.[39]

But while Moses in this rehearsal omitted a large part of the fourth commandment, he referred to the original precept for the whole matter, and then appended

---

[37] Deut. 5: 12–15.   [38] Compare Ex. 19; 20 and Deut. 1.
[39] Ex. 20: 8–11.

to this rehearsal a powerful plea of obligation on the part of the Hebrews to keep the Sabbath. It should be remembered that many of the people had steadily persisted in the violation of the Sabbath, and that this was the last time that Moses spoke in its behalf. He said:—

"And remember that thou wast a servant in the land of Egypt, and that the Lord thy God brought thee out thence through a mighty hand and by a stretched-out arm; therefore the Lord thy God commanded thee to keep the Sabbath-day."

These words are often cited as proof that the Sabbath originated at the departure of Israel from Egypt, and that it was ordained at that time as a memorial of their deliverance from thence. But it will be observed, 1. That this text says not one word respecting the origin of the Sabbath, or rest-day of the Lord; 2. That the facts on this point are all given in the original fourth commandment, and are there referred to creation; 3. That there is no reason to believe that God rested upon the seventh day at the time of this flight from Egypt, nor that he then blessed and hallowed the day; 4. That the Sabbath has nothing in it that would fitly commemorate the deliverance from Egypt, as that was a flight and this is a rest; and that flight was upon the fifteenth of the first month, and this rest is upon the seventh day of each week, one occurring annually, the other, weekly; 5. But that God did ordain a fitting memorial of that deliverance, to be observed by the Hebrews,—the Passover, on the fourteenth day of the first month, in memory of God's passing over them when he smote the Egyptians; and the feast of unleavened bread, in memory of their eating this bread when they fled out of Egypt.[40]

[40] Ex. 12 and 13.

But what, then, do these words imply? Perhaps their meaning may be more readily perceived by comparing them with an exact parallel found in the same book, and from the pen of the same writer :—

" Thou shalt not pervert the judgment of the stranger, nor of the fatherless, nor take a widow's raiment to pledge; but thou shalt remember that thou wast a bondman in Egypt, and the Lord thy God redeemed thee thence; therefore I command thee to do this thing." [41]

It will be seen at a glance that this precept was not given to commemorate the deliverance of Israel from Egyptian bondage; nor could that deliverance give existence to the moral obligation expressed in it. If the language in the one case proves that men were not under obligation to keep the Sabbath before the deliverance of Israel from Egypt, it proves with equal conclusiveness in the other that before that deliverance they were not under obligation to treat with justice and mercy the stranger, the fatherless, and the widow. And if the Sabbath is shown in the one case to be Jewish, in the other, the statute of the great Lawgiver in behalf of the needy and the helpless must share the same fate. It is manifest that this language is in each case an appeal to their sense of gratitude. You were slaves in Egypt, and God rescued you; therefore remember others who are in distress, and oppress them not. You were bondmen in Egypt, and God redeemed you; therefore sanctify unto the Lord the day which he has reserved unto himself,—a most powerful appeal to those who had hitherto persisted in polluting it. Deliverance from abject servi-

---

[41] Deut. 24: 17, 18.

tude was indeed necessary in each case, in order that the things enjoined might be fully observed; but that deliverance did not give existence to either of these duties. Truly, it was one of the acts by which the Sabbath of the Lord was given to that nation, but it was not one of the acts by which God made the Sabbath, nor did it render the rest-day of the Lord a Jewish institution.

That the words engraved upon stone were simply the ten commandments, is evident.

1. It is said of the first tables,—

"And the Lord spake unto you out of the midst of the fire: ye heard the voice cf the words, but saw no similitude; only ye heard a voice. And he declared unto you his covenant, which he commanded you to perform, even ten commandments; and he wrote them upon two tables of stone." [42]

2. The above shows that the first tables of stone contained the ten commandments alone. That the second tables were an exact copy of what was written upon the first, is plainly stated in the following verses :—

"And the Lord said unto Moses, Hew thee two tables of stone like unto the first; and I will write upon these tables the words that were in the first tables, which thou breakest." "And I will write on the tables the words that were in the first tables which thou breakest, and thou shalt put them in the ark." [43]

3. This is confirmed by the decisive testimony found in these verses :—

"And he wrote upon the tables the words of the covenant, the ten commandments" [margin, Heb., *words*]. "And he wrote on the tables, according to the first writing, the ten commandments [margin, *words*], which the Lord spake unto you in

---

[42] Deut. 4: 12, 13.   [43] Ex. 34: 1; Deut. 10: 2.

the mount, out of the midst of the fire in the day of the assembly; and the Lord gave them unto me." [44]

These texts will explain the following language: "And the Lord delivered unto me two tables of stone, written with the finger of God; and on them was written according to all the words which the Lord spake with you in the mount, out of the midst of the fire in the day of the assembly." [45] God is said to have written upon the tables according to all the words which he spoke in the day of the assembly; and these words which he thus wrote are said to have been TEN WORDS. But the preface to the decalogue was not one of these ten words, and hence was not written by the finger of God upon stone. That this distinction must not be overlooked, will be seen by examining the following text and its connection :—

"THESE WORDS the Lord spake unto all your assembly in the mount, out of the midst of the fire, of the cloud, and of the thick darkness, with a great voice; and he added no more. And he wrote them in two tables of stone, and delivered them unto me." [46]

THESE WORDS here brought to view, as written by the finger of God after having been uttered by him in the hearing of all the people, must be understood as one of two things: They are simply the ten words of the law of God, or they are all the words used by Moses in this rehearsal of the decalogue. But they cannot refer to the words used in this rehearsal; for, 1. Moses omits an important part of the fourth precept as given by God in its proclamation from the mount; 2. In this rehearsal

---

[44] Ex. 34: 28; Deut. 10: 4.   [45] Deut. 9: 10.   [46] Deut. 5: 22.

of that precept he cites back to the original for that which is omitted; [47] 3. He appends to this precept an appeal in its behalf to their gratitude, which was not made by God in giving it; 4. This language only purports to be a rehearsal, and not the original itself; and this is further evinced by many verbal deviations from the original decalogue.[48] These facts are decisive as to what was placed upon the tables of stone. That was not an incomplete copy, citing elsewhere for the original, but the original code itself. And hence, when Moses speaks of THESE WORDS as engraved upon the tables, he refers not to the words used by himself in this rehearsal, but to the TEN WORDS of the law of God, and excludes all else.

Thus have we traced the Sabbath through the books of Moses. We have found its origin in paradise, when man was in his uprightness; we have seen the Hebrews set apart from all mankind as the depositaries of divine truth; we have seen the Sabbath and the whole moral law committed as a sacred trust to them; we have seen the Sabbath proclaimed by God as one of the ten commandments; we have seen it written by the finger of God upon stone in the bosom of the moral law; we have seen that law, possessing no Jewish, but simply moral and divine features, placed beneath the mercy-seat in the ark of God's testament; we have seen that various precepts pertaining to the Sabbath were given to the Hebrews, and designed only for them; we have seen that the Hebrews did greatly pollute the Sabbath during their sojourn in the wilderness; and we have heard the final

---

[47] Deut. 5: 12–15 compared with Ex. 20: 8–11.

[48] Deut. 5 compared with Ex. 20.

6

appeal made in its behalf by Moses to that rebellious people.

We rest the foundation of the Sabbatic institution upon its sanctification before the fall of man; the fourth commandment is its great citadel of defense; and its place in the midst of the moral law beneath the mercy-seat shows its immutable obligation and its relation to the atonement.

CHAPTER VII.

THE FEASTS, NEW MOONS, AND SABBATHS OF THE HEBREWS.

Enumeration of the Hebrew festivals—The Passover—The Pentecost—
The Feast of Tabernacles—The new moons—The first and second
annual sabbaths—The third—The fourth—The fifth—The sixth and
seventh—The sabbath of the land—The jubilee—None of these festivals in force until the Hebrews entered their own land—The contrast
between the Sabbath of the Lord and the sabbaths of the Hebrews—
Testimony of Isaiah—Of Hosea—Of Jeremiah—Final cessation of
these festivals.

P to this point we have followed the Sabbath
of the Lord through the books of Moses. A
brief survey of the Jewish festivals is necessary to the complete view of the subject before us. Of
these there were three feasts : the Passover, the Pentecost, and the Feast of Tabernacles ; there was each new
moon, that is, the first day of each month throughout
the year ; then there were seven annual sabbaths,
namely, the first day of unleavened bread, the seventh
day of that feast, the day of Pentecost, the first day of
the seventh month, the tenth day of that month, the fifteenth day of that month, and the twenty-second day of
the same. In addition to all these, every seventh year
was to be the Sabbath of the land, and every fiftieth
year the year of jubilee.

The Passover takes its name from the fact that the angel of the Lord "passed over" the houses of the Hebrews
on that eventful night when the first-born in every

Egyptian family was slain.   This feast was ordained in commemoration of the deliverance of that people from Egyptian bondage.   It began with the slaying of the Paschal lamb on the fourteenth day of the first month, and extended through a period of seven days, in which nothing but unleavened bread was to be eaten.   Its great antitype was reached when Christ, our Passover, was sacrificed for us.[1]

The Pentecost was the second of the Jewish feasts, and occupied but a single day.   It was celebrated on the fiftieth day after the first-fruits of barley harvest had been waved before the Lord.   At the time of this feast, the first-fruits of wheat harvest were offered unto God.   The antitype of this festival was reached on the fiftieth day after the resurrection of Christ, when the great outpouring of the Holy Ghost took place.[2]

The Feast of Tabernacles was the last of the Jewish feasts.   It was celebrated in the seventh month, when they had gathered in the fruit of the land, and extended from the fifteenth to the twenty-first day of that month. It was ordained as a festival of rejoicing before the Lord; and during this period the children of Israel dwelt in booths in commemoration of their dwelling thus during their sojourn in the wilderness.   It probably typifies the great rejoicing after the final gathering of all the people of God into his kingdom.[3]

In connection with these feasts, it was ordained that each new moon, that is, the first day of every month, should be observed with certain specified offerings, and

---

[1] Ex. 12; 1 Cor. 5:7, 8.

[2] Lev. 23:10–21; Num. 28:26–31; Deut. 16:9–12; Acts 2:1–18.

[3] Lev. 23:34–43; Deut. 16:13–15; Neh. 8; Rev. 7:9–14.

with tokens of rejoicing.[4]   The annual sabbaths of the
Hebrews have been already enumerated.   The first two
of these sabbaths were the first and seventh days of the
feast of unleavened bread, that is, the fifteenth and
twenty-first days of the first month.   They were thus
ordained by God :—

" Seven days shall ye eat unleavened bread; even the first
day ye shall put away leaven out of your houses. . . . And in
the first day there shall be an holy convocation, and in the seventh day there shall be an holy convocation to you; no manner
of work shall be done in them, save that which every man must
eat, that only may be done of you." [5]

The third in order of the annual sabbaths was the
day of Pentecost.   This festival was ordained as a rest-
day, in the following language :—

" And ye shall proclaim on the selfsame day, that it may be
an holy convocation unto you: ye shall do no servile work
therein; it shall be a statute forever in all your dwellings
throughout your generations." [6]

The first day of the seventh month was the fourth
annual sabbath of the Hebrews.   Moses was commanded
to—

" Speak unto the children of Israel, saying, In the seventh
month, in the first day of the month, shall ye have a sabbath, a
memorial of blowing of trumpets, an holy convocation.   Ye shall
do no servile work therein; but ye shall offer an offering made by
fire unto the Lord." [7]

The great day of atonement was the fifth of these
sabbaths.   The Lord said unto Moses,—

---

[4] Num. 10: 10; 28: 11–15; 1 Sam. 20: 5, 24, 27; Ps. 81: 3.
[5] Ex. 12: 15, 16; Lev. 23: 7, 8; Num. 28: 17, 18, 25.
[6] Lev. 23: 21; Num. 28: 26.   [7] Lev. 23: 24, 25; Num. 29: 1–6.

" Also on the tenth day of this seventh month there shall be a day of atonement; it shall be an holy convocation unto you. . . . Ye shall do no manner of work; it shall be a statute forever throughout your generations in all your dwellings. It shall be unto you a sabbath of rest, and ye shall afflict your souls; in the ninth day of the month at even, from even unto even, shall ye celebrate your sabbath." [8]

The sixth and seventh of these annual sabbaths were the fifteenth and twenty-second days of the seventh month, that is, the first day of the Feast of Tabernacles; and the day after its conclusion. They were enjoined by God in the following manner :—

" Also in the fifteenth day of the seventh month, when ye have gathered in the fruit of the land, ye shall keep a feast unto the Lord seven days; on the first day shall be a sabbath, and on the eighth day shall be a sabbath." [9]

Besides all these, every seventh year was a sabbath of rest unto the land. The people might labor as usual in other business, but they were forbidden to till the land, that the land itself might rest.[10] After seven of these sabbaths, the following or fiftieth year was to be the year of jubilee, in which every man was to be restored to his inheritance.[11] There is no evidence that the jubilee was ever observed, and it is certain that the sabbatical year was almost entirely disregarded.[12]

Such were the feasts, new moons, and sabbaths of the Hebrews. A few words will suffice to point out the broad distinction between them and the Sabbath of the Lord. The first of the three feasts was ordained in memory of their deliverance from Egyptian bondage, and

---

[8] Lev. 23: 27–32; 16: 29–31; Num. 29: 7.

[9] Lev. 23: 39.   [10] Ex. 23: 10, 11; Lev. 25: 2–7.

[11] Lev. 25: 8–54.   [12] Lev. 26: 34, 35, 43; 2 Chron. 36: 21.

was to be observed when they should enter their own land.[13]   The second feast, as we have seen, could not be observed until after the settlement of the Hebrews in Canaan; for it was to be celebrated when the first-fruits of wheat harvest should be offered before the Lord. The third feast was ordained in memory of their sojourn in the wilderness, and was to be celebrated by them each year after the ingathering of the entire harvest.   Of course, this feast, like the others, could not be observed until the people were settled in their own land.   The new moons, as has been already seen, were not ordained until after these feasts had been instituted.   The annual sabbaths were part of these feasts, and could have no existence until after the feasts to which they belonged had been instituted.   Thus the first and second of these sabbaths were the first and seventh days of the Paschal feast; the third was identical with the feast of Pentecost; the fourth was the same as the new moon in the seventh month; the fifth was the great day of atonement; and the sixth and seventh were the fifteenth and twenty-second days of the seventh month, that is, the first day of the Feast of Tabernacles, and the next day after the close of that feast.   As these feasts were not to be observed until the Hebrews should possess their own land, the annual sabbaths could have no existence until that time.   And so of the sabbaths of the land. These could have no existence until after the Hebrews should possess and cultivate their own land; after six years of cultivation, the land should rest the seventh year, and remain untilled.   After seven of these sabbaths of the land, came the year of jubilee.

---

[13] Ex. 12: 25.

The contrast between the Sabbath of the Lord and these sabbaths of the Hebrews [14] is strongly marked. 1. The Sabbath of the Lord was instituted at the close of the first week of time; while these were ordained in connection with the Jewish feasts. 2. The one was blessed and hallowed by God, because he had rested upon it from the work of creation; the others have no such claim to our regard. 3. When the children of Israel came into the wilderness, the Sabbath of the Lord was an existing institution, obligatory upon them; but the annual sabbaths came into existence only at that time. It is easy to point to the very act of God, while leading that people, that gave existence to these sabbaths; while every reference to the Sabbath of the Lord shows that it had been ordained before God chose that people. 4. The children of Israel were excluded from the promised land for violating the Sabbath of the Lord in the wilderness; but the annual sabbaths were not to be observed until they entered that land. This contrast would be strange indeed were it true that the Sabbath of the Lord was not instituted until the children of Israel came into the wilderness of Sin; for it is certain that two of the annual sabbaths were instituted before they left the land of Egypt.[15] 5. The Sabbath of the Lord was

---

[14] On this point, Mr. Miller uses the following language: "Only one kind of Sabbath was given to Adam, and one only remains for us. See Hosea 2: 11. 'I will also cause all her mirth to cease, her feast days, her new moons, and her sabbaths, and all her solemn feasts.' All the Jewish sabbaths did cease when Christ nailed them to his cross. Col. 2: 14–17. These were properly called Jewish sabbaths. Hosea says 'her sabbaths.' But the sabbath of which we are speaking, God calls 'my sabbath.' Here is a clear distinction between the creation Sabbath and the ceremonial. The one is perpetual; the others were merely shadows of good things to come."—*Life and Views*, pp. 161, 162.

[15] Ex. 12: 16.

made for man; but the annual sabbaths were designed
only for residents in the land of Palestine. 6. The one
was weekly, a memorial of the Creator's rest; the others were annual, connected with the memorials of the
deliverance of the Hebrews from Egypt. 7. The one is
termed "the Sabbath of the Lord," "my Sabbaths,"
"my holy day," and the like; while the others are designated as "your sabbaths," "her sabbaths," and similar
expressions.[16] 8. The one was proclaimed by God as one
of the ten commandments, was written with his finger
in the midst of the moral law upon the tables of stone,
and deposited in the ark beneath the mercy-seat; the
others did not pertain to the moral law, but were embodied in that hand-writing of ordinances which was a
shadow of good things to come. 9. The distinction between these festivals and the Sabbaths of the Lord was
carefully marked by God when he ordained the festivals
and their associated sabbaths; for thus he said: "These
are the feasts of the Lord, which ye shall proclaim to be
holy convocations, . . . BESIDE the Sabbaths of the
Lord." [17]

The annual sabbaths are presented by Isaiah in a
very different light from that in which he presents the
Sabbath of the Lord. Of the one he says:—

"Bring no more vain oblations; incense is an abomination
unto me; the new moons and sabbaths, the calling of assemblies,
I cannot away with; it is iniquity, even the solemn meeting.
Your new moons and your appointed feasts my soul hateth;
they are a trouble unto me; I am weary to bear them." [18]

---

[16] Ex. 20: 10; 31: 13; Isa. 58: 13 compared with Lev. 23: 24, 32, 39; Lam.
1: 7; Hosea 2: 11.

[17] Lev. 23: 37, 38.   [18] Isa. 1: 13, 14.

In striking contrast with this, the same prophet speaks of the Lord's Sabbath :—

" Thus saith the Lord, Keep ye judgment, and do justice; for my salvation is near to come, and my righteousness to be revealed. Blessed is the man that doeth this, and the son of man that layeth hold on it; that keepeth the Sabbath from polluting it, and keepeth his hand from doing any evil. Neither let the son of the stranger, that hath joined himself to the Lord, speak, saying, The Lord hath utterly separated me from his people; neither let the eunuch say, Behold I am a dry tree. For thus saith the Lord unto the eunuchs that keep my Sabbaths, and choose the things that please me, and take hold of my covenant; even unto them will I give in mine house and within my walls a place and a name better than of sons and of daughters; I will give them an everlasting name, that shall not be cut off. Also the sons of the stranger, that join themselves to the Lord, to serve him, and to love the name of the Lord, to be his servants, every one that keepeth the Sabbath from polluting it, and taketh hold of my covenant; even them will I bring to my holy mountain, and make them joyful in my house of prayer; their burnt-offerings and their sacrifices shall be accepted upon mine altar; for mine house shall be called a house of prayer for all people." [19]

Hosea carefully designates the annual sabbaths in the following prediction :—

" I will also cause all her mirth to cease, her feast-days, her new moons, and HER sabbaths, and all her solemn feasts." [20]

This prediction was uttered about B. C. 785. It was fulfilled in part about two hundred years afterward, when Jerusalem was destroyed by Nebuchadnezzar. Of this event, Jeremiah, about B. C. 588, speaks as follows :—

" Her people fell into the hands of the enemy, and none did help her; the adversaries saw her, and did mock at HER sabbaths.

---

[19] Isa. 56: 1–7; 58: 13, 14.　　　　　[20] Hosea 2: 11.

. . . The Lord was an enemy; he hath swallowed up Israel, he hath swallowed up all her palaces, he hath destroyed his strongholds, and hath increased in the daughter of Judah mourning and lamentation. And he hath violently taken away his tabernacle, as if it were of a garden; he hath destroyed his places of the assembly; the Lord hath caused the solemn feasts and sabbaths to be forgotten in Zion, and hath despised in the indignation of his anger the king and the priest. The Lord hath cast off his altar, he hath abhorred his sanctuary, he hath given up into the hand of the enemy the walls of her palaces; they have made a noise in the house of the Lord, as in the day of a solemn feast."[21]

The feasts of the Lord were to be held in the place which the Lord should choose, namely, Jerusalem;[22] and when that city, the place of the solemn assemblies, was destroyed, and the people themselves carried into captivity, the complete cessation of their feasts, and, as a consequence, of the annual sabbaths, which were specified days in those feasts, must occur. The adversaries mocked at her sabbaths by making a " noise in the house of the Lord as in the day of a solemn feast." But the observance of the Lord's Sabbath did not cease with the dispersion of the Hebrews from their own land; for it was not a local institution, like the annual sabbaths. Its violation was one chief cause of the Babylonish captivity;[23] and their final restoration to their own land was made conditional upon their observing it during their dispersion.[24] The feasts, new moons, and annual sabbaths were restored when the Hebrews returned from captivity, and with some interruptions, were kept up until the final destruction of their city and nation by the Romans. But ere the providence of God thus struck out of ex-

---

[21] Lam. 1:7; 2:5–7.   [22] Deut. 16:16; 2 Chron. 7:12; Ps. 122.
[23] Jer. 17:19–27; Neh. 13:15–18.   [24] Isa. 56. See chapter 8 of this work.

istence these Jewish festivals, the whole typical system was abolished, having reached the commencement of its antitype, when our Lord Jesus Christ expired upon the cross. The handwriting of ordinances being thus abolished, no one is to be judged respecting its meats, or drinks, or holy days, or new moons, or sabbaths, " which are a shadow of things to come; but the body is of Christ." But the Sabbath of the Lord did not form a part of this handwriting of ordinances; for it was instituted before sin had entered the world, and consequently before there was any shadow of redemption; it was written by the finger of God, not in the midst of types and shadows, but in the bosom of the moral law; and the day following that on which the typical sabbaths were nailed to the cross, the Sabbath commandment of the moral law is expressly recognized. Moreover, when the Jewish festivals were utterly extinguished with the final destruction of Jerusalem, even then was the Sabbath of the Lord brought to the minds of his people.[25] We have now traced the annual sabbaths until their final cessation, as predicted by Hosea; it remains for us to trace the Sabbath of the Lord until we reach the endless ages of the new earth, when we shall find the whole multitude of the redeemed assembling before God for worship on each successive Sabbath.

---

[25] See chapter 10 of this work.

CHAPTER VIII

THE SABBATH FROM DAVID TO NEHEMIAH.

Silence of six successive books of the Bible relative to the Sabbath—
This silence compared with that of the book of Genesis—The siege of
Jericho—The standing still of the sun—David's act of eating the shew-
bread—The Sabbath of the Lord, how connected with, and how dis-
tinguished from, the annual sabbaths—Earliest reference to the
Sabbath after the days of Moses—Incidental allusions to the Sabbath
—Testimony of Amos—Of Isaiah—The Sabbath a blessing to MAN-
KIND—The condition of being gathered to the Holy Land—The
Sabbath not a local institution—Commentary on the fourth commandment—Testimony of Jeremiah—Jerusalem to be saved if she would
keep the Sabbath—This gracious offer despised—The Sabbath distinguished from the other days of the week—The Sabbath after
the Babylonish captivity—Time for commencing the Sabbath—The
violation of the Sabbath caused the destruction of Jerusalem.

EAVING the books of Moses, there is a long-
continued break in the history of the Sabbath.
No mention of it is found in the books of
Joshua, Judges, Ruth, First Samuel, Second Samuel,
nor First Kings. It is not until we reach the second
book of Kings[1] that the Sabbath is even mentioned. In
the book of First Chronicles, however, which, as a narrative, is parallel to the two books of Samuel, the Sabbath
is mentioned[2] with reference to the events of David's

---

[1] 2 Kings 4: 23.

[2] 1 Chron. 9: 32. It is true that this text relates to the order of things after
the return from Babylon; yet we learn from verse 22 that this order was originally ordained by David and Samuel. See verses 1–32.

life. Yet this leaves a period of five hundred years which the Bible passes in silence respecting the Sabbath.

During this period we have a circumstantial history of the Hebrew people from their entrance into the promised land forward to the establishment of David as their king, embracing many particulars in the life of Joshua, of the elders and judges of Israel, of Gideon, of Barak, of Jephthah, of Samson, of Eli, of Naomi and Ruth, of Hannah and Samuel, of Saul, of Jonathan, and of David. Yet in all this minute record we have no direct mention of the Sabbath.

A favorite argument with anti-Sabbatarians in proof of the total neglect of the Sabbath in the patriarchal age, is that the book of Genesis, which gives a distinct view of the origin of the Sabbath in paradise at the close of the first week of time, does not, in recording the lives of the patriarchs, say anything relative to its observance. Yet in that one book are crowded the events of two thousand three hundred and seventy years. What, then, should they say of the fact that six successive books of the Bible, relating with comparative minuteness the events of five hundred years, and involving many circumstances that would call out a mention of the Sabbath, do not mention it at all? Does the silence of one book, which nevertheless gives the institution of the Sabbath at its very commencement, and which brings into its record almost twenty-four hundred years, prove that there were no Sabbath-keepers prior to Moses? What, then, is proved by the fact that six successive books of the Bible, confining themselves to the events of five hundred years, an average of less than one hundred years apiece, the whole period covered by them being about one-fifth that embraced in the book of Genesis, do nevertheless preserve total silence respecting the Sabbath ?

No one will adduce this silence as evidence of utter neglect of the Sabbath during this period; yet why should they not ? Is it because that, when the narrative, after this long silence, brings in the Sabbath again, it is done incidentally, and not as a new institution ?' Precisely such is the case with the second mention of the Sabbath in the Mosaic record, that is, with its mention after the silence in Genesis.[3] Is it because the fourth commandment had been given to the Hebrews, whereas no such precept had previously been given to mankind ? This answer cannot be admitted, for we have seen that the substance of the fourth commandment was given to the head of the human family; and it is certain that when the Hebrews came out of Egypt, they were under obligation to keep the Sabbath in consequence of existing law.[4] The argument, therefore, is certainly more conclusive that there were no Sabbath-keepers from Moses to David, than that there were none from Adam to Moses; yet no one will attempt to maintain the first position, however many there may be to affirm the latter.

Several facts are narrated in the history of this period of five centuries that have a claim to our notice. The first of these is found in the record of the siege of Jericho.[5] By the command of God, the city was encompassed by the Hebrews each day for seven days; on the last day of the seven, they encompassed it seven times, when by divine interposition the walls were thrown down

---

[3] Compare Ex. 16: 23 and 1 Chron 9: 32.

[4] See chapters 2 and 3.   [5] Josh. 6.

before them, and the city was taken by assault. One day of this seven must have been the Sabbath of the Lord. Did not the people of God, therefore, violate the Sabbath in this instance? Let the following facts answer: 1. That which they did in this case was by direct command of God. 2. That which is forbidden in the fourth commandment is OUR OWN WORK: "Six days shalt thou labor, and do ALL THY WORK; but the seventh day is the Sabbath of the Lord thy God." He who reserved the seventh day unto himself had the right to require its appropriation to his service as he saw fit. 3. The act of encompassing the city was strictly as a *religious* procession. The ark of the covenant of the Lord was borne before the people; and before the ark went seven priests, blowing with trumpets of rams' horns. 4. Nor could the city have been very extensive, else going around it seven times on the last day, and then having time left for its complete destruction, would have been impossible. 5. Nor can we believe that the Hebrews, by God's command carrying the ark before them, which contained simply the ten words of the Most High, were violating the fourth of those words, "Remember the Sabbath-day, to keep it holy." It is certain that one of those seven days on which they encompassed Jericho was the Sabbath; but there is no necessity for supposing it to have been the day in which the city was taken. Nor is this a reasonable conjecture, when all the facts in the case are considered. On this incident, Dr. Clarke remarks as follows:—

"It does not appear that there could be any breach in the Sabbath by the people's simply going around the city, the ark in company, and the priests sounding the sacred trumpets. This was a mere religious procession, performed at the command of God, in which no servile work was done." [6]

At the word of Joshua, it pleased God to arrest the earth in its revolution, and thus cause the sun to remain stationary for a season, that the Canaanites might be overthrown before Israel.[7] Did not this great miracle derange the Sabbath?—Not at all; for the lengthening of one of the six days by God's intervention could not prevent the actual arrival of the seventh day, though it would delay it; nor could it destroy its identity. The case involves a difficulty for those who hold the theory that God sanctified the seventh part of time, and not the seventh day; for in this case the seventh part of time was not allotted to the Sabbath. But there is no difficulty involved for those who believe that God set apart the seventh day to be kept as it arrives, in memory of his own rest. One of the six days was allotted a greater length than ever before or since; yet this did not in the slightest degree conflict with the seventh day, which nevertheless did come. Moreover, all this was while inspired men were upon the stage of action; and it was by the direct providence of God; and what is also to be particularly remembered, it was at a time when no one will deny that the fourth commandment was in full force.

David's eating the shew-bread is a case worthy of notice, as it probably took place upon the Sabbath, and because it is cited by our Lord in a memorable conversation with the Pharisees.[8] The law of the shew-bread enjoined the setting forth of twelve loaves in the sanctuary upon the pure table before the Lord EVERY

---

[6] See Dr. A. Clarke's commentary on Josh. 6: 15.　　[7] Josh. 10: 12–14.

[8] 1 Sam. 21: 1–6; Matt. 12: 3, 4; Mark 2: 25, 26; Luke 6: 3, 4.

7

Sabbath;[9] and when new bread was thus placed before the Lord each Sabbath, the old was taken away to be eaten by the priests.[10] It appears that the shew-bread which was given to David had that day been taken from before the Lord, to put hot bread in its place, and consequently that day was the Sabbath; because when David asked for bread, the priest said, "There is no common bread under mine hand, but there is hallowed bread." And David said, "The bread is in a manner common, especially [as the margin has it] when THIS DAY there is other sanctified in the vessel." And so the sacred writer adds: "The priest gave him hallowed bread; for there was no bread there but the shew-bread, that was taken from before the Lord, to put hot bread in the day when it was taken away." The circumstances of this case, as here enumerated, all favor the view that this was upon the Sabbath: 1. There was NO COMMON bread with the priest, which is not strange when it is remembered that the shew-bread was to be taken from before the Lord each Sabbath, and eaten by the priests; 2. That the priest did not offer to *prepare* other bread is not singular if it be understood that this was the Sabbath; 3. The surprise of the priest in meeting David may have been in part owing to the fact that it was the Sabbath; 4. This may also account for the detention of Doeg that day before the Lord; 5. When our Lord was called upon to pronounce upon the conduct of his disciples who had plucked and eaten the ears of corn upon the Sabbath to satisfy their hunger, he cited this case of David's, and that of the priests' offering sacrifices in the temple upon the Sabbath, as justifying the disciples. There is a

---

[9] Lev. 24: 5–9; 1 Chron. 9: 32.   [10] 1 Sam. 21: 5, 6; Matt. 12:

wonderful propriety and fitness in this citation, if it be understood that this act of David's took place upon the Sabbath. It will be found to present the matter in a very different light from that in which anti-Sabbatarians present it.[11]

A distinction may be here pointed out, which should never be lost sight of. The presentation of the shew-bread and the offering of burnt sacrifices upon the Sabbath, as ordained in the ceremonial law, formed no part of the original Sabbatic institution; for the Sabbath was made before the fall of man; while burnt-offerings and ceremonial rites in the sanctuary were introduced in consequence of the fall. While these rites were in force, they necessarily, to some extent, connected the Sabbath with the festivals of the Jews in which the like offerings were made. This is seen only in those scriptures which record the provision made for these offerings.[12] When the ceremonial law was nailed to the cross, all the Jewish festivals ceased to exist; for they were ordained by it;[13] but the abrogation of that law could only take away those rites which it had appended to the Sabbath, leaving the original institution precisely as it came at first from its Author.

The earliest reference to the Sabbath after the days of Moses is found in what David and Samuel ordained respecting the offices of the priests and Levites at the house of God. It is as follows :—

"And other of their brethren, of the sons of the Kohath-ites, were over the shew-bread, to prepare it every Sabbath."[14]

---

[11] See chapter 10 of this work.

[12] 1 Chron. 23:31; 2 Chron. 2:4; 8:13; 31:3; Neh. 10:31, 33; Eze. 45:17.   [13] See chapter 7 of this work.   [14] 1 Chron. 9:32.

It will be observed that this is only an incidental mention of the Sabbath. Such an allusion, occurring after so long a silence, is decisive proof that the Sabbath had not been forgotten or lost during the five centuries in which it had not been mentioned by the sacred historians. After this, no direct mention of the Sabbath is found from the days of David to those of Elisha the prophet, a period of about one hundred and fifty years. Perhaps the ninety-second psalm is an exception to this statement, as its title, both in Hebrew and English, declares that it was written for the Sabbath-day; [15] and it is not improbable that it was composed by David, the sweet singer of Israel.

The son of the Shunammite woman was dead, and she sought the prophet Elisha. Her husband, not knowing that the child was dead, said to her :—

"Wherefore wilt thou go to him to-day? It is neither new moon nor Sabbath. And she said, It shall be well." [16]

It is probable that the Sabbath of the Lord is here intended, as it is thrice used in a like connection. [17] If this be correct, it shows that the Hebrews were accustomed to visit the prophets of God upon that day for divine instruction,—a very good commentary upon the

---

[15] Cotton Mather says: "There is a psalm in the Bible whereof the title is, 'A Psalm or Song for the Sabbath-day.' Now 'tis a clause in that psalm, 'O Lord, how great are thy works! thy thoughts are very deep.' Ps. 92: 5. That clause intimates what we should make the subject of our meditations on the Sabbath-day. Our thoughts are to be on God's works."—*Discourse on the Lord's Day*, p. 30, A. D. 1703. Hengstenberg says: "This psalm is according to the heading, 'A Song for the Sabbath-day.' The proper positive employment of the Sabbath appears here to be a thankful contemplation of the works of God, a devotional absorption in them which could only exist when ordinary occupations are laid aside."—*The Lord's Day*, pp. 36, 37.

[16] 2 Kings 4: 23.   [17] Isa. 66: 23; Eze. 46: 1; Amos 8: 5.

words used in relation to the gathering of the manna :
" Let no man go out of his place on the seventh day." [18]
Incidental allusion is made to the Sabbath at the accession of Jehoash to the throne of Judah,[19] about B. C.
778. In the reign of Uzziah, the grandson of Jehoash,
the prophet Amos, B. C. 787, uses the following language :—

" Hear this, O ye that swallow up the needy, even to make
the poor of the land to fail, saying, When will the new moon be
gone, that we may sell corn ? and the Sabbath, that we may set
forth wheat, making the ephah small and the shekel great, and
falsifying the balances by deceit ? that we may buy the poor for
silver, and the needy for a pair of shoes; yea, and sell the refuse
of the wheat ? " [20]

These words were spoken more directly concerning
the ten tribes, and indicate the sad state of apostasy
which soon after resulted in their overthrow as a people. About fifty years after this, at the close of the
reign of Ahaz, another allusion to the Sabbath is
found.[21] In the days of Hezekiah, about B. C. 712, the
prophet Isaiah, in enforcing the Sabbath, says:—

" Thus saith the Lord, Keep ye judgment and do justice ; for
my salvation is near to come, and my righteousness to be revealed. Blessed is the man that doeth this, and the son of man
that layeth hold on it ; that keepeth the Sabbath from polluting
it, and keepeth his hand from doing any evil. Neither let the
son of the stranger, that hath joined himself to the Lord, speak,
saying, The Lord hath utterly separated me from his people ;
neither let the eunuch say, Behold, I am a dry tree. For thus
saith the Lord unto the eunuchs that keep my Sabbaths, and
choose the things that please me, and take hold of my covenant,

---

[18] Ex. 16: 29.

[20] Amos 8: 4–6.

[19] 2 Kings 11: 5–9; 2 Chron. 23: 4–8.

[21] 2 Kings 16: 18.

even unto them will I give in mine house and within my walls, a place and a name better than of sons and of daughters; I will give them an everlasting name that shall not be cut off. Also the sons of the stranger, that join themselves to the Lord, to serve him, and to love the name of the Lord, to be his servants, every one that keepeth the Sabbath from polluting it, and taketh hold of my covenant; even them will I bring to my holy mountain, and make them joyful in my house of prayer; their burnt-offerings and their sacrifices shall be accepted upon mine altar; for mine house shall be called a house of prayer for all people. The Lord God which gathereth the outcasts of Israel saith, Yet will I gather others to him, beside those that are gathered unto him." [22]

This prophecy presents several features of peculiar interest: 1. It pertains to a time when the salvation of God is near at hand; [23] 2. It most distinctly shows that the Sabbath is not a Jewish institution; for it pronounces a blessing upon that man, without respect to nationality, who shall keep the Sabbath; and it then particularizes the son of the stranger, that is, the Gentile, [24] and makes a peculiar promise to him if he will keep the Sabbath; 3. This prophecy relates to Israel when they are outcasts, that is, when they are in their dispersion, promising to gather them, and *others*, that is, the Gentiles, with them; but of course, the condition of being gathered to God's holy mountain must be complied with, namely, to love the name of the Lord, to be his servants, and to keep the Sabbath from polluting it; 4. And hence it follows that the Sabbath is not a local institution, susceptible of being observed in the promised land alone, like the annual sabbaths, [25] but one made for

---

[22] Isa. 56: 1–8.

[23] For the coming of this salvation, see Heb. 9: 28; 1 Pet. 1: 9.

[24] Ex. 12: 48, 49; Isa. 14: 1; Eph. 2: 12.   [25] See chapter 7.

mankind, and capable of being observed by the outcasts of Israel when scattered in every land under heaven.[26]

Isaiah again presents the Sabbath; and this he does in language most emphatically distinguishing it from all ceremonial institutions.

"If thou turn away thy foot from the Sabbath, from doing thy pleasure on my holy day; and call the Sabbath a delight, the holy of the Lord, honorable; and shalt honor him, not doing thine own ways, nor finding thine own pleasure, nor speaking thine own words: then shalt thou delight thyself in the Lord; and I will cause thee to ride upon the high places of the earth, and feed thee with the heritage of Jacob thy father; for the mouth of the Lord hath spoken it."[27]

This language is an evangelical commentary on the fourth commandment. It appends to it an exceeding great and precious promise, that takes hold upon the land promised to Jacob, even the new earth.[28]

In the year B. C. 601, thirteen years before the destruction of Jerusalem by Nebuchadnezzar, God made to the Jewish people through Jeremiah the gracious offer, that if they would keep his Sabbath, their city should stand forever. At the same time he testified unto them that if they would not do this, their city should be utterly destroyed. Said the prophet:—

"Hear ye the word of the Lord, ye kings of Judah, and all Judah, and all the inhabitants of Jerusalem, that enter in by these gates. Thus saith the Lord: Take heed to yourselves, and bear no burden on the Sabbath-day, nor bring it in by the gates of Jerusalem;[29] neither carry forth a burden out of your houses

---

[26] Deut. 28: 64; Luke 21: 24.   [27] Isa. 58: 13, 14.

[28] Matt. 8: 11; Heb. 11: 8–16; Rev. 21.

[29] On this text Dr. A. Clarke comments thus: "From this and the following

on the Sabbath-day,[30] neither do ye any work, but hallow ye the
Sabbath-day, as I commanded your fathers. But they obeyed
not, neither inclined their ears, but made their necks stiff, that
they might not hear, nor receive instruction.[31]   And it shall
come to pass, if ye diligently hearken unto me, saith the Lord,
to bring in no burden through the gates of this city on the
Sabbath-day, but hallow the Sabbath-day, to do no work therein ;
then shall there enter into the gates of this city kings and princes
sitting upon the throne of David, riding in chariots and on horses,
they, and their princes, the men of Judah, and the inhabitants of
Jerusalem ; and this city shall REMAIN FOREVER.   And they
shall come from the cities of Judah, and from the places about
Jerusalem, and from the land of Benjamin, and from the plain,
and from the mountains, and from the south, bringing burnt-
offerings, and sacrifices, and meat-offerings, and incense, and
bringing sacrifices of praise unto the house of the Lord.   But if
ye will not hearken unto me to hallow the Sabbath-day, and
not to bear a burden, even entering in at the gates of Jerusalem
on the Sabbath-day ; then will I kindle a fire in the gates thereof,
and it shall devour the palaces of Jerusalem, and it shall not be
quenched." [32]

This gracious offer of the Most High to his rebellious
people was not regarded by them ; for eight years after
this, Ezekiel testifies of them :—

" In thee have they set light by father and mother ; in the
midst of thee have they dealt by oppression with the stranger ;
in thee have they vexed the fatherless and the widow.   Thou
hast despised my holy things, and hast profaned my Sabbaths.

---

verses we find the ruin of the Jews attributed to the breach of the Sabbath ; as
this led to a neglect of sacrifice, the ordinances of religion, and all public worship,
so it necessarily brought with it all immorality.   The breach of the Sabbath was
that which let in upon them all the waters of God's wrath."

[30] For an inspired commentary on this language, see Neh. 13 : 15–18.

[31] This language strongly implies that the violation of the Sabbath had ever
been general with the Hebrews. See Jer. 7 : 23–28.

[32] Jer. 17 : 20–27.

. . . Her priests have violated my law, and have profaned mine holy things; they have put no difference between the holy and profane, neither have they showed difference between the unclean and the clean, and have hid their eyes from my Sabbaths, and I am profaned among them. . . . Moreover, this they have done unto me: they have defiled my sanctuary in the same day, and have profaned my Sabbaths. For when they had slain their children to their idols, then they came the same day into my sanctuary to profane it; and, lo, thus have they done in the midst of mine house." [33]

Idolatry and Sabbath-breaking, which were besetting sins with the Hebrews in the wilderness, and which there laid the foundation for their dispersion from their own land,[34] had ever cleaved unto them. And now, when their destruction was impending from the overwhelming power of the king of Babylon, they were so deeply attached to these and kindred sins that they would not regard the voice of warning. Before entering the Sanctuary of God upon his Sabbath, they first slew their own children in sacrifice to their idols![35] Thus iniquity came to its hight, and wrath came upon them to the uttermost.

"They mocked the messengers of God, and despised his words, and misused his prophets, until the wrath of the Lord arose against his people, till there was no remedy. Therefore he brought upon them the king of the Chaldees, who slew their young men with the sword in the house of their sanctuary, and had no compassion upon young man or maiden, old man, or him that stooped for age: he gave them all into his hand. And all the vessels of the house of God, great and small, and the treasures of the house of the Lord, and the treasures of the king, and of his princes; all these he brought to Babylon, and they burnt the

---

[33] Eze. 22: 7, 8, 26; 23: 38, 39.   [34] Eze. 20: 23, 24; Deut. 32: 16–35.
[35] Eze. 23: 38, 39.

house of God, and brake down the wall of Jerusalem, and burnt all the palaces thereof with fire, and destroyed all the goodly vessels thereof. And them that had escaped from the sword carried he away to Babylon, where they were servants to him and his sons until the reign of the king of Persia." [36]

While the Hebrews were in captivity at Babylon, God made them an offer to restore them to their own land, and give them again a city and a temple under circumstances of wonderful glory.[37] The condition of that offer being disregarded,[33] the proffered glory was never inherited by them. In this offer were several allusions to the Sabbath of the Lord, and also to the festivals of the Hebrews.[39] One of these allusions is worthy of particular notice, for the distinctness with which it discriminates between the Sabbath and the other days of the week :—

"Thus saith the Lord God : The gate of the inner court that looketh toward the east shall be shut THE SIX WORKING DAYS ; but on the Sabbath it shall be opened, and in the day of the new moon it shall be opened." [40]

Six days of the week are by divine inspiration called "the six working days ;" the seventh is called the Sabbath of the Lord. Who shall dare confound this marked distinction ?

After the Jews had returned from their captivity in Babylon, and had restored their temple and city, in a solemn assembly of the whole people they recount, in an address to the Most High, all the great events of God's providence in their past history, testifying respecting the Sabbath as follows :—

---

[36] 2 Chron. 36 : 16–20.   [37] Eze. 40 to 48.   [38] Eze. 43 : 7–11.

[39] Eze. 44 : 24 ; 45 : 17 ; 46 : 1, 3, 4, 12.   [40] Eze. 46 : 1.

" Thou camest down also upon Mount Sinai, and spakest with them from heaven, and gavest them right judgments, and true laws, good statutes and commandments; and madest known unto them thy holy Sabbath, and commandedst them precepts, statutes, and laws by the hand of Moses, thy servant."[41]

Thus were all the people reminded of the great events of Mount Sinai,—the giving of the ten words of the law of God, and the making known of his holy Sabbath. So deeply impressed was the whole congregation with the effect of their former disobedience, that they entered into a solemn covenant to obey God.[42] They pledged themselves to each other in these words :—

" And if the people of the land bring ware or any victuals on the Sabbath-day to sell, that we would not buy it of them on the Sabbath, or on the holy day; and that we would leave the seventh year, and the exaction of every debt."[43]

In the absence of Nehemiah at the Persian court, this covenant was in part, at least, forgotten. Eleven years having elapsed, Nehemiah testifies concerning things when he returned, about B. C. 434 :—

" In those days saw I in Judah some treading wine-presses on the Sabbath, and bringing in sheaves, and lading asses; as also wine, grapes, and figs, and all manner of burdens, which they brought into Jerusalem on the Sabbath-day; and I testified against them in the day wherein they sold victuals. There dwelt men of Tyre also therein, which brought fish, and all manner of ware, and sold on the Sabbath unto the children of Judah, and in Jerusalem. Then I contended with the nobles of Judah, and said unto them, What evil thing is this that ye do, and profane the Sabbath-day ? Did not your fathers thus, and did not our God bring all this evil upon us, and upon this city ? yet ye bring more wrath upon Israel by profaning the Sabbath. And it came to

---

[41] Neh. 9: 13, 14.   [42] Neh. 9: 38; 10: 1–31.   [43] Neh. 10: 31.

pass, that, when the gates of Jerusalem began to be dark before the Sabbath,[44] I commanded that the gates should be shut, and charged that they should not be opened till after the Sabbath: and some of my servants set I at the gates, that there should no burden be brought in on the Sabbath-day. So the merchants and sellers of all kind of ware lodged without Jerusalem once or twice. Then I testified against them, and said unto them, Why lodge ye about the wall? if ye do so again, I will lay hands on you. From that time forth came they no more on the Sabbath. And I commanded the Levites that they should cleanse themselves, and that they should come and keep the gates, to sanctify the Sabbath-day.

---

[44] A few words relative to the time of beginning the Sabbath are here demanded: 1. The reckoning of the first week of time necessarily determines that of all succeeding weeks. The first division of the first day was night; and each day of the first week began with evening; the evening and the morning, an expression equivalent to the night and the day, constituted the day of twenty-four hours. Gen. 1. Hence the first Sabbath began and ended with evening. 2. That the night in the Scriptures is reckoned a part of the day of twenty-four hours, is proved by many texts. Ex. 12:41, 42; 1 Sam. 26:7, 8; Luke 2:8–11; Mark 14:30; Luke 22:34, etc. 3. The 2300 days, symbolizing 2300 years, are each constituted like the days of the first week of time. Dan. 8:14. The margin, which gives the literal Hebrew, calls each of these days an "evening morning." 4. The statute defining the great day of atonement is absolutely decisive that the day begins with evening, and that the night is a part of the day. Lev. 23:32. "It shall be unto you a sabbath of rest, and ye shall afflict your souls: in the ninth day of the month at even, from even unto even shall ye celebrate your sabbath." 5. That evening is at sunset is abundantly proved by the following scriptures: Deut. 16:6; Lev. 22:6, 7; Deut. 23:11; 24:13, 15; Josh. 8:29; 10:26, 27; Judges 14:18; 2 Sam. 3:35; 2 Chron. 18:34; Matt. 8:16; Mark 1:32; Luke 4:40. But does not Neh. 13:19 conflict with this testimony, and indicate that the Sabbath did not begin until after dark?—I think not. The text does not say, "When it began to be dark at Jerusalem before the Sabbath," but it says, "When the *gates* of Jerusalem began to be dark." If it be remembered that the gates of Jerusalem were placed in wide and high walls, it will not be found difficult to harmonize this text with the many here adduced, which prove that the day begins at sunset.

Calmet, in his Bible Dictionary, article, Sabbath, thus states the ancient Jewish method of beginning the Sabbath: "About half an hour before sunset all work is quitted, and the Sabbath is supposed to be begun;" and of the close of the Sabbath he says: "When night comes, and they can discern in the heaven three stars of moderate magnitude, then the Sabbath is ended, and they may return to their ordinary employments."

Remember me, O my God, concerning this also, and spare me according to the greatness of thy mercy."[45]

This scripture is an explicit testimony that the destruction of Jerusalem and the captivity of the Jews at Babylon were in consequence of their profanation of the Sabbath. It is a striking confirmation of the language of Jeremiah, already noticed, in which he testified to the Jews that if they would hallow the Sabbath, their city should stand forever; but that it should be utterly destroyed if they persisted in its profanation. Nehemiah bears testimony to the accomplishment of Jeremiah's prediction concerning the violation of the Sabbath; and with his solemn appeal in its behalf ends the history of the Sabbath in the Old Testament.

---

[45] Neh. 13: 15–22.

CHAPTER IX.

THE SABBATH FROM NEHEMIAH TO CHRIST.

Great change in the Jewish people respecting idolatry and Sabbath-breaking after their return from Babylon—Decree of Antiochus Epiphanes
against the Sabbath—Massacre of a thousand Sabbath-keepers in the
wilderness—Similar massacre at Jerusalem—Decree of the Jewish elders relative to resisting attacks upon the Sabbath—Other martyrdoms—Victories of Judas Maccabeus—How Pompey captured Jerusalem—Teaching of the Jewish doctors respecting the Sabbath—State
of the Sabbatic institution at the first advent of the Saviour.

 PERIOD of almost five centuries intervenes
between the time of Nehemiah and the commencement of the ministry of the Redeemer.
During this time an extraordinary change came over the
Jewish people. Previously, they had been to an alarm-
ing extent idolaters, and out-breaking violators of the
Sabbath. But after their return from Babylon they were
never guilty of idolatry to any extent, the chastisement
of that captivity effecting a cure of this evil.[1] In like
manner did they change their conduct relative to the
Sabbath; and during this period they loaded the Sabbatic institution with the most burdensome and rigorous
ordinances. A brief survey of this period must suffice.
Under the reign of Antiochus Epiphanes, the king of
Syria, B. C. 170, the Jews were greatly oppressed.

---

[1] Speaking of the Babylonish captivity, in his note on Eze. 23: 48, Dr. Clarke
says: "From that time to the present day the Jews never relapsed into idolatry."

" King Antiochus wrote to his whole kingdom, that all should be one people, and every one should leave his laws : so all the heathen agreed according to the commandment of the king. Yea, many also of the Israelites consented to his religion, and sacrificed unto idols, and profaned the Sabbath." [2]

The greater part of the Hebrews remained faithful to God, and as a consequence, were obliged to flee for their lives. The historian continues :—

" Then many that sought after justice and judgment went down into the wilderness, to dwell there, both they, and their children, and their wives, and their cattle ; because afflictions increased sore upon then. Now when it was told the king's servants, and the host that was at Jerusalem, in the city of David, that certain men, who had broken the king's commandment, were gone down into the secret places in the wilderness, they pursued after them a great number, and having overtaken them, they camped against them, and made war against them on the Sabbath-day. And they said unto them, Let that which ye have done hitherto suffice ; come forth, and do according to the commandment of the king, and ye shall live. But they said, We will not come forth, neither will we do the king's commandment, to profane the Sabbath-day. So then they gave them the battle with all speed. Howbeit, they answered them not, neither cast they a stone at them, nor stopped the places where they lay hid ; but said, Let us die all in our innocency : heaven and earth shall testify for us, that ye put us to death wrongfully. So they rose up against them in battle on the Sabbath, and they slew them, with their wives and children, and their cattle, to the number of a thousand people." [3]

In Jerusalem itself a like massacre took place. King Antiochus sent Appollonius with an army of twenty-two thousand,—

" Who, coming to Jerusalem, and pretending peace, did forbear till the holy day of the Sabbath, when, taking the Jews keeping

---

[2] 1 Mac. 1 : 41–43.   [3] 1 Mac. 2 : 29–38 ; Josephus' Antiquities, b. 12, chap. 6.

holy day, he commanded his men to arm themselves.   And so he
slew all them that were gone to the celebrating of the Sabbath,
and running through the city with weapons, slew great multitudes." [4]

In view of these dreadful acts of slaughter, Matta-
thias, " an honorable and great man," the father of Judas
Maccabeus, with his friends decreed thus :—

" Whosoever shall come to make battle with us on the Sabbath-day, we will fight against him ; neither will we die all, as
our brethren that were murdered in the secret places." [5]

Yet some were martyred after this for observing the
Sabbath, as the quotation shows :—

" And others that had run together into caves near by, to
keep the Sabbath-day secretly, being discovered to Philip, were
all burnt together, because they made a conscience to help themselves for the honor of the most sacred day." [6]

After this, Judas Maccabeus did great exploits in
defense of the Hebrews, and in resisting the dreadful
oppression of the Syrian government.   Of one of these
battles the record says :—

" When he had given them this watchword, *The Help of God,*
himself leading the first band, he joined battle with Nicanor.
And by the help of the Almighty they slew above nine thousand
of their enemies, and wounded and maimed the most part of
Nicanor's host, and so put all to flight ; and took their money
that came to buy them, and pursued them far ; but lacking time.
they returned : for it was the day before the Sabbath, and therefore they would no longer pursue them.   So when they had
gathered their armor together, and spoiled their enemies, they
occupied themselves about the Sabbath, yielding exceeding praise
and thanks to the Lord, who had preserved them unto that day,
which was the beginning of mercy distilling upon them.   And

---

[4] 2 Mac. 5 : 25, 26.   [5] 1 Mac. 2 : 41.   [6] 2 Mac. 6 : 11.

after the Sabbath, when they had given part of the spoils to the maimed, and the widows, and orphans, the residue they divided among themselves and their servants." [7]

After this the Hebrews, being attacked upon the Sabbath by their enemies, defeated them with much slaughter.[8]

About B. C. 63 Jerusalem was besieged and taken by Pompey, the general of the Romans. To do this it was necessary to fill an immense ditch, and to raise against the city a bank on which to place the engines of assault. Josephus relates the event as follows :—

"And had it not been our practice, from the days of our forefathers, to rest on the seventh day, this bank could never have been perfected, by reason of the opposition the Jews would have made ; for though our law gives us leave then to defend ourselves against those that begin to fight with us, and assault us, yet does it not permit us to meddle with our enemies while they do anything else. Which thing when the Romans understood, on those days which we call Sabbaths, they threw nothing at the Jews, nor came to any pitched battle with them, but raised up their earthen banks, and brought their engines into such forwardness, that they might do execution the next days." [9]

From this it is seen that Pompey carefully refrained

---

[7] 2 Mac. 8 : 23–28.

[8] 1 Mac. 9 : 43–49; Josephus' Antiquities, b. 13, chap. 1; 2 Mac. 15.

[9] Antiquities of the Jews, b. 14, chap. 4. Here we call attention to one of those historical frauds by which Sunday is shown to be the Sabbath. Dr. Justin Edwards states this case thus : "Pompey, the Roman general, knowing this, when besieging Jerusalem, would not attack them on the Sabbath, but spent the day in constructing his works, and preparing to attack them on Monday, and in a manner that they could not withstand, and so he took the city " (*Sabbath Manual*, p. 216) ; that is to say, the next day after the Sabbath was Monday, and of course Sunday was the Sabbath ! Yet Dr. Edwards well knew that in Pompey's time, 63 years before Christ, Saturday was the only weekly Sabbath, and that Sunday, not Monday, was the day of attack.

from any attack upon the Jews on each Sabbath during the siege, but spent that day in filling the ditch and raising the bank, that he might attack them on the day following each Sabbath, that is, upon Sunday. Josephus further relates that the priests were not at all hindered from their sacred ministrations by the stones thrown among them from the engines of Pompey, even " if any melancholy accident happened ; " and that when the city was taken, and the enemy fell upon them, and cut the throats of those that were in the temples, yet the priests did not run away, or desist from offering the accustomed sacrifices.

These quotations from Jewish history are sufficient to indicate the extraordinary change that came over that people concerning the Sabbath after the Babylonish captivity. A brief view of the teaching of the Jewish doctors respecting the Sabbath at the time when our Lord began his ministry, will conclude this chapter.

" They enumerated about forty primary works, which they said were forbidden to be done on the Sabbath. Under each of these were numerous secondary works, which they said were also forbidden. . . . Among the primary works which were forbidden, were ploughing, sowing, reaping, winnowing, cleaning, grinding, etc. Under the head of grinding was included the breaking or dividing of things which were before united. . . . Another of their traditions was, that, as threshing on the Sabbath was forbidden, the bruising of things, which was a species of threshing, was also forbidden. Of course, it was a violation of the Sabbath to walk on green grass, for that would bruise or thresh it. So, as a man might not hunt on the Sabbath, he might not catch a flea ; for that was a species of hunting. As a man might not carry a burden on the Sabbath, he might not carry water to a thirsty animal, for that was a species of burden ; but he might pour water into a trough, and lead the animal to it. . . . Yet should a sheep fall into a pit, they would readily lift him out, and bear him to a place of safety. . . . They said a man might minister to the sick for the purpose of relieving their distress, but not for the purpose of healing their diseases. He might put a covering on a diseased eye, or anoint it with eye-salve for the purpose of easing the pain, but not to cure the eye." [10]

Such was the remarkable change in the conduct of the Jewish people toward the Sabbath; and such was the teaching of their doctors respecting it. The most merciful institution of God for mankind had become a source of distress; that which God ordained as a delight and a source of refreshment had become a yoke of bondage; the Sabbath, made for man in paradise, was now a most oppressive and burdensome institution. It was time that God should interfere. Next upon the scene of action appears the Lord of the Sabbath.

---

[10] Sabbath Manual of the American Tract Society, pp. 214, 215.

CHAPTER X.

THE SABBATH IN THE TIME OF CHRIST.

Mission of the Saviour—His qualifications as a judge of Sabbatic observance—State of the institution at his advent—The Saviour at Nazareth
—At Capernaum—His discourse in the corn-field—Case of the man
with a withered arm—The Saviour among his relatives—Case of the
impotent man—Of the man born blind—Of the woman bound by
Satan—Of the man who had the dropsy—Object of our Lord's teaching
and miracles relative to the Sabbath—Unfairness of many anti-
Sabbatarians—Examination of Matt. 24:20—The Sabbath not abrogated at the crucifixion—Fourth commandment after that event—
Sabbath not changed at the resurrection of Christ—Examination of
John 20:26—Of Acts 2:1, 2—Redemption furnishes no argument for
the change of the Sabbath—Examination of Ps. 118:22-24—The
Sabbath neither abolished nor changed as late as the close of the
seventy weeks.

N the fullness of time, God sent forth his
Son to be the Saviour of the world. He
who fulfilled this mission of infinite benevolence was both the Son of God and the Son of
man. He was with the Father before the world was,
and by him God created all things.[1] The Sabbath
being ordained at the close of that great work, as a
memorial to keep it in lasting remembrance, the Son of
God, by whom all things were created, could not be
otherwise than a perfect judge of its true design and of
its proper observance. The sixty-nine weeks of Daniel's
prophecy being accomplished, the Redeemer began to

---

[1] Gal. 4:4, 5; John 1:1–10; 17:5, 24; Heb. 1.

preach, saying, " The time is fulfilled." [2] The ministry of the Saviour was at a time when the Sabbath of the Lord had become utterly perverted from its gracious design by the teaching of the Jewish doctors. As we have seen in the previous chapter, it was to the people no longer a source of refreshment and delight, but a cause of suffering and distress. It had been loaded down with traditions by the doctors of the law, until its merciful and beneficent purpose was utterly hidden beneath the rubbish of men's inventions. It being impracticable for Satan, after the Babylonish captivity, to cause the Jewish people, even by bloody edicts, to relinquish the Sabbath and openly profane it, as they had done before that time, he caused their doctors to so pervert it that its real character should be utterly changed, and its observance entirely unlike that which would please God. We shall find that the Saviour never missed an opportunity to correct their false notions respecting the Sabbath; and that he purposely selected the Sabbath as the day on which to perform many of his merciful works. It will be found that no small share of his teaching through his whole ministry was devoted to a determination of what was lawful on the Sabbath,—a singular fact for those to explain who think that he designed its abrogation. At the opening of our Lord's ministry, we read,—

" And Jesus returned in the power of the Spirit into Galilee; and there went out a fame of him through all the region round about. And he taught in their synagogues, being glorified of all. And he came to Nazareth, where he had been brought up; and, as his custom was, he went into the synagogue on the Sabbath-day, and stood up for to read." [3]

---

[2] Dan. 9: 25; Mark 1: 14, 15. [3] Luke 4: 14–16.

Such was the manner of the Saviour relative to the Sabbath. It is evident that in this he intended to show his regard for that day; for it was not necessary to do so in order to gain a congregation, as vast multitudes were ever ready to throng his steps. His testimony being rejected, our Lord left Nazareth for Capernaum. The sacred historian says of this visit :—

"But he, passing through the midst of them, went his way, and came down to Capernaum, a city of Galilee, and taught them on the Sabbath-days. And they were astonished at his doctrine; for his word was with power. And in the synagogue there was a man which had a spirit of an unclean devil; and he cried out with a loud voice, saying, Let us alone; what have we to do with thee, thou Jesus of Nazareth? art thou come to destroy us? I know thee who thou art, the Holy One of God. And Jesus rebuked him, saying, Hold thy peace, and come out of him. And when the devil had thrown him in the midst, he came out of him, and hurt him not. And they were all amazed, and spake among themselves, saying, What a word is this! for with authority and power he commandeth the unclean spirits, and they come out. And the fame of him went out into every place of the country round about. And he arose out of the synagogue, and entered into Simon's house. And Simon's wife's mother was taken with a great fever; and they besought him for her. And he stood over her, and rebuked the fever; and it left her; and immediately she arose and ministered unto them." [4]

According to the record, these are the first miracles performed by the Saviour on the Sabbath. But the strictness of Jewish views relative to the Sabbath is seen in that they waited till sunset, that is, till the Sabbath was passed,[5] before they brought the sick to be healed, as the following account shows :—

---

[4] Luke 4: 30–39; Mark 1: 21–31; Matt. 8: 5–15.

[5] On this point, see conclusion of chapter 8.

" And at even, when the sun did set, they brought unto him all that were diseased, and them that were possessed with devils. And all the city was gathered together at the door. And he healed many that were sick of divers diseases, and cast out many devils; and suffered not the devils to speak, because they knew him." [6]

The next mention of the Sabbath is of peculiar interest :—

" At that time Jesus went on the Sabbath-day through the corn; and his disciples were an hungered, and began to pluck the ears of corn, and to eat. But when the Pharisees saw it, they said unto him, Behold, thy disciples do that which is not lawful to do upon the Sabbath-day. But he said unto them, Have ye not read what David did, when he was an hungered, and they that were with him; how he entered into the house of God, and did eat the shew-bread, which was not lawful for him to eat, neither for them which were with him, but only for the priests? Or have ye not read in the law, how that on the Sabbath-day the priests in the temple profane the Sabbath, and are blameless? But I say unto you that in this place is one greater than the temple. But if ye had known what this meaneth, I will have mercy and not sacrifice, ye would not have condemned the guiltless. For the Son of man is Lord even of the Sabbath-day." [7]

The parallel text in Mark has an important addition to the conclusion as stated by Matthew:—

" And he said unto them, The Sabbath was made for man, and not man for the Sabbath; therefore the Son of man is Lord also of the Sabbath." [8]

The following points should be noted in examining this text :—

1. That the question at issue did not relate to the

---

[6] Mark 1 : 32–34; Luke 4 : 40.

[7] Matt. 12 : 1–8; Mark 2 : 23–28; Luke 6 : 1–5.   [8] Mark 2 : 27, 28.

act of passing through the corn on the Sabbath; for the Pharisees themselves were in the company; and hence it may be concluded that the Saviour and those with him were either going to, or returning from, the synagogue.

2. That the question raised by the Pharisees was this: Whether the disciples, in satisfying their hunger with the corn through which they passed, were not violating the law of the Sabbath.

3. That he to whom this question was proposed was in the highest degree competent to answer it; for he was with the Father when the Sabbath was made.[9]

4. That the Saviour was pleased to appeal to scriptural precedents for the decision of this question, rather than to assert his own independent judgment.

5. That the first case cited by the Saviour was peculiarly appropriate. David, fleeing for his life, entered the house of God upon the Sabbath,[10] and ate the shewbread to satisfy his hunger. The disciples, to relieve their hunger, simply ate of the corn through which they were passing upon the Sabbath. If David did right, though eating in his necessity of that which belonged only to the priests, how little blame could be attached to the disciples, who had not even violated a precept of the ceremonial law!

6. Our Lord's next example is designed to show what labor upon the Sabbath is not a violation of its sacredness; and hence the case of the priests is referred to. The same God who had said in the fourth commandment, " Six days shalt thou labor, and do all THY work,"

---

[9] Comp. John 1:1-3 and Gen. 1:1, 26; 2:1-3.   [10] See chapter 8.

had commanded that the priests should offer certain sacrifices in his temple on the Sabbath.[11] Herein was no contradiction; for the labor performed by the priests upon the Sabbath was simply that necessary for the maintenance of the appointed worship of God in his temple, and was not doing what the commandment calls " THY WORK." Labor of this kind, therefore, the Saviour being judge, was not, and never had been, a violation of the Sabbath.

7. It is highly probable that the Saviour, in this reference to the priests, had his mind not merely upon the sacrifices which they offered upon the Sabbath, but upon the fact that they were required to prepare new shew-bread every Sabbath, when the old was to be removed from the table before the Lord, and eaten by them.[12] This view of the matter would connect the case of the priests with that of David, and both would bear with wonderful distinctness upon the act of the disciples. Then our Lord's argument could be appreciated, when he adds : " But I say unto you, That in this place is one greater than the temple;" so that if the shew-bread was to be prepared each Sabbath for the use of those who ministered in the temple, and those who did this were guiltless, how free from guilt, also, must be the disciples, who, in following HIM who was greater than the temple, but who had not where to lay his head, had eaten of the standing corn upon the Sabbath to relieve their hunger.

8. Our Lord next lays down a principle worthy of the most serious attention, when he adds : " But if ye had known what this meaneth, I will have mercy, and

---

[11] Num. 28: 9, 10.   [12] Lev. 24: 5–9; 1 Chron. 9: 32.

not sacrifice, ye would not have condemned the guiltless." The Most High had ordained certain labor to be
performed upon the Sabbath, in order that sacrifices
might be offered to himself. But Christ affirms, upon
the authority of the Scriptures,[13] that there is something
far more acceptable to God than sacrifices, and that is
acts of mercy. If God held those guiltless who offered
sacrifices upon the Sabbath, how much less would he
condemn those who extend mercy and relief to the dis-
tressed and suffering upon that day.

9. Nor does the Saviour leave the subject even
here; for he adds: " The Sabbath was made for man,
and not man for the Sabbath; therefore the Son of man
is Lord also of the Sabbath." If the Sabbath was *made*,
certain acts were necessary in order to give existence to
it. What were those acts?—(1.) God rested upon the
seventh day, and thus made it the rest-day, or Sabbath,
of the Lord; (2.) He blessed the day, by which it became his holy day; (3.) He sanctified it, or set it apart
to a holy use, making its observance a part of man's duty
toward God. There must have been a time when these
acts were performed; and on this point there is really
no room for controversy. They were not performed at
Sinai, nor in the wilderness of Sin, but in paradise.
And this is strikingly confirmed by the language here
used by the Saviour: " The Sabbath was made for THE
man, not THE man for the Sabbath;"[14] thus citing our
minds to the man Adam who was made of the dust of
the ground, and affirming that the Sabbath was made

---

[13] Hosea 6: 6.

[14] The Greek Testament reads: Καὶ ἔλεγεν αὐτοῖς. Τὸ σάββατον διὰ τὸν
ἄνθρωπον ἐγένετο ᴂχ ὁ ἄνθρωπος διὰ τὸ σάββατον.

for him,—a conclusive testimony that the Sabbath originated in paradise. This fact is happily illustrated by a
statement of the apostle Paul: "Neither was the man
created for the woman; but the woman for the man." [15]
It will not be denied that this language has direct reference to the creation of Adam and Eve. If, then, we
turn back to the beginning, we shall find Adam made of
the dust of the ground, Eve taken from his side, and the
Sabbath made of the seventh day.[16]

In this way the Saviour, to complete the solution of
the question raised by the Pharisees, traces the Sabbath
back to the beginning, as he does the institution of
marriage when the same class proposed for his decision
the lawfulness of divorce.[17] His careful statement of
the design of the Sabbath and of marriage, tracing each
to the beginning, in one case striking down their perversion of the Sabbath, in the other, that of marriage, is the
most powerful testimony in behalf of the sacredness of
each institution. The argument in the case of marriage
stands thus: In the beginning, God created *one* man and
one woman, designing that they TWO should be one flesh.
The marriage relation, therefore, was designed to unite
simply two persons, and this union *should* be sacred and
indissoluble. Such was the bearing of his argument
upon the question of divorce. In relation to the Sabbath,
his argument is this: God made the Sabbath for the man
that he made of the dust of the ground; and being thus
made for an unfallen race, it can only be a merciful and
beneficent institution. He who made the Sabbath for
man before the fall, saw what man needed, and knew
how to supply that want. It was given to him for rest,

---

[15] 1 Cor. 11:9.   [16] Gen. 2:1-3, 7, 21-23.   [17] Matt. 19:3-9.

refreshment, and delight,—a character that it sustained after the fall,[18] but which the Jews had already lost sight of.[19]   Our Lord here lays open his whole heart concerning the Sabbath.   He carefully determines what works are not a violation of the Sabbath; and this he does by Old-Testament examples, that it may be evident that he is introducing no change in the institution; he sets aside their rigorous and burdensome traditions concerning the Sabbath, by tracing it back to its merciful origin in paradise; and having thus disencumbered the Sabbath of Pharisaic rigor, he leaves it upon its paradisiacal foundation, enforced by all the authority and sacredness of that law which he came not to destroy, but to magnify and make honorable.[20]

10. Having divested the Sabbath of all Pharisaic additions, our Lord concludes with this remarkable declaration: " Therefore the Son of man is Lord also of the Sabbath."   (1.) It was not a disparagement to the Sabbath, but an honor, that God's only Son should claim to be its Lord.   (2.) Nor was it derogatory to the character of the Redeemer to be the Lord of the Sabbath; with all the high honors pertaining to his messiahship, he is ALSO Lord of the Sabbath.   Or, if we take the expression in Matthew, he is " Lord EVEN of the Sabbath-day," it shows that it is not a small honor to possess such a title.   (3.) This title implies that the Messiah should be the *protector*, and not the *destroyer*, of the Sabbath; and hence that he was the rightful one to decide the proper nature of Sabbatic observance.   With such

---

[18] Ex. 16: 23; 23: 12; Isa. 58: 13, 14.

[19] See conclusion of chapter 9.   [20] Matt. 5: 17–19; Isa. 42: 21.

memorable words ends our Lord's first discourse concerning the Sabbath.

From this time the Pharisees watched the Saviour to find an accusation against him for violating the Sabbath. The next example will show the malignity of their hearts, their utter perversion of the Sabbath, the urgent need of an authoritative correction of their false teachings respecting it, and the Saviour's unanswerable defense :—

"And when he was departed thence, he went into their synagogue; and, behold, there was a man which had his hand withered. And they asked him, saying, Is it lawful to heal on the Sabbath-days? that they might accuse him. And he said unto them, What man shall there be among you, that shall have one sheep, and if it fall into a pit on the Sabbath-day, will he not lay hold on it, and lift it out? How much then is a man better than a sheep? Wherefore, it is lawful to do well on the Sabbath-days. Then saith he to the man, stretch forth thine hand. And he stretched it forth; and it was restored whole, like as the other. Then the Pharisees went out, and held a council against him how they might destroy him." [21]

What was the act that caused this madness of the Pharisees?—On the part of the Saviour, it was a word; on the part of the man, it was the act of stretching out his arm. Did the law of the Sabbath forbid either of these things?—No one can affirm such a thing. But the Saviour had publicly transgressed that tradition of the Pharisees that forbade the doing of anything whatever toward the healing of the sick upon the Sabbath. And how necessary that such a wicked tradition should be swept away, if the Sabbath itself was to be pre-

---

[21] Matt. 12: 9–14; Mark 3: 1–6; Luke 6: 6–11.

served for man! But the Pharisees were filled with
such madness that they went out of the synagogue, and
consulted how they might destroy Jesus; yet he only
acted in behalf of the Sabbath in setting aside those traditions by which they had perverted it.

After this, our Lord returned into his own country,
and thus we read of him :—

"And when the Sabbath-day was come, he began to teach
in the synagogue; and many hearing him were astonished, saying, From whence hath this man these things? and what wisdom is this which is given unto him, that even such mighty
works are wrought by his hands?" [22]

Not far from this time, we find the Saviour at Jerusalem, and the following miracle was performed upon
the Sabbath :—

"And a certain man was there which had an infirmity thirty
and eight years. When Jesus saw him lie, and knew that he
had been there now a long time in that case, he saith unto him,
Wilt thou be made whole? The impotent man answered him,
Sir, I have no man, when the water is troubled, to put me into the
pool; but while I am coming, another steppeth down before me.
Jesus saith unto him, Rise, take up thy bed, and walk. And
immediately the man was made whole, and took up his bed, and
walked; and on the same day was the Sabbath. The Jews
therefore said unto him that was cured, It is the Sabbath-day:
it is not lawful for thee to carry thy bed. He answered them,
He that made me whole, the same said unto me, Take up thy
bed, and walk. Then asked they him, What man is that which
said unto thee, Take up thy bed, and walk? . . . The man departed and told the Jews that it was Jesus, which had made him
whole. And therefore did the Jews persecute Jesus, and sought
to slay him, because he had done these things on the Sabbath-

----

[22] Mark 6: 1–6.

day. But Jesus answered them, My Father worketh hitherto, and I work. Therefore the Jews sought the more to kill him, because he not only had broken the Sabbath, but said also that God was his Father, making himself equal with God." [23]

Our Lord here stands charged with two crimes: First, He had broken the Sabbath; and secondly, He had made himself equal with God. The first accusation is based on these particulars: 1. By his word he had healed the impotent man. But this violated no law of God; it only set at naught that tradition which forbade anything to be done for curing diseases upon the Sabbath. 2. He had directed the man to carry his bed. But this, as a burden, was a mere trifle,[24] like a cloak or mat, and was designed to show the reality of his cure, and thus to honor the Lord of the Sabbath, who had healed him. Moreover, it was not such a burden as the Scriptures forbid upon the Sabbath.[25] 3. Jesus justified what he had done by comparing his present act of healing to that work which his Father had done HITH-ERTO, *i. e.,* from the beginning of creation. Ever since the Sabbath was sanctified in paradise, the Father, by his providence, had continued to mankind, even upon the Sabbath, all the merciful acts by which the human race has been preserved. This work of the Father's was of precisely the same nature as that which Jesus had now done. These acts did not argue that the Father had *hitherto* lightly esteemed the Sabbath, for he had most solemnly enjoined its observance in the law

---

[23] John 5: 1–18.

[24] See Dr. Bloomfield's Greek Testament on this text; Family Testament of the American Tract Society; and Nevins' Biblical Antiquities, pp. 62, 63.

[25] Compare Jer. 17: 21–27 with Nehemiah 13: 15–20.

and in the prophets; [26] and as our Lord had most expressly recognized their authority, [27] there was no ground to accuse him of disregarding the Sabbath, when he had only followed the example of the Father from the beginning. The Saviour's answer to these two charges will remove all difficulty :—

" Then answered Jesus and said unto them, Verily, verily, I say unto you, The Son can do nothing of himself, but what he seeth the Father do; for what things soever he doeth, these also doeth the Son likewise." [28]

This answer involves two points : 1. That he was following his Father's perfect example, who had ever laid open to him all his works, and hence, as he was doing only that which had ever been the pleasure of the Father to do, he was not engaged in the overthrow of the Sabbath; 2. That by the meek humility of his answer,—" The Son can do nothing of himself, but what he seeth the Father do,"—he showed the groundlessness of their charge of self-exaltation, and left them no chance to answer him again.

Several months after this, the same case of healing was again under discussion.

" Jesus answered and said unto them, I have done one work, and ye all marvel. Moses therefore gave unto you circumcision (not because it is of Moses, but of the fathers); and ye on the Sabbath-day circumcise a man. If a man on the Sabbath-day receive circumcision, that the law of Moses should not be broken, are ye angry at me, because I have made a man every whit whole on the Sabbath-day ? " [29]

---

[26] Gen. 2: 1–3; Ex. 20:8–11; Isa. 56; 58:13, 14; Eze. 20.

[27] Gal. 4:4; Matt. 5:17–19; 7:12; 19:17; Luke 16:17.

[28] John 5:19.   [29] John 7:21–23.

This Scripture contains our Lord's second answer relative to healing the impotent man upon the Sabbath. In his first answer he rested his defense upon the fact that what he had done was precisely the same as that which his Father had done *hitherto,* that is, from the beginning of the world, which implies that the Sabbath had existed from the same point, else the example of the Father during this time would not be relevant. In this, his second answer, a similar point is involved relative to the origin of the Sabbath. His defense this time rests upon the fact that his act of healing no more violated the Sabbath than did the act of circumcising upon the Sabbath. But if circumcision, which was ordained in the time of Abraham, was older than the Sabbath, as it certainly was if the Sabbath originated in the wilderness of Sin, there would be an impropriety in the allusion; for circumcision would be entitled to the priority as the more ancient institution. It would be strictly proper to speak of a more recent institution as involving no violation of an older one; · but it would not be proper to speak of an ancient institution as involving no violation of one more recent. The language therefore implies that the Sabbath was older than circumcision; in other words, more ancient than the days of Abraham. These two answers of the Saviour are certainly in harmony with the unanimous testimony of the sacred writers, that the Sabbath originated with the sanctification of the rest-day of the Lord in Eden.

What had the Saviour done to justify the hatred of the Jewish people toward him ?—Upon the Sabbath he had healed with one word a man who had been helpless thirty-eight years. Was not this act in strict accord-

9

ance with the Sabbatic institution? Our Lord has settled this point in the affirmative by weighty and unanswerable arguments,[30] not in this case alone, but in others already noticed, and also in those which remain to be noticed. Had he left the man in his wretchedness because it was the Sabbath, when a word would have healed him, he would have dishonored the Sabbath, and thrown reproach upon its Author. We shall find the Lord of the Sabbath still further at work in its behalf in rescuing it from the hands of those who had so utterly perverted its design,—a work quite unnecessary, had he designed to nail the institution to his cross.

The next incident to be noticed is the case of the man that was born blind. Jesus, seeing him, said :—

" I must work the works of him that sent me while it is day; the night cometh, when no man can work. As long as I am in the world, I am the light of the world. When he had thus spoken, he spat on the ground, and made clay of the spittle, and he anointed the eyes of the blind man with the clay, and said unto him, Go wash in the pool of Siloam (which is by interpretation, Sent). He went his way, therefore, and washed, and came seeing. . . . And it was the Sabbath-day when Jesus made the clay, and opened his eyes." [31]

Here is the record of another of our Lord's merciful acts upon the Sabbath-day. He saw a man blind from his birth; moved with compassion toward him, he moistened clay, and anointed his eyes, and sent him to the pool to wash; and when he had washed, he received sight. The act was alike worthy of the Sabbath and of its

---

[30] Grotius well says: " If he healed any on the Sabbath, he made it appear, not only from the law, but also from their received opinions, that such works were not forbidden on the Sabbath."—*The Truth of the Christian Religion,* b. 5, sec. 7,

[31] John 9: 1-16,

Lord; and it pertains only to the opponents of the Sabbath *now*, as it pertained only to the enemies of its Lord *then*, to see in this even the slightest violation of the Sabbath.

After this we read as follows :—

" And he was teaching in one of the synagogues on the Sabbath. And, behold, there was a woman which had a spirit of infirmity eighteen years, and was bowed together, and could in no wise lift up herself. And when Jesus saw her, he called her to him, and said unto her, Woman, thou art loosed from thine infirmity. And he laid his hands on her; and immediately she was made straight, and glorified God. And the ruler of the synagogue answered with indignation, because that Jesus healed on the Sabbath-day, and said unto the people; There are six days in which men ought to work; in them therefore come and be healed, and not on the Sabbath-day. The Lord then answered him, and said, Thou hypocrite, doth not each one of you on the Sabbath loose his ox or his ass from the stall, and lead him away to watering ? And ought not this woman, being a daughter of Abraham, whom Satan hath bound, lo, these eighteen years, be loosed from this bond on the Sabbath-day? And when he had said these things, all his adversaries were ashamed: and all the people rejoiced for all the glorious things that were done by him." [32]

This time a daughter of Abraham, that is, a pious woman,[33] who had been bound by Satan eighteen years, was loosed from that bond upon the Sabbath-day. Jesus silenced the clamor of his enemies by an appeal to their own course of action in loosing the ox and leading him to water upon the Sabbath. With this answer our Lord made all his adversaries ashamed, and all the people rejoiced for the glorious things that were done

---

[32] Luke 13: 10–17.   [33] 1 Pet. 3: 6.

by him.   The last of these glorious acts by which Jesus
honored the Sabbath is thus narrated :—

"And it came to pass, as he went into the house of one of
the chief Pharisees to eat bread on the Sabbath-day, that they
watched him.   And, behold, there was a certain man before him
which had the dropsy.   And Jesus answering spake unto the
lawyers and Pharisees, saying, Is it lawful to heal on the Sabbath-day?   And they held their peace.   And he took him, and
healed him, and let him go; and answered them, saying, Which
of you shall have an ass or an ox fallen into a pit, and will not
straightway pull him out on the Sabbath-day?   And they could
not answer him again to these things." [34]

It is evident that the Pharisees and lawyers durst
not answer the question, Is it lawful to heal on the Sabbath-day?   If they said, "Yes," they condemned their
own tradition; if they said, "No," they were unable to
sustain their answer by fair argument; hence they remained silent.   And when Jesus had healed the man, he
asked a second question equally embarrassing: Which
of you shall have an ox fall into a pit, and will not
straightway pull him out on the Sabbath?   And again
they could not answer him.   It is apparent that our
Lord's argument with the Pharisees from time to time,
in relation to the Sabbath, had satisfied them at last that
silence relative to their traditions was wiser than speech.

In his public teaching, the Saviour declared that the
weightier matters of the law were judgment, MERCY, and
faith; [35] and his long-continued and powerful effort in
behalf of the Sabbath was to vindicate it as a MERCIFUL
institution, and to rid it of Pharisaic traditions, by which
it was perverted from its original purpose.   Those who

---

[34] Luke 14: 1 -6.   [35] Matt. 23: 23.

oppose the Sabbath are here guilty of unfairness in two particulars : 1. They represent these Pharisaic rigors as actually belonging to the Sabbatic institution, and by this means turn the minds of men against the Sabbath; 2. Having done this, they represent the effort of the Saviour to set aside those traditions as an effort directed to the overthrow of the Sabbath itself.

And now we come to Christ's memorable discourse upon the mount of Olives, on the very eve of his crucifixion, in which for the last time he mentions the Sabbath :—

"When ye, therefore, shall see the abomination of desolation, spoken of by Daniel the prophet, stand in the holy place (whoso readeth, let him understand), then let them which be in Judea flee into the mountains; let him which is on the house-top not come down to take anything out of his house; neither let him which is in the field return back to take his clothes. And woe unto them that are with child, and to them that give suck in those days! But pray ye that your flight be not in the winter, neither on the Sabbath-day; for then shall be great tribulation, such as was not since the beginning of the world to this time, no, nor ever shall be." [36]

In this language our Lord brings to view the dreadful calamities of the Jewish people, and the destruction of their city and temple, as predicted by Daniel the prophet; [37] and his watchful care over his people as their Lord leads him to point out the means of escape.

1. He gives them a token by which they should know when this terrible overthrow was immediately impending. It was "the abomination of desolation" standing "in the holy place;" or, as expressed by Luke, the

---

[36] Matt. 24: 15–21.   [37] Dan. 9: 26, 27.

token was " Jerusalem compassed with armies." [38]   The fulfillment of this sign is recorded by the historian Josephus.   After stating that Cestius, the Roman commander, at the commencement of the contest between the Jews and the Romans, encompassed the city of Jerusalem with an army, he adds :—

" Who, had he but continued the siege a little longer, had certainly taken the city; but it was, I suppose, owing to the aversion God had already at the city and the sanctuary, that he was hindered from putting an end to the war that very day.   It then happened that Cestius was not conscious either how the besieged despaired of success, or how courageous the people were for him ; and so he recalled his soldiers from the place, and by despairing of any expectation of taking it, without having received any disgrace, he retired from the city, without any reason in the world." [39]

2. This sign being seen, the disciples were to know that the desolation of Jerusalem was nigh.   " Then," says Christ, " let them which be in Judea flee into the mountains."   Josephus records the fulfillment of this injunction :—

" After this calamity had befallen Cestius, many of the most eminent of the Jews swam away from the city, as from a ship when it was going to sink." [40]

Eusebius also relates its fulfillment :—

" The whole body, however, of the church at Jerusalem, having been commanded by a divine revelation, given to men of approved piety there before the war, removed from the city, and dwelt at a certain town beyond the Jordan, called Pella.   Here, those that believed in Christ, having removed from Jerusalem, as if holy men had entirely abandoned the royal city itself, and the whole land of Judea, the divine justice, for their crimes against

---

[38] Luke 21: 20.   [39] Jewish wars, b. 2, chap. 19.   [40] Id., b. 2, chap. 20.

Christ and his apostles, finally overtook them, totally destroying the whole generation of these evil-doers from the earth." [41]

3. So imminent was the danger when this sign should be seen, that not a moment was to be lost. He that was upon the housetop could not even come down to take a single article from his house. The man that was in the field was forbidden to return to the house for his clothes. Not a moment was to be lost; they must flee as they were, and flee for life. And pitiable indeed was the case of those who could not flee.

4. In view of the fact that the disciples must flee the moment the promised token should appear, our Lord directed them to pray for two things; namely, that their flight should not be in the winter, and that it should not be upon the Sabbath-day. Their pitiable situation, should they be compelled to flee to the mountains in the depth of winter, without time to take even their clothes, sufficiently attests the importance of the first of these petitions, and the tender care of Jesus as the Lord of his people. The second of these petitions will be found equally expressive of his care as Lord of the Sabbath.

5. But it is replied that this last petition has reference only to the fact that the Jews would then be keeping the Sabbath strictly, and as a consequence, the city gates would be closed that day, and those be punished with death who should attempt to flee; and hence his petition indicates nothing in proof of Christ's regard for the Sabbath. An assertion so often and so confidently uttered should be well founded in truth; yet a brief examination will show that such is not the case. (1.)

---

[41] Eccl. Hist., b. 3, chap. 5.

The Saviour's language, "Let them which be in Judea
flee into the mountains," has reference to the whole land
of Judea, and not to Jerusalem only. The closing of the
city gates could therefore affect the flight of only a part
of the disciples.   (2.) Josephus states the remarkable
fact, that, when Cestius was marching upon Jerusalem,
in fulfillment of the Saviour's token, and had reached
Lydda, not many miles from Jerusalem, "he found the
city empty of its men; for the whole multitude were
gone up to Jerusalem to the Feast of Tabernacles." [42]
The law of Moses required the presence of every male
in Israel at this feast in Jerusalem; [43] and thus, in the
providence of God, the disciples had no Jewish enemies
left in the country to hinder their flight.   (3.) The
Jewish nation, being thus assembled at Jerusalem, did
most openly violate the Sabbath a few days prior to the
flight of the disciples,—a singular commentary on their
supposed strictness in keeping it at that time. [44] Josephus
says of the march of Cestius upon Jerusalem :—

---

[42] Jewish Wars, b. 2, chap. 19.   [43] Deut. 16: 16.

[44] Mr. Crozier remarks in the *Advent Harbinger* for Dec. 6, 1851: "The reference to the Sabbath in Matt. 24: 20 only shows that the Jews who rejected Christ
would be keeping the Sabbath at the destruction of Jerusalem, and would, in
consequence, add to the dangers of the disciples' flight by punishing them, perhaps
with death, for fleeing on that day."

And Mr. Marsh, forgetting that Christ forbade his disciples to take anything
with them in their flight, uses the following language: "If the disciples should
attempt to flee from Jerusalem on that day, and carry their things, the Jews would
embarrass their flight, and perhaps put them to death. The Jews would be keeping the Sabbath, because they rejected Christ and his gospel."—*Advent Harbinger*,
Jan. 24, 1852. These quotations betray the bitterness of their authors. In honorable distinction from these anti-Sabbatarians, the following is quoted from Mr.
William Miller, himself an observer of the first day of the week:—

"'Neither on the Sabbath-day.' Because it was to be kept as a day of rest,
and no servile work was to be done on that day, nor would it be right for them
to travel on that day. Christ has in this place sanctioned the Sabbath, and
clearly shows us our duty to let no trivial circumstance cause us to break the law

" He pitched his camp at a certain place called Gabao, fifty furlongs distant from Jerusalem. But as for the Jews, when they saw the war approaching to their metropolis, they left the feast, and betook themselves to their arms ; and taking courage greatly from their multitude, went in a sudden and disorderly manner to the fight, with a great noise, and without any consideration had of the rest of the seventh day, although the Sabbath was the day to which they had the greatest regard ; but that rage which made them forget the religious observation [of the Sabbath], made them too hard for their enemies in the fight ; with such violence therefore did they fall upon the Romans, as to break into their ranks, and to march through the midst of them, making a great slaughter as they went." [45] etc.

Thus it is seen that on the eve of the disciples' flight, the rage of the Jews toward their enemies made them utterly disregard the Sabbath ! (4.) But after Cestius encompassed the city with his army, thus giving the Saviour's signal, he suddenly withdrew it, as Josephus says, "without any reason in the world." This was the moment of flight for the disciples, and mark how the providence of God opened the way for those in Jerusalem :—

" But when the robbers perceived this unexpected retreat of his, they resumed their courage, and ran after the hinder parts of his army, and destroyed a considerable number of both their horsemen and footmen ; and now Cestius lay all night at the camp which was at Scopus, and as he went off farther next day, he thereby invited the enemy to follow him, who still fell upon the hindmost, and destroyed them." [46]

---

of the Sabbath. Yet how many who profess to believe in Christ at this present day make it a point to visit, travel, and feast on this day ! What a false-hearted profession must that person make who can thus treat with contempt the moral law of God, and despise the precepts of the Lord Jesus ! We may here learn our obligation to remember the Sabbath-day, to keep it holy."—*Exposition of Matthew 24*, p. 18.

[45] Jewish Wars, b. 2, chap. 19.   [46] Idem.

This sally of the excited multitude in pursuit of the Romans was at the very moment when the disciples were commanded to flee, and could not but afford them the needed facility of escape. Had the flight of Cestius happened upon the Sabbath, undoubtedly the Jews would have pursued him upon that day, as under less exciting circumstances they had, a few days before, gone out several miles to attack him upon the Sabbath. It is seen, therefore, that whether in city or country, the disciples were not in danger of being attacked by their enemies. even had their flight been upon the Sabbath-day.

6. There is, therefore, but one view that can be taken relative to the meaning of these words of our Lord, and that is that he thus spake out of sacred regard for the Sabbath. In his tender care for his people, he had given them a precept that would require them to violate the Sabbath, should the moment for flight happen upon that day; for the command to flee was imperative the instant the promised signal should be seen, and the distance to Pella, where they found a place of refuge, was at least sixty miles. This prayer which the Saviour left with the disciples would cause them to remember the Sabbath whenever they should come before God. It was therefore impossible that the apostolic church should forget the day of sacred rest. Such a prayer, that they might not at a future time be compelled to violate the Sabbath, was a sure and certain means of perpetuating its sacred observance for the coming forty years, until the final destruction of Jerusalem, and was never forgotten by that early church, as we shall hereafter see.[47]

---

[47] See chapter 16.

The Saviour, who had taken unwearied pains during his whole ministry to show that the Sabbath was a merciful institution, and to set aside those traditions by which it had been perverted from its true design, did, in this his last discourse, most tenderly commend the Sabbath to his people, uniting in the same petition their own safety and the sacredness of the rest-day of the Lord.[48]

A few days after this discourse, the Lord of the Sabbath was nailed to the cross as the great sacrifice for the sins of men.[49] The Messiah was thus cut off in the midst of the seventieth week; and by his death he caused the sacrifice and oblation to cease.[50]

Paul describes the abrogation of the typical system at the crucifixion of the Lord Jesus in the following words :—

"Blotting out the handwriting of ordinances that was against us, which was contrary to us, and took it out of the way, nailing it to his cross. . . . Let no man therefore judge you in meat or in drink, or in respect of an holy day, or of the new moon, or of the sabbath-days; which are a shadow of things to come; but the body is of Christ." [51]

The object of this action is declared to be the hand-writing of ordinances. The manner of its abrogation is thus stated: 1. Blotted out; 2. Nailed to the cross; 3.

---

[48] President Edwards says: "A further argument for the perpetuity of the Sabbath we have in Matt. 24: 20: 'Pray ye that your flight be not in the winter, *neither on the Sabbath-day.*' Christ is here speaking of the flight of the apostles and other Christians out of Jerusalem and Judea, just before their final destruction, as is manifest by the whole context, and especially by the 16th verse: 'Then let them which be in Judea flee into the mountains.' But this final destruction of Jerusalem was after the dissolution of the Jewish constitution, and after the Christian dispensation was fully set up. Yet it is plainly implied in these words of our Lord, that even then Christians were bound to a strict observation of the Sabbath."— *Works of President Edwards,* vol. 4, pp. 621, 622, New York, 1849.

[49] Matt. 27; Isa. 53.   [50] Dan. 9: 24–27.   [51] Col. 2: 14–17.

Taken out of the way. Its nature is shown in the words
"against us" and "contrary to us." The things contained in it were meats, drinks, holy days [Greek, ἑορτη,
a feast day], new moons, and sabbaths.[52] The whole is
declared a shadow of good things to come; and the body
which casts this shadow is of Christ. That law which
was proclaimed by the voice of God, and written by his
own finger upon the tables of stone, and deposited beneath the mercy-seat, was altogether unlike that system
of carnal ordinances that was written by Moses in a
book, and placed in the side of the ark.[53] It would be
absurd to speak of the tables of STONE as NAILED to the
cross; or to speak of BLOTTING out what was ENGRAVED in
STONE. It would be blasphemous to represent the Son
of God as pouring out his blood to blot out what the
finger of his Father had written. It would be to confound all the immutable principles of morality, to represent the ten commandments as "contrary" to man's
moral nature. It would be to make Christ the minister
of sin, to represent him as dying to utterly destroy the
moral law. Nor does that man keep truth on his side
who represents the ten commandments as among the
things contained in Paul's enumeration of what was abolished. Nor is there any excuse for those who would
destroy the ten commandments with this statement of
Paul's; for he shows, last of all, that what was thus

---

[52] For an extended view of these Jewish festivals, see chapter 7.

[53] Compare Deut. 10: 4, 5 with 31: 24-26. Thus Morer contrasts the phrase,
"in the ark," which is used with reference to the two tables, with the expression,
"in the side of the ark," as used respecting the book of the law, and says of the
latter: "In the side of the ark, or more critically, in the outside of the ark; or
in a chest by itself on the right side of the ark, saith the Targum of Jonathan."—
Morer's Dialogues on the Lord's Day, p. 211, London, 1701.

abrogated was a shadow of good things to come,—an absurdity, if applied to the moral law. The feasts, new moons, and sabbaths of the ceremonial law, which Paul declared to be abolished in consequence of the abrogation of that code, have been particularly noticed already.[54] That the Sabbath of the Lord is not included in their number, the following facts evince :—

1. The Sabbath of the Lord was made before sin entered our world. It is not, therefore, one of those things that foreshadow redemption from sin.[55]

2. Being made FOR man before the fall, it is not one of those things that are AGAINST him and CONTRARY to him.[56]

3. When the ceremonial sabbaths were ordained, they were carefully distinguished from the Sabbath of the Lord.[57]

4. The Sabbath of the Lord does not owe its exist-ence to the handwriting of ordinances, but is found in the very bosom of that law which Jesus came not to destroy. The abrogation of the ceremonial law could not, therefore, abolish the Sabbath of the fourth commandment.[58]

5. The effort of our Lord through his whole ministry to redeem the Sabbath from the thralldom of the Jewish doctors, and to vindicate it as a merciful institution, is utterly inconsistent with the idea that he nailed it to his cross, as one of those things against man and contrary to him.

6. Our Lord's petition respecting the flight of the

---

[54] See chapter 7.   [55] See chapter 2.   [56] Mark 2 : 27.

[57] Lev. 23 : 37, 38.   [58] Gen. 2 : 1-3 ; Ex. 20 ; Matt. 5 : 17, 19.

disciples from Judea, recognizes the sacredness of the Sabbath many years after the crucifixion of the Saviour.

7. The perpetuity of the Sabbath in the new earth is not easily reconciled with the idea that it was blotted out and nailed to our Lord's cross as one of those things that were contrary to man.[59]

8. Because the authority of the fourth commandment is expressly recognized after the Saviour's crucifixion.[60]

9. And finally, because the royal law, which is unabolished, embodies the ten commandments, and consequently embraces and enforces the Sabbath of the Lord.[61]

When the Saviour died upon the cross, the whole typical system, which had pointed forward to that event as the commencement of its antitype, expired with him. The Saviour being dead, Joseph of Arimathea went to Pilate, and begged the body of Jesus, and with the assistance of Nicodemus, buried it in his own new tomb.[62]

"And that day was the preparation, and the Sabbath drew on. And the women also, which came with him from Galilee, followed after, and beheld the sepulcher, and how his body was laid. And they returned, and prepared spices and ointments; and rested the Sabbath-day according to the commandment. Now upon the first day of the week, very early in the morning, they came unto the sepulcher, bringing the spices which they had prepared, and certain others with them." [63]

This text is worthy of special attention : 1. Because it is an express recognition of the fourth commandment

---

[59] Isa. 66 : 22, 23.   See also the close of chapter 27 of this work.

[60] Luke 23 : 54–56.   [61] James 2 : 8–12 ; Matt. 5 : 17–19 ; Rom. 3 : 19, 31.

[62] Heb. 9 and 10 ; Luke 23 : 46–53 ; John 19 : 38–42.

[63] Luke 23 : 54–56 ; 24 : 1.

after the crucifixion of the Lord Jesus; 2. Because it is the most remarkable case of Sabbatic observance in the whole Bible,—the Lord of the Sabbath was dead, and preparation was being made for embalming him; but when the Sabbath drew on, it was suspended, and they rested, says the sacred historian, according to the commandment; 3. Because it shows that the Sabbath-day, according to the commandment, is the day before the first day of the week, thus identifying the seventh day in the commandment with the seventh day of the New-Testament week; 4. Because it is a direct testimony that the knowledge of the true seventh day was preserved as late as the crucifixion; for they observed the day enjoined in the commandment, and that was the day on which the Most High had rested from the work of creation.

In the course of the day following this Sabbath, that is, upon the first day of the week, it was ascertained that Jesus was risen from the dead. It appears that this event must have taken place upon that day, though it is not thus stated in express terms. At this point of time it is supposed by many that the Sabbath was changed from the seventh to the first day of the week; and that the sacredness of the seventh day was then transferred to the first day of the week, which thenceforth was the Christian Sabbath, enforced by all the authority of the fourth commandment. To judge of the truthfulness of these positions, let us read with care each mention of the first day found in the four evangelists. Matthew writes:—

"In the end of the Sabbath, as it began to dawn toward the first day of the week, came Mary Magdalene and the other Mary to see the sepulcher."

Mark says :—

"And when the Sabbath was past, Mary Magdalene, and Mary the mother of James, and Salome, had bought sweet spices, that they might come and anoint him. And very early in the morning, the first day of the week, they came unto the sepulcher at the rising of the sun. . . . Now when Jesus was risen early the first day of the week, he appeared first to Mary Magdalene."

Luke uses the following language :—

" And they returned, and prepared spices and ointments, and rested the Sabbath-day according to the commandment. Now upon the first day of the week, very early in the morning, they came unto the sepulcher, bringing the spices which they had prepared, and certain others with them."

John bears this testimony :—

" The first day of the week cometh Mary Magdalene early, when it was yet dark, unto the sepulcher, and seeth the stone taken away from the sepulcher. . . . Then the same day at evening, being the first day of the week, when the doors were shut where the disciples were assembled for fear of the Jews, came Jesus and stood in the midst, and saith unto them, Peace be unto you." [64]

In these texts the foundation of the " Christian Sabbath" must be sought, if, indeed, such an institution actually exists ; for there are no other records of the first day which relate to the time when it is supposed to have become sacred. These texts are claimed to prove that at the resurrection of the Saviour, the first day absorbed the sacredness of the seventh, elevating itself from the rank of a secular to that of a sacred day, and abasing the Sabbath of the Lord to the rank of

---

[64] Matt. 28: 1; Mark 16: 1, 2, 9; Luke 23: 56; 24: 1; John 20: 1, 19.

"the six working days."[65] Yet the following facts must be regarded as very extraordinary indeed if this supposed change of the Sabbath here took place :—

1. That these texts should contain no mention of this change of the Sabbath; 2. That they should carefully discriminate between the Sabbath of the fourth commandment and the first day of the week; 3. That they should apply no sacred title to that day, particularly that they should omit the title of Christian Sabbath; 4. That they should not mention the fact that Christ rested upon that day, an act essential to its becoming his "Sabbath;"[66] 5. That they do not relate the act of taking the blessing of God from the seventh day, and placing it upon the first; and, indeed, that they do not mention any act whatever of blessing and hallowing the day; 6. That they omit to mention anything that Christ did To the first day; and that they even neglect to inform us that Christ so much as took the first day of the week upon his lips! 7. That they give no precept in support of first-day observance, nor do they contain a hint of the manner in which the first day of the week can be enforced by the authority of the fourth commandment.

Should it be asserted, however, from the words of John, that the disciples were on this occasion convened for the purpose of honoring the day of the resurrection, and that Jesus sanctioned this act by meeting with them, thus accomplishing the change of the Sabbath, it is sufficient to cite in reply the words of Mark, in which he narrates the interview :—

---

[65] Eze. 46 : 1.   [66] See the origin of the ancient Sabbath in Gen. 2 : 1–3.

" Afterward he appeared unto the eleven as they sat at meat, and upbraided them with their unbelief and hardness of heart, because they believed not them which had seen him after he was risen." [67]

This testimony from Mark shows that the inferences often drawn from the words of John is utterly unfounded. The disciples were assembled for the purpose of eating supper. Jesus came into their midst, and upbraided them with their unbelief respecting his resurrection.

The Scriptures declare that " with God all things are possible ; " yet this statement is limited by the declaration that God cannot lie.[68] Does the change of the Sabbath pertain to those things that are possible with God, or is it excluded by that important limitation, *God cannot lie?* The Lawgiver is the God of truth, and his law is the truth.[69] Whether it would still remain the truth if changed to something else, and whether the Lawgiver would still continue to be the God of truth after he had thus changed it, remains to be seen. The fourth commandment, which is affirmed to have been changed, is thus expressed :—

"Remember the Sabbath-day, to keep it holy. . . . The seventh day is the Sabbath of the Lord thy God. . . . For in six days the Lord made heaven and earth, the sea, and all that in them is, and rested the seventh day; wherefore the Lord blessed the Sabbath-day, and hallowed it."

Now if we insert " first day " in place of " seventh day," we shall bring the matter to a test :—

" Remember the Sabbath-day, to keep it holy. . . . The first

---

[67] Mark 16 : 14.   That this interview was certainly the same as that in John 20 : 19, will be seen from a careful examination of Luke 24.

[68] Matt. 19 : 26; Titus 1 : 2.   [69] Isa. 65 : 16; Ps. 119 : 142, 151.

day is the Sabbath of the Lord thy God. . . . For in six days the Lord made heaven and earth, the sea, and all that in them is, and rested the first day, wherefore the Lord blessed the Sabbath-day, and hallowed it."

This changes the truth of God into a lie; [70] for it is false that God rested upon the first day of the week, and blessed and hallowed it. Nor is it possible to change the rest-day of the Creator from that day on which he did rest to one of the six days on which he did not rest.[71] To change a part of the commandment, and leave the rest unchanged, will not, therefore, answer, as the truth which is left is still sufficient to expose the falsehood which is inserted. A more radical change is needed, like the following :—

" Remember the Christian Sabbath, to keep it holy. The first day is the Sabbath of the Lord Jesus Christ. For on that day he arose from the dead ; wherefore he blessed the first day of the week, and hallowed it."

After such a change, no part of the original Sabbatic institution remains. Not only is the rest-day of the Lord left out, but even the reasons on which the fourth commandment is based are of necessity omitted also. But does such an edition of the fourth commandment exist ?— Not in the Bible, certainly. Is it true that such titles as these are applied to the first day ?—Never, in the Holy Scriptures. Did the Lawgiver bless and hallow that day ?—Most assuredly not. He did not even take the name of it into his lips. Such a change of the

---

[70] Rom. 1: 25.

[71] It is just as easy to change the crucifixion-day from that day of the week on which Christ was crucified to one of the six days on which he was not, as to change the rest-day of the Creator from that day of the week on which he rested to one of the six days on which he wrought in the work of creation.

fourth commandment on the part of the God of truth is impossible ; for it does not merely affirm that which is false, and deny that which is true, but it turns the truth of God itself into a lie. It is simply the act of setting up a rival to the Sabbath of the Lord, which, having neither sacredness nor authority of its own, has contrived to absorb that of the Bible Sabbath itself. Such is the FOUNDATION of the first-day Sabbath. The texts which are employed in rearing the institution upon this foundation will be noticed in their proper order and place. Several of these texts properly pertain to this chapter :—

"And after eight days, again his disciples were within, and Thomas with them ; then came Jesus, the doors being shut, and stood in the midst, and said, Peace be unto you." [72]

It is not asserted that on this occasion our Lord hallowed the first day of the week ; for that act is affirmed to date from the resurrection itself, on the authority of the texts already quoted. But the sacredness of the first day being assumed as the foundation, this text furnishes the first stone for the superstructure—the first pillar in the first-day temple. The argument drawn from it may be stated thus: Jesus selected this day as the one in which to manifest himself to his disciples, and by this act strongly attested his regard for the day. But it is no small defect in this argument that his next meeting with them was on a fishing occasion ; [73] and his last and most important manifestation, when he ascended into heaven, was upon Thursday. [74] The act of the Saviour

---

[72] John 20 : 26.　　　　　　[73] John 21.

[74] Acts 1 : 3. Forty days from the day of the resurrection would expire on Thursday.

in meeting with his disciples, it must therefore be conceded, was insufficient of itself to show that any day is
sacred; for it would otherwise prove the sacredness of
several of the working days.

But a still more serious defect in this argument is
found in the fact that this meeting of Jesus with his disciples does not appear to have been upon the first day of
the week. It was "after eight days" from the previous
meeting of Jesus and the disciples, which, coming at the
very close of the resurrection day, must have extended
into the second day of the week.[75] "After eight days"
from this meeting, if made to signify only one week,
necessarily carries us to the second day of the week.
But a different expression is used by the Spirit of inspiration when simply one week is intended. "After
seven days" is the chosen term of the Holy Spirit when
designating just one week.[76] "After eight days" most
naturally implies the ninth or tenth day;[77] but allowing
it to mean the eighth day, it fails to prove that this ap-

---

[75] When the resurrection day was "far spent," the Saviour and two of the
disciples drew near to Emmaus, a village seven and a half miles from Jerusalem.
They constrained him to go in with them to tarry for the night. While they
were eating supper, they discovered that it was Jesus, when he vanished from
their sight. Then they arose and returned to Jerusalem; and after their arrival,
the first meeting of Jesus with the eleven took place. It could, therefore, have
lacked but little of sunset, which closed the day, if it was not actually upon the
second day, when Jesus came into their midst. Luke 24. In the latter case, the
expression, "the same day at evening, being the first day of the week," would find
an exact parallel in meaning in the expression, "in the ninth day of the
month at even," which actually signifies the evening with which the tenth day of
the month commences. Lev. 23: 32.

[76] Those who were to come before God from Sabbath to Sabbath to minister in
his temple, were said to come "after seven days." 1 Chron. 9: 25; 2 Kings
11: 5.

[77] "After six days," instead of being the sixth day, was about eight days
after. Matt. 17: 1; Mark 9: 2; Luke 9: 28.

pearance of the Saviour was upon the first day of the
week.   To sum up the argument: The first meeting of
Jesus with his disciples in the evening at the close of
first day of the week was mainly if not wholly upon the
second day of the week;[78] the second meeting could not
have been earlier in the week than the second or third
day, and the day seems to have been selected simply
because Thomas was present; the third meeting was
upon a fishing occasion; and the fourth was upon
Thursday, when he ascended into heaven.   The argument for first-day sacredness drawn from this text is
eminently fitted to the foundation of that sacredness
already examined; and the institution of the first-day
Sabbath itself, unless formed of more substantial frame-
work than enters into its foundation, is at best only a
castle in the air.

The text which next enters into the fabric of first-
day sacredness is the following :—

"And when the day of Pentecost was fully come, they were
all with one accord in one place.   And suddenly there came a
sound from heaven as of a rushing mighty wind, and it filled all
the house where they were sitting." [79]

This text is supposed to contribute an important
pillar for the first-day temple, which is furnished as follows: The disciples were convened on this occasion to
celebrate the first-day Sabbath, and the Holy Spirit was
poured out at that time in honor of that day.   To this
deduction there are, however, the most serious objections: 1. There is no evidence that a first-day Sabbath

---

[78] That sunset marks the close of the day, see the close of chapter 8.

[79] Acts 2: 1, 2.

was then in existence; 2. There is no intimation that the disciples came together on this occasion for its celebration; 3. Nor that the Holy Spirit was then poured out in honor of the first-day of the week; 4. From the ascension of Jesus until the day of the Spirit's outpouring, the disciples had continued in prayer and supplication, so that their being convened on this day was nothing materially different from what had been the case for the past ten days or more; [80] 5. Had the sacred writer designed to show that a certain day of the week was honored by the events narrated, he would doubtless have stated that fact, and named the day; 6. Luke was so far from naming the day of the week that it is even now a disputed point, some eminent first-day authors [81] asserting that the day of Pentecost that year came upon the *seventh* day; 7. The one great event which the Holy Spirit designed to mark was the antitype of the feast of Pentecost, the day of the week on which that should occur being wholly immaterial. How widely, therefore, do those err who reverse this order, making the day of the week, which the Holy Spirit has not even named, but which they assume to be the first day, the thing of importance, and passing over in silence that fact which the Holy Spirit has so carefully noted, that this event took place upon the day of Pentecost.

The conclusion to which these facts lead is inevitable; viz., that the pillar furnished from this text for the first-day temple is, like the foundation of that edifice,

---

[80] Luke 24:49–53; Acts 1.

[81] Horatio B. Hackett, D. D., Professor of Biblical Literature in Newton Theological Institution, thus remarks: " It is generally supposed that this Pentecost, signalized by the outpouring of the Spirit, fell on the Jewish Sabbath, our Saturday."—*Commentary on the Original Text of the Acts*, pp. 50, 51.

simply a thing of the imagination, and quite worthy of
a place beside the pillar furnished from the record of our
Lord's second appearance to his disciples.

A third pillar for the first-day edifice is the following : Redemption is greater than creation; therefore the
day of Christ's resurrection should be observed instead
of the day of the Creator's rest. But this proposition
is open to the fatal objection that the Bible says nothing
of the kind.[82] Who, then, knows that it is true ? When
the Creator gave existence to our world, did he not
foresee the fall of man ? and, foreseeing that fall, did he
not entertain the purpose of redeeming him ? Does it
not follow from this that the purpose of redemption was
entertained in that of creation ? Who, then, can affirm
that redemption is greater than creation ?

But as the Scriptures do not decide this point, let it
be assumed that redemption is the greater. Who knows
that a day should be set apart for its commemoration?
The Bible says nothing on the point. But granting that
a day should be set apart for this purpose, what day
should have the preference ? It is said, That day on
which redemption was finished ? It is not true that
redemption is finished; the resurrection of the saints
and the redemption of our earth from the curse are

---

[82] In 1633 William Prynne, a prisoner in the tower of London, composed a
work in defense of first-day observance, entitled, "Dissertation on the Lord's-day
Sabbath." He thus acknowledges the futility of the argument under consideration: "No scripture . . . prefers or advanceth the work of redemption . . .
before the work of creation; both these works being very great and glorious in
themselves; wherefore I cannot believe the work of redemption, or Christ's resurrection alone, to be more excellent and glorious than the work of creation,
without sufficient texts and Scripture grounds to prove it; but may deny it as a
presumptuous fancy or unsound assertion, till satisfactorily proved, as well as
peremptorily averred without proof."—Page 59. This is the judgment of a candid advocate of the first day as a Christian festival.

included in that work.[83]   But granting that redemption should be commemorated before it is finished, by setting apart a day in its honor, the question again arises, What day shall it be?   The Bible is silent in reply.   If the most memorable day in the history of redemption should be selected, undoubtedly the day of the crucifixion, on which the price of human redemption was paid, must have the preference.   Which is the more memorable day, that on which the infinite Lawgiver gave up his only and well-beloved Son to die an ignominious death for a race of rebels who had broken his law, or that day on which he restored that beloved Son to life?   The latter event, though of thrilling interest, is the most natural thing in the world; the crucifixion of the Son of God for sinful men may be safely pronounced the most wonderful event in the annals of eternity.   The crucifixion day is, therefore, beyond all comparison, the more memorable day.   And that redemption itself is asserted of the crucifixion, rather than of the resurrection, is an undoubted fact.   Thus it is written :—

"In whom we have redemption through his blood." "Christ hath redeemed us from the curse of the law, being made a curse for us; for it is written, Cursed is every one that hangeth on a tree." "Thou wast slain, and hast redeemed us to God by thy blood." [84]

If, therefore, any day should be observed in memory of redemption, unquestionably the day of the crucifixion should have the preference.   But it is needless to pursue this point further.   Whether the day of the crucifixion or the day of the resurrection should be preferred, is

---

[83] Luke 21 : 28; Rom. 8 : 23; Eph. 1 : 13, 14; 4 : 30.

[84] Eph. 1 : 7; Gal. 3 : 13; Rev. 5 : 9.

quite immaterial. The Holy Spirit has said nothing in behalf of either of these days, but it has taken care that the *event* in each case should have its own appropriate memorial. Would you commemorate the crucifixion of the Redeemer? You need not change the Sabbath to the crucifixion day. It would be a presumptuous sin in you to do this. Here is the divinely appointed memorial of the crucifixion :—

" The Lord Jesus, the same night in which he was betrayed, took bread; and when he had given thanks, he brake it, and said, Take, eat; this is my body, which is broken for you; this do in remembrance of me. After the same manner also he took the cup, when he had supped, saying, This cup is the new testament in my blood; this do ye, as oft as ye drink it, in remembrance of me. For as often as ye eat this bread and drink this cup, ye do shew the Lord's death till he come." [85]

It is the death of the Redeemer, therefore, and not the day of his death, that the Holy Spirit has thought worthy of commemoration. Would you also commemorate the resurrection of the Redeemer? You need not change the Sabbath of the Bible for that purpose. The great Lawgiver has never authorized such an act. But an appropriate memorial of that event has been ordained.

" Know ye not that so many of us as were baptized into Jesus Christ, were baptized into his death? Therefore we are buried with him by baptism into death; that like as Christ was raised up from the dead by the glory of the Father, even so we also should walk in newness of life. For if we have been planted together in the likeness of his death, we shall be also in the likeness of his resurrection." [86]

To be buried in the watery grave as our Lord was buried in the tomb, and to be raised from the water to

---

[85] 1 Cor. 11: 23–26.   [86] Rom. 6: 3–5; Col. 2: 12.

walk in newness of life, as our Lord was raised from the dead by the glory of the Father, is the divinely authorized memorial of the resurrection of the Lord Jesus. And let it be observed, it is not the day of the resurrection, but the resurrection itself, that was thought worthy of commemoration. The events which lie at the foundation of redemption are the death, burial, and resurrection of the Redeemer. Each of these has its appropriate memorial; while the days on which they severally occurred have no importance attached to them. It was the death of the Redeemer, and not the day of his death, that was worthy of commemoration; and hence the Lord's supper was appointed for that purpose. It was the resurrection of the Saviour, and not the day of the resurrection, that was worthy of commemoration; and hence burial in baptism was ordained as its memorial. It is the change of this memorial to sprinkling that has furnished so plausible a plea for first-day observance in memory of the resurrection.

To celebrate the work of redemption by resting from labor on the first day of the week after six days of toil, it should be true that our Lord accomplished the work of human redemption in the six days prior to that of his resurrection, and that he rested on that day from the work, blessing it, and setting it apart for that reason. Yet not one of these particulars is true. Our Lord's whole life was devoted to this work. He rested temporarily from it, indeed, over the Sabbath following his crucifixion, but resumed the work on the morning of the first day of the week, which he has never since relinquished, and never will, until its perfect accomplishment in the resurrection of the saints and the redemption of the purchased possession. Redemption, therefore, furnishes no plea for a change of the Sabbath, its own memorials being quite sufficient, without destroying the memorial of the great Creator. And thus the third pillar in the temple of first-day sacredness, like the other parts of that structure which have been already examined, is found to be a thing of the imagination only.

A fourth pillar in this temple is taken from an ancient prophecy, in which it is claimed that the Christian Sabbath was foretold :—

" The stone which the builders refused is become the head stone of the corner. This is the Lord's doing ; it is marvelous in our eyes. This is the day which the Lord hath made; we will rejoice and be glad in it." [87]

This text is considered one of the strongest testimonies in support of the Christian Sabbath ; yet it is necessary to assume the very points it is supposed to prove, which are, 1. That the Saviour became the head of the corner by his resurrection ; 2. That the day of his resurrection was made the Christian Sabbath in commemoration of that event ; and 3. That this day, thus ordained, should be celebrated by abstinence from labor, and attendance upon divine worship.

To these extraordinary assumptions it is proper to reply that there is no proof that Jesus became the head of the corner on the day of his resurrection. The Scriptures do not mark the day when this event took place. His being made head of the corner has reference to his becoming the chief corner-stone of that spiritual temple composed of his people ; in other words, it has

---

[87] Ps. 118 : 22–24.

reference to his becoming the head of that living body, the saints of the Most High. It does not appear that he assumed this position until his ascension on high, where he became the chief corner-stone in Zion above, elect and precious.[88] Hence there is no evidence that the first day of the week is even referred to in this text; nor is there the slightest evidence that that day or any other day was set apart as the Christian Sabbath in memory of Christ's resurrection; nor can there well be found a more extraordinary assumption than that this text enjoins the Sabbatic observance of the first day of the week!

This scripture has manifest reference to the Saviour's act of becoming the head of the New-Testament church; and consequently it pertains to the opening of the gospel dispensation. The day in which the people of God rejoice, in view of this relation to the Redeemer, can therefore be understood of no one day of the week; for they are commanded to " rejoice EVERMORE;"[89] but of the whole period of the gospel dispensation. Our Lord uses the word *day* in the same manner when he says :—

" Your father Abraham rejoiced to see my day; and he saw it, and was glad. "[90]

To assert the existence of what is termed the Christian Sabbath on the ground that this text is the prediction of such an institution, is to furnish a fourth pillar for the first-day temple quite as unsubstantial as those already tested.

The seventieth week of Daniel's prophecy extends three and a half years beyond the death of the Re-

---

[88] Eph. 1: 20–23; 2: 20, 21; 1 Pet. 2: 4–7.
[89] 1 Thess. 5: 16.   [90] John 8: 56.

deemer, to the commencement of the great work for the Gentiles. This period of seven years through which we have been passing is the most eventful period in the history of the Sabbath. It embraces the whole history of the Lord of the Sabbath as connected with that institution : his miracles and teaching, by which it is affirmed that he weakened its authority; his death, at which many affirm that he abrogated it; and his resurrection, at which a still larger number declare that he changed it to the first day of the week. We have had the most ample evidence, however, that each of these positions is false, and that the opening of the great work for the Gentiles witnessed the Sabbath of the fourth commandment neither weakened, abrogated, nor changed.

CHAPTER XI.

THE SABBATH DURING THE MINISTRY OF THE APOSTLES.

The knowledge of God preserved in the family of Abraham—The call of the Gentiles—The new covenant puts the law of God into the heart of each Christian—The new covenant has a temple in heaven; and an ark containing the great original of that law which was in the ark upon earth; and before that ark, a priest, whose offering can take away sin—The Old and New Testaments compared—The human family in all ages amenable to the law of God—The good olive-tree shows the intimate relation between the church of the New Testament and the Hebrew church—The apostolic church observed the Sabbath—Examination of Acts 13—The assembly of the apostles at Jerusalem—Sabbatarian origin of the church at Philippi—Of the church of the Thessalonians—Of the church of Corinth—The churches in Judea and in many cases among the Gentiles began with Sabbath-keepers—Examination of 1 Cor. 16:1, 2—Self-contradiction of Dr. Edwards—Paul at Troas—Examination of Rom. 14:1-6—Flight of the disciples from Judea—The Sabbath of the Bible at the close of the first century.

E have now traced the Sabbath through the period of its special connection with the family of Abraham. The termination of the seventy weeks brings us to the call of the Gentiles, and to their admission to equal privileges with the Hebrew race. We have seen that with God there was no injustice in conferring special blessings upon the Hebrews, and at the same time leaving the Gentiles to their own chosen ways.[1] Twice had he given the human family, as a whole, the most ample means of grace that their age of the world admitted, and each time did it result in the

---

[1] See chapter 3.

almost total apostasy of mankind. Then God selected
as his heritage the family of Abraham, his friend, and
by means of that family preserved in the earth the
knowledge of his law, his Sabbath, and himself, until the
coming of the great Messiah. During his ministry the
Messiah solemnly affirmed the perpetuity of his Father's
law, enjoining obedience even to its least commandment;[2]
at his death he broke down that middle wall of partition[3]
by which the Hebrews had been so long preserved as a
separate people in the earth; and when about to ascend
into heaven, he commanded his disciples to go into all
the world, and preach the gospel to every creature,
teaching them to observe all things which he had commanded them.[4] With the expiration of the seventieth
week, the apostles entered upon the execution of this
great commission to the Gentiles.[5] Several facts of
deep interest should be here noticed :—

1. The new covenant, or testament, dates from the
death of the Redeemer. In accordance with the prediction of Jeremiah, it began with the Hebrews alone, and
was confined exclusively to them until the expiration of
the seventieth week. Then the Gentiles were admitted
to a full participation with the Hebrews in its blessings,
being no longer aliens and foreigners, but fellow-citizens
with the saints.[6] God entered into covenant this time
with his people as individuals and not as a nation. The
promises of this covenant embrace two points of great
interest: That God will put his law into the hearts of

---

[2] Matt. 5: 17–19.   [3] Eph. 2: 13–16; Col. 2: 14–17.
[4] Matt. 28: 19, 20; Mark 16: 15.
[5] Dan. 9: 24–27; Acts 9; 10; 11; 26: 12–17; Rom. 11: 13.
[6] 1 Cor. 11: 25; Jer. 31: 31–34; Heb. 8: 8–12; Dan. 9: 27; Eph. 2: 11–22.

his people ; and that he will forgive their sins. These promises being made six hundred years before the birth of Christ, there can be no question relative to what was meant by the law of God. It was the law of God then in existence that should be put into the heart of each new-covenant saint. The new covenant, then, is based upon the perpetuity of the law of God ; it does not abrogate that law, but takes away sin, the transgression of the law from the heart, and puts the law of God in its place.[7] The perpetuity of each precept of the moral law lies, therefore, at the very foundation of the new covenant.

2. As the first covenant had a sanctuary, and within that sanctuary an ark containing the law of God in ten commandments,[8] and had also a priesthood to minister before that ark, to make atonement for the sins of men,[9] even thus it is with the new covenant. Instead of the tabernacle erected by Moses as the pattern of the true, the new covenant has the greater and more perfect tabernacle, which the Lord pitched and not man—the temple of God in heaven.[10] As the great central point in the earthly sanctuary was the ark containing that law which man had broken, even thus it is with the heavenly sanctuary. " The temple of God was opened in heaven, and there was seen in his temple the ark of his testament." [11] Our Lord Jesus Christ, as a great high priest, presents his own blood before the ark of God's testament in the temple in heaven. Respecting this object before which he ministers, let the following points be noted :—

---

[7] Matt. 5: 17–19; 1 John 3: 4, 5; Rom. 4: 15.

[8] Heb. 9: 1–7; Ex. 25: 1–21; Deut. 10: 4, 5; 1 Kings 8: 9.

[9] Heb. 7 to 10; Lev. 16.   [10] Heb. 8: 1–5; 9: 23, 24.

[11] Rev. 11: 19.   11

1. The ark in the heavenly temple is not empty; it contains the testament of God; and hence it is the great center of the sanctuary above, as the ark of God's testament was the center of the sanctuary on earth.[12]

2. The death of the Redeemer for the sins of men, and his work as high priest before the ark in heaven, have direct reference to the fact that within that ark is the law which mankind has broken.

3. As the atonement and priesthood of Christ have reference to the law within that ark before which he ministers, it follows that this law existed and was transgressed before the Saviour came down to die for men.

4. And hence, the law contained in the ark above is not a law which originated in the New Testament; for it necessarily existed long anterior to it.

5. If, therefore, God has revealed this law to mankind, that revelation must be sought in the Old Testament; for while the New Testament makes many references to that law which caused the Saviour to lay down his life for sinful men, and even quotes from it, it never publishes a second edition, but cites us to the Old Testament for the original code.[13]

6. It follows, therefore, that this law is revealed, and that this revelation is to be found in the Old Testament.

7. In that volume will be found an account of (1.) The descent of the Holy One upon Mount Sinai; (2.) The proclamation of his law in ten commandments; (3.) The ten commandments written by the finger of God

---

[12] Ex. 25: 21, 22.

[13] Rom. 3: 19–31; 5: 8–21; 8: 3, 4; 13: 8–10; Gal. 3: 13, 14; Eph. 6: 2, 3; James 2: 8–12; 1 John 3: 4, 5.

upon the two tables of stone; (4.) These tables placed beneath the mercy-seat in the ark of the earthly sanctuary.[14]

8. That this remarkable Old-Testament law which was shut up in the ark of the earthly sanctuary was identical with that in the ark in heaven, may be thus shown: (1.) The mercy-seat which was placed over the ten commandments was the place from which pardon was expected, the great central point in the work of atonement;[15] (2.) The law beneath the mercy-seat was that which made the work of atonement necessary; (3.) There was no atonement that could take away sins, this being only a shadowy, or typical, atonement; (4.) But there was actual sin, and hence a real law which man had broken; (5.) There must, therefore, be an atonement that can take away sins; and that real atonement must pertain to that law which was broken, and respecting which an atonement had been shadowed forth;[16] (6.) The ten commandments are thus set forth in the Old Testament as that law which demanded an atonement; while the fact is ever kept in view that those sacrifices there provided could not avail to take away sins;[17] (7.) But the death of Jesus, as the antitype of those sacrifices, was designed to accomplish precisely what they shadowed forth, but which they could not effect, viz., to make atonement for the transgression of that law which was placed in the ark beneath the mercy-seat.[18]

We are thus brought to the conclusion that the law of God contained in the ark in heaven is identical with

[14] Ex. 19; 20; 24:12; 31:18; Deut. 10.   [15] Lev. 16.
[16] Rom. 3:19-31; 1 John 3:4, 5.   [17] Ps. 40:6-8; Heb. 10.
[18] Heb. 9 and 10.

that law which was contained in the ark upon earth, and that both are identical with that law which the new covenant puts in the heart of each believer.[19]   The Old Testament, therefore, gives us the law of God, and pronounces it perfect; it also provides a typical atonement, but says it is inadequate to take away sins.[20]   Hence what was needed was not a new edition of the law of God; for that which was given already was perfect; but a real atonement, to take away the guilt of the transgressor.   So the New Testament responds precisely to this want, providing a real atonement in the death and intercession of the Redeemer, but giving no new edition of the law of God,[21] though it fails not to cite us to the perfect code given long before.   But although the New Testament does not give a new edition of the law of God, it does show that the Christian dispensation has the great original of·that law in the sanctuary in heaven.

9. We have seen that the new covenant places the law of God in the heart of each believer, and that the original of that law is preserved in the temple in heaven. That all mankind are amenable to the law of God, and that they ever have been, is clearly shown by Paul's epistle to the Romans.   In the first chapter he traces the origin of idolatry to the willful apostasy of the Gentiles, which took place soon after the flood.   In the second chapter he shows that although God gave them up to their own ways, and as a consequence left them without his written law, yet they were not left in utter darkness; for they had by·nature the work of the law written in their hearts; and dim as was this light, their

---

[19] Jer. 31: 33; Rom. 8: 3, 4; 2 Cor. 3: 3.
[20] Ps. 19: 7; James 1: 25; Ps. 40.   [21] Rom. 5.

salvation would be secured by living up to it, or their ruin accomplished by sinning against it. In the third chapter he shows what advantage the family of Abraham had in being taken as the heritage of God, while all other nations were left to their own ways. It was that the oracles of God, the written law, was given them in addition to that work of the law written in the heart, which they had by nature in common with the Gentiles. He then shows that they were no better than the Gentiles, because both classes were transgressors of the law. This he proves by quotations from the Old Testament. Then he shows that the law of God has jurisdiction over all mankind :—

"Now we know that what things soever the law saith, it saith to them who are under the law, that every mouth may be stopped, and all the world may become guilty before God."[22]

He then shows that the law cannot save the guilty, but must condemn them, and that justly. Next, he reveals the great fact that redemption through the death of Jesus is the only means by which God can justify those who seek pardon, and at the same time remain just himself. And finally he exclaims,—

"Do we then make void the law through faith ? God forbid ; yea, we establish the law."[23]

It follows, therefore, that the law of God is unabolished ; that the sentence of condemnation which it pronounces upon the guilty is as extensive as is the offer of pardon through the gospel ; that its work exists in the hearts of men by nature, from which we may conclude that man in his uprightness possessed it in per-

---

[22] Rom. 3: 19.   [23] Rom. 3: 31.

fection, as is further proved by the fact that the new covenant, after delivering men from the condemnation of the law of God, puts that law perfectly into their hearts. From all this it follows that the law of God is the great standard by which sin is shown,[24] and hence the rule of life, by which all mankind, both Jews and Gentiles, should walk.

That the church in the present dispensation is really a continuation of the ancient Hebrew church, is shown by the illustration of the good olive-tree. That ancient church was God's olive-tree, aud it has never been destroyed.[25] Because of unbelief, *some* of its branches were broken off; but the proclamation of the gospel to the Gentiles does not create a new olive-tree; it only grafts into the good tree such of the Gentiles as believe, giving them a place among the original branches, that with them they may partake of its root and fatness. This olive-tree must date from the call of Abraham after the apostasy of the Gentiles, its trunk representing the patriarchs, beginning with the father of the faithful;[26] its branches, the Hebrew people. The ingrafting of the wild olive branches into the place of those branches which were broken off, represents the admission of the Gentiles to equal privileges with the Hebrews after the expiration of the seventy weeks. The Old-Testament church, the original olive-tree, was a kingdom of priests, and an holy nation; the New-Testament church, the olive-tree after the engrafting of the Gentiles, is described in the same terms.[27]

When God gave up the Gentiles to apostasy, before

---

[24] Rom. 3: 20; 1 John 3: 4, 5; 2: 1, 2.   [25] Jer. 11: 16; Rom. 11: 17–24.
[26] Rom. 4: 16–18; Gal. 3: 7–9.   [27] Ex. 19: 5, 9; 1 Pet. 2: 9, 10.

the call of Abraham, he confounded their language, that they should not understand one another, and thus scattered them abroad upon the face of the earth. Standing over against this is the gift of tongues on the day of Pentecost, preparatory to the call of the Gentiles, and their ingrafting into the good olive-tree.[28]

We have followed the Sabbath to the call of the Gentiles, and the opening events of the gospel dispensation. We find the law of God, of which the Sabbath is a part, to be that which made our Lord's death as an atoning sacrifice necessary; and the great original of that law to be in the ark above, before which our Lord ministers as high priest; while a copy of that law is by the new covenant written within the heart of each believer. It is seen, therefore, that the law of God is more intimately connected with the people of God since the death of the Redeemer than before that event.

That the apostolic church did sacredly regard the Sabbath, as well as all the other precepts of the moral law, admits of no doubt. The fact is proved by several considerations: 1. The early Christians were not accused of its violation by their most inveterate enemies; 2. They held sin to be the transgression of the law, and that the law was the great standard by which sin is shown, and that by which sin becomes exceeding sinful,[29]—points which are certainly very decisive evidence that the apostolic church did keep the fourth commandment; 3. The testimony of James relative to the ten commandments, that he who violates one of them becomes guilty of all, is another strong evidence that the primitive church did sacredly regard the whole law of

---

[28] Gen. 11 : 1–9 ; Acts 2 : 1–11.   [29] Rom. 7 : 12, 13.

God;[30] but 4. Besides these facts, we have a peculiar guaranty that the Sabbath of the Lord was not forgotten by the apostolic church. The prayer which our Lord taught his disciples, that their flight from Judea should not be upon the Sabbath, was, as we have seen, designed to impress its sacredness deeply upon their minds, and must have secured that result.[31] In the history of the primitive church we have several important references to the Sabbath. The first of these is as follows :—

"But when they departed from Perga, they came to Antioch in Pisidia, and went into the synagogue on the Sabbath-day, and sat down." [32]

By invitation of the rulers of the synagogue, Paul delivered an extended address, proving that Jesus was the Christ. In the course of these remarks he used the following language :—

"For they that dwell at Jerusalem, and their rulers, because they knew him not, nor yet the voices of the prophets which are read every Sabbath-day, they have fulfilled them in condemning him." [33]

When Paul's discourse was concluded, we read,—

"And when the Jews were gone out of the synagogue, the Gentiles besought that these words might be preached to them the next Sabbath.[34] Now when the congregation was broken up,

---

[30] James 2:8–12.   [31] See chapter 10.   [32] Acts 13:14.   [33] Verse 27.

[34] Dr. Bloomfield has the following note on this text: "The words, εἰς τὸ μεταξὺ σαββ., are by many commentators supposed to mean 'on some intermediate week-day.' But that is refuted by verse 44, and the sense expressed in our common version is, no doubt, the true one. It is adopted by the best recent commentators, and confirmed by the ancient versions."—*Greek Testament with English Notes*, vol. 1, p. 521. Prof. Hackett has a similar note.—*Commentary on Acts*, p. 233.

many of the Jews and religious proselytes followed Paul and Barnabas; who, speaking to them, persuaded them to continue in the grace of God. And the next Sabbath-day came almost the whole city together to hear the word of God." [35]

These texts show, 1. That by the term *Sabbath* in the book of Acts is meant that day on which the Jewish people assembled in the synagogue to listen to the voices of the prophets; 2. That as this discourse was fourteen years after the resurrection of Christ, and the record of it by Luke was some thirty years after that event, hence it follows that the alleged change of the Sabbath at the resurrection of Christ had not, even after many years, come to the knowledge of either Luke or Paul; 3. That here was a remarkable opportunity to mention the change of the Sabbath, were it true that the Sabbath had been changed in honor of Christ's resurrection; for when Paul was asked to preach the same words the next Sabbath, he might have answered that the following day was now the proper day for divine worship; and Luke, in placing this incident upon record, could not well avoid the mention of this new day, had it been true that another day had become the Sabbath of the Lord; 4. That as this second meeting pertained almost wholly to Gentiles, it cannot be said in this case that Paul preached upon the Sabbath out of regard to the Jews; on the contrary, the narrative strongly indicates Paul's regard for the Sabbath as the proper day for divine worship; 5. Nor can it be denied that the Sabbath was well understood by the Gentiles in this city, and that they had some degree of regard for it, a fact which will be corroborated by other texts.

---

[35] Acts 13:42-44.

Several years after these things, the apostles assembled at Jerusalem to consider the question of circumcision.[36] " Certain men which came down from Judea," finding the Gentiles uncircumcised, had "taught the brethren, and said, Except ye be circumcised after the manner of Moses ye cannot be saved." Had they found the Gentiles neglecting the Sabbath, unquestionably this would have first called out their rebuke. It is indeed worthy of notice that no dispute at this time existed in the church relative to the observance of the Sabbath; for none was brought before this apostolic assembly. Yet had it been true that the change of the Sabbath was then advocated, or that Paul had taught the Gentiles to neglect the Sabbath, without doubt those who brought up the question of circumcision would have urged that of the Sabbath with even greater earnestness. That the law of Moses, the observance of which was under discussion in this assembly, is not the ten commandments, is evident from several decisive facts: 1. Because Peter calls the code under consideration a *yoke* which neither their fathers nor themselves were able to bear; whereas James expressly calls the royal law, which, on his own showing, embodies the ten commandments, a law of liberty; 2. Because this assembly did decide against the authority of the law of Moses; and yet James, who was a member of this body, some years afterward solemnly enjoined obedience to the commandments, affirming that he who violated one was guilty of all;[37] 3. Because the chief feature in the law of Moses, as here presented, was circumcision;[38] but circumcision was not in the ten commandments; and were it true that the law of Moses in-

---

[36] Acts 15.   [37] Acts 15: 10, 28, 29 ; James 2: 8–12.   [38] Acts 15: 1, 5.

cluded these commandments, circumcision would not in that case have been a chief feature of that law; 4. Finally, because the precepts still declared obligatory are not properly included in the ten commandments. These were, first, the prohibition of meats offered to idols; secondly, of blood; thirdly, of things strangled; and fourthly, of fornication.[39] All of these precepts may be often found in the books of Moses,[40] and the first and last ones come under the second and seventh commandments respectively; but neither of these covers only a part of that which is forbidden in any commandment. It is evident, therefore, that the authority of the ten commandments was not under consideration in this assembly, and that their decision had no relation to those precepts; for if that were not the case, the apostles released the Gentiles from all obligation to eight of the ten commandments, and from the greater prohibitions contained in the other two.

It is evident that those greatly err who represent the Gentiles as released from the obligation of the Sabbath by this assembly. The question did not come before the apostles on this occasion,—a strong proof that the Gentiles had not been taught to neglect the Sabbath, as they had to omit circumcision, which was the occasion of its being brought before the apostles at Jerusalem. Yet the Sabbath was referred to in this very assembly as an existing institution, and that, too, in connection with the Gentile Christians. When James pronounced sentence upon the question, he used the following language :—

---

[39] Acts 15: 29; 21: 21, 25.

[40] Ex. 34: 15, 16; Num. 25: 2; Lev. 17: 13, 14; Gen. 9: 4; Lev. 3: 17; Gen. 34; Lev. 19: 29.

"Wherefore my sentence is, that we trouble not them, which from among the Gentiles are turned to God; but that we write unto them, that they abstain from pollutions of idols, and from fornication, and from things strangled, and from blood. For Moses of old time hath in every city them that preach him, being read in the synagogues every Sabbath-day." [41]

This last fact is given by James as a reason for the course proposed toward the brethren among the Gentiles. "For Moses of old time hath in every city them that preach him, being read in the synagogues every Sabbath-day." From this it is apparent that the ancient custom of divine worship upon the Sabbath was not only preserved by the Jewish people, and carried with them into every city of the Gentiles, but that the Gentile Christians attended these meetings; for if they did not, the reason assigned by James would lose all its force, as having no application to this case. That they did attend them proves that the Sabbath was the day of divine worship with the Gentile churches.

That the ancient Sabbath of the Lord had neither been abrogated nor changed prior to this meeting of the apostles, is strongly attested by the nature of the dispute here adjusted. And the close of their assembly beheld the Bible Sabbath still sacredly enthroned within the citadel of the fourth commandment. After this, in a vision of the night, Paul was called to visit Macedonia. In obedience to this call, he came to Philippi, which is the chief city of that part of Macedonia. Thus Luke records the visit:—

"And we were in that city abiding certain days. And on the Sabbath we went out of the city by a river side, where prayer

---

[41] Acts 15: 19–21.

was wont to be made; and we sat down, and spake unto the women which resorted thither. And a certain woman named Lydia, a seller of purple, of the city of Thyatira, which worshiped God, heard us; whose heart the Lord opened, that she attended unto the things which were spoken of Paul." [42]

This does not appear to have been a gathering of Jews, but of Gentiles, who, like Cornelius, were worshipers of the true God. Thus it is seen that the church of the Philippians originated with a pious assembly of the Sabbath-keeping Gentiles. And it is likely that Lydia and those employed by her in business, who were evidently observers of the Sabbath, were the means of introducing the gospel into their own city of Thyatira.

"Now when they had passed through Amphipolis and Apollonia, they came to Thessalonica, where was a synagogue of the Jews. And Paul, as his manner was,[43] went in unto them, and three Sabbath-days reasoned with them out of the Scriptures. . . . And some of them believed, and consorted with Paul and Silas; and of the devout Greeks a great multitude, and of the chief women not a few." [44]

Such was the origin of the Thessalonian church. That it was an assembly of Sabbath-keepers at its beginning admits of no doubt; for besides the few Jews who received the gospel through the labors of Paul, there was a great multitude of devout Greeks; that is, of Gentiles, who had united themselves with the Jews in the worship of God upon the Sabbath. In the following words of Paul, addressed to them as a church of Christ, we have

---

[42] Acts 16: 12–14.

[43] Paul's manner is exemplified by the following texts, in all of which it would appear that the meetings in question were upon the Sabbath: Acts 13: 5; 14: 1; 17: 10, 17; 18: 19; 19: 8.

[44] Acts 17: 1–4.

a strong proof of the fact that they continued to observe
the Sabbath after their reception of the gospel :—

"For ye, brethren, became followers of the churches of God
which in Judea are in Christ Jesus." [45]

The churches in Judea, as we have seen, were observers of the Sabbath of the Lord. The first Thessalonian converts, before they received the gospel, were
Sabbath-keepers; and when they became a Christian
church, they took the churches in Judea as their proper
examples. And this church was taken as a pattern by
the churches of Macedonia and Achaia. In this number
were included the churches of Philippi and Corinth.
Paul writes to them :—

"And ye became followers of us and of the Lord, having received the word in much affliction, with joy of the Holy Ghost;
so that ye were ensamples to all that believe in Macedonia and
Achaia. For from you sounded out the word of the Lord, not
only in Macedonia and Achaia, but also in every place your faith
to Godward is spread abroad." [46]

After these things, Paul came to Corinth. Here he
first found Aquila and Priscilla.

"And because he was of the same craft, he abode with them
and wrought; for by their occupation they were tent-makers.
And he reasoned in the synagogue every Sabbath, and persuaded
the Jews and the Greeks." [47]

At this place, also, Paul found Gentiles as well as
Jews in attendance upon the worship of God on the Sabbath. The first members of the church at Corinth were
therefore observers of the Sabbath at the time they received the gospel; and, as we have seen, they followed

---

[45] 1 Thess. 2 : 14.   [46] 1 Thess. 1 : 6–8.   [47] Acts 18 : 3, 4.

the example of the Sabbath-keeping church of Thessalonica, who in turn patterned after the churches in Judea.

The first churches were founded in the land of
Judea. All their members had from childhood been
familiar with the law of God, and well understood the
precept, " Remember the Sabbath-day, to keep it holy."
Besides this precept all these churches had a peculiar
memento of the Sabbath. They knew from our Lord
himself that the time was coming when they must all
suddenly flee from that land ; and in view of this fact
they were to pray that the moment of their sudden flight
might not be on the Sabbath,—a prayer which was designed, as we have seen, to preserve the sacredness of
the Sabbath. That the churches in Judea were composed of Sabbath-keeping members, therefore, admits of
no doubt.

Of the churches founded outside the land of Judea,
whose origin is given in the book of Acts, nearly all began with Jewish converts, who were Sabbath-keepers
when they received the gospel. Among these the Gentile converts were engrafted. And it is worthy of notice
that in a large number of cases, those Gentiles are
termed " devout Greeks," " religious proselytes," persons
that " worshiped God," that " feared God," and that
" prayed to God alway." [48] These Gentiles, at the time
of their conversion to the gospel, were, as we have seen,
worshipers of God upon the Sabbath with the Jewish
people. When James had proposed the kind of letter
that should be addressed by the apostles to the Gentile
converts, he assigned a reason for its adoption, the force
of which can now be appreciated : " For Moses," said he,

---

[48] Acts 10 : 2, 4, 7, 8, 30–35 ; 13 : 43 ;. 14 : 1 ; 16 : 13–15 ; 17 : 4, 10–12.

" of old time hath in EVERY CITY them that preach him, being read in the Synagogue every Sabbath-day." The Sabbatarian character of the apostolic churches is thus clearly shown.

In a letter addressed to the Corinthians, about five years after they had received the gospel, Paul is supposed to contribute a fifth pillar to the first-day temple, as follows :—

" Now concerning the collection for the saints, as I have given order to the churches of Galatia, even so do ye. Upon the first day of the week, let every one of you lay by him in store, as God hath prospered him, that there be no gatherings when I come."[49]

From this text it is argued in behalf of the first-day Sabbath, 1. That this was a public collection ; 2. That hence the first day of the week was the day of public worship in the churches of Corinth and Galatia; 3. And that therefore the Sabbath had been changed to that day. Thus the change of the Sabbath is inferred from the public assemblies for divine worship on the first day at Corinth and Galatia; and the existence of these assemblies on that day is inferred from the words of Paul, " Upon the first day of the week, let every one of you lay *by him* in store."

But what do these words ordain ? Only one answer can be returned : They ordain precisely the *reverse* of a public collection. Each one should lay by himself on each first day of the week, according as God had prospered him, that when Paul should arrive, they might have their bounty ready. Mr. J. W. Morton, late Pres-

---

[49] 1 Cor. 16: 1, 2.

byterian missionary to Hayti, bears the following testimony :—

"The whole question turns upon the meaning of the expression, 'by him;' and I marvel greatly how you can imagine that it means 'in the collection box of the congregation.' Greenfield, in his Lexicon, translates the Greek term, ' *With one's self, i. e., at home.*' Two Latin versions, the Vulgate and that of Castellio, render it ' *apud se,*' with one's self; at home. Three French translations, those of Martin, Osterwald, and De Sacy, '*chez soi,*' at his own house; at home. The German of Luther, ' *bei sich selbst,*' by himself; at home. The Dutch, ' *by hemselven,*' same as the German. The Italian of Diodati, ' *appresso di se,*' in his own presence; at home. The Spanish of Felippe Scio, ' *en su casa,*' in his own house. The Portugese of Ferreira, '*para isso,*' with himself. The Swedish, ' *nœr sig self,*' near himself."[50]

Dr. Bloomfield thus comments on the original : " Παρ ἑαυτῶ, 'by him.' French, *chez lui,* ' at home.' "[51]

The Douay Bible reads : " Let every one of you put apart with himself." Mr. Sawyer translates it : " Let each one of you lay aside by himself." Theodore Beza's Latin version gives it : " *Apud se,*" i. e., at home. The Syriac reads : " Let every one of you lay aside and preserve at home."

It is true that an eminent first-day writer, Justin Edwards, D. D., in a labored effort to prove the change of the Sabbath, brings forward this text to show that Sunday was the day of religious worship with the early church. He says :—

"This laying by in store was NOT laying by AT HOME ; for that would not prevent gatherings when he should come." [52]

---

[50] Vindication of the True Sabbath, third edition, pp. 51, 52.

[51] Greek Testament with English Notes, vol. 2, p. 173.

[52] Sabbath Manual of the American Tract Society, p. 116.

Such is his language as a theologian upon whom has fallen the difficult task of proving the change of the Sabbath by the authority of the Scriptures. But in his Notes on the New Testament, in which he feels at liberty to speak the truth, he squarely contradicts his own language already quoted. Hear him:—

" Lay by him in store; AT HOME. That there be no gatherings; that their gifts might be ready when the apostle should come." [53]

Thus even Dr. Edwards confesses that the idea of a public collection is not found in this scripture. On the contrary, it appears that each individual, in obedience to this precept, would, at the opening of each new week, be found AT HOME laying aside something for the cause of God, according as his worldly affairs would warrant. The change of the Sabbath, as proved by this text, rests wholly upon an idea which Dr. Edwards confesses is not found in it. We have seen that the church at Corinth was a Sabbath-keeping church. It is evident that the change of the Sabbath could never have been suggested to them by this text.

This is the only scripture in which Paul even mentions the first day of the week. It was written nearly thirty years after the alleged change of the Sabbath. Yet Paul omits all title of sacredness, simply designating it as the first day of the week,—a name to which it was entitled as one of " the six working days." [54] It is also worthy of notice that this is the only precept in the Bible in which the first day is even named; and that this precept says nothing relative to the sacredness of the day to which it pertains, even the duty which it en-

---

[53] Family Testament of the American Tract Society.   [54] Eze. 46:1.

joins being more appropriate to a secular than to a sacred day.

Soon after writing his first epistle to the Corinthians, Paul visited Troas. In the record of this visit occurs the last instance in which the first day of the week is mentioned in the New Testament:—

"And we sailed away from Philippi after the days of unleavened bread, and came unto them to Troas in five days;[55] where we abode seven days. And upon the first day of the week, when the disciples came together to break bread, Paul preached unto them, ready to depart on the morrow; and continued his speech until midnight. And there were many lights in the upper chamber, where they were gathered together. And there sat in a window a certain young man named Eutychus, being fallen into a deep sleep; and as Paul was long preaching, he sunk down with sleep, and fell down from the third loft, and was taken up dead. And Paul went down, and fell on him, and embracing him said, Trouble not yourselves; for his life is in him. When he therefore was come up again, and had broken bread, and eaten, and talked a long while, even till break of day, so he departed. And they brought the young man alive, and were not a little comforted. And we went before to ship, and sailed unto Assos, there intending to take in Paul; for so had he appointed, minding himself to go afoot."[56]

This scripture is supposed to furnish a sixth pillar for the first-day temple. The argument may be concisely stated thus: This testimony shows that the first day of the week was appropriated by the apostolic

---

[55] Prof. Hackett remarks on the length of this voyage: "The passage on the apostle's first journey to Europe occupied two days only. See Acts 16:11. Adverse winds or calms would be liable, at any season of the year, to occasion this variation."—*Commentary on Acts*, p. 329. This shows how little ground there is to claim that Paul broke the Sabbath on this voyage. There was ample time to reach Troas before the Sabbath when he started from Philippi, had not providential causes hindered.

[56] Acts 20:6–13.

church to meetings for the breaking of bread in honor
of Christ's resurrection upon that day; from which it is
reasonable to conclude that this day had become the
Christian Sabbath.

If this proposition could be established as an undoubted truth, the change of the Sabbath would not follow as a necessary conclusion; it would even then
amount only to a plausible conjecture. The following
facts will aid us in judging of the truthfulness of this
argument for the change of the Sabbath: 1. This is the
only instance of a religious meeting upon the first day
of the week recorded in the New Testament; 2. No
stress can be laid upon the expression, "*when* the disciples came together," as proving that meetings for the
purpose of breaking bread were held on each first day
of the week; for there is nothing in the original answering to the word "*when*," the whole phrase being translated from three words, the perfect passive participle
συνηγμένων, "being assembled," and τῶν μαθητῶν, "the disciples," the sacred writers simply stating the gathering
of the disciples on this occasion;[57] 3. The ordinance of
breaking bread was not appointed to commemorate the
resurrection of Christ, but to keep in memory his death
upon the cross;[58] therefore the act of breaking bread
upon the first day of the week is not a commemoration
of Christ's resurrection; 4. As the breaking of bread
commemorates our Lord's crucifixion, and was instituted
on the evening with which the crucifixion day began,
when Jesus himself and all the apostles were present,[59]

----

[57] Prof. Whiting renders the phrase: "The disciples being assembled." And
Sawyer has it: "We being assembled."

[58] 1 Cor. 11: 23–26.   [59] Matt. 26.

it is evident that the day of the crucifixion presents greater claims to the celebration of this ordinance than does the day of the resurrection; 5. As our Lord designated no day for this ordinance, and as the apostolic church at Jerusalem is recorded to have celebrated it daily,[60] it is evidently presumption to argue the change of the Sabbath from a single instance of its celebration upon the first day of the week; 6. This instance of breaking bread upon the first day was with evident reference to the immediate and final departure of Paul; for 7. It is a remarkable fact that this, the only instance of a religious meeting on the first day recorded in the New Testament, was a night meeting, which is proved by the fact that many lights were burning in the assembly, and that Paul preached till midnight; 8. From this follows the important consequence that this first-day meeting was upon Saturday night;[61] because the

---

[60] Acts 2: 42–46.

[61] This fact has been acknowledged by many first-day commentators. Prof. Hackett gives the following on this text: "The Jews reckoned the day from evening to morning, and on that principle the evening of the first day of the week would be our Saturday evening. If Luke reckoned so here, as many commentators suppose, the apostle then waited for the expiration of the Jewish Sabbath, and held his last religious service with the brethren at Troas at the beginning of the Christian Sabbath, *i. e.*, on Saturday evening, and consequently resumed his journey on Sunday morning."—*Commentary on Acts*, pp. 329, 330. But he endeavors to shield the first-day Sabbath from this fatal admission by suggesting that Luke probably reckoned time according to the pagan method, rather than by that which is ordained in the Scriptures!

Kitto, in noting the fact that this was an evening meeting, speaks thus: "It has from this last circumstance been inferred that the assembly commenced after sunset on the Sabbath, at which hour the first day of the week had commenced, according to the Jewish reckoning [Jahn's Bibl. Antiq., sec. 398], which would hardly agree with the idea of a commemoration of the resurrection."—*Cyclopedia of Biblical Literature*, article, Lord's day.

Prynne, whose testimony relative to redemption as an argument for the change of the Sabbath has been already quoted, thus states this point: "Because the text saith there were many lights in the upper room where they were gathered

days of the week being reckoned from evening to evening, and evening being at sunset,[62] it is seen that the
first day of the week begins Saturday night at sunset,
and ends at sunset on Sunday; a night meeting, therefore, upon the first day of the week could be only upon
Saturday night; 9. Paul, therefore preached until midnight on Saturday night; for the disciples held a night
meeting at the close of the Sabbath, because he was to
leave in the morning; then, being interrupted by the fall
of the young man, he went down and healed him, then
went up and attended to the breaking of bread; and at
break of day, on Sunday morning, he departed; 10.
Thus are we furnished with conclusive evidence that
Paul and his companions resumed their journey toward
Jerusalem on the morning of the first day of the week;
they taking ship to Assos, and he going on foot (This
fact is an incidental proof of Paul's regard for the Sabbath, in that he waited till it was past before resuming
his journey; and it is a positive proof that he knew

---

together, and that Paul preached from the time of their coming together till midnight, . . . this meeting of the disciples at Troas, and Paul's preaching to
them, began at evening. The sole doubt will be what evening this was. . . .
For my own part I conceive clearly that it was upon Saturday night, as we falsely
call it, and not the coming Sunday night. . . . Because St. Luke records that
it was upon the first day of the week when this meeting was; . . . therefore it
must needs be on the Saturday, not on our Sunday evening, since the Sunday
evening in St. Luke's and the Scripture account was no part of the first, but of
the second day; the day ever beginning and ending at evening."

Prynne notices the objection drawn from the phrase, "ready to depart on the
morrow," as indicating that this departure was not on the same day of the week
with his night meeting. The substance of his answer is this: If the fact be kept
in mind that the days of the week are reckoned from evening to evening, the following texts, in which, in the night, the morning is spoken of as the morrow,
will show at once that another day of the week is not necessarily intended by
the phrase in question. 1 Sam. 19: 11; Esth. 2: 14; Zeph. 3: 3; Acts 23: 31,
32.—*Dissertation on Lord's Day Sabbath*, pp. 36–41, 1633.

[62] See conclusion of chapter 8.

nothing of what in modern times is called the Christian Sabbath); 11. This narrative was written by Luke at least thirty years after the alleged change of the Sabbath. It is worthy of note that Luke omits all titles of sacredness, simply designating the day in question as the first day of the week. This is in admirable keeping with the fact that in his Gospel, when recording the very event which is said to have changed the Sabbath, he not only omits the slightest hint of that fact, but designates the day itself by its secular title of "first day of the week," and at the same time calls the previous day the Sabbath according to the commandment.[63]

The same year that Paul visited Troas, he wrote as follows to the church at Rome :—

"Him that is weak in the faith receive ye, but not to doubtful disputations. For one believeth that he may eat all things; another, who is weak, eateth herbs. Let not him that eateth despise him that eateth not; and let not him which eateth not judge him that eateth; for God hath received him. Who art thou that judgest another man's servant? to his own master he standeth or falleth. Yea, he shall be holden up, for God is able to make him stand. One man esteemeth one day above another; another esteemeth every day alike. Let every man be fully persuaded in his own mind. He that regardeth the day, regardeth it unto the Lord; and he that regardeth not the day, to the Lord he doth not regard it. He that eateth, eateth to the Lord, for he giveth God thanks; and he that eateth not, to the Lord he eateth not, and giveth God thanks." [64]

These words have often been quoted to show that the observance of the fourth commandment is now a matter of indifference, each individual being at liberty to act his pleasure in the matter. So extraordinary a

[63] Luke 23: 56; 24: 1.   [64] Rom. 14: 1–6.

doctrine should be thoroughly tested before being adopted. For as it pleased God to ordain the Sabbath before the fall of man, and to give it a place in his code of ten commandments, thus making it a part of that law to which the great atonement relates; and as the Lord Jesus, during his ministry, spent much time in explaining its merciful design, and took care to provide against its desecration at the flight of his people from the land of Judea, which was ten years in the future when these words were written by Paul; and as the fourth commandment itself is expressly recognized after the crucifixion of Christ,—if, under these circumstances, we could suppose it to be consistent with truth that the Most High should abrogate the Sabbath, we certainly should expect that abrogation to be stated in explicit language. Yet neither the Sabbath nor the fourth commandment are here named. That they are not referred to in this language of Paul, the following reasons will show :—

1. Such a view would make the observance of one of the ten commandments a matter of indifference; whereas James shows that to violate one of them is to transgress the whole;[65] 2. It directly contradicts what Paul had previously written in this epistle; for in treating of the law of ten commandments, he styles it holy, spiritual, just, and good, and states that sin—the transgression of the law—by the commandment becomes "EXCEEDING SINFUL;"[66] 3. Paul in the same epistle affirms the perpetuity of that law which caused our Lord to lay down his life for sinful men;[67] which we have before seen was the ten commandments; 4. Paul in this case

---

[65] James 2 : 8–12.   [66] Rom. 7 : 12, 13; 1 John 3 : 4, 5.   [67] Rom. 3.

not only did not name the Sabbath and the fourth commandment, but certainly was not treating of the moral
law; 5. The topic under consideration, which leads him
to speak as he does of the days in question, was that of
eating all kinds of food, or of refraining from certain
things; 6. The fourth commandment did not stand associated with precepts of such a kind, but with moral laws
exclusively;[68] 7. In the ceremonial law, associated with
the precepts concerning meats, was a large number of
festivals, entirely distinct from the Sabbath of the
Lord;[69] 8. The church of Rome, which began probably
with those Jews that were present from Rome on the
day of Pentecost, had many Jewish members in its communion, as may be gathered from the epistle itself,[70]
and would therefore be deeply interested in the decision
of this question relative to the ceremonial law; as the
Jewish members would feel conscientious in observing
its distinctions, while the Gentile members would have
no such scruples; hence the admirable counsel of Paul
exactly met the case of both classes; 9. Nor can the expression "every day" be claimed as decisive proof that
the Sabbath of the Lord is included. At the very time
when the Sabbath was formally committed to the
Hebrews, just such expressions were used, although
only the six working days were intended. Thus it was
said: "The people shall go out and gather a certain
rate *every* day;" and the narrative says, "They gathered
it *every* morning." Yet when some of them went out to

---

[68] Ex. 20.

[69] Lev. 23. These are particularly enumerated in Col. 2, as we have already
noticed in chapter 7, and in the concluding part of chapter 10.

[70] Acts 2:1-11; Rom. 2:17; 4:1; 7:1.

gather on the Sabbath, God said, " How long refuse ye
to keep my commandments and my laws ? "[71]   The
Sabbath being a great truth, plainly stated, and many
times repeated, it is manifest that Paul, in the expression " every day," speaks of the six working days, among
which a distinction had existed precisely coeval with
that respecting meats; and that he manifestly excepts
that day which from the beginning God had reserved
unto himself.   Just as when Paul quotes and applies to
Jesus the words of David, " All things are put under
him," he adds : " It is manifest that he is excepted
which did put all things under him."[72]   10.   And lastly,
in the words of John, " I was in the Spirit on the Lord's
day," [73] written many years after this epistle of Paul's, we
have an absolute proof that in the gospel dispensation
one day is still claimed by the Most High as his own.[74]

About ten years after this epistle was written, occurred the memorable flight of all the people of God that
were in the land of Judea.   It was not in the winter;
for it occurred just after the Feast of Tabernacles, some
time in October.   And it was not upon the Sabbath; for
Josephus, who speaks of the sudden withdrawal of the
Roman army after it had, by encompassing the city,

---

[71] Ex. 16: 4, 21, 27, 28.   [72] 1 Cor. 15: 27; Ps. 8.   [73] Rev. 1: 10.

[74] To show that Paul regarded Sabbatic observance as *dangerous*, Gal. 4: 10 is
often quoted; notwithstanding, the same individuals claim that Rom. 14 proves
that it is a matter of *perfect indifference;* not seeing that this is to make
Paul contradict himself.   But if the connection be read from verses 8 to 11, it
will be seen that the Galatians before their conversion were not Jews, but heathen;
and that these days, months, times, and years were not those of the Levitical law,
but those which they had regarded with superstitious reverence while they were
heathens.   Observe the stress which Paul lays upon the word " again " in verse
9.   And how many that profess the religion of Christ at the present day super-
stitiously regard certain days as " lucky," or "unlucky," though such notions are derived only from heathen distinctions !

given the very signal for flight which our Lord promised his people, tells us that the Jews rushed out of the city in pursuit of the retreating Romans, which was at the very time when our Lord's injunction of instant flight became imperative upon the disciples. The historian does not intimate that the Jews thus pursued the Romans upon the Sabbath, although he carefully notes the fact that a few days previous to this event they did, in their rage, utterly forget the Sabbath, and rush out to fight the Romans upon that day. These providential circumstances in the flight of the disciples being made dependent upon their asking such interposition at the hand of God, it is evident that the disciples did not forget the prayer which the Saviour taught them relative to this event; and that, as a consequence, the Sabbath of the Lord was not forgotten by them. And thus the Lord Jesus, in his tender care for his people, and in his watchful interest in behalf of the Sabbath, showed that he was alike the Lord of his people and the Lord of the Sabbath.[75]

Twenty-six years after the destruction of Jerusalem, the book of the Revelation was committed to the beloved disciple. It bears the following deeply interesting date as to place and time :—

" I John, who also am your brother, and companion in tribulation, and in the kingdom and patience of Jesus Christ, was in THE ISLE that is called PATMOS, for the word of God and for the testimony of Jesus Christ. I was in the Spirit ON THE LORD'S DAY, and heard behind me a great voice, as of a trumpet, saying, I am Alpha and Omega, the first and the last; and, What thou seest, write in a book." [76]

---

[75] See chapter 10.　　　　[76] Rev. 1: 9–11.

This book is dated on the isle of Patmos, and upon the Lord's day. The place, the day, and the individual have each a real existence, and not merely a symbolical or mystical one. Thus John, almost at the close of the first century, and long after those texts were written which are now adduced to prove that no distinction in days exists, shows that the Lord's day has as real an existence as has the isle of Patmos, or as had the beloved disciple himself.

What day, then, is intended by this designation? Several answers have been returned to this question: 1. It is the gospel dispensation; 2. It is the day of Judgment; 3. It is the first day of the week; 4. It is the Sabbath of the Lord.

The first answer cannot be the true one; for it not only renders the day a mystical term, but it involves the absurdity of representing John as writing to Christians sixty-five years after the death of Christ, that the vision which he had just had was seen by him in the gospel dispensation; as though it were possible for them to be ignorant of the fact that if he had had a vision at all, he must have had it in the existing dispensation.

Nor can the second answer be admitted as the truth; for while it is true that John might have a vision CONCERNING the day of Judgment, it is impossible that he should have a vision ON that day, when it was yet future. If it be no more than an absurdity to represent John as dating his vision on the isle of Patmos, in the gospel dispensation, it becomes a positive untruth if he is made to say that he was in vision on Patmos on the day of Judgment.

The third answer, that the Lord's day is the first day

of the week, is now almost universally received as the truth. The text under examination is brought forward with an air of triumph, as completing the temple of first-day sacredness, and proving beyond all doubt that that day is indeed the Christian Sabbath. Yet, as we have examined this temple with peculiar carefulness, we have discovered that the foundation on which it rests is a thing of the imagination only; and that the pillars by which it is supported exist only in the minds of those who worship at its shrine. It remains to be seen whether the dome which is supposed to be furnished by this text is more real than the pillars on which it rests.

That the first day of the week has no claim to the title of "Lord's day," the following facts will show: 1. As this text does not define the term "Lord's day," we must look elsewhere in the Bible for the evidence that shows the first day to be entitled to such a designation; 2. Matthew, Mark, Luke, and Paul—the other sacred writers who mention the day—use no other designation for it than "first day of the week," a name to which it was entitled as one of the six working days; yet three of these writers mention it at the very time when it is said to have become the Lord's day, and two of them some thirty years after that event; 3. While it is claimed that the Spirit of inspiration, by simply leading John to use the term "Lord's day,"—though he in no way connected the first day of the week therewith—did design to fix this as the proper title of the first day of the week, it is a remarkable fact that after John returned from the isle of Patmos, he wrote his Gospel;[77] and in

---

[77] Dr. Bloomfield, though himself of a different opinion, speaks thus of the views of others concerning the date of John's Gospel: "It has been the general

that Gospel he twice mentioned the first day of the week; yet in each of these instances where it is certain that the first day is intended, no other designation is used than plain "first day of the week,"—a most convincing proof that John did not regard the first day of the week as entitled to this name, or any other expressive of sacredness; 4. What still further decides the point against the first day of the week, is the fact that neither the Father nor the Son have ever claimed the first day in any higher sense than they have any other of the six days which were given to man for labor; 5. And what completes the chain of evidence against the claim of the first day to this title, is the fact that the testimony adduced by first-day advocates to prove that it has been adopted by the Most High in place of that day which he once claimed as his, is found upon examination to have no such meaning or intent. In setting aside the third answer, also, as not being in accordance with truth, the first day of the week may be properly dismissed with it, as having no claim to our regard as a scriptural institution.[78]

---

sentiment, both of ancient and modern inquirers, that it was published about *the close of the first century."—Greek Testament with English Notes*, vol. 1, p. 328.

Morer says that John "penned his Gospel two years later than the Apocalypse, and after his return from Patmos, as St. Augustine, St. Jerome, and Eusebius affirm."—*Dialogues on the Lord's Day*, pp. 53, 54.

The Paragraph Bible of the London Religious Tract Society, in its preface to the book of John, speaks thus: "According to the general testimony of ancient writers, John wrote his Gospel at Ephesus, about the year 97."

In support of the same view, see also Religious Encyclopedia, Barnes's Notes (Gospels), Bible Dictionary, Cottage Bible, Domestic Bible, Mine Explored, Union Bible Dictionary, Comprehensive Bible, Dr. Hales, Horne, Nevins, Olshausen, etc.

[78] The Encyclopedia Britannica, in its article concerning the Sabbath, undertakes to prove that the "religious observation of the first day of the week is of apostolical appointment." After citing and commenting upon all the passages that could be urged in proof of the point, it makes the following candid acknowl-

That the Lord's day is the Bible Sabbath admits of clear and certain proof. The argument stands thus: When God gave to man six days of the week for labor, he expressly reserved for himself the seventh, on which he placed his blessing in memory of his own act of resting upon that day, and thenceforward, through the Bible, has ever claimed it as his holy day. As he has never put away this sacred day and chosen another, the Sabbath of the Lord is still his holy day. These facts may be traced in the following scriptures. At the close of the Creator's rest, it is said :—

"And God blessed the seventh day, and sanctified it; because that in it he had rested from all his work which God created and made." [79]

After the children of Israel had reached the wilderness of Sin, Moses said to them on the sixth day :—

"To-morrow is the rest of the holy Sabbath unto the Lord." [80]

In giving the ten commandments, the Lawgiver thus stated his claim to this day :—

---

edgment: "Still, however, it must be owned that these passages are not sufficient to prove the apostolical institution of the Lord's day, or even the actual observation of it."

The absence of all scriptural testimony relative to the change of the Sabbath, is accounted for by certain advocates of that theory, not by the frank admission that it never was changed by the Lord, but by quoting John 21:25, assuming the change of the Sabbath as an undoubted truth, but that it was left out of the Bible lest it should make that book too large! They think, therefore, that we should go to ecclesiastical history to learn this part of our duty, not seeing that, as the fourth commandment still stands in the Bible unrepealed and unchanged, to acknowledge that that change must be sustained wholly outside of the Bible is to acknowledge that first-day observance is a tradition which makes void the commandment of God. The following chapters of this work will, however, patiently examine the argument for first-day observance drawn from ecclesiastical history.

[79] Gen. 2:3.   [80] Ex. 16:23.

"The seventh day is the Sabbath of the Lord thy God; . . . for in six days the Lord made heaven and earth, the sea, and all that in them is, and rested the seventh day; wherefore the Lord blessed the Sabbath-day, and hallowed it." [81]

He gave to man the six days on which he himself had labored, and reserved as his own that day upon which he had rested from all his work. About eight hundred years after this, God spoke by Isaiah as follows :—

"If thou turn away thy foot from THE SABBATH, from doing thy pleasure on MY HOLY DAY, . . . then shalt thou delight thyself in the Lord; and I will cause thee to ride upon the high places of the earth." [82]

This testimony is perfectly explicit; the Lord's day is the ancient Sabbath of the Bible. The Lord Jesus puts forth the following claim :—

"The Son of man is Lord also of the Sabbath." [83]

Hence, whether it be the Father or the Son whose title is involved, the only day that can be called "the Lord's day" is the Sabbath of the great Creator. [84] And here, at the close of the Bible history of the Sabbath, two facts of deep interest are presented: 1. That John expressly recognizes the existence of the Lord's day at the very close of the first century; 2. That it pleased the Lord of the Sabbath to place a signal honor upon his own day, in that he selected it as the one on which to give that revelation to John which himself alone had been worthy to receive from the Father.

---

[81] Ex. 20: 8–11.   [82] Isa. 58: 13, 14.   [83] Mark 2: 27, 28.

[84] An able opponent of Sabbatic observance speaks as follows relative to the term "Lord's day" of Rev. 1: 10: "If a current day was intended, the only day bearing this definition, in either the Old or New Testaments, is Saturday, the seventh day of the week."— *W. B. Taylor, in the Obligation of the Sabbath,* p. 296.

HISTORY OF THE SABBATH.

PART II.—SECULAR HISTORY.

CHAPTER XII.

EARLY APOSTASY IN THE CHURCH.

General purity of the apostolic churches—Early decline of their piety—
False teachers arose in the church immediately after the apostles—
The great Romish apostasy began before the death of Paul—An evil
thing not rendered good by beginning in the apostolic age—How to
decide between truth and error—Age cannot change the fables of
men into the truth of God—Historical testimony concerning the
early development of the great Apostasy—Such an age no standard
by which to correct the Bible—Testimony of Bower relative to the
traditions of this age—Testimony of Dowling—Dr. Cumming's opinion of the authority of the Fathers—Testimony of Adam Clarke—The
church of Rome has corrupted the writings of the Fathers—Nature
of tradition illustrated—The two rules of faith which divide Christendom—The first-day Sabbath can be sustained only by adopting the
rule of the Romanists.

THE book of Acts is an inspired history of the
church. During the period which is embraced
in its record, the apostles and their fellow-
laborers were upon the stage of action; and under their
watch-care, the churches of Christ preserved, to a great
extent, their purity of life and doctrine. These apostolic churches are thus set forth as examples for all com-

13

ing time.   This book fitly connects the narratives of the
four evangelists with the apostolic epistles, and thus
unites the whole New Testament.   But when we leave
the period embraced in this inspired history, and the
churches which were founded and governed by inspired
men, we enter upon altogether different times.   There
is, unfortunately, great truth in the severe language of
Gibbon :—

"The theologian may indulge the pleasing task of describing
religion as she descended from heaven, arrayed in her native
purity.   A more melancholy duty is imposed on the historian.
He must discover the inevitable mixture of error and corruption,
which she contracted in a long residence upon earth, among a
weak and degenerate race of beings." [1]

What says the book of Acts respecting the time immediately following the labors of Paul?   In addressing
the elders of the Ephesian church, Paul said :—

"For I know this, that after my departing shall grievous
wolves enter in among you, not sparing the flock.   Also of
your own selves shall men arise, speaking perverse things, to
draw away disciples after them." [2]

It follows from this testimony that we are not authorized to receive the teaching of any man simply because
he lived immediately after the apostolic age, or even in
the days of the apostles themselves.   Grievous wolves
were to enter the midst of the people of God, and of
their own selves were men to arise, speaking perverse
things.   If it be asked how these are to be distinguished
from the true servants of God, the proper answer is:
Those who spoke and acted in accordance with the
teachings of the apostles were men of God; those who

---

[1] Decline and Fall of the Roman Empire, chap. 15   [2] Acts 20: 29, 30.

taught otherwise were of that class who should speak perverse things to draw away disciples after them.

What do the apostolic epistles say relative to this apostasy? Paul writes to the Thessalonians :—

"Let no man deceive you by any means; for that day shall not come, except there come a falling away first, and that man of sin be revealed, the son of perdition; who opposeth and exalteth himself above all that is called God, or that is worshiped; so that he as God sitteth in the temple of God, showing himself that he is God. . . . For the mystery of iniquity doth already work; only he who now letteth will let, until he be taken out of the way. And then shall that wicked be revealed, whom the Lord shall consume with the spirit of his mouth, and shall destroy with the brightness of his coming." [3]

To Timothy, in like manner, it is said :-

"Preach the word; be instant in season, out of season; reprove, rebuke, exhort with all long-suffering and doctrine. For the time will come when they will not endure sound doctrine; but after their own lusts shall they heap to themselves teachers, having itching ears; and they shall turn away their ears from the truth, and shall be turned unto fables." [4]

These texts are most explicit in predicting a great apostasy in the church, and in stating the fact that that apostasy had already commenced. The Romish church, the oldest in apostasy, prides itself upon its apostolic character. In the language of Paul to the Thessalonians, already quoted, that great antichristian body may indeed find its claim to an origin in apostolic times vindicated, but its apostolic character is most emphatically denied. And herein is found a striking illustration of the fact that an evil thing is not rendered good by the

---

[3] 2 Thess. 2: 3, 4, 7, 8.
[4] 2 Tim. 4: 2–4; 2 Pet. 2; Jude 4; 1 John 2: 18.

accidental circumstance of its originating in the days of
the apostles.   Everything, at its commencement, is either
right or wrong.   If right, it may be known by its agreement with the divine standard; if wrong at its origin,
it can never cease to be such.   Satan's great falsehood,
which involved our race in ruin, has not yet become the
truth, although six thousand years have elapsed since it
was uttered.   Think of this, ye who worship at the
shrine of venerable error.   When the fables of men obtained the place of the truth of God, he was thereby
dishonored.   How, then, can he accept obedience to
them as any part of that pure devotion which he requires at our hands?   They that worship God must
worship him in Spirit and in truth.   How many ages
must pass over the fables of men before they become
changed into divine truth?   That these predictions of
the New Testament respecting the great apostasy in
the church were fully realized, the pages of ecclesiastical history present ample proof.   Mr. Dowling, in his
"History of Romanism," bears the following testimony :—

"There is scarcely anything which strikes the mind of the
careful student of ancient ecclesiastical history with greater surprise than the comparatively early period at which many of the
corruptions of Christianity, which are embodied in the Romish
system, took their rise; yet it is not to be supposed that when
the first originators of many of these unscriptural notions and
practices planted those germs of corruption, they anticipated or
even imagined they would ever grow into such a vast and hide-
ous system of superstition and error as that of popery. . . .
Each of the great corruptions of the latter ages took its rise in a
manner which it would be harsh to say was deserving of strong
reprehension. . . . The worship of images, the invocation of
saints, and the superstition of relics, were but expansions of the

natural feelings of veneration and affection cherished toward the memory of those who had suffered and died for the truth." [5]

Robinson, author of the "History of Baptism," speaks as follows :—

"Toward the latter end of the second century, most of the churches assumed a new form, the first simplicity disappeared; and insensibly, as the old disciples retired to their graves, their children, along with new converts, both Jews and Gentiles, came forward and new-modeled the cause." [6]

The working of the mystery of iniquity in the first centuries of the Christian church is thus described by a recent writer :—

"During these centuries, the chief corruptions of popery were either introduced in principle, or the seeds of them so effectually sown as naturally to produce those baneful fruits which appeared so plentifully at a later period. In Justin Martyr's time, within fifty years of the apostolic age, the cup was mixed with water, and a portion of the elements sent to the absent. The bread, which at first was sent only to the sick, was, in the time of Tertullian and Cyprian, carried home by the people, and locked up as a divine treasure for their private use. At this time, too, the ordinance of the supper was given to infants of the tenderest age, and was styled the sacrifice of the body of Christ. The custom of praying for the dead, Tertullian states, was common in the second century, and became the universal practice of the following ages; so that it came in the fourth century to be reckoned a kind of heresy to deny the efficacy of it. By this time the invocation of saints, the superstitious use of images, of the sign of the cross, and of consecrated oil, were become established practices, and pretended miracles were confidently adduced in proof of their supposed efficacy. Thus did that mystery of iniquity, which was already working in the

---

[5] Book 2, chap. 1, sec. 1.

[6] Eccl. Researches, chap. 6, p. 51, ed. 1792.

time of the apostles, speedily after their departure, spread its corruptions among the professors of Christianity."[7]

Neander speaks thus of the early introduction of image worship :—

"And yet, perhaps, religious images made their way from domestic life into the churches as early as the end of the third century ; and the walls of the churches were painted in the same way."[8]

The early apostasy of the professed church is a fact which rests upon the authority of inspiration not less than upon that of ecclesiastical history. "The mystery of iniquity," said Paul, "doth already work." We marvel that so large a portion of the people of God were *so soon* removed from the grace of God unto another gospel.

What shall be said of those who go to this period of history, and even to later times, to correct their Bibles ? Paul said that men would rise in the very midst of the elders of the apostolic church, who would speak perverse things, and that men would turn away their ears from the truth, and would be turned unto fables. Are the traditions of this period of sufficient importance to make void God's word ? The learned historian of the popes, Archibald Bower, uses the following emphatic language :—

"To avoid being imposed upon, we ought to treat tradition as we do a notorious and known liar, to whom we give no credit, unless what he says is confirmed to us by some person of undoubted veracity. . . . False and lying traditions are of an

---

[7] The Modern Sabbath Examined, pp. 123, 124.

[8] Rose's Neander, p. 184.

early date, and the greatest men have, out of a pious credulity, suffered themselves to be imposed upon by them." [9]

Mr. Dowling bears a similar testimony :—

" ' The Bible, I say, the Bible only, is the religion of Protestants ! ' Nor is it of any account in the estimation of the genuine Protestant *how early* a doctrine originated, if it is not found in the Bible. He learns from the New Testament itself that there were errors in the time of the apostles, and that their pens were frequently employed in combating those errors. Hence, if a doctrine be propounded for his acceptance, he asks, Is it to be found in the inspired word? Was it taught by the Lord Jesus Christ and his apostles ? . . . More than this, we will add, that though Cyprian, or Jerome, or Augustine, or even the Fathers of an earlier age, Tertullian, Ignatius, or Irenæus, could be plainly shown to teach the unscriptural doctrines and dogmas of popery, which, however, is by no means admitted, still the consistent Protestant would simply ask, Is the doctrine to be found in the Bible? Was it taught by Christ and his apostles ? . . . He who receives a single doctrine upon the mere authority of tradition, let him be called by what name he will, by so doing, steps down from the Protestant rock, passes over the line which separates Protestantism from popery, and can give no valid reason why he should not receive all the earlier doctrines and ceremonies of Romanism upon the same authority." [10]

Dr. Cumming, of London, thus speaks of the authority of the Fathers of the early church :—

" Some of these were distinguished for their genius, some for their eloquence, a few for their piety, and too many for their fanaticism and superstition. It is recorded by Dr. Delahogue (who was Professor in the Roman Catholic College of Maynooth), on the authority of Eusebius, that the Fathers who were really

---

[9] Hist. of the Popes, vol. 1, p. 1, Phila, ed. 1847.
[10] History of Romanism, book 2, chap. 1, secs. 3, 4.

most fitted to be the luminaries of the age in which they lived, were too busy in preparing their flocks for martyrdom to commit anything to writing; and, therefore, by the admission of this Roman Catholic divine, we have not the full and fair exponent of the views of all the Fathers of the earlier centuries, but only of those who were most ambitious of literary distinction, and least attentive to their charges. . . . The most devoted and pious of the Fathers were busy teaching their flocks; the more vain and ambitious occupied their time in preparing treatises. If all the Fathers who signalized the age had committed their sentiments to writing, we might have had a fair representation of the theology of the church of the Fathers; but as only a few have done so (many even of their writings being mutilated or lost), and these not the most devoted and spiritually minded, I contend that it is as unjust to judge of the theology of the early centuries by the writings of the few Fathers who are its only surviving representatives, as it would be to judge of the theology of the nineteenth century by the sermons of Mr. Newman, the speeches of Dr. Candlish, or the various productions of the late Edward Irving." [11]

Dr. Adam Clarke gives the following decisive testimony on the same subject :—

" But of these we may safely state that there is not a *truth* in the most orthodox creed that cannot be proved by their authority; nor a *heresy* that has disgraced the Romish church, that may not challenge them as its abettors. In points of *doctrine*, their authority is, *with me*, nothing. The WORD of God alone contains my creed. On a number of points I can go to the Greek and Latin Fathers of the church to know what *they believed*, and what the people of their respective communions believed; but after all this, I must return to God's word to know what he would have *me* to believe." [12]

In his life, he uses the following strong language :—

" We should take heed how we quote the Fathers in proof of

[11] Lectures on Romanism, p. 203.   [12] Commentary on Prov. 8.

the doctrines of the gospel; because he who knows them best, knows that on many of those subjects they blow hot and cold." [13]

The following testimonies will in part explain the unreliable nature of the Fathers. Thus Ephraim Pagitt testifies :—

" The church of ·Rome, having been conscious of their errors and corruptions, both in faith and manners, have sundry times pretended reformations ; yet their great pride and infinite profit, arising from purgatory, pardons, and such like, hath hindered all such reformations. Therefore, to maintain their greatness, errors, and new articles of faith, 1. They have corrupted many of the ancient Fathers, and, reprinting them, make them speak as they would have them. . . . 2. They have written many books in the names of these ancient writers, and forged many decrees, canons, and councils, to bear false witness to them." [14]

Wm. Reeves testifies to the same fact :—

" The church of Rome has had all the opportunities of time, place, and power to establish the kingdom of darkness; and that in coining, clipping, and washing the primitive records to their own good liking, they have not been wanting to themselves, is notoriously evident." [15]

The traditions of the early church are considered by many quite as reliable as the language of the Holy Scriptures. A single instance taken from the Bible will illustrate the character of tradition, and show the amount of reliance that can be placed upon it :—

" Then Peter, turning about, seeth the disciple whom Jesus loved, following (which also leaned on his breast at supper, and saith, Lord, which is he that betrayeth thee?); Peter, seeing

---

[13] Autobiography of Adam Clarke, LL. D., p. 134.

[14] Christianography, part 2, p. 59, London, 1636.

[15] Translation of the Apologies of Justin Martyr, Tertullian, and others, vol. 2, p. 375.

him, saith to Jesus, Lord, and what shall this man do? Jesus saith unto him, If I will that he tarry till I come, what is that to thee? Follow thou me. Then went this saying abroad among the brethren, that that disciple should not die; yet Jesus said not unto him, He shall not die; but, If I will that he tarry till I come, what is that to thee?" [16]

Here is the account of a tradition which actually originated in the very bosom of the apostolic church, which, nevertheless, handed down to the following generations an entire mistake. Observe how carefully the word of God has corrected this error.

Two rules of faith really embrace the whole Christian world. One of these is the word of God alone; the other is the word of God and the traditions of the church. Here they are:—

I. THE RULE OF THE MAN OF GOD, THE BIBLE ALONE.

"All Scripture is given by inspiration of God, and is profitable for doctrine, for reproof, for correction, for instruction in righteousness; that the man of God may be perfect, thoroughly furnished unto all good works." [17]

II. THE RULE OF THE ROMANIST, THE BIBLE AND TRADITION.

"If we would have the whole rule of Christian faith and practice, we must not be content with those scriptures which Timothy knew from his infancy, that is, with the Old Testament alone; nor yet with the New Testament, without taking along with it the traditions of the apostles, and the interpretation of the church, to which the apostles delivered both the book and the true meaning of it." [18]

It is certain that the first-day Sabbath cannot be sustained by the first of these rules; for the word of

---

[16] John 21: 20–23.　　　　[17] 2 Tim. 3: 16, 17.
[18] Note of the Douay Bible on 2 Tim. 3: 16, 17.

God says nothing respecting such an institution. The second one is necessarily adopted by all who advocate the sacredness of the first day of the week; for the writings of the Fathers and the traditions of the church furnish all the testimony which can be adduced in support of that day. To adopt the first rule is to condemn the first-day Sabbath as a human institution. To adopt the second is virtually to acknowledge that the Romanists are right; for it is by this rule that they are able to sustain their unscriptural dogmas. Mr. W. B. Taylor, an able anti-Sabbatarian writer, states this point with great clearness :—

"The triumph of the consistent Roman Catholic over all observers of Sunday, calling themselves Protestants, is indeed complete and unanswerable. . . . It should present a subject of very grave reflection to Christians of the reformed and evangelical denominations, to find that no single argument or suggestion can be offered in favor of Sunday observance that will not apply with equal force and to its fullest extent in sustaining the various other 'holy days' appointed by 'the church.'" [19]

Listen to the argument of a Roman Catholic :—.

"The word of God commandeth the seventh day to be the Sabbath of our Lord, and to be kept holy: you [Protestants] without any precept of Scripture, change it to the first day of the week, only authorized by our traditions. Divers English Puritans oppose against this point, that the observation of the first day is proved out of Scripture, where it is said 'the first day of the week.' [20] Have they not spun a fair thread in quoting these places? If we should produce no better for purgatory and prayers for the dead, invocation of the saints, and the like, they might have good cause indeed to laugh us to scorn; for where is it written that these were Sabbath-days in which those meetings

---

[19] Obligation of the Sabbath, pp. 254, 255.

[20] Acts 20:7; 1 Cor. 16:2; Rev. 1:10.

were kept? Or where is it ordained they should be always observed? Or, which is the sum of all, where is it decreed that the observation of the first day should abrogate or abolish the sanctifying of the seventh day, which God commanded everlastingly to be kept holy? Not one of those is expressed in the written word of God." [21]

Whoever, therefore, enters the lists in behalf of the first-day Sabbath, must of necessity do this—though perhaps not aware of the fact—under the banner of the church of Rome.

---

[21] A Treatise of Thirty Controversies.

CHAPTER XIII.

THE SUNDAY LORD'S DAY NOT TRACEABLE TO THE APOSTLES.

General statement respecting the Ante-Nicene Fathers—The change of the Sabbath never mentioned by one of these Fathers—Examination of the historical argument for Sunday as the Lord's day—This argument compared with the like argument for the Catholic festival of the Passover.

HE Ante-Nicene Fathers [1] are those Christian writers who flourished after the time of the apostles, and before the council of Nicæa, A. D. 325. Those who govern their lives by the volume of inspiration do not recognize any authority in these Fathers to change any precept of that book, nor to add any new precepts to it. But those whose rule of life is the Bible as modified by tradition, regard the early Fathers of the church as nearly or quite equal in authority to the inspired writers. They declare that the Fathers conversed with the apostles; or if they did not do this, they conversed with some who had seen some

---

[1] The writer has prepared a small work entitled, "The Complete Testimony of the Fathers of the First Three Centuries Concerning the Sabbath and First-day," in which, with the single exception of Origen, some of whose works were not at that time accessible, every passage in the Fathers which gives their views of the Sabbath and first-day is presented. This pamphlet is for sale by the Publishers of the present work for fifteen cents. To save space in this History, a general statement of the doctrine of the Fathers is here made, with brief quotations from them. But in "The Complete Testimony of the Fathers" every passage is given in their own words, and to this little work the reader is referred.

of the apostles; or, at least, they lived within a few generations of the apostles, and so learned by tradition, which involved only a few transitions from father to son, what was the true doctrine of the apostles.

Thus with perfect assurance they supply the lack of inspired testimony in behalf of the so-called Christian Sabbath by plentiful quotations from the early Fathers. What if there be no mention of the change of the Sabbath in the New Testament? and what if there be no commandment for resting from labor on the first day of the week? or, what if there be no method revealed in the Bible by which the first day of the week can be enforced by the fourth commandment? They supply these serious omissions in the Scriptures by testimonies which they say were written by men who lived during the first three hundred years after the apostles.

On such authority as this the multitude dare to change the Sabbath of the fourth commandment. But next to the deception under which men fall when they are made to believe that the Bible may be corrected by the Fathers, is the deception practiced upon them as to what the Fathers actually teach. It is asserted that the Fathers bear explicit testimony to the change of the Sabbath by Christ as a historical fact, and that they knew that this was so because they had conversed with the apostles, or with some who had conversed with them. It is also asserted that the Fathers called the first day of the week the Christian Sabbath, and that they refrained from labor on that day as an act of obedience to the fourth commandment.

Now it is a most remarkable fact that every one of these assertions is false. The people who trust in the

Fathers as their authority for departing from God's commandment, are miserably deceived as to what the Fathers teach.

1. The Fathers are so far from testifying that the apostles told them Christ changed the Sabbath, that not even one of them ever alludes to such a change.

2. No one of them ever calls the first day the Christian Sabbath, nor, indeed, ever calls it a Sabbath of any kind.

3. They never represent it as a day on which ordinary labor was sinful; nor do they represent the observance of Sunday as an act of obedience to the fourth commandment.

4. The modern doctrine of the change of the Sabbath was therefore absolutely unknown in the first centuries of the Christian church.[2]

But though no statement asserting the change of the Sabbath can be produced from the writings of the Fathers of the first three hundred years, it is claimed that their testimony furnishes decisive proof that the first day of the week is the Lord's day of Rev. 1 : 10. The Biblical argument that this term refers to the seventh day and no other, because that day alone is in the Holy Scriptures claimed by the Father and the Son as belonging in a peculiar sense to each, is given in chapter eleven, and is absolutely decisive. But this is set aside without answer, and the claim of the first day to this honorable distinction is substantiated out of the Fathers as follows :—

---

[2] Those who dispute these statements are invited to present the words of the Fathers which modify or disprove them. The reader who may not have access to the writings of the Fathers is referred to the pamphlet already mentioned, in which their complete testimony is given.

The term " Lord's day," as a name for the first day of the week, can be traced back through the first three centuries, from the Fathers who lived toward their close to the ones next preceding, who mention the first day, and so backward by successive steps, till we come to one who lived in John's time, and was his disciple ; and this disciple of John calls the first day of the week the Lord's day. It follows, therefore, that John must have intended the first day of the week by this title, but did not define his meaning because it was familiarly known by that name in his time. Thus by history they claim to prove the first day of the week to be the Lord's day of Rev. 1:10; and then by Rev. 1:10, they attempt to show the first day of the week to be the sacred day of this dispensation; for the spirit of inspiration by which John wrote would not have called the first day by this name if it were only a human institution, and if the seventh day was still by divine appointment the Lord's holy day.

This is a concise statement of the strongest argument for first-day sacredness which can be drawn from ecclesiastical history. It is the argument by which first-day writers prove Sunday to be the day John called the Lord's day. This argument rests upon the statement that " Lord's day," as a name for Sunday, can be traced back to the disciples of John, and that it is the name by which that day was familiarly known in John's time. But this entire statement is false. The truth is, no writer of the first century, and no one of the second, prior to A. D. 194, who is known to speak of the first day of the week, ever calls it the Lord's day ! Yet the first day is seven times mentioned by the sacred writers *before* John's vision upon Patmos, and is twice mentioned by John in his Gospel, which he wrote *after* his return from that island, and is mentioned some sixteen times by ecclesiastical writers of the second century, prior to A. D. 194, and never in a single instance is it called the Lord's day! We give all the instances of its mention in the Bible. Moses, in the beginning, by divine inspiration, gave to the first day its name; and though the resurrection of Christ is said to have made it the Lord's day, yet every sacred writer who mentions the day after that event still adheres to the plain name of "first day of the week." Here are all the instances in which the inspired writers mention the day:—·

Moses, B. C. 1490: "The evening and the morning were the first day." Gen. 1 : 5.

Matthew, A. D. 41: "In the end of the Sabbath, as it began to dawn toward the first day of the week." Matt. 28 : 1.

Paul, A. D. 57: "Upon the first day of the week." 1 Cor. 16 : 2.

Luke, A. D. 60: "Now upon the first day of the week." Luke 24 : 1.

Luke, A. D. 63: "And upon the first day of the week." Acts 20 : 7.

Mark, A. D. 64: "And very early in the morning, the first day of the week." Mark 16 : 2. "Now when Jesus was risen early the first day of the week." Verse 9.

After the resurrection of Christ, and before John's vision, A. D. 96, the day is six times mentioned by inspired men, and every time as plain "first day of the week." It certainly was not familiarly known as "Lord's day" before the time of John's vision. To speak the exact truth, it was not called by that name at all, nor by any other name equivalent to that, nor is there any record of its being set apart by divine authority as such.

But in the year 96, John says, "I was in the Spirit on the Lord's day." Rev. 1:10. Now it is evident that this must be a day which the Lord had set apart for himself, and which he claimed as his. This was all true of the seventh day, but was not in any respect true of the first day. He could not, therefore, call the first day by this name, for it was not such. But if the Spirit of God designed at this point to create a new institution, and to call a certain day the Lord's which before had never been claimed by him, it was necessary that he should specify that new day. He did not define the term, which proves that he was not giving a sacred name to some new institution, but was speaking of a well-known, divinely-appointed day. But *after* John's return from Patmos, he wrote his Gospel,[3] and in that Gospel he twice had occasion to mention the first day of the week. Let us see whether he adheres to the manner of the other sacred writers, or whether, when we know he means the first day, he gives to it a sacred name.

John, A. D. 97: "The first day of the week cometh Mary Magdalene early." John 20:1. "Then the same day at evening, being the first day of the week." Verse 19.

These texts complete the Bible record of the first day of the week. They furnish conclusive evidence

---

[3] See the testimony on page 189 of this work.

that John did not receive new light in vision at Patmos, bidding him call the first day of the week the Lord's day; and when taken with all the instances preceding, they constitute a complete demonstration that the first day was not familiarly known as the Lord's day in John's time, nor indeed known at all by that name. Let us now see whether "Lord's day," as a title for the first day, can be traced back to John by means of the writings of the Fathers.

The following is a concise statement of the testimony by which the Fathers are made to prove that John used the term as a name for the first day of the week. A chain of seven successive witnesses, commencing with one who was the disciple of John, and extending forward through several generations, is made to connect and identify the Lord's day of John with the Sunday Lord's day of a later age. Thus Ignatius, the disciple of John, is made to speak familiarly of the first day as the Lord's day. This is directly connecting the Fathers and the apostles. Then the epistle of Pliny, A. D. 104, in connection with the Acts of the Martyrs, is adduced to prove that the martyrs in his time and forward were tested as to their observance of Sunday, the question being, "Have you kept the Lord's day?" Next, Justin Martyr, A D. 140, is made to speak of Sunday as the Lord's day. After this, Theophilus of Antioch, A. D. 168, is brought forward to bear a powerful testimony to the Sunday Lord's day. Then Dionysius of Corinth, A. D. 170, is made to speak to the same effect. Next Melito of Sardis, A. D. 177, is produced to confirm what the others have said. And finally, Irenæus, A. D. 178, who had been the disciple of Polycarp, one of the disciples of the apostle John, is brought forward to bear a decisive testimony in behalf of Sunday as the Lord's day and the Christian Sabbath.

These are the first seven witnesses who are cited to prove that Sunday is the Lord's day. They bring us nearly to the close of the second century. They constitute the chain of testimony by which the Lord's day of the apostle John is identified with the Sunday Lord's day of later times. First-day writers present these witnesses as proving positively that Sunday is the Lord's day of the Scriptures; and the Christian church accepts this testimony, in the absence of that of the inspired writers. But the folly of the people, and the wickedness of those who lead them, may be set forth in one sentence :—

The first, second, third, fourth, and seventh of these testimonies are inexcusable frauds, while the fifth and sixth have no decisive bearing upon the case.

1. Ignatius, the first of these witnesses, it is said, must have known Sunday to be the Lord's day, for he calls it such, and he had conversed with the apostle John. But in the entire writings of this Father, the term "Lord's day" does not once occur, nor is there in them all a single mention of the first day of the week! The reader will find a critical examination of the epistles of Ignatius in chapter fourteen of this history.

2. It is a pure fabrication that the martyrs in Pliny's time, about A. D. 104, and thence onward, were tested by the question whether they had kept the Sunday Lord's day. No question at all resembling this is to be found in the words of the martyrs, till we come to the fourth century, and then the reference is not at all to

the first day of the week. This is fully shown in chapter fifteen.

3. The Bible Dictionary of the American Tract Society, page 379, brings forward the third of these Sunday Lord's day witnesses in the person of Justin Martyr, A. D. 140. It makes him call Sunday the Lord's day by quoting him as follows :—

"Justin Martyr observes that 'on the Lord's day all Christians in the city or country meet together, because that is the day of our Lord's resurrection.'"

But Justin never gave to Sunday the title of Lord's day, nor, indeed, any other sacred title. Here are his words correctly quoted :—

"And on the day called Sunday, all who live in cities or in the country gather together to one place, and the memoirs of the apostles, or the writings of the prophets, are read, as long as time permits," etc.[4]

Justin speaks of the day called Sunday. But that he may be made to help establish its title to the name of Lord's day, his words are deliberately changed. Thus the third witness to Sunday as the Lord's day, like the first and second, is made such by fraud. But the fourth fraud is even worse than the three which precede.

4. The fourth testimony to the Sunday Lord's day is furnished in Dr. Justin Edwards' Sabbath Manual, p. 114 :—

"Theophilus, bishop of Antioch, about A. D. 162, says: 'Both custom and reason challenge from us that we should honor *the Lord's day*, seeing on that day it was that our Lord Jesus completed his resurrection from the dead.'"

Dr. Edwards does not pretend to give the place in

---

[4] Justin Martyr's First Apology, chap. 67.

Theophilus where these words are to be found. Having carefully and minutely examined every paragraph of the writings of Theophilus several times over, I state emphatically that nothing of the kind is to be found in that writer. He never uses the term "Lord's day," and does not even speak of the first day of the week. These words, which are so well adapted to create the impression that the Sunday Lord's day is of apostolic institution, are put into his mouth by the falsehood of some one.

Here are four frauds, constituting the first four instances of the alleged use of "Lord's day" as a name for Sunday. Yet it is by means of these very frauds that the Sunday Lord's day of later ages is identified with the Lord's day of the Bible. Somebody invented these frauds. The use to which they are put plainly indicates the purpose for which they were framed. The title of Lord's day must be proved to pertain to Sunday by apostolic authority. For this purpose these frauds were a necessity. The case of the Sunday Lord's day may be fitly illustrated by that of the long line of popes. Their apostolic authority as head of the Catholic church depends on their being able to identify the apostle Peter as the first of their line, and to prove that his authority was transmitted to them. There is no difficulty in tracing their line back to the early ages, though the earliest Roman bishops were modest, unassuming men, wholly unlike the popes of after times. But when they come to make Peter the head of their line, and to identify his authority and theirs, they can do it only by fraudulent testimonials. And such is the case with first-day observance. It may be traced back as a festival to the time of Justin Martyr, A. D. 140, but the day had then no sacred name, and claimed no apostolic authority. These must be secured, however, at any cost; and so its title of " Lord's day " is, by a series of fraudulent testimonials, traced to the apostle John, as in like manner the authority of the popes is traced to the apostle Peter.

5. The fifth witness of this series is Dionysius, of Corinth, A. D. 170. Unlike the four which have been already examined, Dionysius actually uses the term " Lord's day," though he says nothing identifying it with the first day of the week. His words are these :—

" To-day we have passed the Lord's holy day, in which we have read your epistle; in reading which we shall always have our minds stored with admonition, as we shall, also, from that written to us before by Clement." [5]

The epistle of Dionysius to Soter, bishop of Rome, from which this sentence is taken, has perished. Eusebius, who wrote in the fourth century, has preserved to us this sentence, but we have no knowledge of its connection. First-day writers quote Dionysius as the fifth of their witnesses that Sunday is the Lord's day. They say that Sunday was so familiarly known as such in the time of Dionysius, that he calls it by that name without even stopping to tell what day he meant.

But it is not honest to present Dionysius as a witness to the Sunday Lord's day, for he makes no application of the term. Yet it is said he certainly meant Sunday, because that was the familiar name of the day in his time, as is indicated by the fact that he did not

---

[5] Eusebius's Eccl. Hist., book 4, chap. 23.

define the term. And how is it known that "Lord's day" was the familiar name for Sunday in the time of Dionysius? The four witnesses already examined furnish all the evidence in proof of this, for there is no writer this side of Dionysius who calls Sunday the Lord's day until almost the entire period of a generation has elapsed. So Dionysius constitutes the fifth witness of the series by virtue of the fact that the first four witnesses prove that in his time, "Lord's day" was the common name for the first day of the week. But the first four testify to nothing of the kind until the words are by fraud put into their mouths! Dionysius is a witness for the Sunday Lord's day, because four fraudulent testimonials from the generations preceding him fix this as the meaning of his words! And the name "Lord's day" must have been a very common one for the first day of the week, because Dionysius does not define the term! And yet those who say this know that this *one* sentence of his epistle remains, while the connection, which doubtless fixed his meaning, has perished.

But Dionysius does not merely use the term "Lord's day." He uses a stronger term than this,—"the Lord's *holy* day:" Even for a long period after Dionysius, no writer gives to Sunday so sacred a title as "the Lord's holy day." Yet this is the very title given to the Sabbath in the Holy Scriptures, and it is a well-ascertained fact that at this very time it was extensively observed, especially in Greece, the country of Dionysius, and that, too, as an act of obedience to the fourth commandment.[6]

6. The sixth witness in this remarkable series is

---

[6] See chapter 18 of this History.

Melito, of Sardis, A. D. 177. The first four, who never
use the term "Lord's day," are by direct fraud made to
call Sunday by that name; the fifth, who speaks of the
Lord's holy day, is claimed, on the strength of these
frauds, to have meant Sunday; while the sixth is not
certainly proved to have spoken of any day! Melito
wrote several books which are now lost, but their titles
have been preserved by Eusebius.[7] One of these, as
given in the English version of Eusebius, is "On the
Lord's Day." Of course, first-day writers claim this was
a treatise concerning Sunday, though down to this point
no writer calls Sunday by this name. But it is an important fact that the word *day* formed no part of the title of Melito's book. It was a discourse on something
pertaining to the Lord,—*ὁ περι τῆς κυριακῆς λόγος*,—but the
essential word, *ἡμερας (day)*, is wanting. It may have
been a treatise on the life of Christ, for Ignatius thus
uses these words in connection : *κμριακὴν ζωὴν (Lord's life)*.
Like the sentence from Dionysius, it would not even
seem to help the claim of Sunday to the title of Lord's
day were it not for the series of frauds in which it
stands.

7. The seventh witness summoned to prove that
"Lord's day" was the apostolic title of Sunday, is
Irenæus. Dr. Justin Edwards professes to quote him
as follows :—[8]

"Hence Irenæus, bishop of Lyons, a disciple of Polycarp,
who had been the companion of the apostles, A. D. 167 [it should
be A. D. 178], says that the Lord's day was the Christian Sabbath. His words are, 'On the Lord's day every one of us

---

[7] See his Ecclesiastical History, book 4, chap. 26.

[8] Sabbath Manual, p. 114.

Christians keeps the Sabbath, meditating on the law, and rejoicing in the works of God.'"

This witness is brought forward in a manner to give the utmost weight and authority to his words. He was the disciple of that eminent Christian martyr, Polycarp, and Polycarp was the companion of the apostles. What Irenæus says is therefore, in the estimation of many, as worthy of our confidence as though we could read it in the writings of the apostles. Does not Irenæus call Sunday the Christian Sabbath and the Lord's day? Did he not learn these things from Polycarp? And did not Polycarp get them from the fountain head? What need have we of further witness that "Lord's day" is the apostolic name for Sunday? What if the six earlier witnesses have failed us? Here is one that says all that can be asked, and he had his doctrine from a man who had his from the apostles! Why, then, does not this establish the authority of Sunday as the Lord's day?

The first reason is that neither Irenæus nor any other man can add to or change one precept of the word of God, on any pretense whatever. We are never authorized to depart from the words of the inspired writers on the testimony of men who conversed with the apostles, or rather, who conversed with some who had conversed with them. And the second reason is that every word of this pretended testimony of Irenæus is a fraud! Nor is there a single instance in which the term "Lord's day" is to be found in any of his works, nor in any fragment of his works preserved in other authors![9]

---

[9] See chapter 16 of this work; and also "Testimony of the Fathers," pp. 44–52.

And this completes the seven witnesses by whom the Lord's day of the Catholic church is traced back to, and identified with, the Lord's day of the Bible! It is not till A. D. 194, sixteen years after the latest of these witnesses, that we meet the first instance in which Sunday is called the Lord's day. In other words, Sunday is not called the Lord's day till ninety-eight years after John was upon Patmos, and one hundred and sixty-three years after the resurrection of Christ!

But is not this owing to the fact that the records of that period have perished? By no means; for the day is six times mentioned by the inspired writers between the resurrection of Christ, A. D. 31, and John's vision upon Patmos, A. D. 96; namely, by Matthew, A. D. 41; by Paul, A. D. 57; by Luke, A. D. 60 and 63; and by Mark, A. D. 64; and always as the first day of the week. John, after his return from Patmos, A. D. 97, twice mentions the day, still calling it the first day of the week.

After John's time, the day is next mentioned in the so-called epistle of Barnabas, written probably as early as A. D. 140, and is there called "the eighth day." Then it is spoken of by Justin Martyr in his apology, A. D. 140, once as "the day on which we all hold our common assembly;" once as "the first day on which God . . . made the world;" once as "the same day [on which Christ] rose from the dead;" once as "the day after that of Saturn;" and three times as "Sunday," or "the day of the sun." Again he refers to it in his dialogue with Trypho, A. D. 155, in which he twice calls it the "eighth day;" once "the first of all the days;" once as "the first" "of all the days of the [weekly] cycle;" and twice as "the first day after the Sabbath."

It is once mentioned by Irenæus, A. D. 178, who calls it simply the "first day of the week." And next it is introduced once by Bardesanes, who likewise calls it simply "the first of the week." The variety of names by which the day is mentioned during this time is remarkable; but it is *never* called "Lord's day," nor is it ever designated by *any sacred* name.

Though Sunday is mentioned in so many different ways during the second century, it is not till we come almost to the close of the second century that we find the first instance in which it is called "Lord's day." Clement, of Alexandria, A. D. 194, uses this title with reference to "the eighth day." If he speaks of a natural day, he no doubt means Sunday. It is not certain, however, that he speaks of a natural day, for his explanation gives to the term an entirely different sense. Here are his words :—

"And the Lord's day Plato prophetically speaks of, in the tenth book of the *Republic*, in these words : ' And when seven days have passed to each of them in the meadow, on the eighth they are to set out, and arrive in four days.' By the meadow is to be understood the fixed sphere, as being a mild and genial spot, and the locality of the pious; and by the seven days, each motion of the seven planets, and the whole practical art which speeds to the end of rest. But after the wandering orbs, the journey leads to heaven, that is, to the eighth motion and day. And he says that souls are gone on the fourth day, pointing out the passage through the four elements. But the seventh day is recognized as sacred, not by the Hebrews only, but also by the Greeks ; according to which the whole world of all animals and plants revolve." [10]

Clement was originally a heathen philosopher, and

---

[10] The Miscellanies of Clement, book 5, chap. 14.

these strange mysticisms which he here puts forth upon the words of Plato are only modifications of his former heathen notions. Though Clement says that Plato speaks of the Lord's day, it is certain that he does not understand him to speak of literal days nor of a literal meadow. On the contrary, he interprets the meadow to represent "the fixed sphere, as being a mild and genial spot, and the locality of the pious;" which must refer to their future inheritance. The seven days are not so many literal days, but they represent "each motion of the seven planets, and the whole practical art which speeds to the end of rest." This seems to represent the present period of labor which is to end in the rest of the saints; for he adds: "But after the wandering orbs [represented by Plato's seven days] the journey leads to *heaven*, that is, to *the eighth* motion and *day*." The seven days, therefore, do here represent the period of the Christian's pilgrimage, and the eighth day of which Clement here speaks is not Sunday, but heaven itself! Here is the first instance of "Lord's day" as a name for the eighth day, but this eighth day is a mystical one, and means heaven!

But Clement uses the term "Lord's day" once more, and this time clearly, as representing, not a literal day, but the whole period of our regenerate life. For he speaks of it in treating of fasting, and he sets forth fasting as consisting of abstinence from sinful pleasures, not only in deeds, to use his distinction, as forbidden by the law, but in thoughts, as forbidden by the gospel. Such fasting pertains to the entire life of the Christian. And thus Clement sets forth what is involved in observing this duty in the gospel sense:—

" He, in fulfillment of the precept, according to the gospel, keeps the Lord's day, when he abandons an evil disposition, and assumes that of the Gnostic, glorifying the Lord's resurrection in himself." [11]

From this statement we learn, not merely his idea of fasting, but also that of celebrating the Lord's day, and glorifying the resurrection of Christ. This, according to Clement, does not consist in paying special honors to Sunday, but in abandoning an evil disposition, and in assuming that of the Gnostic, a Christian sect to which he belonged. Now it is plain that this kind of Lord's-day observance pertains to no one day of the week, but embraces the entire life of the Christian. Clement's Lord's day was not a literal, but a mystical day, embracing, according to this, his second use of the term, the entire regenerate life of the Christian; and according to his first use of the term, embracing also the future life in heaven. And this view is confirmed by Clement's statement of the contrast between the Gnostic sect to which he belonged and other Christians. He says of their worship that it was " NOT ON SPECIAL DAYS, as some others, but *doing this continually* in our whole life." And he speaks further of the worship of the Gnostic, that it was "*not* in a specified place, or selected temple, or at certain festivals, and on appointed days, *but during his whole life*." [12]

It is certainly a very remarkable fact that the first writer who speaks of the Lord's day as the eighth day, uses the term, not with reference to a literal, but a mystical day. It is not Sunday, but the Christian's life, or

---

[11] The Miscellanies of Clement, book 7, chap. 12; Testimony of the Fathers, p. 61.

[12] The Miscellanies, book 7, chap. 7; Testimony of the Fathers, p. 62.

heaven itself! This doctrine of a perpetual Lord's day we shall find alluded to in Tertullian, and expressly stated in Origen, who are the next two writers that use the term. But Clement's mystical or perpetual Lord's day shows that he had no idea that John meant Sunday by his use of these words; for in that case he must have recognized that as the true Lord's day, and the Gnostics' special day of worship.

Tertullian, A. D. 200, is the next writer who uses the term "Lord's day." He defines his meaning, and fixes the name upon the day of Christ's resurrection. Kitto [13] says this is "the earliest authentic instance" in which the name is thus applied, and we have proved this true by actual examination of every writer, unless the reader can discover some reference to Sunday in Clement's mystical eighth day. Tertullian's words are these :—

"We, however (just as we have received), only on the Lord's day of the resurrection [*solo die dominico resurrexionis*] ought to guard, not only against kneeling, but every posture and office of solicitude; deferring even our business, lest we give any place to the devil. Similarly, too, in the period of Pentecost; which period we distinguish by the same solemnity of exultation." [14]

Twice more does Tertullian use the term "Lord's day," and once more does he define it, this time calling it the "eighth day." And in each of these two cases he places the day which he calls the Lord's day in the same rank with the Catholic festival of Pentecost, as he does in the instance already quoted. As the second instance of Tertullian's use of "Lord's day," we quote a portion of the rebuke which he addressed to his brethren for

---

[13] Kitto's Cyclopedia of Biblical Literature, original edition, article, Lord's day.
[14] Tertullian on Prayer, chap. 23 ; Testimony of the Fathers, p. 67.

mingling with the heathen in their festivals. He
says :—

"Oh! better fidelity of the nations to their own sects, which
claims no solemnity of the Christians for itself! Not the Lord's
day, not Pentecost, *even if they had known them,* would they
have shared with us; for they would fear lest they should seem
to be Christians. *We* are not apprehensive lest we seem to be
heathens! If any indulgence is to be granted to the flesh, you
have it. I will not say your own days, but more too; for to the
heathens each festive day occurs but once annually; *you* have a
festive day every eighth day." [15]

The festival which Tertullian here represents as
coming every eighth day was no doubt the one which he
has just called the Lord's day. Though he elsewhere [16]
speaks of the Sunday festival as observed at least by
some portion of the heathen, he here speaks of the
Lord's day as unknown to those of whom he now writes.
This strongly indicates that the Sunday festival had but
recently begun to be called by the name of "Lord's day."
Once more he speaks of it :—

"As often as the anniversary comes round, we make offerings
for the dead as birth-day honors. We count fasting or kneeling
in worship on the Lord's day to be unlawful. We rejoice in the
same privilege also from Easter to Whitsunday [the Pentecost].
We feel pained should any wine or bread, even though our own,
be cast upon the ground. At every forward step and movement,
at every going in and out, when we put on our clothes and shoes,
when we bathe, when we sit at table, when we light the lamps,
on couch, on seat, in all the ordinary actions of daily life, we
trace upon the forehead the sign [of the cross].

"If for these and other such rules, you insist upon having

---

[15] On Idolatry, chap. 14 ; Testimony of the Fathers, p. 66.
[16] *Ad Nationes,* book 1, chap. 13 ; Testimony of the Fathers, p. 70.

positive Scripture injunction, you will find none. Tradition will be held forth to you as the *originator* of them, custom as their strengthener, and faith as their observer. That reason will support tradition, and custom, and faith, you will either yourself perceive, or learn from some one who has." [17]

This completes the instances in which Tertullian uses the term " Lord's day," except a mere allusion to it in his discourse on Fasting. It is very remarkable that in each of the three cases, he puts it on a level with the festival of Whitsunday, or Pentecost. He also associates it directly with " offerings for the dead " and with the use of " the sign of the cross." When asked for authority from the Bible for these things, he does not answer, " We have the authority of John for the Lord's day, though we have nothing but tradition for the sign of the cross and offerings for the dead." On the contrary, he said there was no Scripture injunction for any of them. If it be asked, How could the title of " Lord's day " be given to Sunday except by tradition derived from the apostles? the answer will be properly returned, What was the origin of offerings for the dead? and how did the sign of the cross come into use among Christians? The title of " Lord's day " as a name for Sunday is no nearer apostolic than is the sign of the cross, and offerings for the dead; for it can be traced no nearer to apostolic times than can these most palpable errors of the great apostasy.

Clement taught a perpetual Lord's day; Tertullian held a similar view, asserting that Christians should celebrate a perpetual Sabbath, not by abstinence from

---

[17] *De Corona*, secs. 3 and 4; Testimony of the Fathers, pp. 68, 69.

labor, but from sin.[18]   Tertullian's method of Sunday observance will be noticed hereafter.

Origen, A. D. 231, is the third of the ancient writers who call "the eighth day" the Lord's day.   He was the disciple of Clement, the first writer who makes this application.   It is not strange, therefore, that he should teach Clement's doctrine of a perpetual Lord's day, nor that he should state it even more distinctly than did Clement himself.   Origen, having represented Paul as teaching that all days are alike, continues thus :

"If it be objected to us on this subject that we ourselves are accustomed to observe certain days, as for example the Lord's day, the Preparation, the Passover, or the Pentecost, I have to answer, that to the perfect Christian, who is ever in his thoughts, words, and deeds serving his natural Lord, God the Word, all his days are the Lord's, and he is always keeping the Lord's day." [19]

This was written some forty years after Clement had propounded his doctrine of the Lord's day.   The imperfect Christian might honor a Lord's day which stood in the same rank with the Preparation, the Passover, and the Pentecost.   But the perfect Christian observed the true Lord's day, which embraced all the days of his regenerate life.   Origen uses the term "Lord's day" for two different days : 1. For a natural day, which in his judgment stood in the same rank with the Preparation day, the Passover, and the Pentecost; 2. For a mystical day, as did Clement, which is the entire period of the Christian's life.   The mystical day, in his estimation, was the true "Lord's day."   It therefore follows

---

[18] An Answer to the Jews, chap. 4; Testimony of the Fathers, p. 73.

[19] Against Celsus, book 8, chap. 22; Testimony of the Fathers, p. 87.

that he did not believe Sunday to be the Lord's day by apostolic appointment. But, after Origen's time, "Lord's day" became a common name for the so-called eighth day. Yet these three men—Clement, Tertullian, and Origen—who first make this application, not only do not claim that this name was given to the day by the apostles, but plainly indicate that they had no such idea. Offerings for the dead and the use of the sign of the cross are found as near to the apostolic times as is the use of "Lord's day" as a name for Sunday. The three have a common origin, as shown by Tertullian's own words. Origen's views of the Sabbath and of the Sunday festival will be noticed hereafter.

Such is the case with the claim of Sunday to the title of "Lord's day." The first instance of its use, if Clement be supposed to refer to Sunday, is not till almost one century after John was in vision upon Patmos. Those who first called it by that name had no idea that it was such by divine or apostolic appointment, as they plainly show. In marked contrast with this is the Catholic festival of the Passover. Though never commanded in the New Testament, it can be traced back to men who say that they had it from the apostles!

The churches of Asia Minor had the festival from Polycarp, who, as Eusebius states the claim of Polycarp, had "observed it with John, the disciple of our Lord, and the rest of the apostles with whom he associated."[20] Socrates says of them that they maintain that this observance "was delivered to them by the apostle John."[21] Anatolius says of these Asiatic Christians that they re-

---

[20] Eusebius's Eccl. Hist., book 5, chap. 24.
[21] Socrates's Eccl. Hist., book 5, chap. 22.

ceived "the rule from an unimpeachable authority, to wit, the evangelist John." [22]

Nor was this all. The Western churches also, with the church of Rome at their head, were strenuous observers of the Passover festival. They also traced the festival to the apostles. Thus Socrates says of them: "The Romans and those in the western parts assure us that their usage originated with the apostles Peter and Paul." [23] But he says these parties cannot prove this by written testimony. Sozomen says of the Romans, with respect to the Passover festival, that they "have never deviated from their original usage in this particular, the custom having been handed down to them by the holy apostles, Peter and Paul." [24]

If the Sunday Lord's day could be traced to a man who claimed to have celebrated it with John and other of the apostles, how confidently would this be cited as proving positively that it is an apostolic institution! And yet this can be done in the case of the Passover festival! Nevertheless, a single fact in the case of this very festival is sufficient to teach us the folly of trusting in tradition. Polycarp claimed that John and other of the apostles taught him to observe the festival on the fourteenth day of the first month, whatever day of the week it might be; while the elders of the Roman church asserted that Peter and Paul taught them that it must be observed on the Sunday following Good Friday! [25]

The "Lord's day" of the Catholic church can be

---

[22] Anatolius, Tenth Fragment.   [23] Socrates's Eccl. Hist., book 5, chap. 22.

[24] Sozomen's Eccl. Hist., book 7, chap. 18; see also Mosheim, book 1, cent. 2, part 2, chap. 4, sec. 9.

[25] Socrates's Eccl. Hist., book 5, chap. 22; Mc Clintock and Strong's Cyclo pedia, vol. 3, p. 13; Bingham's Antiquities, p. 1149.

traced no nearer to John than A. D. 194, or perhaps, in strict truth, to A. D. 200, and those who then use the name show plainly that they did not believe it to be the Lord's day by apostolic appointment. To hide these fatal facts by seeming to trace the title back to Ignatius, the disciple of John, and thus to identify Sunday with the Lord's day of that apostle, a series of remarkable frauds has been committed, which we have had occasion to examine. But even could the Sunday Lord's day be traced to Ignatius, the disciple of John, it would then come no nearer being an apostolic institution than does the Catholic festival of the Passover, which can be traced to Polycarp, another of John's disciples, who claimed to have received it from John himself!

CHAPTER XIV.

THE FIRST WITNESSES FOR SUNDAY.

Origin of Sunday observance the subject of present inquiry—Contradict-
ory statements of Mosheim and Neander—The question between
them stated, and the true data for deciding that question—The New
Testament furnishes no support for Mosheim's statement—Epistle of
Barnabas a forgery—The testimony of Pliny determines nothing in
the case—The epistle of Ignatius probably spurious, and certainly interpolated so far as it is made to sustain Sunday—Decision of the
question.

UNDAY, the first day of the week, is now
almost universally observed as the Christian
Sabbath. The origin of this institution is
still before us as the subject of inquiry. This is presented by two eminent church historians ; but so directly
do they contradict each other, that it is a question of
curious interest to determine which of them states the
truth. Thus Mosheim writes respecting the first century :—[1]

"All Christians were unanimous in setting apart the first day
of the week, on which the triumphant Saviour arose from the
dead, for the solemn celebration of public worship. This pious
custom, which was derived from the example of the church of

---

[1] Maclaine's Mosheim, cent. 1, part 2, chap. 4, sec. 4. I have given Maclaine's
translation, not because it is an accurate version of Mosheim, but because it is so
much used in support of the first-day Sabbath. Maclaine, in his preface to
Mosheim, says : "I have sometimes taken considerable liberties with my author."
And he tells us what these liberties are by saying that he "often added a
few sentences to render an observation more striking, a fact more clear, a portrait

Jerusalem, was founded upon the express appointment of the apostles, who consecrated that day to the same sacred purpose, and was observed universally throughout the Christian churches, as appears from the united testimonies of the most credible writers."

Now let us read what Neander, the most distinguished of church historians, says of this apostolic authority for Sunday observance :—

" The festival of Sunday, like all other festivals, was always only a human ordinance, and it was far from the intentions of the apostles to establish a divine command in this respect, far from them, and from the early apostolic church, to transfer the laws of the Sabbath to Sunday. Perhaps at the end of the second century a false application of this kind had begun to take place; for men appear by that time to have considered laboring on Sunday as a sin." [2]

---

more finished." The present quotation is an instance of these liberties. Dr. Murdock, of New Haven, who has given " a close, literal version " of Mosheim, gives the passage thus :—

" The Christians of this century, assembled for the worship of God, and for their advancement in piety, on the first day of the week, the day on which Christ reassumed his life; for that this day was set apart for religious worship by the apostles themselves, and that, after the example of the church at Jerusalem, it was generally observed, we have unexceptionable testimony."—*Murdock's Mosheim*, cent. 1, part 2, chap. 4, sec. 4.

[2] Neander's Church History, translated by H. J. Rose, p. 186. To break the force of this strong statement of Neander, that " the festival of Sunday, like all other festivals, was always only a human ordinance, and it was far from the intentions of the apostles to establish a divine command in this respect, far from them, and from the early apostolic church, to transfer the laws of the Sabbath to Sunday," two things have been said :—

1. That Neander, in a later edition of his work, retracted this declaration. It is true that in re-writing his work, he omitted this sentence. But he inserted nothing of a contrary character, and the general tenor of the revised edition is in this place precisely the same as in that from which this out-spoken statement is taken.

In proof of this, we cite from the later edition of Neander his statement in this very place of what constituted Sunday observance in the early church. He says:—

How shall we determine which of these historians is in the right? Neither of them lived in the apostolic age of the church. Mosheim was a writer of the eighteenth century, and Neander, of the nineteenth. Of necessity, therefore, they must learn the facts in the case from the writings of that period which have come down to us. These contain all the testimony which can have any claim to be admitted in deciding this case. These are, first, the inspired writings of the New Testament; secondly, the reputed productions of such writers of that age as are supposed to mention the first day; viz., the epistle of Barnabas, the letter of Pliny, governor of Bythinia, to the emperor Trajan, and the epistle of Ignatius. These are all the writings prior to the middle of the second century—and this is late enough to amply cover the ground of Mosheim's statement—which can be introduced as even referring to the first day of the week.

The questions to be decided by this testimony are these: Did the apostles set apart Sunday for divine worship, as Mosheim affirms? or does the evidence in the case show that the festival of Sunday, like all other

---

"Sunday was distinguished as a day of joy, by being exempted from fasts, and by the circumstance that prayer was performed on this day in a standing and not in a kneeling posture, as Christ, by his resurrection, had raised up fallen man again to heaven."—*Torrey's Neander,* vol. 1, p. 295, ed. 1852.

This is an accurate account of early Sunday observance, as we shall hereafter show; and that such observance was only a human ordinance, of which no feature was ever commanded by the apostles, will be very manifest to every person who attempts to find any precept for any particular of it in the New Testament.

2. But the other method of setting aside this testimony of Neander is to assert that he did not mean to deny that the apostles established a divine command for Sunday as the Christian Sabbath, but meant to assert that they did not establish a divine command for Sunday as a Catholic festival! Those who make this assertion must know that it is false. Neander expressly denies that the apostles either constituted or recognized Sunday as a Sabbath, and he represents Sunday as a mere festival from the very first of its observance, and established only by human authority.

festivals, was always only a human ordinance, as is affirmed by Neander?

It is certain that the New Testament contains no appointment of Sunday for the solemn celebration of public worship. And it is equally true that there is no example of the church of Jerusalem on which to found such observance. The New Testament, therefore, furnishes no support[3] for the statement of Mosheim.

The three epistles which have come down to us purporting to have been written in the apostolic age, or immediately subsequent to that age, next come under examination. These are all that remain to us of a period more extended than that embraced in the statement of Mosheim. He speaks of the first century only; but we summon all the writers of that century, and of the following one prior to the time of Justin Martyr, A. D. 140, who are even supposed to mention the first day of the week. Thus the reader is furnished with all the data in the case. The epistle of Barnabas speaks as follows in behalf of the first-day observance :—

" Lastly he saith unto them, Your new moons and your sabbaths I cannot bear them. Consider what he means by it; the sabbaths, says he, which ye now keep, are not acceptable unto me, but those which I have made; when resting from all things, I shall begin the eighth day, that is, the beginning of the other world; for which cause we observe the eighth day with gladness, in which Jesus arose from the dead, and having manifested himself to his disciples, ascended into heaven." [4]

It might be reasonably concluded that Mosheim would place great reliance upon this testimony as coming

---

[3] See chapters 10 and 11, in which the New Testament has been carefully examined on this point.

[4] Epistle of Barnabas, 13: 9, 10; or as others divide the epistle, chapter 15.

from an apostle, and as being somewhat better suited to sustain the sacredness of Sunday than anything previously examined by us. Yet he frankly acknowledges that this epistle is spurious. Thus he says :—

"The epistle of Barnabas was the production of some Jew who, most probably, lived in this century, and whose mean abilities and superstitious attachment to Jewish fables, show, notwithstanding the uprightness of his intentions, that he must have been a very different person from the true Barnabas, who was St. Paul's companion." [5]

In another work, Mosheim says of this epistle :—

"As to what is suggested by some, of its having been written by that Barnabas who was the friend and companion of St. Paul, the futility of such a notion is easily to be made apparent from the letter itself; several of the opinions and interpretations of Scripture which it contains having in them so little of either truth, dignity, or force as to render it impossible that they could ever have proceeded from the pen of a man divinely instructed." [6]

Neander speaks thus of this epistle :—

"It is impossible that we should acknowledge this epistle to belong to that Barnabas who was worthy to be the companion of the apostolic labors of St. Paul." [7]

Prof. Stuart bears a similar testimony :—

"That a man by the name of Barnabas wrote this epistle I doubt not; that the chosen associate of Paul wrote it, I, with many others, must doubt." [8]

Dr. Killen, Professor of Ecclesiastical History, to the General Assembly of the Presbyterian church of Ireland, uses the following language :—

---

[5] Eccl. Hist., cent. 1, part 2, chap. 2, sec. 21.

[6] Historical Commentaries, cent. 1, sec. 53. [7] Rose's Neander, p. 407.

[8] Note appended to Gurney's History, Authority and Use of the Sabbath, p. 86.

"The tract known as the Epistle of Barnabas was probably composed in A. D. 135. It is the production, apparently, of a convert from Judaism who took special pleasure in allegorical interpretation of Scripture."[9]

Prof. Hackett bears this testimony:—

"The letter still extant, which was known as that of Barnabas even in the second century, cannot be defended as genuine."[10]

Mr. Milner speaks of the reputed epistle of Barnabas as follows:—

"It is a great injury to him to apprehend the epistle, which goes by his name, to be his."[11]

Kitto speaks of this production as—

"The so-called epistle of Barnabas, probably a forgery of the second century."[12]

Says the Encyclopedia of Religious Knowledge, speaking of the Barnabas of the New Testament:—

"He could not be the author of a work so full of forced allegories, extravagant and unwarrantable explications of Scripture, together with stories concerning beasts, and such like conceits, as make up the first part of this epistle."[13]

Eusebius, the earliest of church historians, places this epistle in the catalogue of spurious books. Thus he says:—

"Among the spurious must be numbered both the books called, 'The Acts of Paul,' and that called, 'Pastor,' and 'The Revelation of Peter.' Besides these, the books called, 'The Epistle

---

[9] Ancient Church, pp. 367, 368.   [10] Commentary on Acts, p. 251.

[11] History of the Church, cent. 1, chap. 15.

[12] Cyclopedia Biblical Literature, art. Lord's day, tenth ed., 1858.

[13] Encyclopedia of Religious Knowledge, art., Barnabas's Epistle.

of Barnabas,' and what are called, 'The Institutions of the Apostles.' " [14]

Sir Wm. Domville speaks as follows :—

" But the epistle was not written by Barnabas ; it was not merely unworthy of him, it would be a disgrace to him; and what is of much more consequence, it would be a disgrace to the Christian religion, as being the production of one of the authorized teachers of that religion in the times of the apostles, which circumstance would seriously damage the evidence of its divine origin. Not being the epistle of Barnabas, the document is, as regards the Sabbath question, nothing more than the testimony of some unknown writer to the practice of Sunday observance by some Christians of some unknown community, at some uncertain period of the Christian era, with no sufficient ground for believing that period to have been the first century." [15]

Coleman bears the following testimony :—

" The epistle of Barnabas, bearing the honored name of the companion of Paul in his missionary labors, is evidently spurious. It abounds in fabulous narratives, mystic, allegorical interpretations of the Old Testament, and fanciful conceits, and is generally agreed by the learned to be of no authority." [16]

As a specimen of the unreasonable and absurd things contained in this epistle, the following passage is quoted :—

" Neither shalt thou eat of the hyena : that is, again, be not an adulterer ; nor a corrupter of others ; neither be like to such. And wherefore so ! Because that creature every year changes its kind, and is sometimes male, and sometimes female." [17]

---

[14] Eccl. Hist., book 3, chap. 25.

[15] The Sabbath, or an Examination of the Six Texts commonly adduced from the New Testament in proof of a Christian Sabbath, p. 233.

[16] Ancient Christianity, chap. 1, sec. 2.

[17] Epistle of Barnabas, 9 : 8. In some editions it is chap. 10.

Thus first-day historians being allowed to decide the case, we are authorized to treat this epistle as a forgery. And whoever will read its ninth chapter (for it will not bear quoting) will acknowledge the justice of the conclusion. This epistle is the only writing purporting to come from the first century, except the New Testament, in which the first day is even referred to. That this furnishes no support for Sunday observance, even Mosheim acknowledges.

The next document that claims our attention is the letter of Pliny, the Roman Governor of Bythinia, to the emperor Trajan. It was written about A. D. 104. He says of the Christians of his province :—

"They affirmed that the whole of their guilt or error was, that they met on a certain stated day, before it was light, and addressed themselves in a form of prayer to Christ, as to some god, binding themselves by a solemn oath, not for the purposes of any wicked design, but never to commit any fraud, theft, or adultery ; never to falsify their word, nor deny a trust when they should be called upon to deliver it up; after which it was their custom to separate, and then re-assemble to eat in common a harmless meal." [18]

This epistle of Pliny certainly furnishes no support for Sunday observance. The case is presented in a candid manner by Coleman. He says of this extract:—

"This statement is evidence that these Christians kept a day as holy time, but whether it was the last or the first day of the week, does not appear." [19]

Charles Buck, an eminent first-day writer, saw no evidence in this epistle of first-day observance, as is

[18] Coleman's Ancient Christianity, pp. 35, 36.

[19] Ancient Christianity Exemplified, chap. 26, sec. 2.

manifest from the indefinite translation which he gives it. Thus he cites the epistle :—

" These persons declare that their whole crime, if they are guilty, consists in this : that on certain days they assemble before sunrise to sing alternately the praises of Christ as of God." [20]

Tertullian, who wrote A. D. 200, speaks of this very statement of Pliny's thus :—

" He found in their religious services nothing but meetings *at early morning* for singing hymns to Christ and God, and sealing home their way of life by a united pledge to be faithful to their religion, forbidding murder, adultery, dishonesty, and other crimes." [21]

Tertullian certainly found in this no reference to the festival of Sunday.

Mr. W. B. Taylor speaks of this stated day as follows :—

" As the Sabbath-day appears to have been quite as commonly observed at this date as the sun's day (if not even more so), it is just as probable that this ' stated day ' referred to by Pliny was the seventh day, as that it was the first day ; though the latter is generally *taken for granted*." [22]

Taking for granted the very point that should be proved, is no new feature in the evidence thus far examined in support of first-day observance. Although Mosheim relies on this expression of Pliny's as a chief support of Sunday, yet he speaks thus of the opinion of another learned man :—

" B. Just. Hen. Boehmer would indeed have us to understand this day to have been the same with the Jewish Sabbath." [23]

[20] Buck's Theological Dictionary, article, Christians.

[21] Tertullian's Apology, sec. 2.   [22] Obligation of the Sabbath, p. 300.

[23] Historical Commentaries, cent. 1, sec. 47.

This testimony of Pliny was written a few years subsequent to the time of the apostles. It relates to a church which probably had been founded by the apostle Peter.[24] It is certainly far more probable that this church, only forty years after the death of Peter, was keeping the fourth commandment, than that it was observing a day never enjoined by divine authority. It must be conceded that this testimony from Pliny proves nothing in support of Sunday observance; for it does not designate what day of the week was thus observed.

The epistles of Ignatius of Antioch, so often quoted in behalf of first-day observance, next claim our attention. He is represented as saying :—

" Wherefore if they who are brought up in these ancient laws came nevertheless to the newness of hope, no longer observing sabbaths, but keeping the Lord's day, in which also our life is sprung up by him, and through his death, whom yet some deny (by which mystery we have been brought to believe, and therefore wait that we may be found the disciples of Jesus Christ, our only master): how shall we be able to live different from him; whose disciples the very prophets themselves being, did by the Spirit expect him as their master." [25]

Two important facts relative to this quotation are worthy of particular notice : 1. That the epistles of Ignatius are acknowledged to be spurious by first-day writers of high authority; and those epistles which some of them except as possibly genuine, do not include in their number the epistle to the Magnesians, from which the above quotation is made, nor do they say anything relative to first-day observance; 2. That the

---

[24] 1 Pet. 1:1. See Clarke's Commentary, preface to the epistles of Peter.

[25] Ignatius to the Magnesians, 3:3-5; or, as others divide the epistle, chap. 9.

epistle to the Magnesians would say nothing of any day, were it not that the word *day* had been fraudulently inserted by the translator! In support of the first of these propositions, the following testimony from **Dr. Killen** is adduced :—

"In the sixteenth century, fifteen letters were brought out from beneath the mantle of a hoary antiquity, and offered to the world as the productions of the pastor of Antioch. Scholars refused to receive them on the terms required, and forthwith eight of them were admitted to be forgeries. In the seventeenth century, the seven remaining letters, in a somewhat altered form, again came forth from obscurity, and claimed to be the works of Ignatius. Again discerning critics refused to acknowledge their pretensions ; but curiosity was roused by this second apparition, and many expressed an earnest desire to obtain a sight of the real epistles. Greece, Syria, Palestine, and Egypt were ransacked in search of them, and at length three letters are found. The discovery creates general gratulation; it is confessed that four of the epistles so lately asserted to be genuine, are apocryphal ; and it is boldly said that the three now forthcoming are above challenge. But truth still refuses to be compromised, and sternly disowns these claimants for her approbation. The internal evidence of these three epistles abundantly attests that, like the last three books of the Sibyl, they are only the last shifts of a grave imposture." [26]

The same writer thus states the opinion of Calvin:—

"It is no mean proof of sagacity of the great Calvin, that, upwards of three hundred years ago, he passed a sweeping sentence of condemnation on these Ignatian epistles." [27]

Of the three epistles of Ignatius still claimed as genuine, Prof. C. F. Hudson speaks as follows :—

"Ignatius of Antioch was martyred probably A. D. 115. Of

[26] Ancient Church, pp. 413, 414.   [27] Id., p. 427.

the eight epistles ascribed to him, three are genuine ; viz., those addressed to Polycarp, the Ephesians, and the Romans." [28]

It will be observed that the three epistles which are here mentioned as genuine do not include that epistle from which the quotation in behalf of Sunday is taken, and it is a fact, also, that they contain no allusion to Sunday. Sir Wm. Domville, an anti-Sabbatarian writer, uses the following language :—

" Every one at all conversant with such matters is aware that the works of Ignatius have been more interpolated and corrupted than those of any other of the ancient Fathers ; and also that some writings have been attributed to him which are wholly spurious." [29]

Robinson, an eminent English Baptist writer of the last century, expresses the following opinion of the epistles ascribed to Ignatius, Barnabas, and others :—

" If any of the writings attributed to those who are called apostolic Fathers, as Ignatius, teacher at Antioch, Polycarp, at Smyrna, Barnabas, who was half a Jew, and Hermas, who was a brother to Pius, teacher at Rome, if any of these be genuine, of which there is great reason to doubt, they only prove the piety and illiteracy of the good men. Some are worse, and the best not better, than the godly epistles of the lower sort of Baptists and Quakers in the time of the civil war in England. Barnabas and Hermas both mention baptism ; but both of these books are contemptible reveries of wild and irregular geniuses." [30]

The doubtful character of these Ignatian epistles is thus sufficiently attested. The quotation in behalf of Sunday is not taken from one of the three epistles that are still claimed as genuine ; and what is still further to be observed, it would say nothing in behalf of any

---

[28] Future Life, p. 290.   [29] Examination of the Six Texts, p. 237.
[30] Ecclesiastical Researches, chap. 6, pp. 50, 51, ed. 1792.

16

day were it not for an extraordinary license, not to
say fraud, which the translator has used in inserting the
word *day*. This fact is shown with critical accuracy by
Kitto, whose Cyclopedia is in high repute among first-
day scholars. He presents the original of Ignatius, with
comments and a translation, as follows :—

" We must here notice one other passage . . . as bearing on the
subject of the Lord's day, though it certainly contains no mention
of it. It occurs in the epistle of Ignatius to the Magnesians
(about A. D. 100). The whole passage is confessedly obscure,
and the text may be corrupt. . . . The passage is as follows :—

" Εἰ οὖν ὁι ἐν παλαιοῖς πράγμασιν ἀναστραφέντες, εἰς καινότητα ἐλπίδος ἦλθον—
μηκέτι σαββατίζοντες, ἀλλὰ κατὰ κυριακὴν ζωὴν ζῶντες—(ἐν ᾗ καὶ ἡ ζωὴ ἡμῶν
ἀνέτειλεν δἰ αὐτοῦ, etc.)[31]

" Now many commentators assume (on what ground does not
appear), that after κυριακὴν [Lord's] the word ἡμέραν [day] is to be
understood. . . . Let us now look at the passage simply as it
stands. The defect of the sentence is the want of a substantive to
which αὐτοῦ can refer. This defect, so far from being remedied, is
rendered still more glaring by the introduction of ἡμέρα. Now if
we take κυριακὴ ζωὴ as simply ' the life of the Lord,' having a more
personal meaning, it certainly goes nearer to supplying the substantive to αὐτοῦ. . . . Thus upon the whole the meaning might
be given thus :—

" If those who lived under the old dispensation have come to
the newness of hope, no longer keeping sabbaths, but living according to our Lord's life (in which, as it were, our life has risen
again through him, etc.). . . . On this view the passage does
not refer at all to the Lord's day ; but even on the opposite supposition, it cannot be regarded as affording any positive evidence
to the early use of the term ' Lord's day ' (for which it is often
cited), since the material word ἡμέρα [day] is purely conject-
ural." [32]

---

[31] Ignatius ad Magnesios, sec. 9.
[32] Cyclopedia Biblical Literature, article. Lord's Day.

The learned Morer, a clergyman of the church of England, confirms this statement of Kitto. He renders Ignatius thus :—

" If, therefore, they who were well versed in the works of ancient days came to newness of hope, not sabbatizing, but living according to the dominical life, etc. . . . The Medicean copy, the best and most like that of Eusebius, leaves no scruple, because ζωὴν is expressed, and determines the word *dominical* to the person of Christ, and not to the day of his resurrection." [33]

Sir Wm. Domville speaks on this point as follows :—

" Judging, therefore, by the tenor of the epistle itself, the literal translation of the passage in discussion, ' no longer observing sabbaths,' but living according to the Lord's life, appears to give its true and proper meaning ; and if this be so, Ignatius, whom Mr. Gurney [34] puts forward as a material witness to prove the observance of the Lord's day in the beginning of the second century, fails to prove any such fact, it appearing on a thorough examination of his testimony that he does not even mention the Lord's day, nor in any way allude to the religious observance of it, whether by that name or by any other." [35]

It is manifest, therefore, that this famous quotation has no reference whatever to the first day of the week, and that it furnishes no evidence that that day was known in the time of Ignatius by the title of Lord's day.[36] The evidence is now before the reader which must determine whether Mosheim or Neander spoke in

---

[33] Dialogues on the Lord's Day, pp. 206, 207.

[34] A first-day writer, author of the " History, Authority, and Use of the Sabbath."

[35] Examination of the Six Texts, pp. 250, 251.

[36] For a fuller statement of the case of Ignatius, see " Testimony of the Fathers," pp. 26–30. The quotation from Ignatius examined in this chapter is there shown, according to the connection, to relate, not to New-Testament Christians, but to the ancient prophets.

accordance with the facts in the case. And thus it appears that in the New Testament, and in the uninspired writings of the period referred to, there is absolutely nothing to sustain the strong Sunday statement of Mosheim. When we come to the fourth century, we shall find a statement by him which essentially modifies what he has here said. Of the epistles ascribed to Barnabas, Pliny, and Ignatius, we have found that the first is a forgery; that the second speaks of a stated day without defining what one; and that the third, which is probably a spurious document, would say nothing relative to Sunday, if the advocates of first-day sacredness had not interpolated the word *day* into the document! We can hardly avoid the conclusion that Mosheim spoke on this subject as a doctor of divinity, and not as a historian; and with the firmest conviction that we speak the truth, we say with Neander, " The festival of Sunday was always only a human ordinance."

CHAPTER XV.

EXAMINATION OF A FAMOUS FALSEHOOD.

Were the martyrs in Pliny's time and afterward tested by the question whether they had kept Sunday or not?—Argument in the affirmative quoted from Edwards—Its origin—No facts to sustain such an argument prior to the fourth century—A single instance at the opening of that century all that can be claimed in support of the assertion—Sunday not even alluded to in that instance—Testimony of Mosheim relative to the work in which this is found.

CERTAIN doctors of divinity have made a special effort to show that the "stated day" of Pliny's epistle is the first day of the week. For this purpose they adduce a fabulous narrative which the more reliable historians of the church have not deemed worthy of record. The argument is this: In Pliny's time and afterward, that is, from the close of the first century and onward, whenever the Christians were brought before their persecutors for examination, they were asked whether they had kept the Lord's day, this term being used to designate the first day of the week. And hence two facts are asserted to be established: 1. That when Pliny says that the Christians who were examined by him were accustomed to meet on a stated day, that day was undoubtedly the first day of the week; 2. That the observance of the first day of the week was the grand test by which Christians were known to their heathen persecutors; 3. That "Lord's

day" was the name by which the first day of the week
was known in the time of Pliny, a few years after the
death of John.   To prove these points, Dr. Edwards
makes the following statement :—

"Hence the fact that their persecutors, when they wished to
know whether men were Christians, were accustomed to put to
them this question; viz., '*Dominicum servasti* (Hast thou kept
the Lord's day)?' If they had, they were Christians.   This was
the badge of their Christianity, in distinction from Jews and
pagans.   And if they said they had, and would not recant, they
must be put to death.   And what, when they continued steadfast, was their answer? '*Christianus sum; intermittere non pos-
sum* (I am a Christian; I cannot omit it).' It is a badge of my
religion, and the man who assumes it must of course keep the
Lord's day, because it is the will of his Lord; and should he
abandon it, he would be an apostate from his religion." [1]

Mr. Gurney, an English first-day writer of some
note, uses the same argument and for the same purpose.[2]   The importance attached to this statement, and
the prominence given to it by the advocates of first-day
sacredness, render it proper that its merits should be
examined.   Dr. Edwards gives no authority for his
statement; but Mr. Gurney traces the story to Dr.
Andrews, bishop of Winchester, who claimed to have
taken it from the *Acta Martyrum,* an ancient collection
of the acts of the martyrs.   It was in the early part of
the seventeenth century that Bishop Andrews first
brought this forward in his speech in the court of Star
Chamber, against Thraske, who was accused before that
arbitrary tribunal of maintaining the heretical opinion
that Christians are bound to keep the seventh day as

---

[1] Sabbath Manual, p. 120.

[2] See his "History, Authority, and Use of the Sabbath," chap. 4, pp. 87, 88

the Sabbath of the Lord. The story was first produced, therefore, for the purpose of confounding an observer of the Sabbath when on trial by his enemies for keeping that day. Sir Wm. Domville, an able anti-Sabbatarian writer, thus traces out the matter:—

" The bishop, as we have seen, refers to the *Acta* of the martyrs as justifying his assertion respecting the question, *Dominicum servasti ?* but he does not cite a single instance from them in which that question was put. We are left, therefore, to hunt out the instances for ourselves, wherever, if anywhere, they are to be found. The most complete collection of the memoirs and legends still extant, relative to the lives and sufferings of the Christian martyrs, is that by Ruinart, entitled, ' *Acta primorum Martyrum sincera et selecta.*' I have carefully consulted that work, and I take upon myself to affirm that among the questions there stated to have been put to the martyrs in and before the time of Pliny, and for nearly two hundred years afterwards, the question, *Dominicum servasti ?* does not once occur ; nor any equivalent question." [3]

This shows at once that no proof can be obtained from this quarter, either that the " stated day " of Pliny was the first day of the week, or that the martyrs of the early church were tested by the question whether they had observed it or not. It also shows the statement to be false that the martyrs of Pliny's time called Sunday the Lord's day, and kept it as such. After quoting all the questions put to martyrs in and before Pliny's time, and thus proving that no such question as is alleged was put to them, Domville says :—

" This much may suffice to show that *Dominicum servasti ?* was no question in Pliny's time, as Mr. Gurney intends us to believe it was. I have, however, still other proof of Mr. Gur-

---

[3] Examination of the Six Texts, pp. 258–261.

ney's unfair dealing with the subject, but I defer stating it for
the present, that I may proceed in the inquiry, What may have
been the authority on which Bishop Andrews relied when stating
that *Dominicum servasti?* was ever a usual question put by the
heathen persecutors? I shall with this view pass over the martyrdoms which intervened between Pliny's time and the fourth
century, as they contain nothing to the purpose, and shall come
at once to that martyrdom the narrative of which was, I have no
doubt, the source from which Bishop Andrews derived his question, '*Dominicum servasti* (Hold you the Lord's day)?' This
martyrdom happened A. D. 304.[4] The sufferers were Saturninus
and his four sons, and several other persons. They were taken
to Carthage, and brought before the proconsul Amulinus. In
the account given of their examinations by him, the phrases,
'CELEBRARE *Dominicum*,' and 'AGERE *Dominicum*,' frequently
occur, but in no instance is the verb '*servare*' used in reference
to *Dominicum*. I mention this chiefly to show that when Bishop
Andrews, alluding, as no doubt he does, to the narrative of this
martyrdom, says the question was, *Dominicum servasti?* it is
very clear he had not his author at hand, and that in trusting to
his memory, he coined a phrase of his own." [5]

Domville quotes at length the conversation between
the proconsul and the martyrs, which is quite similar in
most respects to Gurney's and Edward's quotation from
Andrews. He then adds :—

"The narrative of the martyrdom of Saturninus being the
only one which has the appearance of supporting the assertion
of Bishop Andrews that, 'Hold you the Lord's day?' was the
usual question to the martyrs, what if I should prove that even
this narrative affords no support to that assertion? yet nothing
is more easy than this proof; for Bishop Andrews has quite mistaken the meaning of the word *Dominicum* in translating it 'the
Lord's day.' It had no such meaning. It was a barbarous

---

[4] The date in Baronius is A. D. 303.

[5] Examination of the Six Texts, pp. 263–265.

word in use among some of the ecclesiastical writers in, and subsequent to, the fourth century, to express sometimes a church, and at other times the Lord's supper, but NEVER the Lord's day.[6] My authorities on this point are—

"1. Ruinart, who, upon the word *Dominicum*, in the narrative of the martyrdom of Saturninus, has a note, in which he says it is a word signifying the Lord's supper [7] ('*Dominicum vero desinat sacra mysteria*'), and he quotes Tertullian and Cyprian in support of this interpretation.

"2. The editors of the Benedictine edition of St. Augustine's works. They state that the word *Dominicum* has the two meanings of a church and the Lord's supper. For the former, they quote, among other authorities, a canon of the council of Neo Cesarea. For the latter meaning, they quote Cyprian, and refer also to St. Augustine's account of his conference with the Donatists, in which allusion is made to the narrative of the martyrdom of Saturninus.[8]

"3. Gesner, who, in his Latin Thesaurus, published in 1749,

---

[6] Note by Domville. "*Dominicum* is not, as may at first be supposed, an adjective, of which *diem* [day] is the understood substantive. It is itself a substantive, neuter, as appears from the passage, '*Quia non potest intermitti Dominicum*,' in the narrative respecting Saturninus. The Latin adjective *Dominicus*, when intended to refer to the Lord's day, is never, I believe, used without its substantive *dies* [day] being expressed. In all the narratives contained in Ruinart's *Acta Martyrum*, I find but two instances of mention being made of the Lord's day, and in both these instances the substantive *dies* [day] is expressed."

[7] This testimony is certainly decisive. It is the interpretation of the compiler of the *Acta Martyrum* himself, and is given with direct reference to the particular instance under discussion. An independent confirmation of Domville's authorities may be found in Lucius's Eccl. Hist., cent. 4, chap. 6: "Fit mentio aliquoties locorum istorum in quibus convenerint Christiani. in historia persecutionis sub Diocletiano et Maximino. Et apparet, ante Constantinum etiam, locos eos fuisse mediocriter exstructos atque exornatos: quos seu Templa appellarunt seu Dominica; ut apud Eusebium (li. 9, c. 10) et Ruffinum (li. 1, c. 3)."

It is certain that *Dominicum* is here used as designating a place of divine worship. Dr. Twisse, in his "Morality of the Fourth Commandment," p. 122, says: "The ancient Fathers, both Greek and Latin, called temples by the name of *dominica* and κυριακα."

[8] Domville cites St. Augustine's Works, vol. 5, pp. 116, 117, Antwerp ed. A. D. 1700.

gives both meanings to the word *Dominicum*. For that of the Lord's supper, he quotes Cyprian; for that of a church, he quotes Cyprian and also Hillary.[9]

Domville states other facts of interest bearing on this point, and then pays his respects to Mr. Gurney as follows :—

"It thus appearing that the reference made by Bishop Andrews to the 'Acts of Martyrs' completely fails to establish his dictum respecting the question alleged to have been put to the martyrs, and it also appearing that there existed strong and obvious reasons for not placing implicit reliance upon that dictum, what are we to think of Mr. Gurney's regard for truth, when we find he does not scruple to tell his readers that the 'stated day' mentioned in Pliny's letter as that on which the Christians held their religious assemblies, was 'clearly the first day of the week,' as is proved by the very question which it was customary for the Roman persecutors to address to the martyrs, '*Dominicum servasti* (Hast thou kept the Lord's day)?' For this unqualified assertion, prefixed as it is by the word 'clearly,' in order to make it the more impressive, Mr. Gurney is without any excuse." [10]

The justice of Domville's language cannot be questioned, when he characterizes this favorite first-day argument as—

"One of those daring misstatements of facts so frequent in theological writings, and which, from the confident tone so generally assumed by the writers on such occasions, are usually received without examination, and allowed, in consequence, to pass current for truth." [11]

The investigation to which this statement has been subjected, shows, 1. That no such question as, Hast

----

[1] Examination of the Six Texts, pp. 267, 268.

[10] Id., pp. 270, 271.　　　　　　　[11] Id., pp. 272, 273.

thou kept the Lord's day? is upon record, as proposed to the martyrs in the time of Pliny; 2. That no such question was asked to any martyr prior to the commencement of the fourth century; 3. That a single instance of martyrdom in which any question of the kind was asked, is all that can be claimed; 4. That in this one case, which is all that has even the slightest appearance of sustaining the story under examination, a correct translation of the original Latin shows that the question had no relation whatever to the observance of Sunday! All this has been upon the assumption that the *Acta Martyrum*, in which this story is found, is an authentic work. Let Mosheim testify relative to the character of this work for veracity :—

"As to those accounts which have come down to us under the title of *Acta Martyrum*, or the Acts of the Martyrs, their authority is certainly for the most part of a very questionable nature ; indeed, speaking generally, it might be coming nearer to the truth, perhaps, were we to say that they are entitled to no sort of credit whatever." [12]

Such is the authority of the work from which this story is taken. It is not strange that first-day historians should leave the repetition of it to theologians.

Such are the facts respecting this extraordinary falsehood. They constitute so complete an exposure of this famous historical argument for Sunday as to consign it to the just contempt of all honest men. But this is too valuable an argument to be lightly surrendered, and, moreover, it is as truthful as are certain other of the historical arguments for Sunday. It will not do to give up this argument because of its dishonesty; for others will have to go with it for possessing the same character.

---

[12] Historical Commentaries, cent. 1, sec. 32.

Since the publication of Domville's elaborate work, James Gilfillan, of Scotland, has written a large volume entitled, " The Sabbath," which has been extensively circulated both in Europe and America, and is esteemed a standard work by the American Tract Society and by first-day denominations in general. Gilfillan had read Domville, as appears from his statements on pages 10, 142, 143, 616, of his volume. He was therefore acquainted with Domville's exposure of the fraud respecting " *Dominicum servasti?* " But though he was acquainted with this exposure, he offers not one word in reply. On the contrary, he repeats the story with as much assurance as though it had not been proved a falsehood. But as Domville had shown up the matter from the *Acta Martyrum,* it was necessary for Gilfillan to trace it to some other authority, and so he assigns it to Cardinal Baronius. Here are Gilfillan's words :—

" From the days of the apostles downward for many years, the followers of Christ had no enemies more fierce and unrelenting than that people [the Jews], who cursed them in the synagogue, sent out emissaries into all countries to calumniate their Master and them, and were abbettors, wherever they could, to the martyrdom of men, such as Polycarp, of whom the world was not worthy. Among the reasons of this deadly enmity was the change of the Sabbatic day. The Romans, though they had no objection on this score, punished the Christians for the faithful observance of their day of rest, one of the testing questions put to the martyrs being, ' *Dominicum servasti* (Have you kept the Lord's day)? '—*Baron. An. Eccles.,* A. D. 303, Num. 35, etc." [13]

Gilfillan having reproduced this statement, and assigned as his authority the annalist Baronius, more recent first-day writers take courage, and repeat the story

[13] The Sabbath, by James Gilfillan, p. 7.

after him. Now they are all right, as they think. What if the *Acta Martyrum* has failed them? Domville ought to have gone to Baronius, who, in their judgment, is the true source of information in this matter. Had he done this, they say, he would have been saved from misleading his readers. But let us ascertain what evil Domville has done in this case. It all consists in the assertion of two things out of the *Acta Martyrum* :—[14]

1. That no such question as " *Dominicum servasti?* " was addressed to any martyr till the early part of the fourth century, some two hundred years after the time of Pliny.

2. That the question even then did not relate to what is called the Lord's day, but to the Lord's supper.

Now it is a remarkable fact that Gilfillan has virtually admitted the truth of the first of these statements, for the earliest instance which he could find in Baronius is A. D. 303, as his reference plainly shows. It differs only one year from the date assigned in Ruinart's *Acta Martyrum,* and relates to the very case which Domville has quoted from that work! Domville's first and most important statement is therefore vindicated by

[14] To break the force of Domville's statement, in which he exposes the story originally told by Bishop Andrews as coming from the *Acta Martyrum,* it is said that Domville used Ruinart's *Acta Martyrum,* and that Ruinart was not born till thirty-one years after Bishop Andrews's death, so that Domville did not go to the same book that was used by the bishop, and therefore failed to find what he found. Those who raise this point betray their ignorance or expose their dishonesty. The *Acta Martyrum* is a collection of the memoirs of the martyrs, written by their friends from age to age. Ruinart did not write a new work, but simply edited "the most valued collection" of these memoirs that has ever appeared. (See McClintock and Strong's Cyclopedia, vol. 1, pp. 56, 57.) Domville used Ruinart's edition, because, as he expresses it, it is "the most complete collection of the memoirs and legends still extant, relative to the lives and sufferings of the Christian Martyrs." Domville's use of Ruinart was, therefore, in the highest degree just and right.

Gilfillan himself, though he has not the frankness to say this in so many words.

Domville's second point is that *Dominicum*, when used as a noun, as in the present case, signifies either a church or the Lord's supper, but never signifies Lord's day. He establishes the fact by incontestible evidence. Gilfillan was acquainted with all this. He could not answer Domville, and yet he was not willing to abandon the falsehood which Domville had exposed. So he turns from the *Acta Martyrum*, in which the compiler directly defines the word to mean precisely what Domville asserts, and brings forward the great Romish annalist, Cardinal Baronius. Now, say our first-day friends, we are to have the truth from a high authority. Gilfillan has found in Baronius an express statement that the martyrs were tested by the question, "Have you kept the Lord's day?" No matter, then, as to the *Acta Martyrum*, from which Bishop Andrews first produced this story. That, indeed, has failed us, but we have in its stead the weighty testimony of the great Baronius. To be sure, he fixes this test no earlier than the fourth century, which renders it of no avail as proof that Pliny's stated day was Sunday; but it is worth much to have Baronius bear witness that certain martyrs in the fourth century were put to death because they observed the Sunday Lord's day.

But these exultant thoughts are vain. I must state a grave fact in plain language : Gilfillan has deliberately falsified the testimony of Baronius ! That historian records at length the martyrdom of Saturninus and his company in Northern Africa in A. D. 303. It is the very story which Domville has cited from the *Acta Martyrum*, and

Baronius repeatedly indicates that he himself copied it from that work. He gives the various questions propounded by the proconsul, and the several answers which were returned by each of the martyrs. I copy from Baronius the most important of these. They were arrested while celebrating the Lord's sacrament according to custom.[15] The following is the charge on which they were arrested: They had celebrated the *Collectam Dominicum* against the command of the emperors.[16] The proconsul asked the first whether he had celebrated the *Collectam*, and he replied that he was a Christian, and had done this.[17] Another says, " I have not only been in the *Collecta*, but I have celebrated the *Dominicum* with the brethren, because I am a Christian."[18] Another says, " We have celebrated the *Dominicum*, because the *Dominicum* cannot be neglected." [19] Another said that the *Collecta* was made [or observed] at his house.[20] The proconsul, questioning again one of those already examined, received this answer: " The *Dominicum* cannot be disregarded; the law so commands." [21] When one was asked whether the *Collecta* was made [or observed] at his house, he answered, " In

---

[15] Ibique celebrantes ex more Dominica Sacramenta.—*Baronius*, Tome 3, p. 848, A. D. 303, No. 36, Lucæ, A. D. 1738.

[16] Qui contra edictum Imperatorum, et Cæsarum Collectam Dominicam celebrassent.—*Baronius*, Tome 3, p. 348, A. D. 303, No. 39.

[17] Utrum Collectam fecisset. Qui cum se Christianum, et in Collecta fuisse profiteretur.—Id.

[18] Nam et in Collecta fui, et Dominicum cum fratribus celebravi, quia Christiana sum.—Id., No. 43, p. 344. This was spoken by a female martyr.

[19] Dominicum celebravimus. Proconsul ait: Quare? respondit: Quia non potest intermitti Dominicum.—Id., No. 46, p. 350.

[20] In cujus dome Collecta facta fuit.—Id., No. 47, p. 350.

[21] Intermitti Dominicum non potest, ait. Lex sic jubet.—Id.

my house we have celebrated the *Dominicum.*" He
added, " Without the *Dominicum,* we cannot be," or live.[22]
To another, the proconsul said that he did not wish to
know whether he was a Christian, but whether he par-
ticipated in the *Collecta.*   His reply was : " As if one
could be a Christian without the *Dominicum,* or as if the
Dominicum can be celebrated without the Christian." [23]
And he said further to the proconsul : " We have observed the *Collecta* most sacredly ; we have always convened in the *Dominicum* for reading the Lord's word." [24]
Another said : " I have been in [literally, have made]
the *Collecta* with my brethren, I have celebrated the
Dominicum." [25]   After him, another proclaimed the
Dominicum to be the hope and safety of the Christian ;
and when tortured as the others, he exclaimed, " I have
celebrated the *Dominicum* with a devoted heart, and
with my brethren I have made the *Collecta* because I
am a Christian." [26]   When the proconsul again asked
one of these whether he had conducted the *Dominicum,*
he replied that he had, because Christ was his Saviour.[27]

   I have thus given the substance of this famous ex-

---

[22] In tua, inquit proconsul, domo Collectæ factæ sunt, contra praecepta Imperatorum?   Cui Emeritus sancto Spiritu inundatus: In domo mea, inquit, egimus
Dominicum. . . . Quioniam sine Dominico esse non possumus.—Id. No. 49, pp.
350, 351.

[23] Non quaero an Christianus sis sed an Collectam feceris. . . . Quasi Christianus sine Dominico esse possit.—Id. No. 51, p. 351.

[24] Collectam, inquit, religiosissime celebravimus; ad scripturas Dominicas
legendas in Dominicum convenimus semper.—Id.

[25] Cum fratribus feci Collectam, Dominicum celebravi.—Id. No. 52, p. 351.

[26] Post quem junior Felix, spem salutemque Christianorum Dominicum esse
proclamans. . . . Ego, inquit, devota menta celebravi Dominicum; collectam
cum fratribus feci, quia Christianus sum.—Id. No. 53.

[27] Utrum egeris Dominicum. Cui respondit Saturninus: Egi Dominicum, quia
Salvator est Christus.—Id., p. 352.

amination, and have set before the reader the references therein made to the *Dominicum*. It is to be observed that *Collecta* is used as another name for *Dominicum*. Now does Baronius use either of these words to signify the Lord's day? It so happens that he has defined these words with direct reference to this very case no less than seven times. Now let us read these seven definitions :—

When Baronius records the first question addressed to these martyrs, he there defines these words as follows : " By the words *Collectam, Collectionem,* and *Dominicum,* the author always understands the sacrifice of the Mass." [28] After recording the words of that martyr who said that the law commanded the observance of the *Dominicum,* Baronius defines his statement thus : "Evidently the Christian law concerning the *Dominicum,* no doubt about celebrating the sacrifice." [29] Baronius, by the Romish words *sacrifice* and *Mass,* refers to the celebration of the Lord's supper by these martyrs. At the conclusion of the examination, he again defines the celebration of the *Dominicum.* He says : " It has been shown above in relating these things that the Christians were moved, even in the time of severe persecution, to celebrate the *Dominicum.* Evidently, as we have declared elsewhere in many places, it was a sacrifice without bloodshed, and of divine appointment." [30] He pres-

---

[28] Per Collectam namque, et Collectionem, et Dominicum, intelligit semper auctor sacrificium Missæ.—*Baronius*, Tome 3, A. D. 303, No. 39, p. 348.

[29] Scilicet lex Christiana de Dominico, nempe sacrificio celebrando.—Id., No. 47, p. 350.

[30] De celebratione Dominici; Quod autem superius in recitatis actis sit demonstratum, flagrantis persecutionis etiam tempore solicitos fuisse Christianos celebrare Dominicum, nempe (ut alias pluribus declararimus) ipsum sacrosanctum sacrificum incruentum.—Id., No. 83, p. 358.

17

ently defines *Dominicum* again, saying, " Though it is a
fact that the same expression was employed at times
with reference to the *temple* of God, yet since all the
churches upon the earth have united in this matter, and
from other things related above, it has been sufficiently
shown concerning the celebration of the *Dominicum,
that only the sacrifice of the Mass can be understood.*" [31]
Observe this last statement. He says, Though the
word has been employed to designate the temple of the
Lord, yet in the things here related it can *only* signify
the sacrifice of the Mass. These testimonies are exceedingly explicit. But Baronius has not yet finished.
In the index to Tome 3, he explains these words again
with direct reference to this very martyrdom. Under
Collecta is this statement: " The *Collecta*, the *Dominicum*,
the Mass, the same [A. D.] 303, xxxix." [32]   Under
Missa: " The Mass is the same as the *Collecta*, or
Dominicum [A. D.] 303, xxxix." [33]   Under *Dominicum:*
" To celebrate the *Dominicum* is the same as to conduct
the Mass, [A. D.] 303, xxxix.; xlix.; li." [34]

It is not possible to mistake the meaning of Baronius.
He says that *Dominicum* signifies the Mass! The celebration of the supper by these martyrs was doubtless
very different from the pompous ceremony which the
church of Rome now observes under the name of Mass.
But it was the sacrament of the Lord's supper, concern-

---

[31] Quod etsi sciamus eamdem vocem pro Dei templo interdum accipi soli-
tam; tamen quod ecclesiæ omnes solo æquatæ fuissent; ex aliis superius recitatis
de celebratione Dominici, nonisi sacrificium missæ posse intelligo, satis est dec-
laratum.—Id., No. 84, p. 359.

[32] Collecta, Dominicum, Missa, idem, 303, xxxix., p. 677.

[33] Missa idem quod Collecta, sive Dominicum, 303, xxxix., p. 702.

[34] Dominicum celebrare idem quod Missas agere, 303, xxxix.; xlix.; li., p. 684.

ing which they were tested, and for observing which they were put to a cruel death. The word *Dominicum* signifies "the sacred mysteries," as Ruinart defines it; and Baronius, in *seven* times affirming *this* definition, though acknowledging that it has sometimes been used to signify *temple of God*, plainly declares that in this record, it can have *no other meaning* than that service which the Romanists call the sacrifice of the Mass. Gilfillan had read all this, yet he dares to quote Baronius as saying that these martyrs were tested by the question, "Have you kept Lord's day?" He could not but know that he was writing a direct falsehood; but he thought the honor of God, and the advancement of the cause of truth, demanded this act at his hands.

Before Gilfillan wrote his work, Domville had called attention to the fact that the sentence, "*Dominicum servasti?*" does not occur in the *Acta Martyrum,* a different verb being used every time. But this is the popular form of this question, and must not be given up. So Gilfillan declares that Baronius uses it in his record of the martyrdoms in A. D. 303. But we have cited the different forms of questions recorded by Baronius, and find them to be precisely the same as those of the *Acta Martyrum.* "*Dominicum servasti?*" does not occur in that historian, and Gilfillan, in stating that it does, is guilty of untruth. This, however, is comparatively unimportant. But for asserting that Baronius speaks of "Lord's day" under the name of *Dominicum,* Gilfillan stands convicted of inexcusable falsehood in matters of serious importance.

CHAPTER XVI.

ORIGIN OF FIRST-DAY OBSERVANCE.

Sunday a heathen festival from remote antiquity—Origin of the name—
Reasons which induced the leaders of the church to adopt this festival
—It was the day generally observed by the Gentiles in the first cent-
uries of the Christian era—To have taken a different day would have
been exceedingly inconvenient—They hoped to facilitate the conver-
sion of the Gentiles by keeping the same day that they observed—
Three voluntary weekly festivals in the church in memory of the
Redeemer—Sunday soon elevated above the other two—Justin Martyr
—Sunday observance first found in the church of Rome—Irenæus—
First act of papal usurpation was in behalf of Sunday—Tertullian—
Earliest trace of abstinence from labor on Sunday—General statement
of facts—The Roman church made its first great attack upon the Sab-
bath by turning it into a fast.

ORE ancient than the Christian religion is the
festival of Sunday, its origin being lost in remote antiquity.   It did not originate, however,
from any divine command, nor from piety toward
God; on the contrary, it was set apart as a sacred day
by the heathen world in honor of their chief god, the sun.
It is from this fact that the first day of the week has
obtained the name of Sunday, a name by which it is
known in many languages.   Webster thus defines the
word :—

" Sunday ; so called because this day was anciently dedicated
to the sun or to its worship.   The first day of the week ; the
Christian Sabbath ; a day consecrated to rest from secular employments, and to religious worship ; the Lord's day."

And Worcester, in his large dictionary, uses similar language :—

"Sunday; so named because anciently dedicated to the sun or to its worship. The first day of the week; the Christian Sabbath, consecrated to rest from labor and to religious worship; the Lord's day."

These lexicographers call Sunday the Christian Sabbath, etc., because in the general theological literature of our language it is thus designated, though never so termed in the Bible. Lexicographers do not undertake to settle theological questions, but simply to define terms as currently used in a particular language. Though all the other days of the week have heathen names, Sunday alone was a conspicuous heathen festival in the days of the early church. The *North British Review*, in a labored attempt to justify the observance of Sunday by the Christian world, styles that day, "THE WILD SOLAR HOLIDAY [*i. e.*, festival in honor of the sun] OF ALL PAGAN TIMES." [1]

Verstegan says :—

"The most ancient Germans being pagans, and having appropriated their first day of the week to the peculiar adoration of the sun, whereof that day doth yet in our English tongue retain the name of Sunday, and appropriated the next day unto it, unto the special adoration of the moon, whereof it yet retaineth with us the name of Monday; they ordained the next day to these most heavenly planets to the particular adoration of their great reputed god, Tuisco, whereof we do yet retain in our language the name of Tuesday." [2]

The same author thus speaks concerning the idols of our Saxon ancestors :—

---

[1] Vol. 18, p. 409.   [2] Verstegan's Antiquities, p. 10, London, 1628.

"Of these, though they had many, yet seven among the rest they especially appropriated unto the seven days of the week. . . . Unto the day dedicated unto the special adoration of the idol of the sun, they gave the name of Sunday, as much as to say the sun's day, or the day of the sun. This idol was placed in a temple, and there adored and sacrificed unto, for that they believed that the sun in the firmament did with or in this idol correspond and co-operate." [3]

Jennings makes this adoration of the sun more ancient than the deliverance of Israel from Egypt. For, in speaking of the time of that deliverance, he refers to the Gentiles as—

"The idolatrous nations who, in honor to their chief god, the sun, began their day at his rising." [4]

He represents them also as setting apart Sunday in honor of the same object of adoration :—

"The day which the heathens in general consecrated to the worship and honor of their chief god, the sun, which, according to our computation, was the first day of the week." [5]

The *North British Review* thus defends the introduction of this ancient heathen festival into the Christian church :—

"That very day was the Sunday of their heathen neighbors and respective countrymen; and patriotism gladly united with expediency in making it at once their Lord's day and their Sabbath. . . . If the authority of the church is to be ignored altogether by Protestants, there is no matter; because opportunity and common expediency are surely argument enough for so cere-

---

[3] Antiquities, p. 68.

[4] Jewish Antiquities, book 3, chap. 1. See also McClintock and Strong's Cyclopedia, 4, 472, art., Idolatry : Dr. A. Clarke and Dr. Gill on Job 31 : 26; Webster under the word *Sabianism*, and Worcester under *Sabian*.

[5] Id., book 3, chap. 3.

monial a change as the mere day of the week for the observance of the rest and holy convocation of the Jewish Sabbath. That primitive church, in fact, was shut up to the adoption of the Sunday, until it became established and supreme, when it was too late to make another alteration; and it was no irreverent nor undelightful thing to adopt it, inasmuch as the first day of the week was their own high day at any rate: so that their compliance and civility were rewarded by the redoubled sanctity of their quiet festival." [6]

It would seem that something more potent than "patriotism" and "expediency" would be requisite to transform this heathen festival into the Christian Sabbath, or even to justify its introduction into the Christian church. A further statement of the reasons which prompted its introduction, and a brief notice of the earlier steps toward transforming it into a Christian institution, will occupy the remainder of this chapter. Chafie, a clergyman of the English Church, in 1652, published a work in vindication of first-day observance, entitled, "The Seventh-day Sabbath." After showing the general observance of Sunday by the heathen world in the early ages of the church, Chafie thus states the reasons which forbid the Christians' attempting to keep any other day :—

"1. Because of the contempt, scorn, and derision they thereby should be had in, among all the Gentiles with whom they lived. . . . How grievous would be their taunts and reproaches against the poor Christians living with them and under their power for their new set sacred day, had the Christians chosen any other than the Sunday. . . . 2. Most Christians then were either servants or the poorer sort of people; and the Gentiles, most probably, would not give their servants liberty to cease from working on any other set day constantly, except on their Sunday. . . . 3.

Because had they assayed such a change, it would have been but labor in vain; . . . they could never have brought it to pass."[7]

Thus it is seen that at the time when the early church began to apostatize from God and to foster in its bosom human ordinances, the heathen world—as they had long done—very generally observed the first day of the week in honor of the sun. Many of the early Fathers of the church had been heathen philosophers. Unfortunately, they brought with them into the church many of their old notions and principles. Particularly did it occur to them that by uniting with the heathen in the day of weekly celebration they should greatly facilitate their conversion. The reasons which induced the church to adopt the ancient festival of the heathen as something made ready to hand, are thus stated by Morer :—

" It is not to be denied but we borrow the name of this day from the ancient Greeks and Romans, and we allow that the old Egyptians worshiped the sun, and as a standing *memorial* of their veneration, dedicated this day to him. And we find by the influence of their examples, *other* nations, and among them the Jews themselves, doing him homage;[8] yet these abuses did not hinder the Fathers of the Christian church simply to repeal, or altogether lay by, the day or its name, but only to sanctify and improve both, as they did also the pagan temples polluted before with idolatrous services, and other instances wherein those good men were always tender to work any other change than what was evidently necessary, and in such things as were plainly inconsistent with the Christian religion; so that Sunday being the day on which the Gentiles solemnly adored that planet, and called it Sunday, partly from its influence on that day especially, and partly in respect to its divine body (as they conceived it), the

---

[7] Pp. 61, 62.   [8] 2 Kings 23: 5; Jer. 43: 23, margin.

Christians thought fit to keep the same day and the same name of it, that they might not appear causelessly peevish, and by that means hinder the conversion of the Gentiles, and bring a greater prejudice than might be otherwise taken against the gospel." [9]

In the time of Justin Martyr, Sunday was a weekly festival, widely celebrated by the heathen in honor of their god, the sun. And so, in presenting to the heathen emperor of Rome an "Apology" for his brethren, Justin takes care to tell him thrice that the Christians held their assemblies on this day of general observance.[10] Sunday, therefore, makes its first appearance in the Christian church as an institution identical in time with the weekly festival of the heathen, and Justin, who first mentions this festival, had been a heathen philosopher. Sixty years later, Tertullian acknowledges that it was not without an appearance of truth that men declared the sun to be the God of the Christians. But he answered that though they worhiped toward the east, like the heathen, and devoted Sunday to rejoicing, it was for a reason far different from sun-worship.[11] And on another occasion, in defending his brethren from the charge of sun-worship, he acknowledges that these acts—prayer toward the east, and making Sunday a day of festivity—did give men a chance to think the sun was the God of the Christians.[12] Tertullian is therefore a witness to the fact that Sunday was a heathen festival when it obtained a foothold in the Christian church, and that the Christians, in consequence of observing it, were

---

[9] Dialogues on the Lord's day, pp. 22, 23.

[10] Apology, chap. 67; Testimony of the Fathers, pp. 34, 35.

[11] Apology, sec. 16; Testimony of the Fathers, pp. 64, 65.

[12] *Ad Nationes*, book 1, chap. 13 ; Testimony of the Fathers, p. 70.

taunted with being sun-worshipers. It is remarkable that in his replies he never claims for their observance any divine precept or apostolic example. His principal point was that they had as good a right to do it as the heathen had. One hundred and twenty-one years after Tertullian, Constantine, while yet a heathen, put forth his famous edict in behalf of the heathen festival of the sun, which day he pronounced "venerable." And this heathen law caused the day to be observed everywhere throughout the Roman empire, and firmly established it both in church and State. It is certain, therefore, that at the time of its entrance into the Christian church, Sunday was an ancient weekly festival of the heathen world.

That this heathen festival was upon the day of Christ's resurrection, doubtless powerfully contributed to aid " patriotism " and " expediency " in transforming it into the Lord's day, or Christian Sabbath. For, with pious motives, as we may reasonably conclude, the professed people of God early paid a voluntary regard to several days, memorable in the history of the Redeemer. Mosheim, whose testimony in behalf of Sunday has been presented already, uses the following language relative to the crucifixion day :—

" It is also probable that Friday, the day of Christ's crucifixion, was early distinguished by particular honors from the other days of the week." [13]

Of the second century he says :—

" Many also observed the fourth day of the week, on which Christ was betrayed ; and the sixth, which was the day of his crucifixion." [14]

---

[13] Eccl. Hist., cent. 1, part 2, chap. 4, note ‡ to sec. 4.
[14] Eccl. Hist., cent. 2, part 2, chap. 1, sec. 12.

Dr. Peter Heylyn says of those who chose Sunday :—

"Because our Saviour rose that day from among the dead, so chose they Friday for another, by reason of our Saviour's passion; and Wednesday on the which he had been betrayed: the Saturday, or ancient Sabbath, being meanwhile retained in the Eastern churches." [15]

Of the comparative sacredness of these three voluntary festivals, the same writer testifies :—

"If we consider either the preaching of the word, the ministration of the sacraments, or the public prayers, the Sunday in the Eastern churches had no great prerogative above other days, especially above the Wednesday and the Friday, save that the meetings were more solemn, and the concourse of people greater than at other times, as is most likely." [16]

And besides these three weekly festivals, there were also two annual festivals of great sacredness. These were the Passover and the Pentecost. And it is worthy of special notice that although the Sunday festival can be traced no higher in the church than Justin Martyr, A. D. 140, the Passover can be traced to a man who claimed to have received it from the apostles. (See chapter thirteen.) Among these festivals, considered simply as voluntary memorials of the Redeemer, Sunday had very little pre-eminence; for it is well stated by Heylyn,—

"Take which you will, either the Fathers or the moderns, and we shall find no Lord's day instituted by any apostolic mandate; no Sabbath set on foot by them upon the first day of the week." [17]

---

[15] History of the Sabbath, part 2, chap. 1, sec. 12.

[16] Id., part 2, chap. 3, sec. 4.

[17] Hist. of the Sabbath, part 2, chap. 1, sec. 10.

Domville bears the following testimony, which is worthy of lasting remembrance :—

"Not any ecclesiastical writer of the first three centuries attributed the origin of Sunday observance either to Christ or to his apostles."[18]

"Patriotism" and "expediency," however, erelong elevated immeasurably above its fellows that one of these voluntary festivals which corresponded to "the wild solar holiday" of the heathen world, making that day, at last, "the Lord's day" of the Christian church. The earliest testimony in behalf of first-day observance that has *any* claim to be regarded as genuine, is that of Justin Martyr, written about A. D. 140. Before his conversion, he was a heathen philosopher. The time, place, and occasion of his first Apology or Defense of the Christians, addressed to the Roman emperor, is thus stated by an eminent Roman Catholic historian. He says that Justin Martyr—

"Was at Rome when the persecution that was raised under the reign of Antoninus Pius, the successor of Adrian, began to break forth, where he composed an excellent apology in behalf of the Christians."[19]

Of the works ascribed to Justin Martyr, Milner says :—

"Like many of the ancient Fathers, he appears to us under the greatest disadvantage. Works really his have been lost ; and others have been ascribed to him, part of which are not his, and the rest, at least, of ambiguous authority."[20]

---

[18] Examination of the Six Texts, Supplement, pp. 6, 7.

[19] Du Pin's Eccl. Hist., vol. 1, p. 50.

[20] Hist. Church, cent. 2, chap. 3.

If the writings ascribed to him are genuine, there is little propriety in the use made of his name by the advocates of the first-day Sabbath. He taught the abrogation of the Sabbatic institution; and there is no intimation in his words that the Sunday festival which he mentions was other than a voluntary observance. Thus he addresses the emperor of Rome :—

"And upon the day called Sunday, all that live either in city or country meet together at the same place, where the writings of the apostles and prophets are read as much as time will give leave; when the reader has done, the bishop makes a sermon, wherein he instructs the people, and animates them to the practice of such lovely precepts: at the conclusion of this discourse, we all rise up together, and pray; and prayers being over, as I now said, there is bread and wine and water offered, and the bishop, as before, sends up prayers and thanksgivings, with all the fervency he is able, and the people conclude all with the joyful acclamation of Amen. Then the consecrated elements are distributed to, and partaken of by, all that are present, and sent to the absent by the hands of the deacons. But the wealthy and the willing, for every one is at liberty, contribute as they think fitting; and this collection is deposited with the bishop, and out of this he relieves the orphan and the widow, and such as are reduced to want by sickness or any other cause, and such as are in bonds, and strangers that come from far; and, in a word, he is the guardian and almoner to all the indigent. Upon Sunday we all assemble, that being the first day in which God set himself to work upon the dark void, in order to make the world, and in which Jesus Christ our Saviour rose again from the dead; for the day before Saturday he was crucified, and the day after, which is Sunday, he appeared unto his apostles and disciples, and taught them what I have now proposed to your consideration." [21]

---

[21] Justin Martyr's First Apology, translated by Wm. Reeves, p. 127, secs. 87, 88, 89.

This passage, if genuine, furnishes the earliest reference to the observance of Sunday as a religious festival in the Christian church. It should be remembered that this language was written at Rome, and addressed directly to the emperor. It shows, therefore, what was the practice of the church in that city and vicinity, but does not determine how extensive this observance was. It contains strong incidental proof that apostasy had made progress at Rome, the institution of the Lord's supper being changed in part already to a human ordinance, water being now as essential to the Lord's supper as the wine or the bread. And what is still more dangerous, as perverting the institution of Christ, the consecrated elements were sent to the absent,—a step which speedily resulted in their becoming objects of superstitious veneration, and finally of worship. Justin tells the emperor that Christ thus ordained; but such a statement is a grave departure from the truth of the New Testament.

This statement of reasons for Sunday observance is particularly worthy of attention. He tells the emperor that they assembled upon the day called Sunday. This was equivalent to saying to him, We observe the day on which our fellow-citizens offer their adoration to the sun. Here both "patriotism" and "expediency" discover themselves in the words of Justin, which were addressed to a persecuting emperor in behalf of the Christians. But as if conscious that the observance of a heathen festival as the day of Christian worship was not consistent with their profession as worshipers of the Most High, Justin bethinks himself for reasons in defense of this observance. He assigns no divine precept nor apostolic example for this festival; for his reference to what Christ taught his disciples, as appears from the connection, was to the general system of the Christian religion, and not to the observance of Sunday. If it be said that Justin might have learned from tradition what is not to be found in the New Testament relative to Sunday observance, and that, after all, Sunday may be a divinely-appointed festival, it is sufficient to answer, 1. That this plea would show only tradition in favor of the Sunday festival; 2. That Justin Martyr is a very unsafe guide, his testimony relative to the Lord's supper differing from that of the New Testament; and 3. That the American Tract Society, in a work published against Romanism, bears the following testimony relative to the point before us :—

"Justin Martyr appears, indeed, peculiarly unfitted to lay claim to authority. It is notorious that he supposed a pillar erected on the island of the Tiber to Semo Sanchus, an old Sabine Deity, to be a monument erected by the Roman people in honor of the impostor, Simon Magus. Were so gross a mistake to be made by a modern writer in relating a historical fact, exposure would immediately take place, and his testimony would thenceforward be suspected. And assuredly, the same measure should be meted to Justin Martyr, who so egregiously errs in reference to a fact alluded to by Livy, the historian." [22]

Justin assigns the following reasons in support of Sunday observance : "That being the first day in which God set himself to work upon the dark void in order to make the world, and in which Jesus Christ our Saviour rose again from the dead." Bishop Jeremy Taylor most fittingly replies to this :—

[22] The Spirit of Popery, pp. 44, 45.

" The first of these looks more like an excuse than a just reason ; for if anything of the creation were made the cause of a Sabbath, it ought to be the end, not the beginning ; it ought to be the rest, not the first part of the work ; it ought to be that which God assigned, not [that] which man should take by way of after justification." [23]

It is to be observed, therefore, that the first trace of Sunday as a Christian festival is found in the church of Rome. Soon after this time, and thenceforward, we shall find " the bishop" of that church making vigorous efforts to suppress the Sabbath of the Lord. and to elevate in its stead the festival of Sunday.

It is proper to note the fact, also, that Justin was a decided opponent of the ancient Sabbath. In his " Dialogue with Trypho the Jew," he thus addressed him :—

" This new law teaches you to observe a perpetual Sabbath ; and you, when you have spent one day in idleness, think you have discharged the duties of religion. . . . If any one is guilty of adultery, let him repent, then he hath kept the true and delightful Sabbath unto God. . . . For we really should observe that circumcision, which is in the flesh, and the Sabbath, and all the feasts, if we had not known the reason why they were imposed upon you, namely, upon the account of your iniquities. . . . It was because of your iniquities, and the iniquities of your fathers, that God appointed you to observe the Sabbath. . . . You see that the heavens are not idle, nor do they observe the Sabbath. Continue as ye were born. For if before Abraham there was no need of circumcision, nor of the sabbaths, nor of feasts, nor of offerings before Moses ; so now in like manner there is no need of them, since Jesus Christ, the Son of God, was by the determinate counsel of God, born of a virgin of the seed of Abraham without sin." [24]

---

[23] Ductor Dubitantium, part 1, book 2, chap. 2, rule 6, sec. 45.
[24] Brown's Translation, pp. 43, 44, 52, 59, 63, 64.

This reasoning of Justin deserves no reply. It shows, however, the unfairness of Dr. Edwards, who quotes Justin Martyr as a witness for the change of the Sabbath; [25] whereas Justin held that God made the Sabbath on account of the wickedness of the Jews, and that he totally abrogated it in consequence of the first advent of Christ, the Sunday festival of the heathen being evidently adopted by the church at Rome from motives of "expediency" and perhaps of "patriotism." The testimony of Justin, if genuine, is peculiarly valuable in one respect. It shows that, as late as A. D. 140, the first day of the week had acquired no title of sacredness; for Justin several times mentions the day, thrice as "the day called Sunday," and twice as "the eighth day," and by other terms also, but never by any sacred name. [26]

The next important witness in behalf of first-day sacredness is thus presented by Dr. Edwards :—

"Hence Irenæus, bishop of Lyons, a disciple of Polycarp, who had been the companion of the apostles, A. D. 167, says that the Lord's day was the Christian Sabbath. His words are, 'On the Lord's day every one of us Christians keeps the Sabbath, meditating on the law, and rejoicing in the works of God.'" [27]

This testimony is highly valued by first-day writers, and is often and prominently set forth in their publications. Sir Wm. Domville, whose elaborate treatise on the Sabbath has been several times quoted, states the following important fact relative to this quotation :—

"I have carefully searched through all the extant works of Irenæus, and can with certainty state that no such passage, or

---

[25] Sabbath Manual, p. 121.   [26] Dialogue with Trypho, p. 65.

[27] Sabbath Manual, p. 114.

18

any one at all resembling it, is there to be found. The edition I consulted was that by Massuet (Paris, 1710); but to assure myself still further, I have since looked to the editions by Erasmus (Paris, 1563), and Grabe (Oxford, 1702), and in neither do I find the passage in question." [28]

It is a remarkable fact that those who quote this as the language of Irenæus, if they give any reference, cite their readers to Dwight's Theology, instead of referring them to the place in the works of Irenæus where it is to be found. It was Dr. Dwight who first enriched the theological world with this invaluable quotation. Where, then, did Dwight obtain this testimony which has so many times been given as that of Irenæus? On this point, Domville remarks :—

"He had the misfortune to be afflicted with a disease in his eyes from the early age of twenty-three, a calamity (says his biographer) by which he was deprived of the capacity for reading and study. . . . The knowledge which he gained from books after the period above mentioned [by which the editor must mean his age of twenty-three] was almost exclusively at second hand, by the aid of others." [29]

Domville states another fact which gives us unquestionably the origin of this quotation :—

"But although not to be found in Irenæus, there are, in the writings ascribed to another Father, namely, in the interpolated epistle of Ignatius to the Magnesians, and in one of its interpolated passages, expressions so clearly resembling those of Dr. Dwight's quotation as to leave no doubt of the source from which he quoted." [30]

Such, then, is the end of this famous testimony of Irenæus, who had it from Polycarp, who had it from the

---

[28] Examination of the Six Texts, pp. 131, 132.

[29] Id., p. 128.　　　[30] Id., p. 130.

apostles! It was furnished the world by a man whose eyesight was impaired; who, in consequence of this infirmity, took at second hand an interpolated passage from an epistle falsely ascribed to Ignatius, and published it to the world as the genuine testimony of Irenæus. Loss of eyesight, as we may charitably believe, led Dr. Dwight into the serious error which he has committed; but by the publication of this spurious testimony, which seemed to come in a direct line from the apostles, he has rendered multitudes as incapable of reading aright the fourth commandment, as he, by loss of natural eyesight, was of reading Irenæus for himself. This case admirably illustrates tradition as a religious guide; it is the blind leading the blind until both fall into the ditch.

Nor is this all that should be said in the case of Irenæus. In all his writings there is *no instance* in which he calls Sunday the Lord's day! And what is also very remarkable, there is no sentence extant, written by him, in which he even mentions the first day of the week![31] It appears, however, from several statements in ancient writers, that he did mention the day, though no sentence of *his* in which it is mentioned is in existence. He held that the Sabbath was a typical institution, which pointed to the seventh thousand years as the great day of rest to the church;[32] he said that Abraham was " without observance of Sabbaths; "[33] and yet he makes the origin of the Sabbath to be the sanctification of the seventh day.[34] But he expressly asserts the perpetuity

[31] See his full statement in the Testimony of the Fathers, pp. 44–52.

[32] Against Heresies, book 4, chap. 16, secs. 1, 2; book 5, chap. 28, sec. 3.

[33] Id., book 4, chap. 16, secs. 1, 2.   [34] Id., book 5, chap. 33, sec. 2.

and authority of the ten commandments, declaring
that they are identical with the law of nature implanted
from the beginning in mankind, that they remain permanently with us, and that if any one does not observe
them, he has no salvation." [35]

It is a remarkable fact that the first instance upon
record in which the bishop of Rome attempted to rule
the Christian church was by AN EDICT IN BEHALF OF
SUNDAY. It had been the custom of all the churches to
celebrate the Passover, but with this difference : that
while the Eastern churches observed it upon the fourteenth day of the first month, no matter what day of the
week this might be, the Western churches kept it upon
the Sunday following that day, or rather, upon the
Sunday following Good Friday. Victor, bishop of
Rome, in the year 196,[36] took upon him to impose the
Roman custom upon all the churches ; that is, to compel
them to observe the Passover upon Sunday. "This
bold attempt," says Bower, "we may call the first essay
of papal usurpation." [37] Dowling terms it the "earliest
instance of Romish assumption." [38] The churches of
Asia Minor informed Victor that they could not comply
with his lordly mandate. Then, says Bower,—

"Upon the receipt of this letter, Victor, giving the reins to
an impotent and ungovernable passion, published bitter invectives
against all the churches of Asia, declared them cut off from his
communion, sent letters of excommunication to their respective
bishops ; and, at the same time, in order to have them cut off

---

[35] Against Heresies, book 4, chap. 15, sec. 1 ; chap. 13, sec. 4.

[36] Bower's History of the Popes, vol. 1, pp. 18, 19 ; Rose's Neander, pp. 188–
190 ; Dowling's History of Romanism, book 1, chap. 2, sec. 9.

[37] History of the Popes, vol. 1, p. 18.

[38] History of Romanism, heading of page 32.

from the communion of the whole church, wrote to the other bishops, exhorting them to follow his example, and forbear communicating with their refractory brethren of Asia." [39]

The historian informs us that "not one followed his example or advice; not one paid any sort of regard to his letters, or showed the least inclination to second him in such a rash and uncharitable attempt." He further says :—

" Victor being thus baffled in his attempt, his successors took care not to revive the controversy; so that the Asiatics peaceably followed their ancient practice till the council of Nicæa, which, out of complaisance to Constantine the Great, ordered the solemnity of Easter to be kept everywhere on the same day, after the custom of Rome." [40]

The victory was not obtained for Sunday in this struggle, as Heylyn testifies,—

" Till the great council of Nicæa [A. D. 325], backed by the authority of as great an emperor [Constantine], settled it better than before ; none but some scattered schismatics, now and then appearing, that durst oppose the resolution of that famous synod." [41]

Constantine, by whose powerful influence the council of Nicæa was induced to decide this question in favor of the Roman bishop, that is, to fix the Passover upon Sunday, urged the following strong reason for the measure :—

" Let us, then, have nothing in common with the most hostile rabble of the Jews." [42]

---

[39] History of the Popes, vol. 1, p. 18.

[40] Id., pp. 18, 19; Gieseler's Eccl. Hist., vol. 1, p. 57.

[41] History of the Sabbath, part 2, chap. 2, secs. 4, 5.

[42] Boyle's Historical View of the Council of Nicæa, p. 52, ed. 1842.

This sentence is worthy of notice. A determination to have nothing in common with the Jews had very much to do with the suppression of the Sabbath in the Christian church. Those who rejected the Sabbath of the Lord, and chose in its stead the more popular and more convenient Sunday festival of the heathen, were so infatuated with the idea of having nothing in common with the Jews, that they never even questioned the propriety of a festival in common with the heathen.

This festival was not weekly, but annual; but the removal of it from the fourteenth of the first month to the Sunday following Good Friday was the first legislation attempted in honor of Sunday as a Christian festival; and, as Heylyn quaintly expresses it, " The Lord's day found it no small matter to obtain the victory." [43]   In a brief period after the council of Nicæa, by the laws of Theodosius, capital punishment was inflicted upon those who should celebrate the feast of the Passover upon any other day than Sunday.[44]   The Britons of Wales were long able to maintain their ground against this favorite project of the Roman church, and as late as the sixth century " obstinately resisted the imperious mandates of the Roman pontiffs." [45]

Four years from the commencement of the struggle just narrated, bring us to the testimony of Tertullian, the oldest of the Latin Fathers, who wrote about A. D. 200.   Dr. Clarke tells us that the Fathers " blow hot and cold."   Tertullian is a fair example of this.   He places the origin of the Sabbath at the creation, but elsewhere

---

[43] Hist. Sab., part 2, chap. 2, sec. 5.
[44] Decline and Fall of the Roman Empire, chap. 27.
[45] Id., chap. 38.

says that the patriarchs did not keep it. He says that Joshua broke the Sabbath at Jericho, and afterward shows that he did not break it. He says that Christ broke the Sabbath, and in another place proves that he did not. He represents the eighth day as more honorable than the seventh, and elsewhere states the reverse. He states that the law is abolished, and in other places teaches its perpetuity and authority. He declares that the Sabbath was abrogated by Christ, and afterward asserts that " Christ did not at all rescind the Sabbath," but imparted " an additional sanctity " to " the Sabbathday itself, which from the beginning had been consecrated by the benediction of the Father." And he goes on to say that Christ " furnished to this day divine safeguards,—a course which his adversary would have pursued for some other days, to avoid honoring the Creator's Sabbath."

This last statement is very remarkable. The Saviour furnished additional safeguards to the Creator's Sabbath. But " his adversary" would have done this to some other days. Now it is plain, first, that Tertullian did not believe that Christ sanctified some other day to take the place of the Sabbath; and secondly, that he believed the consecration of another day to be the work of the the adversary of God! When he wrote these words, he certainly did not believe in the sanctification of Sunday by Christ. But Tertullian and his brethren found themselves observing as a festival that day on which the sun was worshiped, and they were, in consequence, taunted with being worshipers of the sun. Tertullian denies the charge, though he acknowledges that it had some appearance of truth. He says :—

" Others, again, certainly with more information and greater verisimilitude, believe that the sun is our God. We shall be counted Persians, perhaps, though we do not worship the orb of day painted on a piece of linen cloth having himself everywhere in his own disk. The idea, no doubt, has originated from our being known to turn to the east in prayer. But you, many of you, also, under pretense sometimes of worshiping the heavenly bodies, move your lips in the direction of the sunrise. In the same way, if we devote Sunday to rejoicing, from a far different reason than sun-worship, we have some resemblance to those of you who devote the day of Saturn to ease and luxury, though they, too, go far away from Jewish ways of which they are ignorant." [46]

Tertullian pleads no divine command nor apostolic example for this practice. In fact, he offers no reason for the practice, though he intimates that he had one to offer. But he finds it necessary in another work to repel this same charge of sun-worship, because of Sunday observance. In his second answer to this charge he states the ground of defense more distinctly, and here we shall find his best reason :—

" Others, with greater regard to good manners, it must be confessed, suppose that the sun is the God of the Christians, because it is a well-known fact that we pray toward the east, or because we make Sunday a day of festivity. What then? Do you do less than this? Do not many among you, with an affectation of sometimes worshiping the heavenly bodies likewise, move your lips in the direction of the sunrise? It is you, at all events, who have even admitted the sun into the calendar of the week; and you have selected its day [Sunday] in preference to the preceding day, as the most suitable in the week for either an entire abstinence from the bath, or for its postponement until the evening, or for taking rest, and for banqueting. By resorting to these customs, you deliberately deviate from your own religious rites to those of strangers." [47]

---

[46] Tertullian's Apology, sec. 16. [47] Tertullian's *Ad Nationes*, book 1, chap. 13.

Tertullian, in this discourse, addresses himself to the nations still in idolatry. With some of these, Sunday was an ancient festival; with others it was of comparatively recent date. But some of these heathen reproached the Sunday Christians with being sun-worshipers. And now observe the answer. He does not say, " We Christians are commanded to celebrate the first day of the week in honor of Christ's resurrection." His answer is doubtless the best that he knew how to frame. It is a mere retort, and consists in asserting, first, that the Christians had done no more than their accusers, the heathen ; and secondly, that they had as good a right to make Sunday a day of festivity as had the heathen !

The origin of first-day observance has been the subject of inquiry in this chapter. We have found that Sunday from remote antiquity was a heathen festival in honor of the sun, and that in the first centuries of the Christian era this ancient festival was in general veneration in the heathen world. We have learned that patriotism and expediency, and a tender regard for the conversion of the Gentile world, caused the leaders of the church to adopt as their religious festival the day observed by the heathen, and to retain the same name which the heathen had given it. We have seen that the earliest instance upon record of the actual observance of Sunday in the Christian church, is found in the church of Rome about A. D. 140. The first great effort in its behalf, A. D. 196, is by a singular coincidence the first act of papal usurpation. The first instance of a sacred title being applied to this festival, and the earliest trace of abstinence from labor on that day, are found in the writings of Tertullian at the close of the second century.

The origin of the festival of Sunday is now before the reader; the steps by which it has ascended to supreme power will be pointed out in their proper order and place.

One fact of deep interest will conclude this chapter. The first great effort made to put down the Sabbath was the act of the church of Rome in turning it into a fast, while Sunday was made a joyful festival. While the Eastern churches retained the Sabbath, a portion of the Western churches, with the church of Rome at their head, turned it into a fast. As a part of the Western churches refused to comply with this ordinance, a long struggle ensued, the result of which is thus stated by Heylyn:—

" In this difference it stood a long time together, till in the end the Roman church obtained the cause, and Saturday became a fast almost through all the parts of the Western world. I say the Western world, and of that alone, the Eastern churches being so far from altering their ancient custom that in the sixth council of Constantinople, A. D. 692, they did admonish those of Rome to forbear fasting on that day upon pain of censure." [48]

Wm. James, in a sermon before the University of Oxford, thus states the time when this fast originated:—

" The Western church began to fast on Saturday at the beginning of the third century." [49]

Thus it is seen that this struggle began with the third century, that is, immediately after the year 200. Neander thus states the motive of the Roman church:—

---

[48] History of the Sabbath, part 2, chap. 2, sec. 3.
[49] Sermons on the Sacraments and Sabbath, p. 166

"In the Western churches, particularly the Roman, where opposition to Judaism was the prevailing tendency, this very opposition produced the custom of celebrating the Saturday in particular as a fast-day." [50]

By Judaism, Neander meant the observance of the seventh day as the Sabbath. Dr. Charles Hase, of Germany, states the object of the Roman church in very explicit language :—

"The Roman church regarded Saturday as a fast-day in direct opposition to those who regarded it as a Sabbath. Sunday remained a joyful festival in which all fasting and worldly business was avoided as much as possible, but the original commandment of the decalogue respecting the Sabbath was not then applied to that day." [51]

Lord King attests this fact in the following words :—

"Some of the Western churches, that they might not seem to Judaize, fasted on Saturday, as Victorinus Petavioncnsis writes: We use to fast on the seventh day. And it is our custom then to fast, that we may not seem, with the Jews, to observe the Sabbath." [52]

Thus the Sabbath of the Lord was turned into a fast in order to render it despicable before men. Such was the first great effort of the Roman church toward the suppression of the ancient Sabbath of the Bible.

---

[50] Neander, p. 186.

[51] Ancient Church History, part 1, div. 2, A. D. 100–312, sec. 69.

[52] Enquiry into the Constitution of the Primitive Church, part 2, chap. 7, sec. 11. See also Schaff's "History of the Christian Church," vol. 1, p. 373.

CHAPTER XVII.

THE NATURE OF EARLY FIRST-DAY OBSERVANCE.

The history of first-day observance compared with that of the popes—
First-day observance defined in the very words of each of the early
Fathers who mention it—The reasons which each had for its observ-
ance stated in his own words—Sunday in their judgment of no higher
sacredness than Easter or Whitsunday, or even than the fifty days
between those festivals—Sunday not a day of abstinence from labor
—The reasons which are offered by those of them who rejected the
Sabbath stated in their own words.

N apt illustration of the history of first-day
observance in the Christian church is that of
the bishops of Rome. The Roman bishop now
claims supreme power over all the churches of Christ.
He asserts that this power was given to Peter, and by
him was transmitted to the bishops of Rome; or rather
that Peter was the first Roman bishop, and that a succession of such bishops from his time to the present
have exercised this absolute power in the church.
They are able to trace back their line to apostolic times,
and they assert that the power now claimed by the
pope was claimed and exercised by the first pastors of
the church of the Romans. Those who now acknowledge the supremacy of the pope believe this assertion,
and with them it is a conclusive evidence that the pope
is by divine right possessed of supreme power. But
the assertion is absolutely false. The early pastors,
or bishops, or elders, of the church of the Romans were

modest, unassuming ministers of Christ, wholly unlike the arrogant bishop of Rome, who now usurps the place of Christ as the head of the Christian church.

The first day of the week now claims to be the Christian Sabbath, and enforces its authority by means of the fourth commandment, having set aside the seventh day, which that commandment enjoins, and usurped its place. Its advocates assert that this position and this authority were given to it by Christ. As no record of such a gift is found in the Scriptures, the principal argument in its support is furnished by tracing first-day observance back to the early Christians, who, it is said, would not have hallowed the day if they had not been instructed to do it by the apostles; and the apostles would not have taught them to do it if Christ had not, in their presence, changed the Sabbath.

But first-day observance can be traced no nearer to apostolic times than A. D. 140, while the bishops of Rome can trace their line to the very times of the apostles. Herein is the papal claim to apostolic authority better than is that of the first-day Sabbath. But with this exception, the historical argument in behalf of each is the same. Both began with very moderate pretensions, and gradually gaining in power and sacredness, grew up in strength together.

Let us now go to those who were the earliest observers of Sunday, and learn from them the nature of that observance at its commencement. We shall find, 1. That no one claimed for first-day observance any divine authority; 2. That none of them had ever heard of the change of the Sabbath, and none believed the first-day festival to be a continuation of the Sabbatic institution; 3. That labor on that day is never set forth as sinful, and that abstinence from labor is never mentioned as a feature of its observance, nor even implied, only so far as is necessary in order to spend a portion of the day in worship; 4. That if we put together all the hints respecting Sunday observance which are scattered through the Fathers of the first three centuries (for no one of them gives more than two of these, and generally a single hint is all that is found in one writer), we shall find just four items : (1.) An assembly on that day in which the Bible was read and expounded, and the supper celebrated, and money collected; (2.) The day must be one of rejoicing; (3.) It must not be a day of fasting; and (4.) The knee must not be bent in prayer on that day.

The following are all the hints respecting the nature of first-day observance during the first three centuries. The epistle falsely ascribed to Barnabas simply says : "We keep the eighth day with joyfulness." [1]   Justin Martyr, in words already quoted at full length, describes the kind of meeting which they held at Rome and in that vicinity on that day, and this is all that he connects with its observance. [2]   Irenæus taught that to commemorate the resurrection, the knee must not be bent on that day, and mentions nothing else as essential to its honor.   This act of standing in prayer was a symbol of the resurrection, which was to be celebrated only on that day, as he held. [3]   Bardesanes, the Gnostic, represents the Christians as everywhere meeting for worship on that day, but he does not describe that worship, and he gives

---

[1] Epistle of Barnabas, chap. 15.   [2] Justin Martyr's First Apology, chap. 67.
[3] Lost Writings of Irenæus, Fragments 7 and 50.

no other honor to the day.[4] Tertullian describes Sunday observance as follows : " We devote Sunday to rejoicing ; " and he adds, " We have some resemblance to those of you who devote the day of Saturn to *ease* and *luxury.*" [5] In another work he gives us a further idea of the festive character of Sunday. Speaking to his brethren, he says : " If any *indulgence is to be granted to the flesh,* you have it. I will not say your own days, but more too; for to the heathens each festive day occurs but once annually ; you have *a festive* day *every eighth day.*" [6] Dr. Heylyn spoke the truth when he said :—

" Tertullian tells us that they did devote the Sunday partly unto mirth and recreation, not to devotion altogether; when in a hundred years after Tertullian's time there was no law or constitution to restrain men from labor on this day in the Christian church." [7]

The Sunday festival in Tertullian's time was not like the modern first-day Sabbath, but was essentially the German festival of Sunday, a day for worship and for recreation, and one on which labor was not sinful. But Tertullian speaks further respecting Sunday observance, and the following extract has been used as proof that labor on that day was counted sinful. This is the only statement that can be found prior to Constantine's Sunday law that has such an appearance, and the proof is decisive that its meaning is not what is claimed. Here are his words :—

" We, however (just as we have received), only on the day of

---

[4] Book of the Laws of Countries.

[5] Tertullian's Apology, sec. 16. [6] On Idolatry, chap. 14.

[7] Hist. Sab., part 2, chap. 8, sec. 13.

the Lord's resurrection, ought to guard, not only against kneeling, but every posture and office of solicitude, deferring even our businesses, lest we give any place to the devil.   Similarly, too, in the period of Pentecost; which period we distinguish by the same solemnity of exultation." [8]

He speaks of " deferring even our businesses ; " but this does not necessarily imply anything more than its postponement during the hours devoted to religious services.   It falls very far short of saying that labor on Sunday is a sin.   But we will quote Tertullian's next mention of Sunday observance before noticing further the words last quoted :—

" We count fasting or kneeling in worship on the Lord's day to be unlawful. We rejoice in the same privilege also from Easter to Whitsunday." [9]

These two things, fasting and kneeling, are the only acts which the Fathers set down as unlawful on Sunday, unless, indeed, mourning may be included by some in the list.   It is certain that labor is never thus mentioned.   And observe that Tertullian repeats the important statement of the previous quotation, that the honor due to Sunday pertains also to the "period of Pentecost," that is, to the fifty days between Easter, or Passover, and Whitsunday, or Pentecost.   If, therefore, labor on Sunday was in Tertullian's estimation sinful, the same was true for the period of Pentecost, a space of fifty days !   But this is not possible.   We can conceive of the deferring of business for one religious assembly each day for fifty days, and also that men should neither fast nor kneel during that time, which was precisely what the religious celebration of Sunday actually

---

[8] On Prayer, chap. 23.   [9] *De Corona*, sec. 3.

was. But to make Tertullian assert that labor on Sunday was a sin is to make him declare that such was the case for fifty days together, which no one will venture to say was the doctrine of Tertullian.

In another work, Tertullian gives us one more statement respecting the nature of Sunday observance : " We make Sunday a day of festivity. What then ? Do you do less than this ? "[10] His language is very extraordinary when it is considered that he was addressing heathen. It seems that Sunday as a Christian festival was so similar to the festival which these heathen observed that he challenged them to show wherein the Christians went further than did these heathen whom he here addressed.

The next Father who gives us the nature of early Sunday observance is Peter of Alexandria. He says :—

" But the Lord's day we celebrate as a day of joy, because on it he rose again, on which day we have received it for a custom not even to bow the knee." [11]

He marks two things as essential : it must be a day of joy; and Christians must not kneel on that day. Zonaras, an ancient commentator on these words of Peter, explains the day of joy by saying, " We ought not to fast; for it is a day of joy for the resurrection of the Lord." [12] Next in order, we quote the so-called Apostolical Constitutions. These command Christians to assemble for worship every day, " but principally on the Sabbath-day; and on the day of our Lord's resurrection, which is the Lord's day, meet more diligently,

---

[10] *Ad Natione*, book 1, chap. 13.   [11] Canon 15.
[12] Ante-Nicene Library, vol. 14, p. 322.

sending praise to God," etc.   The object of assembling was "to hear the saving word concerning the resurrection," to "pray thrice standing," to have the prophets read, to have preaching and also the supper.[13]   These " Constitutions " not only give the nature of the worship on Sunday as just set forth, but they also give an idea of Sunday as a day of festivity :—

" Now we exhort you, brethren and fellow-servants, to avoid vain talk and obscene discourses, and jestings, drunkenness, lasciviousness, luxury, unbounded passions, with foolish discourses *since we do not permit you so much as on the Lord's days,* which are days of joy, to speak or act anything unseemly." [14]

This language plainly implies that the so-called Lord's day was a day of greater mirth than the other days of the week.   Even on the Lord's day they must not speak or act anything unseemly, though it is evident that their license on that day was greater than on other days.

Once more these " Constitutions " give us the nature of Sunday observance : " Every Sabbath-day, excepting one, and every Lord's day hold your solemn assemblies, and rejoice ; for he will be guilty of sin who fasts on the Lord's day." [15]   But no one can read so much as once that " he is guilty of sin who performs work on this day."

Next, we quote the epistle to the Magnesians in its longer form, which, though not written by Ignatius, was actually written about the time that the Apostolical Constitutions were committed to writing.   Here are the words of this epistle :—

" And after the observance of the Sabbath, let every friend

---

[13] Apostolical Constitutions, book 2, sec. 7, par. 59.

[14] Id., book 5, sec 2, par. 10.   [15] Id., book 5, sec. 3, par. 20.

of Christ keep the Lord's day as a festival, the resurrection day, the queen and chief of all the days." [16]

The writer of the Syriac Documents concerning Edessa comes last, and he defines the services of Sunday as follows : " On the first [day] of the week, let there be service, and the reading of the Holy Scriptures, and the oblation." [17]   These are all the passages in the writings of the first three centuries which describe early first-day observance.   Let the reader judge whether we have correctly stated the nature of that observance. Next we invite attention to the several reasons offered by these Fathers for celebrating the festival of Sunday.

The reputed epistle of Barnabas supports the Sunday festival by saying that it was the day " on which Jesus rose again from the dead," and it intimates that it prefigures the eight thousand years, when God shall create the world anew.[18]

Justin Martyr has four reasons :—

1. " It is the first day on which God, having wrought a change in the darkness and matter, made the world." [19]

2. " Jesus Christ our Saviour on the same day rose from the dead." [20]

3. " It is possible for us to show how the eighth day possessed a certain mysterious import, which the seventh day did not possess, and which was promulgated by God through these rites," [21] *i. e.*, through circumcision.

4. " The command of circumcision, again, bidding [them] always circumcise the children on the eighth day,

---

[16] Epistle to the Magnesians (longer form), chap. 9.

[17] Syriac Documents, p. 38.   [18] Epistle of Barnabas, chap. 15.

[19] Justin's First Apology, chap. 67.   [20] Id.

[21] Dialogue with Trypho, chap. 24.

was a type of the true circumcision, by which we are circumcised from deceit and iniquity through Him who rose from the dead on the first day after the Sabbath." [22]

Clement, of Alexandria, appears to treat solely of a mystical eighth day, or Lord's day. It is perhaps possible that he has some reference to Sunday. Therefore we quote what he says in behalf of this day, calling attention to the fact that he produces his testimony, not from the Bible, but from a heathen philosopher :—

" And the Lord's day Plato prophetically speaks of in the tenth book of the *Republic,* in these words : 'And when seven days have passed to each of them in the meadow, on the eighth day they are to set out, and arrive in four days.' " [23]

Clement's reasons for Sunday are found outside the Scriptures. The next Father will give us a good reason for Clement's action in this case.

Tertullian is the next writer who gives reasons for the Sunday festival. He is speaking of " offerings for the dead," the manner of Sunday observance, and the use of the sign of the cross upon the forehead. Here is the ground on which these observances rest :—

"If, for these and other such rules, you insist upon having positive Scripture injunction, you will find none. Tradition will be held forth to you as the originator of them, custom as their strengthener, and faith as their observer. That reason will support tradition, and custom, and faith, you will either yourself perceive, or learn from some one who has." [24]

Tertullian's frankness is to be commended. He had no Scripture to offer, and he acknowledged the fact. He depended on tradition, and he was not ashamed to

---

[22] Dialogue with Trypho, chap. 41.

[23] Clement's Miscellanies, book 5, chap. 14.   [24] *De Corona,* sec. 4.

confess it. Following Tertullian is Origen, who gives Scripture evidence in support of the Sunday festival. Here are his words :—

" The manna fell on the Lord's day, and not on the Sabbath, to show the Jews that even then the Lord's day was preferred before it." [25]

Origen seems to have been of Tertullian's judgment as to the inconclusiveness of the arguments adduced by his predecessors. He therefore coined an original argument, which seems to have been very conclusive in his estimation, as he offers this alone. But he must have forgotten that the manna fell on all the six working days, or he would have seen that while his argument does not elevate Sunday above the other five working days, it does make the Sabbath the least reputable day of the seven ! And yet the miracle of the manna was expressly designed to set forth the sacredness of the Sabbath, and to establish its authority before the people.

Cyprian is the next Father who gives an argument for the Sunday festival. He contents himself with one of Justin's old arguments, viz., the one drawn from circumcision. Thus he says :—

" For in respect of the observance of the eighth day in the Jewish circumcision of the flesh, a sacrament was given beforehand in shadow and in usage; but when Christ came, it was fulfilled in truth. For because the eighth day, that is, the first day after the Sabbath, was to be that on which the Lord should rise again, and should quicken us, and give us circumcision of the Spirit, the eighth day, that is, the first day after the Sabbath,

---

[25] *Origen's Opera*, Tome 2, p. 158, Paris, A. D. 1733, " Quod si ex Divinis Scripturis hoc constat, quod die Dominica Deus pluit manna de cælo et in Sabbato non pluit, intelligant Judæi jam tunc prælatam esse Dominicam nostram Judaico Sabbato."

and the Lord's day, went before in the figure; which figure
ceased when by and by the truth came, and spiritual circumcision
was given to us." [26]

Such is the only argument adduced by Cyprian in
behalf of the first-day festival. The circumcision of infants when eight days old was, in his judgment, a type
of infant baptism. But he did not hold that circumcision on the eighth day of the child's life, signified that baptism need to be deferred till the infant was eight days
old, but, as here stated, did signify that the eighth day
was to be the Lord's day! But the eighth day, on
which circumcision took place, was not the first day of
the week, but the eighth day of each child's life, whatever day of the week that might be.

The next Father who gives a reason for celebrating
Sunday as a day of joy, and refraining from kneeling on
it, is Peter, of Alexandria, who simply says, " Because
on it he rose again." [27]

Then come the Apostolical Constitutions, which assert
that the Sunday festival is a memorial of the resurrection :—

" But keep the Sabbath, and the Lord's day festival; because
the former is a memorial of the creation, and the latter of the resurrection." [28]

The writer, however, offers no proof that Sunday
was set apart by divine authority in memory of the resurrection. But the next person who gives his reasons
for keeping Sunday " as a festival," is the writer of the
longer form of the reputed epistle of Ignatius to the
Magnesians. He finds the eighth day prophetically set

---

[26] Cyprian's Epistle, No. 58, sec. 4.   [27] Peter's Canons, No. 15.
[28] Apostolical Constitutions, book 7, sec. 2, par. 23.

forth in the title to the sixth and twelfth psalms! In the margin, the word *Sheminith* is translated "the eighth." Here is this writer's argument for Sunday:—

"Looking forward to this, the prophet declared, ' To the end for the eighth day,' on which our life both sprang up again, and the victory over death was obtained in Christ." [29]

There is yet another of the Fathers of the first three centuries who gives the reasons then used in support of the Sunday festival, and that is the writer of the Syriac Documents concerning Edessa. He comes next in order, and closes the list. Here are four reasons:—

1. "Because on the first day of the week our Lord rose from the place of the dead."
2. "On the first day of the week he arose upon the world," *i. e.*, he was born upon Sunday.
3. "On the first day of the week he ascended up to heaven."
4. "On the first day of the week he will appear at last with the angels of heaven." [30]

The first of these reasons is as good a one as man can devise out of his own heart for doing what God never commanded; the second and fourth are mere assertions of which mankind know nothing; while the third is a positive untruth, for the ascension was upon Thursday.

We have now presented every reason for the Sunday festival which can be found in all the writings of the first three centuries. Though generally very trivial, and sometimes worse than trivial, they are nevertheless worthy of careful study. They constitute a decisive testimony that the change of the Sabbath by Christ or

[29] Epistle to the Magnesians, chap. 9.　　[30] Syriac Documents, p. 38.

by his apostles from the seventh to the first day of the
week was absolutely unknown during that entire period.
But were it true that such a change had been made, they
must have known it. Had they believed that Christ
changed the Sabbath to commemorate his resurrection,
how emphatically would they have stated that fact, instead of offering reasons for the festival of Sunday which
are so worthless as to be, with one or two exceptions,
entirely discarded by modern first-day writers. Or
had they believed that the apostles honored Sunday as
the Sabbath, or Lord's day, how would they have produced these facts in triumph! But Tertullian said that
they had no positive Scripture injunction for the Sunday
festival; and the others, by offering reasons that were
only devised in their own hearts, corroborated his testimony, and all of them together establish the fact that,
even in their own estimation, the day was only sustained
by the authority of the church. They were totally un-
acquainted with the modern doctrine that the seventh
day in the commandment means simply one day in seven,
and that the Saviour, to commemorate his resurrection,
appointed the first day of the week to be that one of the
seven to which the commandment should apply!

We have given every statement in the Fathers of the
first three centuries in which the manner of celebrating
the Sunday festival is set forth. We have also given
every reason for that observance which is to be found in
any of them. These two classes of testimonies show
clearly that ordinary labor was not one of the things
which were forbidden on that day. We now offer direct
proof that other days, which on all hands are accounted
nothing but church festivals, were expressly declared by

the Fathers to be equal, if not superior, in sacredness to the Sunday festival.

The " Lost Writings of Irenæus " gives us his mind concerning the relative sacredness of the festival of Sunday and of either Easter or Pentecost. This is the statement :—

" Upon which [feast] we do not bend the knee, because it is of *equal significance* with the Lord's day, for the reason already alleged concerning it." [31]

Tertullian, in a passage already quoted, which, by omitting the sentence we are about to quote, has been used as the strongest testimony to the first-day Sabbath in the Fathers, expressly makes the period of Pentecost —a space of fifty days—equal in sacredness with the festival which he calls " Lord's day." Thus he says :—

" Similarly, too, in the period of Pentecost; which period we distinguish by *the same solemnity of exultation.*" [32]

He states the same fact in another work :—

" We count fasting or kneeling in worship on the Lord's day to be unlawful. We rejoice *in the same privilege* also from Easter to Whitsunday." [33]

Origen classes the so-called Lord's day with three other church festivals :—

" If it be objected to us on this subject that we ourselves are accustomed to observe certain days, as for example the Lord's day, the Preparation, the Passover, or Pentecost, I have to answer, that to the perfect Christian, who is ever in his thoughts, words, and deeds, serving his natural Lord, God the Word, all

---

[31] Fragment 7.   [32] Tertullian on Prayer, chap. 23.

[33] *De Corona,* sec. 3.

his days are the Lord's, and he is always keeping the Lord's day." [34]

Irenæus and Tertullian make the Sunday Lord's day equal in sacredness with the period from the Passover to the Pentecost; but Origen, after classing the day with several church festivals, virtually confesses that it has no pre-eminence above other days.

Commodianus, who once uses the term "Lord's day," speaks of the Catholic festival of the Passover as "Easter, that day of ours *most blessed*." [35]   This certainly indicates that in his estimation no other sacred day was superior in sanctity to Easter.

The "Apostolical Constitutions" treat the Sunday festival in the same manner that it is treated by Irenæus and Tertullian.   They make it equal to the sacredness of the period from Easter to the Pentecost.   Thus they say :—

"He will be guilty of sin who fasts on the Lord's day, being the day of the resurrection, or during the time of Pentecost, or in general, who is sad on a festival day to the Lord." [36]

These testimonies prove conclusively that the festival of Sunday, in the judgment of such men as Irenæus, Tertullian, and others, stood in the same rank with that of Easter or Whitsunday.   They had no idea that one was commanded by God, while the others were only ordained by the church.   Indeed, Tertullian, as we have seen, expressly declares that there is no precept for Sunday observance. [37]

---

[34] Origen against Celsus, book 8, chap. 22.

[35] Instructions of Commodianus, sec. 75.

[36] Apostolical Constitutions, book 5, sec. 3, par. 20.

[37] *De Corona*, secs. 3 and 4.

Besides these important facts, we have decisive evidence that Sunday was not a day of abstinence from labor, and our first witness is Justin, the earliest witness to the Sunday festival in the Christian church. Trypho, the Jew, said to Justin, by way of reproof, "You observe no festivals or Sabbaths." [38] This was exactly adapted to bring out from Justin the statement that, though he did not observe the seventh day as the Sabbath, he did thus rest on the first day of the week, if it were true that that day was with him a day of abstinence from labor. But he gives no such answer. He sneers at the very idea of abstinence from labor, declaring that "God does not take pleasure in such observances." Nor does he intimate that this is because the Jews did not rest upon the right day; but he condemns the very idea of refraining from labor for a day, stating that "the new law," which has taken the place of the commandments given on Sinai,[39] requires a perpetual Sabbath, and this is kept by repenting of sin, and refraining from its commission. Here are his words :—

"The new law requires you to keep a perpetual Sabbath, and you, *because you are idle for one day*, suppose you are pious, not discerning why this has been commanded you; and if you eat unleavened bread, you say the will of God has been fulfilled. The Lord our God does not take pleasure in such observances : if there is any perjured person or a thief among you, let him cease to be so; if any adulterer, let him repent; then he has kept the sweet and true Sabbaths of God." [40]

This language plainly implies that Justin did not believe that any day should be kept as a Sabbath by abstinence from labor, but that all days should be kept

---

[38] Dialogue with Trypho, chap. 10.   [39] Id., chap. 11.   [40] Id., chap. 12.

as sabbaths by abstinence from sin. This testimony is decisive, and it is in exact harmony with the facts already adduced from the Fathers, and with others yet to be presented. Moreover, it is confirmed by the express testimony of Tertullian. He says :—

"By us (to whom *Sabbaths are strange,* and the new moons, and festivals formerly beloved by God the) Saturnalia and new year's and mid-winter's festivals and Matronalia are frequented." [41]

And he adds in the same paragraph, in words already quoted :—

" If *any indulgence is to be granted to the flesh,* you have it. I will not say *your own days,* but *more too ;* for to the *heathens* each festive day occurs but once annually; you have a *festive day every eighth day.*" [42]

Tertullian tells his brethren in plain language that they kept no sabbaths, but did keep many heathen festivals. If the Sunday festival, which was a day of "indulgence" to the flesh, and which he here mentions as the "eighth day," was kept by them as the Christian Sabbath in place of the ancient seventh day, then he would not have asserted that to us "sabbaths are strange." But Tertullian has precisely the same Sabbath as Justin Martyr. He does not keep the first day in place of the seventh, but he keeps a "perpetual sabbath," in which he professes to refrain from sin every day, and actually abstains from labor on none. Thus, after saying that the Jews teach that "from the beginning God sanctified the seventh day," and therefore observe that day, he says :—

"Whence we [Christians] understand that we still more

---

[41] Tertullian on Idolatry, chap. 14.   [42] Id.

ought to observe a Sabbath from all 'servile work' always, and not only every seventh day, but through all time."[43]

Tertullian certainly had no idea that Sunday was the Sabbath in any other sense than were all the seven days of the week. We shall find a decisive confirmation of this when we come to quote Tertullian respecting the origin of the Sabbath. We shall also find that Clement expressly makes Sunday a day of labor.

Several of the early Fathers wrote in opposition to the observance of the seventh day. We now give the reasons assigned by each for that opposition. The writer called Barnabas did not keep the seventh day, not because it was a ceremonial ordinance unworthy of being observed by a Christian, but because it was so pure an institution that even Christians cannot truly sanctify it till they are made immortal. Here are his words :—

"Attend, my children, to the meaning of this expression, 'He finished in six days.' This implieth that the Lord will finish all things in six thousand years, for a day is with him a thousand years. And he himself testifieth, saying, 'Behold, to-day will be as a thousand years.' Therefore, my children, in six days, that is, in six thousand years, all things will be finished. 'And he rested on the seventh day.' This meaneth: When his Son, coming [again], shall destroy the time of the wicked man, and judge the ungodly, and change the sun, and the moon, and the stars, then shall he truly rest on the seventh day. Moreover, he says, 'Thou shalt sanctify it with pure hands and a pure heart.' If, therefore, any one can now sanctify the day which God hath sanctified, except he is pure in heart in all things, we are deceived. Behold, therefore: certainly one properly resting sanctifies it, when we ourselves, having received the promise, wickedness no longer existing, and all things having been made new by the Lord, shall be able to work righteousness. Then we

---

[43] Tertullian against the Jews, chap. 4.

shall be able to sanctify it, having been first sanctified ourselves. Further he says to them, 'your new moons and your sabbaths I cannot endure.' Ye perceive how he speaks: Your present sabbaths are not acceptable to me, but that is which I have made [namely this], when giving rest to all things, I shall make a beginning of the eighth day, that is, a beginning of another world, wherefore, also, we keep the eighth day with joyfulness, the day, also, on which Jesus rose again from the dead." [44]

Observe the points embodied in this statement of doctrine: 1. He asserts that the six days of creation prefigure the six thousand years which our world shall endure in its present state of wickedness; 2. He teaches that at the end of that period, Christ will come again, and make an end of wickedness, and " then shall he truly rest on the seventh day;" 3. That no "one can now sanctify the day which God hath sanctified, except he is pure in heart in all things;" 4. But that cannot be the case until the present world shall pass away, " when we ourselves, having received the promise, wickedness no longer existing, and all things having been made new by the Lord, shall be able to work righteousness: then we shall be able to sanctify it, having been first sanctified ourselves;" therefore men cannot keep the Sabbath while this wicked world lasts; 5. So he says, " Your present sabbaths are not acceptable," not because they are not pure, but because you are not now able to keep them as purely as their nature demands; 6. That is to say, the keeping of the day which God has sanctified is not possible in such a wicked world as this; 7. But though the seventh day cannot now be kept, the eighth day can be, and ought to be, because when the seven thousand years are past, there will be at the beginning of the

---

[44] Epistle of Barnabas, chap. 15.

eighth thousand, the new creation; 8. Therefore, he did not attempt to keep the seventh day, which God had sanctified; for that is too pure to be kept in the present wicked world, and can only be kept after the Saviour comes, at the commencement of the seventh thousand years; but he kept the eighth day with joyfulness, on which Jesus arose from the dead; 9. So it appears that the eighth day, which God never sanctified, is exactly suitable for observance in our world during its present state of wickedness; 10. But when all things have been made new, and we are able to work righteousness, and wickedness no longer exists, then we shall be able to sanctify the seventh day, having first been sanctified ourselves.

The reason Barnabas gives for not observing the Sabbath of the Lord is not that the commandment enjoining it is abolished, but that the institution is so pure that men in their present imperfect state cannot acceptably sanctify it. They will keep it, however, in the new creation; but in the meantime they keep with joyfulness the eighth day, which, having never been sanctified by God, is not difficult to keep in the present state of wickedness.

Justin Martyr's reasons for not observing the Sabbath are not at all like those of the so-called Barnabas, for Justin seems to have heartily despised the Sabbatic institution. He denies that it was obligatory before the time of Moses, and declares that it was abolished by the advent of Christ. He teaches that it was given to the Jews because of their wickedness, and he expressly affirms the abolition of both the Sabbath and the law. So far is he from teaching the change of the Sabbath from the seventh to the first day of the week, or from making the Sunday festival a continuation of the ancient Sabbatic institution, that he sneers at the very idea of days of abstinence from labor, or days of idleness; and though God gives as his reason for the observance of the Sabbath, that that was the day on which he rested from all his work, Justin gives as his first reason for the Sunday festival that that was the day on which God began his work! Of abstinence from labor as an act of obedience to the Sabbath, Justin says :—

"The Lord our God does not take pleasure in such observances." [45]

A second reason for not observing the Sabbath is thus stated by him :—

"For we, too, would observe the fleshly circumcision, and the Sabbaths, and in short, all the feasts, if we did not know for what reason they were enjoined you; namely, on account of your transgressions and the hardness of your hearts." [46]

As Justin never discriminates between the Sabbath of the Lord and the annual sabbaths, he doubtless here means to include it as well as them. But what a falsehood it is to assert that the Sabbath was given to the Jews because of their wickedness! The truth is, it was given to the Jews because of the universal apostasy of the Gentiles.[47] But in the following paragraph, Justin gives three more reasons for not keeping the Sabbath :—

"Do you see that the elements are not idle, and keep no Sabbaths? Remain as you were born. For if there was no need of circumcision before Abraham, or of the observance of Sabbaths, of feasts and sacrifices, before Moses, no more need is there of

---

[45] Dialogue with Trypho, chap. 12.   [46] Id., chap. 18.
[47] See chapter 3 of this History.

them now, after that, according to the will of God, Jesus Christ, the son of God, has been born without sin, of a virgin sprung from the stock of Abraham." [48]

Here are three reasons : 1. "That the elements are not idle, and keep no Sabbaths;" though this reason is simply worthless as an argument against the seventh day, it is a decisive confirmation of the fact already proved, that Justin did not make Sunday a day of abstinence from labor; 2. His second reason here given is that there was no observance of Sabbaths before Moses; and yet we know that God, at the beginning, did appoint the Sabbath to a holy use,—a fact to which, as we shall see, quite a number of the Fathers testify, and we also know that in that age were men who kept all the precepts of God; 3. There is no need of Sabbatic observance since Christ. Though this is mere assertion, it is by no means easy for those to meet it fairly who represent Justin as maintaining the Christian Sabbath.

Another argument of Justin against the obligation of the Sabbath is, that God "directs the government of the universe on this day equally as on all others!" [49] as though this were inconsistent with the present sacredness of the Sabbath, when it is also true that God thus governed the world in the period when Justin acknowledges the Sabbath to have been obligatory. Though this reason is trivial as an argument against the Sabbath, it does show that Justin could have attached no Sabbatic character to Sunday. But he has yet one more argument against the Sabbath. The ancient law has been done away by the new and final law, and the old cove-

[48] Dialogue with Trypho, chap. 23.   [49] Id., chap. 29.

20

nant has been superseded by the new.[50]　But he forgets
that the design of the new covenant was not to do away
with the law of God, but to put that law into the heart
of every Christian.　And many of the Fathers, as we
shall see, expressly repudiate this doctrine of the abrogation of the decalogue.

Such were Justin's reasons for rejecting the ancient
Sabbath.　But though he was a decided asserter of the
abrogation of the law, and of the Sabbatic institution
itself, and kept Sunday only as a festival, modern first-
day writers cite him as a witness in support of the
doctrine that the first day of the week should be observed
as the Christian Sabbath on the authority of the fourth
commandment.

Now let us learn what stood in the way of Irenæus's
observance of the Sabbath.　It was not that the commandments were abolished, for we shall presently learn
that he taught their perpetuity.　Nor was it that he believed in the change of the Sabbath, for he gives no hint
of such an idea.　The Sunday festival, in his estimation,
appears to have been simply of " equal significance " with
the Pentecost.[51]　Nor was it that Christ broke the Sabbath; for Irenæus says that he did not.[52]　But because
the Sabbath is called a sign, he regarded it as significant
of the future kingdom, and appears to have considered
it no longer obligatory, though he does not expressly say
this.　Thus he sets forth the meaning of the Sabbath as
held by him :—

" Moreover, the Sabbath of God, *that is, the kingdom*, was,
as it were, indicated by created things," etc.[53]

---

[50] Dialogue with Trypho, chap. 11.　　[51] Lost Writings of Irenæus, Fragment 7.
[52] Against Heresies, book 4, chap. 8, sec. 2.　　[53] Id., book 4, chap. 16, sec. 1.

" These [promises to the righteous] are [to take place] in *the times of the kingdom*, that is, upon the seventh day, which has been sanctified, in which God rested from all the works which he created, which is the true Sabbath of the righteous," [54] etc.

" For the day of the Lord is as a thousand years; and in six days created things were completed; it is evident, therefore, that they will come to an end at the six thousandth year." [55]

But Irenæus did not notice that the Sabbath, as a sign, does not point forward to the restitution, but backward to the creation, that it may signify that the true God is the Creator.[56] Nor did he observe the fact that when the kingdom of God shall be established under the whole heaven, all flesh shall hallow the Sabbath.[57]

But he says that those who lived before Moses were justified " without observance of Sabbaths," and offers as proof that the covenant at Horeb was not made with the Fathers. Of course, if this proves that the patriarchs were free from obligation toward the fourth commandment, it is equally good as proof that they might violate any other. These things indicate that Irenæus was opposed to Sabbatic observance, though he did not in express language assert its abrogation, and did in most decisive terms assert the continued obligation of the ten commandments.

Tertullian offers numerous reasons for not observing the Sabbath, but there is scarcely one of these that he does not in some other place expressly contradict. Thus he asserts that the patriarchs before Moses did not observe the Sabbath.[58] But he offers no proof, and he elsewhere dates the origin of the Sabbath at the creation,

---

[54] Irenæus against Heresies, book 5, chap. 33, sec. 2.

[55] Id., book 5, chap. 28, sec. 3. [56] Ex. 31: 17; Eze. 20: 12, 20.

[57] Isa. 66: 22, 23; Dan. 7: 18, 27. [58] Answer to the Jews, chap. 2.

as we shall show hereafter.[59]   In several places he teaches
the abrogation of the law, and seems to set aside moral
law as well as ceremonial.   But elsewhere he bears express testimony that the ten commandments are still
binding as the rule of the Christian's life.[60]   He quotes
the words of Isaiah, in which God is represented as hat-
ing the feasts, new-moons, and sabbaths observed by
the Jews,[61] as proof that the seventh-day Sabbath was a
temporary institution abrogated by Christ.   But in another place he says: " *Christ did not at all rescind the
Sabbath :* he kept the law thereof." [62]   And he also explains this very text by stating that God's aversion toward the Sabbaths observed by the Jews was " because
they were celebrated without the fear of God, by a people full of iniquities ;" and he adds that the prophet, in
a later passage, speaking of Sabbaths celebrated according to God's commandment, " declares them to be true,
delightful, and inviolable." [63]   Another statement is that
Joshua violated the Sabbath in the siege of Jericho.[64]
Yet he elsewhere explains this very case, showing that
the commandment forbids our own work, not God's.
Those who acted at Jericho did " not do their own work,
but God's, which they executed, and that, too, from his
express commandment." [65]   He also both asserts and denies that Christ violated the Sabbath.[66]   Tertullian was

---

[59] Tertullian against Marcion, book 4, chap. 12.

[60] Compare his works as follows: Answer to the Jews, chaps. 2, 3, 4, 6;
Against Marcion, book 1, chap. 20; book 5, chaps. 4, 19; with *De Anima*, chap.
37; on Modesty, chap. 5.

[61] Isa. 1: 13, 14.

[62] Answer to the Jews, chap. 4; Against Marcion, book 4, chap. 12.

[63] Isa. 56: 2; 58: 13.

[64] Answer to the Jews, chap. 4; Against Marcion, book 4, chap. 12.

[65] Against Marcion, book 2, chap. 21.   [66] Id., book 4, chap. 12.

a double-minded man. He wrote against the law and the Sabbath, but contradicted and exposed his own errors.

Origen attempts to prove that the ancient Sabbath is to be understood mystically or spiritually, not literally :—

" ' Ye shall sit, every one in your dwellings : no one shall move from his place on the Sabbath-day.' Which precept it is impossible to observe literally; for no man can sit a whole day so as not to move from the place where he sat down." [67]

Great men are not always wise. There is no such precept in the Bible. Origen referred to that which forbade the people to go out for manna on the Sabbath, but which did not conflict with another that commanded holy convocations or assemblies for worship on the Sabbath. [68]

Victorinus is the latest of the Fathers before Constantine, who offers reasons against the observance of the Sabbath. His first reason is that Christ said by Isaiah that his soul hated the Sabbath; which Sabbath he in his body abolished; and these assertions we have seen answered by Tertullian. [69] His second reason is that "Jesus [Joshua] the son of Nave [Nun], the successor of Moses, himself broke the Sabbath-day;" [70] which is false. His third reason is that "Matthias [a Maccabean] also, prince of Judah, broke the Sabbath;" [71] which is doubtless false, but is of no consequence as authority. His fourth argument is original, and may fitly close the list of reasons assigned by the Fathers for not observing the Sabbath. It is given in full without an answer :—

"And in Matthew we read, that it is written Isaiah also and the rest of his colleagues broke the Sabbath." [72]

---

[67] *De Principiis*, book 4, chap. 1, sec. 17. [68] Ex. 16:29; Lev. 23:3.
[69] Creation of the World, sec. 4. [70] Id., sec. 5. [71] Id.
[72] Creation of the World, sec. 5.

CHAPTER XVIII.

THE SABBATH IN THE RECORD OF THE EARLY FATHERS.

The first reasons for neglecting the Sabbath are now mostly obsolete—A portion of the early Fathers taught the perpetuity of the decalogue, and made it the standard of moral character—What they say concerning the origin of the Sabbath at creation—Their testimony concerning the perpetuity and observance of the ancient Sabbath—Enumeration of the things which caused the suppression of the Sabbath, and the elevation of Sunday.

HE reasons offered by the early Fathers for neglecting the observance of the Sabbath, show conclusively that they had no special light on the subject by reason of living in the first centuries, which we in this later age do not possess. The fact is, so many of the reasons offered by them are manifestly false and absurd that those who in these days discard the Sabbath, do also discard the most of the reasons offered by these Fathers for this same course. We have also learned from such of the early Fathers as mention first-day observance, the exact nature of the Sunday festival, and all the reasons which in the first centuries were offered in its support. Very few indeed of these reasons are now offered by modern first-day writers.

But some of the Fathers bear emphatic testimony to the perpetuity of the ten commandments, and make their observance the condition of eternal life. Some also distinctly assert the origin of the Sabbath at creation. Several of them, moreover, bear witness to the existence of Sabbath-keepers, or give decisive testimony to the perpetuity and obligation of the Sabbath, or define the nature of proper Sabbatic observance, or connect the observance of the Sabbath and first-day together. Let us now hear the testimony of those who assert the authority of the ten commandments. Irenæus asserts their perpetuity, and makes them a test of Christian character. Thus he says :—

" For God at the first, indeed, warning them [the Jews] by means of *natural precepts*, which *from the beginning he had implanted in mankind*, that is, by means of *the* DECALOGUE (*which, if any one does not observe, he has no salvation*), did then demand nothing more of them." [1]

This is a very strong statement. He makes the ten commandments the law of nature implanted in man's being at the beginning; and so inherited by all mankind. This is no doubt true. It is the presence of the carnal mind or law of sin and death, implanted in man by the fall, that has partially obliterated this law, and made the work of the new covenant a necessity.[2] He again asserts the perpetuity and authority of the ten commandments in the following words :—

" Preparing man for this life, the Lord himself did speak in his own person to all alike the words of the decalogue : and therefore, in like manner, do they remain permanently with us, receiving, by means of his advent in the flesh, extension and increase, but not abrogation." [3]

By the " extension " of the decalogue, Irenæus doubt-

---

[1] Irenæus against Heresies, book 4, chap. 15, sec.1.

[2] Jer. 31: 33; Rom. 7: 21–25; 8: 1–7.

[3] Irenæus against Heresies, book 4, chap. 16, sec. 4.

less means the exposition which the Saviour gave of the meaning of the commandments in his sermon on the mount.[4] Theophilus speaks in like manner concerning the decalogue :—

"For God has given us a law and holy commandments ; and *every one* who *keeps* these *can be saved,* and, obtaining the resurrection, can inherit incorruption."[5]

"We have learned a holy law ; but we have as Lawgiver him who is really God, who teaches us to act righteously, and to be pious, and to do good."[6]

"Of this great and wonderful law which tends to all righteousness, the TEN HEADS are such as we have already rehearsed."[7]

Tertullian calls the ten commandments "the rules of our regenerate life," that is to say, the rules which govern the life of a converted man :—

"They who theorize respecting numbers, honor the number ten as the parent of all the others, and as imparting perfection to the human nativity. For my own part, I prefer viewing this measure of time in reference to God, as if implying that the ten months rather initiated man into *the ten commandments ;* so that the numerical estimate of the time needed to consummate our natural birth should correspond to the numerical classification of *the rules of our regenerate life.*"[8]

In showing the deep guilt involved in the violation of the seventh commandment, Tertullian speaks of the sacredness of the commandments which precede it, naming several in particular, and among them the fourth, and then says of the precept against adultery that—

It stands "in the very forefront of *the most holy law,* among the *primary counts* of the *celestial edict.*"[9]

---

[4] Matt., chapters 5, 6, 7.   [5] Theophilus to Autolycus, book 2, chap. 27.
[6] Id., book 3, chap. 9.   [7] Id.   [8] *De Anima,* chap. 37.
[9] On Modesty, chap. 5.

Clement of Rome, or rather the author whose works have been ascribed to this Father, speaks thus of the decalogue as a test :—

" On account of those, therefore, who, by neglect of their own salvation, please the evil one, and those, who, by study of their own profit, seek to please the good One, ten things have been prescribed as a test to this present age, according to the number of ten plagues which were brought upon Egypt." [10]

Novatian, who wrote about A. D. 250, is accounted the founder of the sect called *Cathari*, or Puritans. He wrote a treatise on the Sabbath, which is not extant. There is no reference to Sunday in any of his writings. He makes the following striking remarks concerning the moral law :—

" The law was given to the children of Israel for this purpose, that they might profit by it, and RETURN *to those virtuous manners* which, although *they had received them from their fathers*, they had corrupted in Egypt, by reason of their intercourse with a barbarous people. Finally, also, those *ten commandments* on the tables teach nothing *new*, but *remind them of what had been obliterated*—that righteousness in them, which had been put to sleep, might revive again, as it were, by the afflatus of the law, after the manner of a fire [nearly extinguished]." [11]

It is evident that in the judgment of Novatian, the ten commandments enjoined nothing that was not sacredly regarded by the patriarchs before Jacob went down into Egypt. It follows, therefore, that in his opinion the Sabbath was made, not at the fall of the manna, but when God sanctified the seventh day ; and that holy men from the earliest ages observed it.

The Apostolical Constitutions, written about the third

---

[10] Recognitions of Clement, book 3, chap. 55.
[11] Novatian on the Jewish Meats, chap. 3.

century, give us an understanding of what was widely
regarded in the third century as apostolic doctrine.
They speak thus of the ten commandments :—

" Have before thine eyes the fear of God, and always remember the ten commandments of God,—to love the one and only
Lord God with all thy strength ; to give no heed to idols, or any
other beings, as being lifeless gods, or irrational beings or
dæmons." [12]

" He gave a plain law to assist the law of nature, such a one
as is pure, saving, and holy, in which his own name was inscribed,
perfect, which is never to fail, being complete in ten commands,
unspotted, converting souls." [13]

This writer, like Irenæus, believed in the identity of
the decalogue with the law of nature. These testimonies show that in the writings of the early Fathers are
some of the strongest utterances in behalf of the perpetuity and authority of the ten commandments. Now let
us hear what they say concerning the origin of the Sabbath at creation. The epistle ascribed to Barnabas
says :—

" And he says in another place, ' If my sons keep the Sabbath, then will I cause my mercy to rest upon them.' The Sabbath is mentioned at the beginning of the creation [thus]: ' And
God made in six days the works of his hands, and made an end
on the seventh day, and rested on it, and sanctified it.' " [14]

Irenæus seems plainly to connect the origin of the
Sabbath with the sanctification of the seventh day :—

" These [things promised] are [to take place] in the times of
the kingdom, that is, upon the seventh day, which has been sanctified, in which God rested from all his works which he created,

---

[12] Apostolical Constitutions, book 2, scc. 4, par. 36.
[13] Id., book 6, sec. 4, par. 19.   [14] Epistle of Barnabas, chap. 15.

which is the true Sabbath, in which they shall not be engaged in any earthly occupation." [15]

Tertullian, likewise, refers the origin of the Sabbath to "the benediction of the Father" :—

"But inasmuch as birth is also completed with the seventh month, I more readily recognize in this number than in the eighth the honor of a numerical agreement with the Sabbatical period; so that the month in which God's image is sometimes produced in a human birth, shall in its number tally with the day on which God's creation was completed and *hallowed.*" [16]

"For even in the case before us, he [Christ] fulfilled the law, while interpreting its condition; [moreover] he exhibits in a clear light the different kinds of work, while doing what the law excepts from the sacredness of the Sabbath, [and] while imparting to the Sabbath-day itself which *from the beginning had been consecrated by the benediction of the Father,* an additional sanctity by his own beneficent action." [17]

Origen, who, as we have seen, believed in a mystical Sabbath, did nevertheless fix its origin at the sanctification of the seventh day :—

"For he [Celsus] knows nothing of the day of the Sabbath and rest of God, which follows the completion of the world's creation, and which lasts during the duration of the world, and in which all those will keep festival with God who have done all their works in their six days." [18]

The testimony of Novatian, which has been given relative to the sacredness and authority of the decalogue, plainly implies the existence of the Sabbath in the patriarchal ages, and its observance by those holy men of old. It was given to Israel that they might " RETURN to those

---

[15] Irenæus against Heresies, book 5, chap. 33, sec. 2.

[16] *De Anima,* chap. 37. [17] Tertullian against Marcion, book 4, chap. 12.

[18] Origen against Celsus, book 6, chap. 61.

virtuous manners which, although *they had received them from their fathers,* they had corrupted in Egypt." And he adds, " Those ten commandments on the tables teach *nothing new,* but *remind* them of what had been obliterated." [19]   He did not, therefore, believe the Sabbath to have originated at the fall of the manna, but counted it one of those things which were practiced by their fathers before Jacob went down to Egypt.

Lactantius places the origin of the Sabbath at creation :—

" God completed the world and this admirable work of nature in the space of six days (as is contained in the secrets of holy Scripture), and CONSECRATED the seventh day, on which he had rested from his works. But this is the Sabbath-day, which, in the language of the Hebrews, received its name from the number, whence the seventh is the legitimate and complete number." [20]

In a poem on Genesis, written about the time of Lactantius, but by an unknown author, we have an explicit testimony to the divine appointment of the seventh day to a holy use while man was yet in Eden, the garden of God :—

> " The seventh came, when God
>   At his work's end did rest, DECREEING IT
>   SACRED UNTO THE COMING AGE'S JOYS." [21]

The Apostolical Constitutions, while teaching the present obligation of the Sabbath, plainly indicate its origin to have been at creation :—

" O Lord Almighty, thou hast created the world by Christ, and *hast appointed the Sabbath in memory thereof,* because that

---

[19] Novatian on the Jewish Meats, chap. 3.
[20] Divine Institutes of Lactantius, book 7, chap. 14.
[21] Poem on Genesis, Lines 51–53.

on that day thou hast made us rest from our works, for the meditation upon thy laws." [22]

Such are the testimonies of the early Fathers to the primeval origin of the Sabbath, and to the sacredness and perpetual obligation of the ten commandments. We now call attention to what they say relative to the perpetuity of the Sabbath, and to its observance in the centuries during which they lived. Tertullian defines Christ's relation to the Sabbath :—

" He was called ' Lord of the Sabbath' because he maintained the Sabbath as his own institution." [23]

He affirms that Christ did not abolish the Sabbath :—

" Christ did not at all rescind the Sabbath: he kept the law thereof, and both in the former case did a work which was beneficial to the life of his disciples (for he indulged them with the relief of food when they were hungry), and in the present instance, cured the withered hand ; in each case intimating by facts, ' I came not to destroy the law, but to fulfill it.' " [24]

Nor can it be said that while Tertullian denied that Christ abolished the Sabbath, he did believe that he transferred its sacredness from the seventh day of the week to the first; for he continues thus :—

" He [Christ] exhibits in a clear light the different kinds of work, while doing what the law excepts from the sacredness of the Sabbath, [and] while imparting to the Sabbath-day itself, which from the beginning had been consecrated by the benediction of the Father, an additional sanctity by his own beneficent action. For he furnished *to this day* DIVINE SAFEGUARDS—*a course which his adversary would have pursued for some other days*, to avoid honoring the Creator's Sabbath, and restoring to the Sabbath the works which were proper for it." [25]

---

[22] Apostolical Constitutions, book 7, sec. 2, par. 36.
[23] Tertullian against Marcion, book 4, chap. 12.   [24] Id.
[25] Tertullian against Marcion, book 4, chap. 12.

This is a very remarkable statement. The modern doctrine of the change of the Sabbath was unknown in Tertullian's time. Had it then been in existence, there could be no doubt that in the words last quoted he was aiming at it a heavy blow; for the very thing which he asserts Christ's adversary, Satan, would have had him do, that modern first-day writers assert he did do in consecrating another day instead of adding to the sanctity of his Father's Sabbath.

Archelaus, of Cascar in Mesopotamia, emphatically denies the abolition of the Sabbath :—

"Again, as to the assertion that the Sabbath has been abolished, we deny that he has abolished it plainly; for he was himself also Lord of the Sabbath." [26]

Justin Martyr, as we have seen, was an outspoken opponent of Sabbatic observance, and of the authority of the law of God. He was by no means always candid in what he said. He has occasion to refer to those who observed the seventh day, and he does it with contempt. Thus he says :—

"But if some, through weak-mindedness, wish to observe such institutions as were given by Moses (from which they expect some virtue, but which we believe were appointed by reason of the hardness of the people's hearts), along with their hope in this Christ, and [wish to perform] the eternal and natural acts of righteousness and piety, yet choose to live with the Christians and the faithful, as I said before, not inducing them either to be circumcised like themselves, or to keep the Sabbath, or to observe any other such ceremonies, then I hold that we ought to join ourselves to such, and associate with them in all things as kinsmen and brethren." [27]

These words are spoken of Sabbath-keeping Chris-

---

[26] Disputation with Manes, sec. 42.   [27] Dialogue with Trypho, chap. 47.

tians. Such of them as were of Jewish descent no doubt generally retained circumcision. But there were many Gentile Christians who observed the Sabbath, as we shall see; and it is not true that they observed circumcision. Justin speaks of this class as acting from " weakmindedness ; " yet he inadvertently alludes to the keeping of the commandments as the performance of " the ETERNAL and NATURAL ACTS OF RIGHTEOUSNESS," a most appropriate designation indeed. Justin would fellowship those who act thus, provided they would fellowship him in the contrary course. But though Justin, on this condition, could fellowship these " weak-minded " brethren, he says that there are those who " *do not venture to have any intercourse with, or to extend hospitality to, such persons :* but I do not agree with them." [28] This shows the bitter spirit which prevailed in some quarters toward the Sabbath, even as early as Justin's time. Justin has no word of condemnation for these intolerant professors ; he is only solicitous lest those persons who perform "the eternal and natural acts of righteousness and piety " should condemn those who do not perform them.

Clement, of Alexandria, though a mystical writer, bears an important testimony to the perpetuity of the ancient Sabbath, and to man's present need thereof. He comments thus on the fourth commandment :—

" And the fourth word is that which intimates that the world was created by God, and that *he gave us the seventh day as a rest*, on account of the trouble that there is in life. For God is incapable of weariness, and suffering, and want. *But we who bear flesh need rest.* The seventh day, therefore, is proclaimed

---

[28] Dialogue with Trypho, chap. 47.

a rest—abstraction from ills—preparing for the primal day, our true rest." [29]

Clement recognized the authority of the moral law; for he treats of the ten commandments one by one, and shows what each enjoins. He plainly teaches that the Sabbath was made for man, and that he now needs it as a day of rest, and his language implies that it was made at the creation. But in the next paragraph he makes some curious suggestions, which deserve notice :—

" Having reached this point, we must mention these things by the way; since the discourse has turned on the seventh and the eighth. For the eighth may possibly turn out to be properly the seventh, and the seventh manifestly the sixth, and the latter properly the Sabbath, and the seventh a day of work. For the creation of the world was concluded in six days." [30]

This language has been adduced to show that Clement called the eighth day, or Sunday, the Sabbath. But first-day writers in general have not dared to commit themselves to such an interpretation, and some of them have expressly discarded it. Let us notice this statement with especial care. He speaks of the ordinals *seventh* and *eighth* in the abstract, but probably with reference to the days of the week. Observe, then,—

1. That he does not intimate that the eighth day has *become* the Sabbath in place of the seventh which was *once* such, but he says that the eighth day may possibly turn out to be properly the seventh.

2. That in Clement's time, A. D. 194, there was not any confusion in the minds of men as to which day was the ancient Sabbath, and which one was the first day of

---

[29] Clement's Miscellanies, book 6, chap. 16.   [30] Id.

the week, or eighth day, as it was often called, nor does he intimate that there was.

3. But Clement, from some cause, says that possibly the eighth day should be counted the seventh, and the seventh day the sixth. Now, if this should be done, it would change the numbering of the days, not only as far back as the resurrection of Christ, but all the way back to the creation.

4. If, therefore, Clement, in this place, designed to teach that Sunday is the Sabbath, he must also have held that it always had been such.

5. But observe that, while he changes the numbering of the days of the week, he does not change the Sabbath from one day to another. He says the eighth may possibly be the seventh, and the seventh, properly the sixth, and the latter, or this one [Greek, ἡ μὲν κυρίως εἶναι σάββατον_, properly the Sabbath, and the seventh a day of work.

6. By the latter must be understood the day last mentioned, which he says should be called, not the seventh, but the sixth; and by the seventh must certainly be intended that day which he says is not the eighth, but the seventh, that is to say, Sunday.

There remains but one difficulty to be solved, and that is why he should suggest the changing of the numbering of the days of the week by striking one from the count of each day, thus making the Sabbath the sixth day in the count instead of the seventh; and making Sunday the seventh day in the count instead of the eighth. The answer seems to have eluded the observation of the first-day and anti-Sabbatarian writers who have sought to grasp it. But there is a fact which solves the difficulty. Clement's commentary on the fourth commandment, from which these quotations are taken, is principally made up of curious observations on " the perfect number six," " the number seven motherless and childless," and the number eight, which is " a cube," and the like matters, and is taken, with some change of arrangement, almost word for word from Philo Judæus, a teacher who flourished at Alexandria about one century before Clement. Whoever will take pains to compare these two writers will find in Philo nearly all the ideas and illustrations which Clement has used, and the very language also in which he has expressed them.[31] Philo was a mystical teacher to whom Clement looked up as to a master. A statement which we find in Philo, in immediate connection with several curious ideas, which Clement quotes from him, gives, beyond all doubt, the key to Clement's suggestion that possibly the eighth day should be called the seventh, and the seventh day called the sixth. Philo said that, according to God's purpose, the first day of time was not to be numbered with the other days of the creation week. Thus he says :—

" And he allotted each of the six days to one of the portions of the whole, TAKING OUT THE FIRST DAY, which he does not even call the first day, *that it may not be numbered with the others*, but entitling it ONE, he names it rightly, perceiving in it, and ascribing to it, the nature and appellation of the limit." [32]

This would simply change the numbering of the days, as counted by Philo, and afterward partially

---

[31] Compare Clement of Alexandria, vol. 2, pp. 386–390, Ante-Nicene library edition, or the Miscellanies of Clement, book 4, chap. 16, with Bohn's edition of Philo, vol. 1, pp. 3, 4, 29, 30, 31, 32, 54, 55; vol. 3, p. 159; vol. 4, p. 452.

[32] Bohn's edition of Philo Judæus, vol. 1, p. 4.

adopted by Clement, and make the Sabbath, not the seventh day, but the sixth, and Sunday, not the eighth day, but the seventh; but it would still leave the Sabbath-day and the Sunday the same identical days as before. It would, however, give the Sabbath the name of sixth day, because the first of the six days of creation was not counted; and it would cause the eighth day, so called in the early church because of its coming next after the Sabbath, to be called seventh day. Thus the Sabbath would be the sixth day, and the seventh a day of work, and yet the Sabbath would be the identical day that it has ever been, and the Sunday, though called seventh day, would still, as ever before, remain a day on which ordinary labor was lawful. Of course, Philo's idea that the first day of time should not be counted, is wholly false; for there is not one fact in the Bible to support it, but many which expressly contradict it, and even Clement, with all deference to Philo, only timidly suggests it. But when the matter is laid open, it shows that Clement had no thought of calling Sunday the Sabbath, and that he does expressly confirm what we have fully proved out of other of the Fathers, that Sunday was a day on which, in their judgment, labor was not sinful.

Tertullian, at different periods of his life, held different views respecting the Sabbath, and committed them all to writing. We last quoted from him a decisive testimony to the perpetuity of the Sabbath, coupled with an equally decisive testimony against the sanctification of the first day of the week. In another work, from which we have already quoted his statement that Christians should not kneel on Sunday, we find another state-

ment that " some few " abstained from kneeling on the
Sabbath. This has probable reference to Carthage, where
Tertullian lived. He speaks thus :—

" In the matter of *kneeling* also, prayer is subject to diversity
of observance, through the act of some few who abstain from
kneeling on the Sabbath ; and since this dissension is particularly on its trial before the churches, the Lord will give his grace
that the dissentients may either yield, or else indulge their opinion without offense to others." [33]

The act of standing in prayer was one of the chief
honors conferred upon Sunday. Those who refrained
from kneeling on the seventh day, without doubt did it
because they desired to honor that day. This particular act is of no consequence ; for it was adopted in imitation of those who, from tradition and custom, thus
honored Sunday ; but we have in this an undoubted
reference to Sabbath-keeping Christians. Tertullian
speaks of them, however, in a manner quite unlike that
of Justin in his reference to the commandment-keepers
of his time.

Origen, like many others of the Fathers, was far
from being consistent with himself. Though he has
spoken against Sabbatic observance, and has honored
the so-called Lord's day as something better than the
ancient Sabbath, he has nevertheless given a discourse
expressly designed to teach Christians the proper
method of observing the Sabbath. Here is a portion of
this sermon :—

" But what is the feast of the Sabbath except that of which
the apostle speaks, ' There remaineth therefore a Sabbatism,'
that is, the observance of the Sabbath, by the people of God ?

---

[33] Tertullian on Prayer, chap. 23.

Leaving the Jewish observances of the Sabbath, let us see how the Sabbath ought to be observed by a Christian. On the Sabbath-day all worldly labors ought to be abstained from. If, therefore, you cease from all secular works, and execute nothing worldly, but give yourselves up to spiritual exercises, repairing to church, attending to sacred reading and instruction, thinking of celestial things, solicitous for the future, placing the Judgment to come before your eyes, not looking to things present and visible, but to those which are future and invisible, this is the observance of the Christian Sabbath." [34]

This is by no means a bad representation of the proper observance of the Sabbath. Such a discourse addressed to Christians is a strong evidence that many did then hallow that day. Some, indeed, have claimed that these words were spoken concerning Sunday. They would have it that he contrasts the observance of the first day with that of the seventh. But the contrast is not between the different methods of keeping two days, but between two methods of observing one day. The Jews in Origen's time spent the day mainly in mere abstinence from labor, and often added sensuality to idleness. But the Christians were to observe it in divine worship, as well as sacred rest. What day he intends cannot be doubtful. It is DIES SABBATI, a term which can signify only the seventh day. Here is the first instance of the term Christian Sabbath, *Sabbati Christiani,*

[34] *Origen's Opera*, Tome 2, p. 358, Paris, 1733, " Quæ est autem festivitas Sabbati nisi illa dequa Apostolus dicit, 'relinqueretur ergo Sabbatismus,' hoc, est, Sabbati observatio, 'populo Dei'? Relinquentes ergo Judaicas Sabbati observationes, qualis debeat esse Christiano Sabbati observatio, videamus. Die Sabbati nihil ex omnibus mundi actibus oportet operari. Si ergo desinas ab omnibus sæcularibus operibus, et nihil mundanum geras, sed spiritalibus operibus vaces, ad ecclesiam convenias, lectionibus divinis et tractatibus aurem præbeas, et de cœlestibus cogites, de futura, spe sollicitudinem geras, venturum judicium præ oculis habeas, non respicias ad præ sentia et visibilia, sed ad invisibilia et futura, hæc est observatio Sabbati Christiani."—*Origenis in Numeras Homilia 23.*

and it is expressly applied to the seventh day observed
by Christians.

The longer form of the reputed epistle of Ignatius to
the Magnesians was not written till after Origen's time;
but though not written by Ignatius, it is valuable for
the light it throws upon the existing state of things at
the time of its composition, and for marking the progress
which apostasy had made with respect to the Sabbath. Here is its reference to the Sabbath and first
day :—

" Let us therefore no longer keep the Sabbath after the Jewish manner, and rejoice in days of idleness; for ' he that does
not work, let him not eat.' For say the [holy] oracles, ' in the
sweat of thy face shalt thou eat thy bread.' But let every one
of you keep the Sabbath after a spiritual manner, rejoicing in
meditation on the law, not in relaxation of the body, admiring
the workmanship of God, and not eating things prepared the day
before, nor using lukewarm drinks, and walking within a prescribed space, nor finding delight in dancing and plaudits which
have no sense in them. And after the observance of the Sabbath, let every friend of Christ keep the Lord's day as a festival,
the resurrection day, the queen and chief of all the days [of the
week]. Looking forward to this, the prophet declared, ' To the
end, for the eighth day,' on which our life both sprang up again,
and the victory over death was obtained in Christ." [35]

This writer specifies the different things which made
up the Jewish observance of the Sabbath. They may
be summed up under two heads: 1. Strict abstinence
from labor; 2. Dancing and carousal. Now in the light
of what Origen has said, we can understand the contrast
which this writer draws between the Jewish and the
Christian observance of the Sabbath. The error of the

---

[35] Epistle to the Magnesians (longer form), chap. 9.

Jews in the first part of this was that they contented themselves with mere bodily relaxation, without raising their thoughts to God, the Creator, and this mere idleness soon gave place to sensual folly.

The Christian, as Origen draws the contrast, refrains from labor on the Sabbath that he may raise his heart in grateful worship; or, as this writer expresses it, the Christian keeps the Sabbath in "a spiritual manner," rejoicing in meditation on the law; but to do thus, he must hallow it in the manner which the law commands, that is, in the observance of a sacred rest which commemorates the rest of the Creator. The writer evidently believed in the observance of the Sabbath as an act of obedience to that law on which they were to meditate on that day. And the nature of the epistle indicates that it was observed, at all events, in the country where it was written. But mark the work of apostasy. The so-called Lord's day, for which the writer could offer nothing better than an argument drawn from the title of the sixth psalm (see its marginal reading), is exalted above the Lord's holy day, and made the queen of all days!

The Apostolical Constitutions, though not written in apostolic times, were in existence as early as the third century, and were then very generally believed to express the doctrine of the apostles. They do, therefore, furnish important historical testimony to the practice of the church at that time, and also indicate the great progress which apostasy had made. Guericke speaks thus of them :—

"This is a collection of ecclesiastical statutes purporting to be the work of the apostolic age, but in reality formed gradually in the second, third, and fourth centuries, and is of much value in reference to the history of polity, and Christian archæology generally." [36]

Mosheim says of them :—

" The matter of this work is unquestionably ancient; since the manners and discipline of which it exhibits a view are those which prevailed amongst the Christians of the second and third centuries, especially those resident in Greece and the oriental regions." [37]

These Constitutions indicate that the Sabbath was extensively observed in the third century. They also show the standing of the Sunday festival in that century. After solemnly enjoining the sacred observance of the ten commandments, they thus enforce the Sabbath :—

" Consider the manifold workmanship of God, which received its beginning through Christ. Thou shalt observe the Sabbath, on account of Him who ceased from his work of creation, but ceased not from his work of providence: it is a rest for meditation of the law, not for idleness of the hands." [38]

This is sound Sabbatarian doctrine. To show how distinctly these Constitutions recognize the decalogue as the foundation of Sabbatic authority, we quote the words next preceding the above, though they have been already quoted :—

" Have before thine eyes the fear of God, and always remember the ten commandments of God,—to love the one and only Lord God with all thy strength; to give no heed to idols, or any other beings, as being lifeless gods, or irrational beings or dæmons." [39]

---

[36] Ancient Church, p. 212.   [37] Historical Commentaries, cent. 1, sec. 51.
[38] Apostolical Constitutions, book 2, sec. 4, par. 36.   [39] Id.

But though these Constitutions thus recognize the authority of the decalogue and the sacred obligation of the seventh day, they elevate the Sunday festival in some respects to higher honor than the Sabbath, though they claim for it no precept of the Scriptures. Thus they say :—

"But keep the Sabbath, and the Lord's day festival; because the former is the memorial of the creation, and the latter of the resurrection." [40]

" For the Sabbath is the ceasing of the creation, the completion of the world, the inquiry after laws, and the grateful praise to God for the blessings he has bestowed upon men. All which the Lord's day excels, and shows the Mediator himself, the Provider, the Lawgiver, the Cause of the resurrection, the First-born of the whole creation." [41]

"So that the Lord's day commands us to offer unto thee, O Lord, thanksgiving for all. For this is the grace afforded by thee, which, on account of its greatness, has obscured all other blessings." [42]

Tested by his own principles, the writer of these Constitutions was far advanced in apostasy ; for he held a festival, for which he claimed no divine authority, more honorable than one which he acknowledged to be ordained of God. There could be but one step more in this course, and that would be to set aside the commandment of God for the ordinance of man, and this step was, not very long afterward, actually taken. One other point should be noticed. It is said :—

" Let the slaves work five days ; but on the Sabbath-day and the Lord's day let them have leisure to go to church for instruction in piety." [43]

---

[40] Apostolical Constitutions, book 7, sec. 2, par. 23.
[41] Id., book 7, sec. 2, par. 36.   [42] Id., book 2, sec. 4, par. 36.
[43] Id., book 8, sec. 4, par. 33.

The question of the sinfulness of labor on either of these days is not here taken into the account; for the reason assigned is that the slaves may have leisure to attend public worship.   But while these Constitutions elsewhere forbid labor on the Sabbath on the authority of the decalogue, they do not forbid it upon the first day of the week.   Take the following as an example :—

"O Lord Almighty, thou hast created the world by Christ, and hast appointed the Sabbath in memory thereof, because that *on that day* thou hast made us *rest from our works*, for the meditation upon thy laws." [44]

The Apostolical Constitutions are valuable to us, not as authority respecting the teaching of the apostles, but as giving us a knowledge of the views and practices which prevailed in the third century.   As these Constitutions were extensively regarded as embodying the doctrine of the apostles, they furnish conclusive evidence that, at the time when they were put in writing, the ten commandments were very generally revered as the immutable rule of right, and that the Sabbath of the Lord was by many observed as an act of obedience to the fourth commandment, and as the divine memorial of the creation.   They also show that the first-day festival had, in the third century, attained such strength and influence as to clearly indicate that ere long it would claim the entire ground.   But observe that the Sabbath and the so-called Lord's day were then regarded as distinct institutions, and that no hint of the change of the Sabbath from the seventh day to the first is even once given.

Thus much out of the Fathers concerning the author-

---

[44] Apostolical Constitutions, book 7, sec. 2, par. 36.

ity of the decalogue, and concerning the perpetuity and observance of the ancient Sabbath. The suppression of the Sabbath of the Bible, and the elevation of Sunday to its place, has been shown to be in no sense the work of the Saviour. But so great a work required the united action of powerful causes, and these causes we will now enumerate :—

1. *Hatred toward the Jews.*—This people, who retained the ancient Sabbath, had slain Christ. It was easy for men to forget that Christ, as Lord of the Sabbath, had claimed it as his own institution, and to call the Sabbath a Jewish institution which Christians should not regard.[45]

2. *The hatred of the church of Rome toward the Sabbath, and its determination to elevate Sunday to the highest place.*—This church, as the chief in the work of apostasy, took the lead in the earliest effort to suppress the Sabbath by turning it into a fast. And the very first act of papal aggression was by an edict in behalf of Sunday. Thenceforward, in every possible form, this church continued this work until the pope announced that he had received a divine mandate for Sunday observance [the very thing lacking] in a roll which fell from heaven.

3. *The voluntary observance of memorable days.*—In the Christian church, almost from the beginning, men voluntarily honored the fourth, the sixth, and the first days of the week, and also the anniversary of the Passover and the Pentecost, to commemorate the betrayal, the death, and the resurrection, of Christ, and the descent of the

---

[45] Victorinus says, "Let the sixth day become a rigorous fast, lest we should appear to observe any Sabbath with the Jews."—*On the Creation of the World*, sec. 4. And Constantine says, "It becomes us to have nothing in common with the perfidious Jews."—*Socrates's Eccl. Hist.*, book 5, chap. 22.

Holy Spirit, which acts in themselves could not be counted sinful.

4. *Making tradition of equal authority with the Script-ures.*—This was the great error of the early church, and the one to which that church was specially exposed, as having in it those who had seen the apostles, or who had seen those who had seen them. It was this which rendered the voluntary observance of memorable days a dangerous thing; for what began as a voluntary observance became, after the lapse of a few years, a standing custom, established by tradition, which must be obeyed because it came from those who had seen the apostles, or from those who had seen others who had seen them. This is the origin of the various errors of the great apostasy.

5. *The entrance of the no-law heresy.*—This is seen in Justin Martyr, the earliest witness to the Sunday festival, and in the church of Rome, of which he was then a member.

6. *The extensive observance of Sunday as a heathen festival.*—The first day of the week corresponded to the widely observed heathen festival of the sun. It was therefore easy to unite the honor of Christ in the observance of the day of his resurrection, with the convenience and worldly advantage of his people, in having the same festival day with their heathen neighbors, and to make it a special act of piety in that the conversion of the heathen was thereby facilitated, while the neglect of the ancient Sabbath was justified by stigmatizing that divine memorial as a Jewish institution with which Christians should have no concern.

CHAPTER XIX.

THE SABBATH AND FIRST-DAY DURING THE FIRST FIVE CENTURIES.

Origin of the Sabbath and of the festival of the sun contrasted—Entrance of that festival into the church—The moderns with the ancients—The Sabbath observed by the early Christians—Testimony of Morer—Of Twisse—Of Giesler—Of Mosheim—Of Coleman—Of Bishop Taylor—The Sabbath loses ground before the Sunday festival—Several bodies of decided Sabbatarians—Testimony of Brerewood —Constantine's Sunday law—Sunday a day of labor with the primitive church—Constantine's edict a heathen law, and himself at that time a heathen—The bishop of Rome authoritatively confers the name of Lord's day upon Sunday—Heylyn narrates the steps by which Sunday arose to power—A marked change in the history of that institution—Paganism brought into the church—The Sabbath weakened by Constantine's influence—Remarkable facts concerning Eusebius—The Sabbath recovers strength again—The council of Laodicea pronounces a curse upon the Sabbath-keepers—The progress of apostasy marked—Authority of church councils considered— Chrysostom—Jerome—Augustine—Sunday edicts—Testimony of Socrates relative to the Sabbath about the middle of the fifth century.— Of Sozomen—Effectual suppression of the Sabbath at the close of the fifth century.

E now have the origin of the Sabbath and of the festival of Sunday distinctly before us. In the beginning, when God made the world, he gave to man the Sabbath that he might not forget the Creator of all things. When men apostatized from God, Satan turned them to the worship of the sun, and, as a standing memorial of their veneration for that luminary, caused them to dedicate to his honor the first day of the

week.   When the elements of apostasy had sufficiently
matured in the Christian church, this ancient festival
stood forth as a rival to the Sabbath of the Lord.   The
manner in which it obtained a foothold in the Christian
church has been already shown; and many facts which
have an important bearing upon the struggle between
these rival institutions have also been given.   We have,
in the preceding chapters, given the statements of the
most ancient Christian writers respecting the Sabbath
and first-day in the early church.   As we now trace the
history of these two days during the first five centuries
of the Christian era, we shall give the statements of
modern church historians, covering the same ground with
the early Fathers, and shall also quote, in continuation
of the ancient writers, the testimonies of the earliest
church historians.   The reader can thus discover how
nearly the ancients and moderns agree.   Of the observance of the Sabbath in the early church, Morer speaks
as follows :—

"The primitive Christians had a great veneration for the
Sabbath, and spent the day in devotion and sermons.   And it is
not to be doubted but they derived this practice from the apostles
themselves, as appears by several scriptures to that purpose; who,
keeping both that day and the first of the week, gave occasion to
the succeeding ages to join them together, and make it one festival, though there was not the same reason for the continuance
of the custom as there was to begin it." [1]

A learned English first-day writer of the seventeenth
century, William Twisse, D. D., thus states the early
history of these two days :—

"Yet for some hundred years in the primitive church, not

[1] Dialogues on the Lord's day, p. 189.

the Lord's day only, but the seventh day also, was religiously observed, not by Ebion and Cerinthus only, but by pious Christians also, as Baronius writeth, and Gomarus confesseth, and Rivet also, that we are bound in conscience under the gospel, to allow for God's service a better proportion of time than the Jews did under the law, rather than a worse." [2]

That the observance of the Sabbath was not confined to Jewish converts, the learned Gieseler explicitly testifies :—

" While the Jewish Christians of Palestine retained the entire Mosaic law, and consequently the Jewish festivals, the Gentile Christians observed also *the Sabbath* and the Passover,[3] with reference to the last scenes of Jesus' life, but without Jewish superstition. In addition to these, Sunday, as the day of Christ's resurrection, was devoted to religious services." [4]

The statement of Mosheim may be thought to contradict that of Giesler. He says :—

" The seventh day of the week was also observed as a festival, not by the Christians in general, but by such churches only as were principally composed of Jewish converts, nor did the other Christians censure this custom as criminal and unlawful." [5]

It will be observed that Mosheim does not deny that the Jewish converts observed the Sabbath. He denies that this was done by the Gentile Christians. The proof on which he rests this denial is thus stated by him :—

---

[2] Morality of the Fourth Commandment, p. 9, London, 1641.

[3] 1 Cor. 5: 6-8.   [4] Eccl. Hist., vol. 1, chap. 2, sec. 30.

[5] Eccl. Hist., book 1, cent. 1, part 2, chap. 4, sec. 4. Dr. Murdock's translation is more accurate than that above by Maclaine. He gives it in these words : " Moreover, those congregations which either lived intermingled with Jews, or were composed in great measure of Jews, were accustomed also to observe the *seventh day* of the week as a SACRED day, for doing which the other Christians taxed them with no wrong."

"The churches of Bithynia, of which Pliny speaks, in his letter to Trajan, had only one stated day for the celebration of public worship; and that was undoubtedly the first day of the week, or what we call the Lord's day." [6]

The proposition to be proved is this: The Gentile Christians did not observe the Sabbath. The proof is found in the following fact: The churches of Bithynia assembled on a stated day for the celebration of divine worship. It is seen, therefore, that the conclusion is gratuitous, and wholly unauthorized by the testimony.[7] But this instance shows the dexterity of Mosheim in drawing inferences, and gives us some insight into the kind of evidence which supports some of these sweeping statements in behalf of Sunday. Who can say that this "stated day" was not the very day enjoined in the fourth commandment? Of the Sabbath and first-day in the early ages of the church, Coleman speaks as follows:—

"The last day of the week was strictly kept in connection with that of the first day for a long time after the overthrow of the temple and its worship. Down even to the fifth century the observance of the Jewish Sabbath was continued in the Christian church, but with a rigor and solemnity gradually diminishing until it was wholly discontinued." [8]

This is a most explicit acknowledgment that the Bible Sabbath was long observed by the body of the Christian church. Coleman is a first-day writer, and therefore not likely to state the case too strongly in behalf of the seventh day. He is a modern writer, but we

---

[6] Eccl. Hist., book 1, cent. 1, part 2, chap. 4, sec. 4, margin.

[7] See chapter 14 of this History.

[8] Ancient Christianity Exemplified, chap. 26, sec. 2.

have already proved his statements true by those of the ancients. It is true that Coleman speaks also of the first day of the week, yet his subsequent language shows that it was a long while before this became a sacred day. Thus he says :—

"During the early ages of the church, it was never entitled 'the Sabbath,' this word being confined to the seventh day of the week, the Jewish Sabbath, which, as we have already said, continued to be observed for several centuries by the converts to Christianity." [9]

This fact is made still clearer by the following language, in which this historian admits Sunday to be nothing but a human ordinance :— .

"No law or precept appears to have been given by Christ or the apostles, either for the abrogation of the Jewish Sabbath, or the institution of the Lord's day, or the substitution of the first for the seventh day of the week." [10]

Coleman does not seem to realize that in making this truthful statement he has directly acknowledged that the ancient Sabbath is still in full force as a divine institution, and that first-day observance is only authorized by the traditions of men. He next relates the manner in which this Sunday festival, which had been nourished in the bosom of the church, usurped the place of the Lord's Sabbath,—a warning to all Christians of the tendency of human institutions, if cherished by the people of God, to destroy those which are divine. Let this important language be carefully pondered. His words are,—

"The observance of the Lord's day was ordered while yet the Sabbath of the Jews was continued; nor was the latter superseded until the former had acquired the same solemnity and im-

---

[9] Anc. Christ. Exem., chap. 26, sec. 2.   [10] Id.

portance which belonged, at first, to that great day which God originally ordained and blessed. . . . But in time, after the Lord's day was fully established, the observance of the Sabbath of the Jews was gradually discontinued, and was finally denounced as heretical." [11]

Thus is seen the result of cherishing this harmless Sunday festival in the church. It asked only toleration at first; but gaining strength by degrees, it gradually undermined the Sabbath of the Lord, and finally denounced its observance as heretical.

Jeremy Taylor, a distinguished bishop of the Church of England, and a man of great erudition, but a decided opponent of Sabbatic obligation, confirms the testimony of Coleman. He affirms that the Sabbath was observed by the Christians of the first three hundred years, but denies that they did this out of respect to the authority of the law of God. But we have shown from the Fathers that those who hallowed the Sabbath did it as an act of obedience to the fourth commandment, and that the decalogue was acknowledged as of perpetual obligation, and as the perfect rule of right. As Bishop Taylor denies that this was their ground of observance, he should have shown some other; which he has not done. He speaks as follows :—

"The Lord's day did not succeed in the place of the Sabbath, but the Sabbath was wholly abrogated, and the Lord's day was merely an ecclesiastical institution. It was not introduced by virtue of the fourth commandment, because they for almost three hundred years together kept that day which was in that commandment; but they did it also without any opinion of prime obligation, and therefore they did not suppose it moral." [12]

---

[11] Anc. Christ. Exem., chap. 26, sec. 2.

[12] *Ductor Dubitantium*, part 1, book 2, chap. 2, rule 6, sec. 51.

That such an opinion relative to the obligation of the fourth commandment had gained ground extensively among the leaders of the church, as early at least as the fourth century, and probably in the third, is sufficiently attested by the action of the council of Laodicea, A. D. 364, which anathematized those who should observe the Sabbath, as will be noticed in its place. That this loose view of the morality of the fourth commandment was resisted by many, is shown by the existence of various bodies of steadfast Sabbatarians in that age, whose memory has come down to us; and also by the fact that that council made such a vigorous effort to put down the Sabbath. Coleman has clearly portrayed the gradual depression of the Sabbath, as the first-day festival arose in strength, until Sabbath-keeping became heretical, when, by ecclesiastical authority, the Sabbath was suppressed, and the festival of Sunday became fully established as a new and different institution. The natural consequence of this is seen in the rise of distinct sects, or bodies, who were distinguished for their observance of the seventh day. That they should be denounced as heretical, and falsely charged with many errors, is not surprising, when we consider that their memory has been handed down to us by their opponents, and that Sabbath-keepers in our own time are not unfrequently treated in this very manner. The first of these ancient Sabbatarian bodies was the Nazarenes. Of these, Morer testifies that—

They "retained the Sabbath; and though they pretended to believe as Christians, yet they practiced as Jews, and so were in reality neither one nor the other." [13]

---

[13] Dialogues on the Lord's Day, p. 66.

Dr. Francis White, Lord Bishop of Ely, mentions the Nazarenes as one of the ancient bodies of Sabbath-keepers who were condemned by the church leaders for that heresy; and he classes them with heretics, as Morer has done.[14]   Yet the Nazarenes have a peculiar claim to our regard, as being in reality the apostolic church of Jerusalem, and its direct successors.   Thus Gibbon testifies :—

"The Jewish converts, or, as they were afterwards called, the Nazarenes, who had laid the foundations of the church, soon found themselves overwhelmed by the increasing multitudes, that from all the various religions of polytheism enlisted under the banner of Christ. . . . The Nazarenes retired from the ruins of Jerusalem to the little town of Pella beyond the Jordan, where that ancient church languished above sixty years in solitude and obscurity." [15]

It is not strange that the church which fled out of Judea at the word of Christ [16] should long retain the Sabbath, as it appears that they did, even as late as the fourth century.   Morer mentions another class of Sabbath-keepers in the following language :—

"About the same time were the Hypsistarii, who closed with these as to what concerned the Sabbath, yet would by no means accept circumcision as too plain a testimony of ancient bondage. All these were heretics, and so adjudged to be by the Catholic church.   Yet their hypocrisy and industry were such as gained them a considerable footing in the Christian world." [17]

---

[14] A Treatise of the Sabbath-day, containing a "Defense of the Orthodoxal Doctrine of the Church of England against Sabbatarian Novelty," p. 8.   It was written in 1635, at the command of the king, in reply to Brabourne, a minister of the established church, whose work, entitled, "A Defense of that most Ancient and Sacred Ordinance of God's, the Sabbath-day," was dedicated to the king, with a request that he would restore the Bible Sabbath!   See the preface to Dr. White's Treatise.

[15] Decline and Fall, chap. 15.   [16] See chapter 10.

[17] Dialogues on the Lord's Day, p. 67.

The Bishop of Ely names these also as a body of Sabbath-keepers whose heresy was condemned by the church.[18] The learned Joseph Bingham, M. A., gives the following account of them :—

"There was another sect which called themselves Hypsistarians, that is, worshipers of the most high God, whom they worshiped as the Jews only in one person. And they observed their Sabbaths, and used distinction of meats, clean and unclean, though they did not regard circumcision, as Gregory Nazianzen, whose father was one of this sect, gives the account of them." [19]

It must ever be remembered that these people, whom the Catholic church adjudged to be heretics, are not speaking for themselves : their enemies who condemned them have transmitted to posterity all that is known of their history. It would be well if heretics, who meet with little mercy at the hand of ecclesiastical writers, could at least secure the impartial justice of a truthful record.

Another class are thus described by Cox in his elaborate work, entitled, " Sabbath Laws and Sabbath Duties " :—

" In this way [that is, by presenting the testimony of the Bible on the subject] arose the ancient Sabbatarians, a body, it is well known, of very considerable importance in respect both to numbers and influence, during the greater part of the third and the early part of the next century." [20]

The close of the third century witnessed the Sabbath much weakened in its hold upon the church in general, and the festival of Sunday, although possessed of no

---

[18] Treatise of the Sabbath-day, p. 8.

[19] Antiquities of the Christian Church, book 16, chap. 6, sec. 2.

[20] Page 280. Cox here quotes the work entitled, " The Modern Sabbath Examined."

divine authority, steadily gaining in strength and in sacredness. The following historical testimony from a member of the English Church, Edward Brerewood, professor in Gresham College, London, gives a good general view of the matter, though the author's anti-Sabbatarian views are mixed with it. He says :—

"The ancient Sabbath did remain and was observed together with the celebration of the Lord's day by the Christians of the East church above three hundred years after our Saviour's death; and besides that, no other day for more hundreds of years than I spake of before, was known in the church by the name of Sabbath but that: let the collection thereof and conclusion of all be this: The Sabbath of the seventh day, as touching the alligations of God's solemn worship to time, was ceremonial; that Sabbath was religiously observed in the East church three hundred years and more after our Saviour's passion. That church, being the great part of Christendom, and having the apostles' doctrine and example to instruct them, would have restrained it if it had been deadly." [21]

Such was the case in the Eastern churches at the end of the third century; but in such of the Western churches as sympathized with the church of Rome, the Sabbath had been treated as a fast from the beginning of that century, to express their opposition toward those who observed it according to the commandment.

In the early part of the fourth century, an event occurred which could not have been foreseen, but which threw an immense weight in favor of Sunday into the balances already trembling between the rival institutions, the Sabbath of the Lord and the festival of the sun. This was nothing less than an edict from the throne of the Roman empire in behalf of "the venerable day of

---

[21] Learned Treatise of the Sabbath, p. 77, Oxford, 1631.

the sun." It was issued by the emperor Constantine in A. D. 321, and is thus expressed :—

" Let all the judges and town people, and the occupation of all trades rest on the venerable day of the sun ; but let those who are situated in the country, freely and at full liberty attend to the business of agriculture ; because it often happens that no other day is so fit for sowing corn and planting vines ; lest, the critical moment being let slip, men should lose the commodities granted by Heaven. Given the seventh day of March ; Crispus and Constantine being consuls, each of them for the second time." [22]

Of this law, a high authority speaks as follows :—

" It was Constantine the Great who first made a law for the proper observance of Sunday ; and who, according to Eusebius, appointed it should be regularly celebrated throughout the Roman empire. Before him, and even in his time, they observed the Jewish Sabbath, as well as Sunday ; both to satisfy the law of Moses, and to imitate the apostles who used to meet together on the first day. By Constantine's law, promulgated in 321, it was decreed that for the future the Sunday should be kept as a day of rest in all cities and towns ; but he allowed the country people to follow their work." [23]

Another eminent authority thus states the purport of this law :—

---

[22] This edict is the original fountain of first-day authority, and in many respects answers to the festival of Sunday what the fourth commandment is to the Sabbath of the Lord. The original of this edict may be seen in the library of Harvard College, and is as follows :—

IMP. CONSTANT. A. ELPIDIO.

Omnes Judices, urbanæque plebes, et cunctarum artium officia venerabili die solis quiescant. Ruri tamen positi agrorum culturæ libere licenterque inserviant : quoniam frequenter evenit, ut non aptius alio die frumenta sulcis, aut vineæ scrobibus mandentur, ne occasione momenti pereat commoditas coelesti provisione concessa. Dat. Nonis Mart. Crispo. 2 & Constantino 2. Coss. 321. Corpus Juris Civilis Codicis lib. iii tit. 12. 3.

[23] Encyc. Brit., art., Sunday, seventh edition, 1842.

" Constantine the Great made a law for the whole empire (A. D. 321) that Sunday should be kept as a day of rest in all cities and towns; but he allowed the country people to follow their work on that day." [24]

Thus the fact is placed beyond all dispute that this decree gave full permission to all kinds of agricultural labor. The following testimony of Mosheim is therefore worthy of strict attention :—

" The first day of the week, which was the ordinary and stated time for the public assemblies of the Christians, was in consequence of a peculiar law enacted by Constantine, observed with greater solemnity than it had formerly been." [25]

What will the advocates of first-day sacredness say to this? They quote. Mosheim respecting Sunday observance in the first century,—which testimony has been carefully examined in this work,[26]—and they seem to think that his language in support of first-day sacredness is nearly equal in authority to the language of the New Testament; in fact, they regard it as supplying an important omission in that book. Yet Mosheim states respecting Constantine's Sunday law, promulgated in the fourth century,—which restrained merchants and mechanics, but allowed all kinds of agricultural labor on that day,—that it caused the day to be " observed with greater solemnity than it had formerly been." It follows, therefore, on Mosheim's own showing, that Sunday, during the first three centuries, was not a day of abstinence from labor in the Christian church. On this point, Bishop Taylor thus testifies :—

" The primitive Christians did all manner of works upon the

---

[24] Encyc. Am., art., Sabbath.
[25] Eccl. Hist., cent. 4, part 2, chap. 4, sec. 5.   [26] Chap. 14.

Lord's day, even in the times of persecution, when they are the strictest observers of all the divine commandments; but in this they knew there was none; and therefore, when Constantine the emperor had made an edict against working upon the Lord's day, yet he excepts and still permitted all agriculture or labors of the husbandman whatsoever." [27]

Morer tells us respecting the first three centuries, that is to say, the period before Constantine, that—

" The Lord's day had no command that it should be sanctified, but it was left to God's people to pitch on this or that day for the public worship. And being taken up and made a day of meeting for religious exercises, yet for three hundred years there was no law to bind them to it, and for want of such a law, the day was not wholly kept in abstaining from common business; nor did they any longer rest from their ordinary affairs (such was the necessity of those times) than during the divine service." [28]

And Sir Wm. Domville says :—

" Centuries of the Christian era passed away before the Sunday was observed by the Christian church as a Sabbath. History does not furnish us with a single proof or indication that it was at any time so observed previous to the Sabbatical edict of Constantine in A. D. 321. " [29]

What these able modern writers set forth as to labor on Sunday before the edict of Constantine was promulgated, we have fully proved in the preceding chapters out of the most ancient ecclesiastical writers. That such an edict could not fail to strengthen the current already strongly set in favor of Sunday, and greatly to weaken the influence of the Sabbath, cannot be doubted. Of this fact, an able writer bears witness :—

---

[27] Duct. Dubitant., part 1, book 2, chap. 2, rule 6, sec. 59.

[28] Dialogues on the Lord's Day, p. 233.

[29] Examination of the Six Texts, p. 291.

" Very shortly after the period when Constantine issued his edict enjoining the general observance of Sunday throughout the Roman empire, the party that had contended for the observance of the seventh day dwindled into insignificance. The observance of Sunday as a public festival, during which all business, with the exception of rural employments, was intermitted, came to be more and more generally established ever after this time, throughout both the Greek and the Latin churches. There is no evidence, however, that either at this, or at a period much later, the observance was viewed as deriving any obligation from the fourth commandment; it seems to have been regarded as an institution corresponding in nature with Christmas, Good Friday, and other festivals of the church; and as resting with them on the ground of ecclesiastical authority and tradition." [30]

This extraordinary edict of Constantine's caused Sunday to be observed with greater solemnity than it had formerly been. Yet we have the most indubitable proof that this law was a heathen enactment; that it was put forth in favor of Sunday as a heathen institution, and not as a Christian festival; and that Constantine himself not only did not possess the character of a Christian, but was at that time in truth a heathen. It is to be observed that Constantine did not designate the day which he commanded men to keep, as Lord's day, Christian Sabbath, or the day of Christ's resurrection; nor does he assign any reason for its observance which would indicate that it was a Christian festival. On the contrary, he designates the ancient heathen festival of the sun in language that cannot be mistaken. Dr. Hessey thus sustains this statement :—

" Others have looked at the transaction in a totally different light, and refused to discover in the document, or to suppose in

---

[30] Cox's Sabbath Laws, etc., pp. 280, 281. He quotes the Modern Sabbath Examined.

the mind of the enactor, any recognition of the Lord's day as a matter of divine obligation. They remark, and *very truly*, that Constantine designates it by its *astrological* or *heathen* title, Dies Solis, and insist that the epithet *venerabilis*, with which it is introduced, has reference to the rites performed on that day in honor of *Hercules*, *Apollo*, and *Mithras*." [31]

On this important point, Milman, the learned editor of Gibbon, thus testifies :—

"The rescript commanding the celebration of the Christian Sabbath, bears no allusion to its peculiar sanctity as a Christian institution. It is the day of the sun which is to be observed by the general veneration ; the courts were to be closed, and the noise and tumult of public business and legal litigation were no longer to violate the repose of the sacred day. But the believer in the new paganism, of which the solar worship was the characteristic, might acquiesce without scruple in the sanctity of the first day of the week." [32]

In a subsequent chapter he adds :—

"In fact, as we have before observed, the day of the sun would be willingly hallowed by almost all the pagan world, especially that part which had admitted any tendency toward the Oriental theology." [33]

On the seventh day of March, Constantine published his edict commanding the observance of that ancient festival of the heathen, the venerable day of the sun. On the following day, March eighth,[34] he issued a second decree in every respect worthy of its heathen predecessor.[35] The purport of it was this: That if any

---

[31] Hessey's Bampton Lectures, p. 60.

[32] History of Christianity, book 3, chap. 1.   [33] Id., book 3, chap. 4.

[34] These dates are worthy of marked attention. See Blair's Chronological Tables, p. 193, ed. 1856; Rosse's Index of Dates, p. 830.

[35] *Imp. Constantinus A. Ad Maximum.* Si quid de Palatio Nostro, aut ceteris operibus publicis, degustatum fulgore esse constiterit, retento more veteris obser-

royal edifice should be struck by lightning, the ancient
ceremonies of propitiating the deity should be practiced,
and the *haruspices* were to be consulted to learn the
meaning of the awful portent.[36] The *haruspices* were
soothsayers who foretold future events by examining
the entrails of beasts slaughtered in sacrifice to the
gods![37] The statute of the seventh of March, enjoining
the observance of the venerable day of the sun, and that
of the eighth of the same month, commanding the
consultation of the *haruspices*, constitute a noble pair of
well-matched heathen edicts. That Constantine himself
was a heathen at the time these edicts were issued, is
shown not only by the nature of the edicts themselves,
but by the fact that his nominal conversion to Christianity is placed by Mosheim two years after his Sunday
law, as the following will show :—

" After well considering the subject, I have come to the conclusion, that *subsequently to the death of Licinius, in the year
323*, when *Constantine* found himself sole emperor, *he became an
absolute Christian*, or one who believes no religion but the
Christian to be acceptable to God. He had previously considered
the religion of one God as more excellent than the other religions,
and believed that Christ ought especially to be worshiped ; yet
he supposed there were also inferior deities, and that to these
some worship might be paid, in the manner of the fathers, with-

vantiæ. Quid portendat, ob Haruspicibus requiratur, et diligentissime scriptura
collecta ad Nostram Scientiam referatur. Ceteris etiam usurpandæ huius con-
suetudinis licentia tribuenda: dummodo sacrificiis domesticis abstineant, quae
specialiter prohibita sunt. Eam autem denunciationem adque interpretationem,
quae de tactu Amphitheatri scriba est, de qua ad Heraclianum Tribunum, et
Magistrum Officiorum scripseras, ad nos scias esse perlatum. Dat. 16, Kal. Jan.
Serdicae Acc. 8, Id. Mart. Crispo 2, et Constantino 2. C. C. Coss. 321. Cod.
Theodos. 16, 10, 1.—*Library of Harvard College.*

[36] See Jortin's Eccl. Hist., vol. 1, sec. 31; Milman's Hist. Christianity, book
3, chap. 1.

[37] See Webster; for an ancient record of the act, see Eze. 21: 19–22.

out fault or sin. And who does not know that, in those times, many others also combined the worship of Christ with that of the ancient gods, whom they regarded as the ministers of the supreme God in the government of human and earthly affairs ? " [38]

As a heathen, Constantine was the worshiper of Apollo, or the sun, a fact that sheds much light upon his edit enjoining men to observe the venerable day of the sun. Thus Gibbon testifies :—

" The devotion of Constantine was more peculiarly directed to the genius of the sun, the Apollo of Greek and Roman mythology ; and he was pleased to be represented with the symbols of the god of light and poetry. . . . The altars of Apollo were crowned with the votive offerings of Constantine ; and the credulous multitude were taught to believe that the emperor was permitted to behold with mortal eyes the visible majesty of their tutelar deity. . . . The sun was universally celebrated as the invincible guide and protector of Constantine." [39]

His character as a professor of Christianity is described in these words :—

" The sincerity of the man, who, in a short period, effected such amazing changes in the religious world, is best known to Him who searches the heart. Certain it is that his subsequent life furnished no evidence of conversion to God. He waded without remorse through seas of blood, and was a most tyrannical prince." [40]

A few words relative to his character as a man will complete our view of his fitness to legislate for the church. This man, when elevated to the highest place of earthly power, caused his eldest son, Crispus, to be privately murdered, lest the fame of the son should

---

[38] Historical Commentaries, cent. 4, sec. 7.

[39] Decline and Fall of the Roman Empire, chap. 20.

[40] Marsh's Eccl. Hist., period 3, chap. 5.

eclipse that of the father. In the same ruin was involved his nephew Licinius, " whose rank was his only crime," and this was followed by the execution " perhaps of a guilty wife." [41]

Such was the man who elevated Sunday to the throne of the Roman empire; and such the nature of the institution which he thus elevated. A recent English writer says of Constantine's Sunday law that it " would seem to have been rather to promote heathen than Christian worship." And he shows, in the following extract, how this heathen emperor became a Christian, and how .this heathen statute became a Christian law :—

" At a LATER PERIOD, carried away by the current of opinion, he declared himself a convert to the church. Christianity, then, or what he was pleased to call by that name, became the law of the land, and the edict of A. D. 321, being unrevoked, was enforced as a Christian ordinance." [42]

Thus it is seen that a law, enacted in support of a heathen institution, after a few years came to be considered a Christian ordinance; and Constantine himself, four years after his Sunday edict, was able to control the church, as represented in the general council of Nicæa, so as to cause the members of that council to establish their annual festival of the Passover upon Sunday. [43] Paganism had prepared the institution from ancient days, and had now elevated it to supreme power; its work was accomplished.

We have proved that the Sunday festival in the

---

[41] Decline and Fall of the Roman Empire, chap. 18.

[42] Sunday and the Mosaic Sabbath, p. 4, published by R. Groombridge & Sons, London.   [43] See chap. 18.

Christian church had no Sabbatical character before the time of Constantine. We have also shown that heathenism, in the person of Constantine, first gave to Sunday its Sabbatical character, and, in the very act of doing it, designated it as a heathen, and not as a Christian, festival, thus establishing a heathen Sabbath. It was now the part of popery authoritatively to effect its transformation into a Christian institution,—a work which it was not slow to perform. Sylvester was the bishop of Rome while Constantine was emperor. How faithfully he acted his part in transforming the festival of the sun into a Christian institution is seen in that, by his apostolic authority, he changed the name of the day, giving it the imposing title of " LORD'S DAY." [44] To Constantine and Sylvester, therefore, the advocates of first-day observance are greatly indebted. The one elevated it as a heathen festival to the throne of the empire, making it a day of rest from most kinds of business; the other changed it into a Christian institution, giving it the dignified appellation of " Lord's day." It is not a sufficient reason for denying that Pope Sylvester, not far from A. D. 325, authoritatively conferred on Sunday the name of Lord's day, to say that one of the Fathers, as early as A. D. 200, calls the day by that name, and that some seven different writers, between A. D. 200 and A. D. 325, viz., Tertullian, Origen, Cyprian, Anatolius, Commo-

---

[44] Omnium vero dierum per septimanam appellationes (ut Solis, Lunae, Martis, etc.), mutasse in ferias: ut Polydorus (li. 6, c. 5) indicat. Metaphrastes vero, nomina dierum Hebraeis usitata retinuisse eum, tradit; SOLIUS PRIMI DIEI APPELLATIONE MUTATA, QUEM DOMINICUM DIXIT. Historia Ecclesiastica per M. Ludovicum Lucium, cent. 4, cap. 10, pp. 739, 740, Ed. Basilea, 1624.—*Library of Andover Theological Seminary.* The Ecclesiastical History of Lucius is simply the second edition of the famous " Magdeburg Centuries," which was published under his supervision.

dianus, Victorinus, and Peter of Alexandria, can be adduced, who give this name to Sunday.

No one of these Fathers ever claims for this title any apostolic authority; and it has been already shown that they could not have believed the day to be the Lord's day by divine appointment. So far, therefore, is the use of this term by these persons as a name for Sunday from conflicting with the statement that Sylvester, by his apostolic authority, established this name as the rightful title of that day, that it shows the act of Sylvester to be exactly suited to the circumstances of the case. Indeed, Nicephorus asserts that Constantine, who considered himself quite as much the head of the church as was the pope, "directed that the day which the Jews considered the first day of the week, and which the Greeks dedicated to the sun, should be called the Lord's day."[45] The circumstances of the case render the statements of Lucius and Nicephorus in the highest degree probable. They certainly do not indicate that the pope would deem such an act on his part unnecessary.

Take a recent event in papal history as an illustration of this case. Only a few years since, Pius IX. decreed that the virgin Mary was born without sin. This had long been asserted by many distinguished writers in the papal church, but it lacked authority as a dogma of that church until the pope, A. D. 1854, gave it his official sanction.[46] It was the work of Constantine and Sylvester, in the early part of the fourth century to establish the festival of the sun to be a day of rest by the authority of the empire, and to render it a Christian institution by the authority of St. Peter.

[45] Quoted in Elliott's Horæ Apocalypticæ, fifth edition, vol. 4, p. 603.

[46] McClintock and Strong's Cyclopedia, vol. 4, p. 506.

The following from Dr. Heylyn, a distinguished member of the Church of England, is worthy of particular attention. In most forcible language he traces the steps by which the Sunday festival arose to power, contrasting it in this respect with the ancient Sabbath of the Lord; and then, with equal truth and candor, he acknowledges that, as the festival of Sunday was set up by the emperor and the church, the same power can take it down whenever it sees fit:—

"Thus do we see upon what grounds the Lord's day stands; ON CUSTOM FIRST, and VOLUNTARY consecration of it to religious meetings: that custom countenanced by the authority of the church of God, which TACITLY approved the same; and FINALLY CONFIRMED and RATIFIED BY CHRISTIAN PRINCES throughout their empires. And as the day for rest from labors, and restraint from business upon that day, [it] received its greatest strength from the supreme magistrate as long as he retained that power which to him belongs; as after from the canons and decrees of councils, the decretals of popes and orders of particular prelates, when the sole managing of ecclesiastical affairs was committed to them.

"I hope it was not so with the former Sabbath, which neither took original from custom, that people being not so forward to give God a day; nor required any countenance or authority from the kings of Israel to confirm and ratify it. The Lord had spoke the word, that he would have one day in seven, precisely the seventh day from the world's creation, to be a day of rest unto all his people; which said, there was no more to do but gladly to submit and obey his pleasure. . . . But thus it was not done in our present business. The Lord's day had no such command that it should be sanctified, but was left plainly to God's people to pitch on this, or *any other*, for the public use. And being taken up amongst them, and made a day of meeting in the congregation for religious exercises; yet for three hundred years there was neither law to bind them to it, nor any rest from labor or from worldly business required upon it.

23

" And when it seemed good unto Christian princes, the nursing fathers of God's church, to lay restraints upon their people, yet at the first they were not general; but only thus, that certain men in certain places should lay aside their ordinary and daily works, to attend God's service in the church; those whose employments were most toilsome and most repugnant to the true nature of a Sabbath, being allowed to follow and pursue their labors because most necessary to the commonwealth.

" And in the following times, when as the prince and prelate, in their several places endeavored to restrain them from that also, which formerly they had permitted, and interdicted almost all kinds of bodily labor upon that day; it was not brought about without much struggling and an opposition of the people; more than a thousand years being past, after Christ's ascension, before the Lord's day had attained that state in which now it standeth. . . . And being brought into that state, wherein now it stands, it doth not stand so firmly and on such sure grounds, but that those powers which raised it up may take it lower if they please, yea take it quite away as unto the time, and settle it on any other day as to them seems best." [47]

Constantine's edict marks a signal change in the history of the Sunday festival.   Dr. Heylyn testifies :—

" Hitherto have we spoken of the Lord's day as taken up by the common consent of the church ; not instituted or established by any text of Scripture, or edict of emperor, or decree of council. . . . In that which followeth, we shall find both emperors and councils very frequent in ordering things about this day and the service of it." [48]

After his professed conversion to Christianity, Constantine still further exerted his power in behalf of the venerable day of the sun, now formally transformed into the Lord's day, by the apostolic authority of the Roman bishop.   Heylyn again says :—

---

[47] Hist. Sab., part 2, chap. 3, sec. 12.   [48] Id., sec. 1.

"So natural a power it is in a Christian prince to order things about religion, that he not only took upon him to command the day, but also to prescribe the service." [49]

The influence of Constantine powerfully contributed to the aid of those church leaders who were intent upon bringing the forms of pagan worship into the Christian church. Gibbon thus places upon record the motives of these men, and the result of their action :—

"The most respectable bishops had persuaded themselves that the ignorant rustics would more cheerfully renounce the superstition of paganism, if they found some resemblance, some compensation, in the bosom of Christianity. The religion of Constantine achieved, in less than a century, the final conquest of the Roman empire; but the victors themselves were insensibly subdued by the arts of their vanquished rivals." [50]

The body of nominal Christians, which resulted from this strange union of pagan rites with Christian worship, arrogated to itself the title of Catholic church; while the true people of God, who resisted these dangerous innovations, were branded as heretics, and cast out of the church. It is not strange that the Sabbath should lose ground in such a body, in struggling with its rival, the festival of the sun. Indeed, after a brief period, the history of the Sabbath will be found only in the almost obliterated records of those whom the Catholic church cast out and stigmatized as heretics. Of the Sabbath in Constantine's time, Heylyn says :—

"As for the Saturday, that retained its wonted credit in the Eastern churches, little inferior to the Lord's day, if not plainly equal; not as a Sabbath, think not so ; but as a day designed unto sacred meetings." [51]

---

[49] Hist. Sab., part 2, chap. 3, sec. 1.   [50] Decline and Fall, chap. 28.
[51] Hist. Sab., part 2, chap. 3, sec. 5.

There is no doubt that, after the great flood of worldliness which entered the church at the time of Constantine's pretended conversion, and after all that was done by himself and by Sylvester in behalf of Sunday, the observance of the Sabbath became, with many, only a nominal thing. But the action of the council of Laodicea, to which we shall presently refer, proves conclusively that the Sabbath was still observed, not simply as a festival, as Heylyn would have it, but as a day of abstinence from labor, as enjoined in the commandment.

The work of Constantine, however, marks an epoch in the history of the Sabbath and of Sunday. Constantine was hostile to the Sabbath, and his influence told powerfully against it with all those who sought worldly advancement. The historian Eusebius was the special friend and eulogist of Constantine. This fact should not be overlooked in weighing his testimony concerning the Sabbath. He speaks of it as follows :—

" They [the patriarchs] did not, therefore, regard circumcision, nor observe the Sabbath, nor do we; neither do we abstain from certain foods, nor regard other injunctions which Moses subsequently delivered to be observed in types and symbols, because such things as these do not belong to Christians." [52]

This testimony shows precisely the views of Constantine and the imperial party relative to the Sabbath. But it does not give the views of Christians as a whole; for we have seen that the Sabbath had been extensively retained up to this point, and we shall soon have occasion to quote other historians, the contemporaries and successors of Eusebius, who record its continued observance. Constantine exerted a controlling influence

---

[52] Eccl. Hist., book 1, chap. 4.

in the church, and was determined to "have nothing in common with that most hostile rabble of the Jews." Happy would it have been had his aversion been directed against the festivals of the heathen, rather than against the Sabbath of the Lord.

Before Constantine's time, there is no trace of the doctrine of the change of the Sabbath. On the contrary, we have decisive evidence that Sunday was a day on which ordinary labor was considered lawful and proper. But Constantine, while yet a heathen, commanded that every kind of business excepting agriculture should be laid aside on that day. His law designated the day as a heathen festival, which it actually was. But within four years after its enactment, Constantine had become, not merely a professed convert to the Christian religion, but, in many respects, practically the head of the church, as the course of things at the council of Nicæa plainly showed. His heathen Sunday law, being unrevoked, was thenceforward enforced in behalf of that day as a Christian festival. This law gave to the Sunday festival, for the first time, something of a Sabbatic character. It was now a rest-day from most kinds of business, by the law of the Roman empire. God's rest-day was thenceforward more in the way than ever before.

But now we come to a fact of remarkable interest. The way having been prepared, as we have just seen, for the doctrine of the change of the Sabbath, and the circumstances of the case demanding its production, it was at this very point brought forward for the *first time*. Eusebius, the special friend and flatterer of Constantine, was the man who first put forth this doctrine. In his "Commentary on the Psalms" he makes the following statement on Psalm 92, respecting the change of the Sabbath :—

" Wherefore as they [the Jews] rejected it [the Sabbath law], the Word [Christ], by the new covenant, TRANSLATED and TRANSFERRED the feast of the Sabbath to the morning light, and gave us the symbol of true rest, viz., the saving Lord's day, the first [day] of the light, in which the Saviour of the world, after all his labors among men, obtained the victory over death, and passed the portals of heaven, having achieved a work superior to the six-days' creation." [53]

" On this day, which is the first [day] of light and of the true Sun, we assemble, after an interval of six days, and celebrate holy and spiritual Sabbaths, even all nations redeemed by him throughout the world, and do those things according to the spiritual law, which were decreed for the priests to do on the Sabbath." [54]

" And all things whatsoever that it was duty to do on the Sabbath, these we have transferred to the Lord's day, as more appropriately belonging to it, because it has a precedence and is first in rank, and more honorable than the Jewish Sabbath." [55]

Eusebius was under the strongest temptation to please and even to flatter Constantine; for he lived in the sunshine of imperial favor. On one occasion he went so far as to say that the city of Jerusalem, which Constantine had rebuilt, might be the New Jerusalem predicted in the prophecies! [56] But perhaps there was no act of Eusebius that could give Constantine greater pleasure than his publication of such doctrine as this respecting the change of the Sabbath. The emperor had,

---

[53] Eusebius's Commentary on the Psalms, quoted in Cox's Sabbath Literature, vol. 1, p. 361; also in Justin Edward's Sabbath Manual, pp. 125-127.

[54] Id.   [55] Id.

[56] Eusebius's Life of Constantine, 3, 33, quoted in Elliott's Horæ Apocalypticæ, Vol. 1, p. 256.

by the civil law, given to Sunday a Sabbatical character. Though he had done this while yet a heathen, he found it to his interest to maintain this law after he obtained a commanding position in the Catholic church. When, therefore, Eusebius came out and declared that Christ transferred the Sabbath to Sunday, a doctrine never before heard of, and in support of which he had no Scripture to quote, Constantine could not but feel in the highest degree flattered that his own Sabbatical edict pertained to the very day which Christ had ordained to be the Sabbath in place of the seventh. It was a convincing proof that Constantine was divinely called to his high position in the Catholic church, that he should thus exactly identify his work with that of Christ, though he had no knowledge at the time that Christ had done any work of the kind.

As no writer before Eusebius had ever hinted at the doctrine of the change of the Sabbath; and as there is the most convincing proof, as we have shown, that before his time Sunday possessed no Sabbatic character; and as Eusebius does not claim that this doctrine is asserted in the Scriptures, nor in any preceding ecclesiastical writer, it is certain that he was the father of the doctrine. This new doctrine was not put forth without some motive.' That motive could not have been to bring forward some neglected passages of the Scriptures; for he does not quote a single text in its support. But the circumstances of the case plainly reveal the motive. The new doctrine was exactly adapted to the new order of things introduced by Constantine. It was, moreover, peculiarly suited to flatter that emperor's pride, the very thing which Eusebius was under the strongest temptation to do.

It is remarkable, however, that Eusebius, in the very connection in which he announces this new doctrine, unwittingly exposes its falsity. He first asserts that Christ changed the Sabbath, and then virtually contradicts it by indicating the real authors of the change. Thus he says :—

"All things whatsoever that it was duty to do on the Sabbath, these WE have transferred to the Lord's day." [57]

The persons here referred to as the authors of this work are the Emperor Constantine, and such bishops as Eusebius, who loved the favor of princes, and Sylvester, the pretended successor of Saint Peter. Two facts refute the assertion of Eusebius that Christ changed the Sabbath : 1. Eusebius, who lived three hundred years after the alleged change, is the first man who mentions such a change ; 2. Eusebius testifies that himself and others made this change, which they could not have done had Christ made it at the beginning. But though the doctrine of the change of the Sabbath was thus announced by Eusebius, it was not seconded by any writer of that age. The doctrine had never been heard of before, and Eusebius had simply his own assertion, but no passage of the Holy Scriptures to offer in its support.

But after Constantine, the Sabbath began to recover strength, at least in the Eastern churches. Prof. Stuart, in speaking of the period from Constantine to the council of Laodicea, A. D. 364, says :—

"The practice of it [the keeping of the Sabbath] was continued by Christians who were jealous for the honor of the Mosaic law, and finally became, as we have seen, predominant throughout Christendom. It was supposed at length that the fourth

---

[57] Cox's Sabbath Literature, vol. 1, p. 361.

commandment did require the observance. of the seventh-day Sabbath (not merely a seventh part of time), and reasoning as Christians of the present day are wont to do, viz., that *all* which belonged to the ten commandments was immutable and perpetual, the churches in general came gradually to regard the seventh-day Sabbath as altogether sacred." [58]

Prof. Stuart, however, connects with this the statement that Sunday was honored by all parties. But the council of Laodicea struck a heavy blow at this Sabbath-keeping in the Eastern church. Mr. James, in addressing the University of Oxford, bears this witness :—

"When the practice of keeping Saturday Sabbaths, which had become so general at the close of this century, was evidently gaining ground in the Eastern church, a decree was passed in the council held at Laodicea [A. D. 364] 'that members of the church should not rest from work on the Sabbath, like Jews; but should labor on that day, and preferring in honor the Lord's day, then, if it be in their power, should rest from work as Christians.' " [59]

This shows conclusively that at that period the observance of the Sabbath according to the commandment was extensive in the Eastern churches. But the Laodicean council not only forbade the observance of the Sabbath, but they even pronounced a curse on those who should obey the fourth commandment! Prynne thus testifies :—

"It is certain that Christ himself, his apostles, and the primitive Christians for some good space of time, did constantly observe the seventh-day Sabbath: . . . the evangelists and St. Luke in the Acts ever styling it the Sabbath-day, . . . and making mention of its . . . solemnization by the apostles and other

[58] Appendix to Gurney's History, etc., of the Sabbath, pp. 115, 116.
[59] Sermons on the Sacraments and Sabbath, pp. 122, 123.

Christians, ...it being still solemnized by many Christians
after the apostles' times, even till the council of Laodicea [A. D.
364], as ecclesiastical writers and the twenty-ninth canon of that
council testify, which runs thus: [60] 'Because Christians ought
not to Judaize, and to rest in the Sabbath, but to work in that
day (which many did refuse at that time to do). But preferring
in honor the Lord's day (there being then a great controversy
among Christians which of these two days . . . should have pre-
cedency), if they desired to rest, they should do this as Christians.
Wherefore if they shall be found to Judaize, let them be accursed
from Christ.' . . . The seventh-day Sabbath was . . . solemnized by Christ, the apostles, and primitive Christians, till the
Laodicean council did in a manner quite abolish the observation
of it. . . . The council of Laodicea [A. D. 364] . . . first settled
the observation of the Lord's day, and prohibited . . . the keeping of the Jewish Sabbath under an anathema." [61]

The action of this council did not extirpate the Sabbath from the Eastern churches, though it did materially
weaken its influence, and cause its observance to become
with many only a nominal thing, while it did most effectually enhance the sacredness and the authority of the
Sunday festival. That it did not wholly extinguish
Sabbath-keeping is thus certified by an old English
writer, John Ley :—

"From the apostles' time until the council of Laodicea, which
was about the year 364, the holy observation of the Jews' Sabbath continued, as may be proved out of many authors ; yea,
notwithstanding the decree of that council against it." [62]

And Gregory, bishop of Nyssa, about A. D. 372, uses
this expostulation :—

---

[60] Quod non oportet Christianos Judaizere et otiare in Sabbato, sed operari in
eodem die. Preferentes autem in veneratione Dominicum diem si vacare volu-
erint, ut Christiani hoc faciat ; quod si reperti fuerint Judaizare Anathema sint
a Christo.

[61] Dissertation on the Lord's day Sabbath, pp. 33, 34, 44. 1633.

[62] Sunday a Sabbath, p. 163. 1640.

" With what eyes can you behold the Lord's day, when you despise the Sabbath? Do you not perceive that they are sisters, and that in slighting the one, you affront the other? " [63]

This testimony is valuable in that it marks the progress of apostasy concerning the Sabbath. The Sunday festival entered the church, not as a divine institution, but as a voluntary observance. Even as late as A. D. 200, Tertullian said that it had only tradition and custom in its support. [64]

But in A. D. 372 this human festival had become the sister and equal of that day which God hallowed in the beginning, and solemnly commanded in the moral law. How worthy to be called the sister of the Sabbath the Sunday festival actually was, may be judged from what followed. When this self-styled sister had gained an acknowledged position in the family, she expelled the other, and trampled her in the dust. In our days, the Sunday festival claims to be the very day intended in the fourth commandment.

The following testimonies exhibit the authority of church councils in its true light. Jortin is quoted by Cox as saying :—

" In such assemblies, the best and the most moderate men seldom have the ascendant, and they are often led or driven by others who are far inferior to them in good qualities." [65]

The same writer gives us Baxter's opinion of the famous Westminster Assembly. Baxter says :—

" I have lived to see an assembly of ministers, where three or four leading men were so prevalent as to form a confession in the

---

[63] Dialogues on the Lord's Day, p. 188; Hessey's Bampton Lectures, pp. 72, 304, 305.

[64] Tertullian's *De Corona*, sections 3 and 4.   [65] Sabbath Laws, etc., p. 138.

name of the whole party, which had that in it which particular members did disown. And when about a controverted article, one man hath charged me deeply with questioning the words of the church, others, who were at the forming of that article, have laid it all on that same man, the rest being loth to strive much against him ; and so it was, he himself was the church whose authority he so much urged." [66]

Such has been the nature of councils in all ages ; yet they have ever claimed infallibility, and have largely used that infallibility in the suppression of the Sabbath and the establishment of the festival of Sunday. Of first-day sacredness prior to, and as late as, the time of Chrysostom, Kitto thus testifies :—

" Though in later times we find considerable reference to a sort of *consecration of the day*, it does not seem at any period of the ancient church to have assumed the form of such an observance as some modern religious communities have contended for. Nor do these writers in any instance pretend to allege *any divine command, or even apostolic practice* in support of it. . . . Chrysostom (A. D. 360) concludes one of his Homilies by dismissing his audience to their respective ordinary occupations." [67]

It was reserved for modern theologians to discover the divine or apostolic authority for Sunday observance. The ancient doctors of the church were unaware that any such authority existed ; and hence they deemed it lawful and proper to engage in usual worldly business on that day, when their religious worship was concluded. Heylyn bears witness concerning St. Chrysostom that he—

" Confessed it to be lawful for a man to look unto his worldly business on the Lord's day, after the congregation was dismissed." [68]

---

[66] Sabbath Laws, etc., p. 138.

[67] Cyclopedia Biblical Literature, article, Lord's Day; Heylyn's Hist. Sab., part 2, chap. 2, sec. 7.   [68] Hist. Sab., part 2, chap. 3, sec. 9.

St. Jerome, a few years after this, at the opening of the fifth century, in his commendation of the lady Paula, shows his own opinion of Sunday labor. Thus he says :—

"Paula, with the women, as soon as they returned home on the Lord's day, they sat down severally to their work, and made clothes for themselves and others." [69]

Morer justifies this Sunday labor in the following terms :—

"If we read they did any work on the Lord's day, it is to be remembered that this application to their daily tasks was not till their worship was quite over, when they might with innocency enough resume them, because the length of time or the number of hours assigned for piety was not then so well explained as in after ages. The state of the church is vastly different from what it was in those early days. Christians then, for some centuries of years, were under persecution and poverty; and besides their own wants, they had many of them severe masters, who compelled them to work, and made them bestow less time in spiritual matters than they otherwise would. In St. Jerome's age, their condition was better, because Christianity had got into the throne as well as into the empire. Yet for all this, the entire sanctification of the Lord's day proceeded slowly; and that it was the work of time to bring it to perfection, appears from the several steps the church made in her constitutions, and from the decrees of emperors and other princes, wherein the prohibitions from servile and civil business advanced by degrees from one species to another, till the day had got a considerable figure in the world. Now, therefore, the case being so much altered, the most proper use of citing those old examples is only, in point of doctrine, to show that ordinary work, as being a compliance with Providence for the support of natural life, is not sinful even on the Lord's day, when necessity is loud, and the laws of that church and nation where we live are not against it. This is what the first Chris-

---

[69] Dialogues on the Lord's Day, p. 234; Hist. Sab., part 2, chap. 3, sec. 7.

tians had to say for themselves, in the works they did on that
day. And if those works had been then judged a profanation
of the festival, I dare believe, they would have suffered martyrdom rather than been guilty." [70]

The bishop of Ely thus testifies :—

"In St. Jerome's days, and in the very place where he was
residing, the devoutest Christians did ordinarily work upon the
Lord's day, when the service of the church was ended." [71]

St. Augustine, the contemporary of Jerome, gives a
synopsis of the argument in that age for Sunday observance, in the following words :—

"It appears from the sacred Scriptures, that this day was a
solemn one; it was the first day of the age, that is, of the existence of our world; in it the elements of the world were formed;
on it the angels were created; on it Christ rose also from the
dead; on it the Holy Spirit descended from heaven upon the
apostles, as manna had done in the wilderness. For these and
other such circumstances the Lord's day is distinguished; and
therefore the holy doctors of the church have decreed that all the
glory of the Jewish Sabbath is transferred to it. Let us therefore keep the Lord's day as the ancients were commanded to do
the Sabbath." [72]

It is to be observed that Augustine does not assign
among his reasons for first-day observance, the change
of the Sabbath by Christ or his apostles, or that the
apostles observed that day, or that John had given it
the name of "Lord's day." These modern first-day arguments were unknown to Augustine. He gave the
credit of the work, not to Christ or his inspired apostles,
but to the holy doctors of the church, who, of their own
accord, had transferred the glory of the ancient Sabbath

---

[70] Dialogues on the Lord's Day, pp. 236, 237.
[71] Treatise of the Sabbath, p. 219.   [72] Sabbath Laws, etc., p. 284.

to the venerable day of the sun. In the fifth century, the first day of the week was considered the most proper day for giving holy orders; that is, for ordinations; and about the middle of this century, says Heylyn,—

"A law [was] made by Leo, then pope of Rome, and generally since taken up in the Western church, that they should be conferred upon no day else." [73]

According to Dr. Justin Edwards, this same pope made also this decree in behalf of Sunday :—

"WE ORDAIN, according to the true meaning of the Holy Ghost, and of the apostles as thereby directed, that on the sacred day wherein our own integrity was restored, all do rest and cease from labor." [74]

Soon after this edict of the pope, the Emperor Leo, A. D. 469, put forth the following decree :—

"It is our will and pleasure, that the holy days dedicated to the most high God, should not be spent in sensual recreations, or otherwise profaned by suits of law, especially the Lord's day, which we decree to be a venerable day, and therefore free it of all citations, executions, pleadings, and the like avocations. Let not the circus or theater be opened, nor combating with wild beasts be seen on it. . . . If any will presume to offend in the premises, if he be a military man, let him lose his commission; or if other, let his estate or goods be confiscated." [75]

And this emperor determined to mend the breach in Constantine's law, and thus prohibit agriculture on Sunday; so he adds :—

"We command, therefore, all, as well husbandmen as others, to forbear work on this day of our restoration." [76]

---

[73] Hist. Sab., part 2, chap. 4, sec. 8.   [74] Sabbath Manual, p. 123.
  [75] Dialogues on the Lord's Day, p. 259.   [76] Id., p. 260.

The holy doctors of the church had by this time very
effectually despoiled the Sabbath of its glory, transfer-
ring it to the Lord's day of Pope Sylvester, as Augustine
testifies; yet was not Sabbatical observance wholly extinguished even in the Catholic church. The historian
Socrates, who wrote about the middle of the fifth century, says :—

" For although almost all churches throughout the world celebrate the sacred mysteries on the Sabbath of every week, yet the
Christians of Alexandria and at Rome, on account of some ancient
tradition, refuse to do this. The Egyptians in the neighborhood
of Alexandria, and the inhabitants of Thebais, hold their religious
meetings on the Sabbath, but do not participate of the mysteries
in the manner usual among Christians in general; for, after having eaten and satisfied themselves with food of all kinds, in the
evening, making their oblations, they partake of the mysteries." [77]

As the church of Rome had turned the Sabbath into
a fast some two hundred years before this, in order to
oppose its observance, it is probable that this was the
ancient tradition referred to by Socrates. And Sozomen, the contemporary of Socrates, speaks on the same
point as follows :—

" The people of Constantinople, and of several other cities, assemble together on the Sabbath, as well as on the next day;
which custom is never observed at Rome, or at Alexandria.
There are several cities and villages in Egypt, where, contrary to
the usages established elsewhere, the people meet together on
Sabbath evenings; and although they had dined previously, partake of the mysteries." [78]

On the statement of these historians, Cox remarks :—

---

[77] Socrates, book 5, chap. 22.
[78] Sozomen, book 7, chap. 19; Lardner, vol. 4, chap. 85, p. 217.

"It was their practice to Sabbatize on Saturday, and to celebrate Sunday as a day of rejoicing and festivity. While, however, in some places a respect was thus generally paid to both of these days, the Judaizing practice of observing Saturday was by the leading churches expressly condemned, and all the doctrines connected with it steadfastly resisted."[79]

The time has now come, when, as stated by Coleman, the observance of the Sabbath was deemed heretical; and the close of the fifth century witnessed its effectual suppression in the great body of the Catholic church.

[79] Sabbath Laws, p. 280.

24

CHAPTER XX.

SUNDAY DURING THE DARK AGES.

The pope becomes the head of all the churches—The people of God re-
tire into the wilderness—Sunday to be traced through the Dark Ages
in the history of the Catholic church—State of that festival in the sixth
century—It did not acquire the title of Sabbath for many ages—Time
when it became a day of abstinence from labor in the East—When in
the West—Sunday canon of the first council of Orleans—Of the council of Arragon—Of the third council of Orleans—Of a council at Mascon—At Narbon—At Auxerre—Miracles establishing the sacredness
of Sunday—The pope advises men to atone, by the pious observance
of Sunday, for the sins of the previous week—The Sabbath and Sunday both strictly kept by a class at Rome, who were put down by the
pope—According to Twisse, they were two distinct classes—The Sabbath, like its Lord, crucified between two thieves—Council of Chalons
—Council at Toledo, in which the Jews were forbidden to keep the
Sabbath, and commanded to keep Sunday—First English law for Sunday—Council at Constantinople—In England—In Bavaria—Canon of
the archbishop of York—Statutes of Charlemange, and canons of councils which he called—The pope aids in the work—Council at Paris
originates a famous first-day argument—The councils fail to establish
Sunday sacredness—The emperors besought to send out some more
terrible edict in order to compel the observance of that day—The pope
takes the matter in hand in earnest, and gives Sunday an effectual establishment—Other statutes and canons—Sunday piety of a Norwegian
king—Sunday consecrated to the mass—Curious but obsolete first-day
arguments—The eating of meat forbidden upon the Sabbath by the
pope—Pope Urban II. ordains the Sabbath of the Lord to be a festival for the worship of the Virgin Mary—Apparition from St. Peter—
The pope sends Eustace into England with a roll that fell from heaven,
commanding Sunday observance under direful penalties—Miracles
which followed—Sunday established in Scotland—Other Sunday laws
down to the Reformation—Sunday always only a human ordinance.

HE opening of the sixth century witnessed the
development of the great apostasy to such an
extent that the man of sin might be plainly

seen sitting in the temple of God.[1] The Western Roman empire had been broken up into ten kingdoms, and
the way was now prepared for the work of the little
horn.[2] In the early part of this century, the bishop of
Rome was made head over the entire church by the emperor of the East, Justinian.[3] The dragon gave unto the
beast his power, and his seat, and great authority. From
this accession to supremacy by the Roman pontiff, date
the " time, times, and dividing of time," or twelve hundred and sixty years, of the prophecies of Daniel and
John.[4]

The true people of God now retired for safety into
places of obscurity and seclusion, as represented by the
prophecy : " The woman fled into the wilderness, where
she hath a place prepared of God, that they should feed
her there a thousand two hundred and three-score days."[5]
Leaving their history for the present, let us follow that
of the Catholic church, and trace in its record the history of the Sunday festival through the period of the
Dark Ages. Of the fifth and sixth centuries, Heylyn
bears the following testimony :—

" The faithful, being united better than before, became more
uniform in matters of devotion ; and in that uniformity did agree
together to give the Lord's day all the honors of an holy festival.
Yet was not this done all at once, but by degrees ; the fifth and
sixth centuries being well-nigh spent before it came into that
height which hath since continued. The emperors and the prelates in these times had the same affections ; both [being] earnest to advance this day above all other ; and to the edicts of the

---

[1] 2 Thess. 2. [2] Dan. 7.

[3] Shimeall's Bible Chronology, part 2, chap. 9, sec. 5, pp. 175, 176; Croly
on the Apocalypse, pp. 167–173.

[4] Dan. 7 : 8, 24, 25 ; Rev. 13 : 1–5. [5] Rev. 12.

one, and ecclesiastical constitutions of the other, it stands indebted for many of those privileges and exemptions which it still enjoyeth." [6]

But Sunday had not yet acquired the title of Sabbath. Brerewood gives this testimony :—

" The name of the Sabbath remained appropriated to the old Sabbath ; and was never attributed to the Lord's day, not of many hundred years after our Saviour's time." [7]

And Heylyn says of the term " Sabbath" in the ancient church :—

" The Saturday is called among them by no other name than that which formerly it had, the *Sabbath.* So that whenever for a thousand years and upwards, we meet with *Sabbatum* in any writer of what name soever, it must be understood of no day but *Saturday.*" [8]

Dr. Francis White, bishop of Ely, also testifies :—

" When the ancient Fathers distinguish and give proper names to the particular days of the week, they always style the Saturday, *Sabbatum,* the Sabbath ; and the Sunday, or first day of the week, *Dominicum,* the Lord's day." [9]

It should be observed, however, that the earliest mention of Sunday as the Lord's day, is in the writings of Tertullian ; Justin Martyr, some sixty years before, styling it " the day called Sunday ; " while the authoritative application of that term to Sunday was by Sylvester, bishop of Rome, more than one hundred years after the time of Tertullian. The earliest mention of Sunday as the Christian Sabbath is thus noted by Heylyn :—

---

[6] Hist. Sab., part 2, chap. 4, sec. 1.
[7] Learned Treatise of the Sabbath, p. 73, ed. 1631.
[8] Hist. Sab., part 2, chap. 2, sec. 12.
[9] Treatise of the Sabbath-Day, p. 202.

" The first who ever used it to denote the Lord's day (the first that I have met with in all this search) is one Petrus Alfonsus—he lived about the time that Rupertus did [which was the beginning of the twelfth century]—who calls the Lord's day by the name of Christian Sabbath." [10]

Of Sunday labor in the Eastern church, Heylyn says :—

" It was near nine hundred years from our Saviour's birth, if not quite so much, before restraint of husbandry on this day had been first thought of in the East; and probably being thus restrained, did find no more obedience there than it had done before in the Western parts." [11]

Of Sunday labor in the Western church, Dr. Francis White speaks as follows :—

" The Catholic church, for more than six hundred years after Christ, permitted labor, and gave license to many Christian people to work upon the Lord's day at such hours as they were not commanded to be present at the public service by the precept of the church." [12]

But let us trace the several steps by which the festival of Sunday increased in strength until it attained its complete development. These will be found at present mostly in the edicts of emperors, and the decrees of councils. Morer tells us that—

" Under Clodoveus, king of France, met the bishops in the first council of Orleans [A. D. 507], where they obliged themselves and their successors to be always at the church on the Lord's day, except in case of sickness or some great infirmity. And because they, with some other of the clergy in those days, took cognizance of judicial matters, therefore by a council at Arragon, about the year 518, in the reign of Theodorick, king of the Goths, it

---

[10] Hist. Sab., part 2, chap. 5, sec. 13.   [11] Id., part 2, chap. 5, sec. 6.
[12] Treatise of the Sabbath-Day, pp. 217, 218.

was decreed that 'No bishop or other person in holy orders should examine or pass judgment in any civil controversy on the Lord's day.' " [13]

This shows that civil courts were sometimes held on Sunday by the bishops in those days; otherwise such a prohibition would not have been put forth. Hengstenberg, in his notice of the third council of Orleans, gives us an insight into the then existing state of the Sunday festival :—

" The third council of Orleans, A. D. 538, says in its twenty-ninth canon : 'The opinion is spreading amongst the people, that it is wrong to ride, or drive, or cook food, or do anything to the house or the person on the Sunday. But since such opinions are more Jewish than Christian, that shall be lawful in future which has been so to the present time. On the other hand, agricultural labor ought to be laid aside, *in order that the people may not be prevented from attending church.*' " [14]

Observe the reason assigned. It is not lest they violate the law of the Sabbath, but it is that they may not be kept from church. Another authority states the case thus :—

" Labor in the country [on Sunday] was not prohibited till the council of Orleans, A. D. 538. It was thus an institution of the church, as Dr. Paley has remarked. The earlier Christians met in the morning of that day for prayer and singing hymns, in commemoration of Christ's resurrection, and then went about their usual duties." [15]

In A. D. 588 another council was held, the occasion of which is given in the following extract :—

" And because, notwithstanding all this care, the day was not duly observed, the bishops were again summoned to Mascon, a town in Burgundy, by King Gunthrum, and there they framed this

---

[13] Dialogues on the Lord's Day, pp. 263, 264.   [14] The Lord's Day, p. 58.
[15] Dictionary of Chronology, p. 813, art. Sunday.

canon: 'Notice is taken that Christian people very much neglect and slight the Lord's day, giving themselves, as on other days, to common work, to redress which irreverence, for the future, we warn every Christian who bears not that name in vain, to give ear to our advice, knowing we have a concern on us for your good, and a power to hinder you to do evil. Keep, then, the Lord's day, the day of our new birth.' " [16]

Further legislation being necessary, we find that—

" About a year forward, there was a council at Narbon, which forbid all persons of what country or quality soever, to do any servile work on the Lord's day. But if any man presumed to disobey this canon, he was to be fined if a freeman, and if a servant, severely lashed. Or, as Surius represents the penalty in the edict of King Recaredus, which he put out, near the same time, to strengthen the decrees of the council, 'Rich men were to be punished with a loss of a moiety of their estates, and the poorer sort with perpetual banishment,' in the year of grace 590. Another synod was held at Auxerre, a city in Champain, in the reign of Clotair, king of France, where it was decreed . . . 'that no man should be allowed to plow, nor cart, or do any such thing on the Lord's day.' " [17]

Such were some of the efforts made in the sixth century to advance the sacredness of the Sunday festival. And Morer tells us that,—

" For fear the doctrine should not take without miracles to support it, Gregory of Tours [about A. D. 590] furnishes us with several to that purpose." [18]

Mr. Francis West, an English first-day writer, gravely adduces one of these miracles in support of first-day sacredness :—

" Gregory of Tours reporteth, 'that a husbandman, who upon

---

[16] Dialogues on the Lord's Day, p. 265.

[17] Id., pp. 265, 266; Hist. Sab., part 2, chap. 4, sec. 7.

[18] Dialogues on the Lord's Day, p. 68.

the Lord's day went to plough his field, as he cleansed his plough with an iron, the iron stuck so fast in his hand that for two years he could not be delivered from it, but carried it about continually, to his exceeding great pain and shame.' " [19]

In the conclusion of the sixth century, Pope Gregory exhorted the people of Rome to " expiate on the day of our Lord's resurrection what was remissly done for the six days before." [20]   In the same epistle, this pope condemned a class of men at Rome who advocated the strict observance of both the Sabbath and the Sunday, styling them the preachers of Antichrist.[21]   This shows the intolerant feeling of the papacy toward the Sabbath, even when joined with the strict observance of Sunday.   It also shows that there were Sabbath-keepers even in Rome itself as late as the seventh century, although so far bewildered by the prevailing darkness that they joined with its observance a strict abstinence from labor on Sunday.

In the early part of the seventh century, arose another foe to the Bible Sabbath in the person of Mahomet.   To distinguish his followers alike from those who observed the Sabbath and those who observed the festival of Sun-

---

[19] Historical and Practical Discourse on the Lord's Day, p. 174.

[20] Dialogues on the Lord's Day, p. 282.

[21] Fleury, Hist. Eccl., Tome 8, Livre 36, sec. 22; Heylyn's Hist. Sab., part 2, chap. 5, sec. 1.   Dr. Twisse, however, asserts that the pope speaks of two classes. He gives Gregory's words as follows: " Relation is made unto me that certain men of a perverse spirit have sowed among you some corrupt doctrines contrary to our holy faith ; so as to forbid any work to be done on the Sabbath-day: these men we may well call the preachers of Antichrist. . . . Another report was brought unto me; and what was that?—That some perverse persons preach among you, that on the Lord's day none should be washed.   This is clearly another point maintained by other persons, different from the former."—*Morality of the Fourth Commandment*, pp. 19, 20.   If Dr. Twisse is right, the Sabbath-keepers in Rome about the year 600 were not chargeable with the Sunday observance above mentioned.

day, he selected Friday, the sixth day of the week, as their religious festival. And thus "the Mohammedans and the Romanists crucified the Sabbath, as the Jews and the Romans did the Lord of the Sabbath, between two thieves, the sixth and the first days of the week;" [22] for Mohammedanism and Romanism each suppressed the Sabbath over a wide extent of territory. About the middle of the seventh century, we have further canons of the church in behalf of Sunday :—

" At Chalons, a city in Burgundy, about the year 654, there was a provincial synod which confirmed what had been done by the third council of Orleans, about the observation of the Lord's day, namely, that 'none should plow or reap, or do any other thing belonging to husbandry, on pain of the censures of the church; which was the more minded, because backed with the secular power, and by an edict menacing such as offended herein; who, if bondmen, were to be soundly beaten, but if free, had three admonitions, and then if faulty, lost the third part of their patrimony, and if still obstinate, were made slaves for the future. And in the first year of Eringius, about the time of Pope Agatho, there sat the twelfth council of Toledo in Spain, A. D. 681, where the Jews were forbidden to keep their own festivals, but so far at least observe the Lord's day as to do no manner of work on it, whereby they might express their contempt of Christ or his worship.' " [23]

These were weighty reasons indeed for Sunday observance! Nor can it be thought strange that in the Dark Ages a constant succession of such things should eventuate in the universal observance of that day. Even the Jews were to be compelled to desist from Sabbath

---

[22] The idea is suggested by the language of an anonymous first-day writer of the seventeenth century, Irenæus Philalethes, in a work entitled, " *Sabbato-Dominica*," pref., p. 11, London, 1643.

[23] Dialogues on the Lord's Day, p. 267.

observance, and to honor Sunday by resting on that day from their labor. The earliest mention of Sunday in English statutes appears to be the following :—

A. D. 692. " Ina, king of the West Saxons, by the advice of Cenred his father, and Heddes and Erkenwald his bishops, with all his aldermen and sages, in a great assembly of the servants of God, for the health of their souls, and common preservation of the kingdom, made several constitutions, of which this was the third : ' If a servant do any work on Sunday by his master's or-der, he shall be free, and the master pay thirty shillings ; but if he went to work on his own head, he shall be either beaten with stripes, or ransom himself with a price.   A freeman, if he works on this day, shall lose his freedom, or pay sixty shillings; if he be a priest, double.' " [24]

The same year that this law was enacted in England, the sixth general council convened at Constantinople, which decreed that,—

" If any bishop or other clergyman, or any of the laity, ab-sented himself from the church three Sundays together, except in cases of very great necessity, if a clergyman, he was to be de-posed ; if a layman, debarred the holy communion." [25]

In the year 747 a council of the English clergy was called under Cuthbert, archbishop of Canterbury, in the reign of Egbert, king of Kent, and this constitution made :—

" It is ordered that the Lord's day be celebrated with due veneration, and wholly devoted to the worship of God.   And that all abbots and priests, on this most holy day, remain in their re-spective monasteries and churches, and there do their duty ac-cording to their places." [26]

Another ecclesiastical statute of the eighth century

---

[24] Dialogues, etc., p. 283.   [25] Id., p. 268.   [26] Id., pp. 283, 284.

was enacted at Dingosolinum in Bavaria, where a synod met about 772, which decreed that,—

" If any man shall work his cart on this day, or do any such common business, his team shall be presently forfeited to the public use ; and if the party persists in his folly, let him be sold for a bondman." [27]

The English were not behind their neighbors in the good work of establishing the sacredness of Sunday. Thus we read :—

A. D. 784. "Egbert, archbishop of York, to show positively what was to be done on Sundays, and what the laws designed by prohibiting ordinary work to be done on such days, made this canon : ' Let nothing else, saith he, be done on the Lord's day, but to attend on God in hymns and psalms and spiritual songs. Whoever marries on Sunday, let him do penance for seven days.' " [28]

In the conclusion of the eighth century, further efforts were made in behalf of this favored day :—

" Charles the Great summoned the bishops to Friuli, in Italy, where . . . they decreed [A. D. 791] that all people should, with due reverence and devotion, honor the Lord's day. . . . Under the same prince, another council was called three years later at Frankford in Germany, and there the limits of the Lord's day were determined from Saturday evening to Sunday evening." [29]

The five councils of Mentz, Rheims, Tours, Chalons, and Arles were all called in the year 813 by Charlemagne. It would be too irksome to the reader to dwell upon the several acts of these councils in behalf of Sunday. They are of the same character as those already quoted. The council of Chalons, however, is worthy of being noticed, in that, according to Morer,—

---

[27] **Dialogues**, etc., p. 268.   [28] Id., p. 284.   [29] Id., p. 269.

"They entreated the help of the secular power, and desired the emperor [Charlemagne] to provide for the stricter observation of it [Sunday]. Which he accordingly did, and left no stone unturned to secure the honor of the day. His care succeeded; and during his reign, the Lord's day bore a considerable figure. But after his day, it put on another face." [30]

The pope lent a helping hand in checking the profanation of Sunday :—

"And thereupon Pope Eugenius, in a synod held at Rome about 826, . . . gave directions that the parish priest should admonish such offenders, and wish them to go to church and say their prayers, lest otherwise they might bring some great calamity on themselves and neighbors." [31]

All this, however, was not sufficient; and so another council was summoned. At this council was brought forward—perhaps for the first time—the famous first-day argument now so familiar to all, that Sunday is proved to be the true Sabbath because men are struck by lightning who labor on that day. Thus we read :—

"But these paternal admonitions turning to little account, a provincial council was held at Paris three years after, . . . in 829, wherein the prelates complain that 'the Lord's day was not kept with reverence as became religion, . . . which was the reason that God had sent several judgments on them, and in a very remarkable manner punished some people for slighting and abusing it. For, say they, many of us by our own knowledge, and some by hearsay, know that several countrymen, following their husbandry on this day, have been killed with lightning; others, being seized with convulsions in their joints, have miserably perished. Whereby it is apparent how high the displeasure of God was upon their neglect of this day.' And at last they conclude that 'in the first place the priests and

---

[30] Dialogues, etc., p. 270.   [31] Id., p. 271.

ministers, then kings and princes, and all faithful people, be beseeched to use their utmost endeavors and care that the day be restored to its honor, and, for the credit of Christianity, more devoutly observed for the time to come.' " [32]

Further legislation being necessary,—

"It was decreed about seven years after, in a council at Aken, under Lewis the Godly, that neither pleadings nor marriages should be allowed on the Lord's day." [33]

But the law of Charlemagne, though backed by the authority of the church, as expressed in the canons of the councils already quoted, became very feeble by the remissness of Lewis, his successor. It is evident that canons and decrees of councils, though fortified with the mention of terrible judgments that had befallen transgressors, were not yet sufficient to enforce the sacred day. Another and more terrific statute than any yet issued was sought at the hands of the emperor, as here expressed :—

"Thereupon an address was made to the emperors, Lewis and Lotharius, that they would be pleased to take some care in it, and send out some precept or injunction more severe than what was hitherto extant, to strike terror into their subjects, and force them to forbear their ploughing, pleading, and marketing, then grown again into use; which was done about the year 853; and to that end, a synod was called at Rome under the popedom of Leo IV." [34]

The advocates of the first-day Sabbath have in all ages sought for a law capable of striking terror into those who do not hallow that day. They still continue the vain endeavor. But if they would honor the day

---

[32] Dialogues, etc., p. 271; Hist. Sab., part 2, chap. 5, sec. 7.

[33] Dialogues, etc., p. 272.   [34] Id., p. 261.

which God set apart for the Sabbath, they would find in that law of fire which proceeded from his right hand a statute which renders all human legislation entirely unnecessary.[35]

At this synod, the pope took the matter in hand in good earnest. Heylyn testifies that under the emperors Lewis and Lotharius, a synod was held at Rome, A. D. 853, under Pope Leo IV.,—

"Where it was ordered more precisely than in former times that no man should from thenceforth dare to make any markets on the Lord's day, no, not for things that were to eat; neither to do any kind of work that belonged to husbandry. Which canon being made at Rome, confirmed at Compeigne, and afterwards incorporated, as it was, into the body of the canon law, became to be admitted, without further question, in most parts of Christendom, especially when the popes had attained their height, and brought all Christian princes to be at their devotion. For then the people, who before had most opposed it, might have justly said, 'Behold, two kings stood not before him, how then shall we stand?' Out of which consternation all men presently obeyed, tradesmen of all sorts being brought to lay by their labors; and amongst those, the miller, though his work was easiest, and least of all required his presence." [36]

This was a most effectual establishment of first-day sacredness. Five years after this we read as follows :—

A. D. 858. "The Bulgarians sent some questions to Pope Nicholas, to which they desired answers. And that [answer] which concerned the Lord's day was that they should desist from all secular work, etc." [37]

Morer informs us respecting the civil power, that—

"In this century the Emperor [of Constantinople] Leo, surnamed the philosopher, restrained the works of husbandry, which,

---

[35] Ex. 20: 8–11; Deut. 33: 2.
[36] Hist. Sab., part 2, chap. 5, sec. 7; Morer, p. 272.   [37] Ib.

according to Constantine's toleration, were permitted in the Eas The same care was taken in the West by Theodorius, king of the Bavarians, who made this order, that ' If any person on the Lord's day yoked his oxen, or drove his wain, his right-side ox should be forthwith forfeited; or if he made hay and carried it in, he was to be twice admonished to desist, which if he did not, he was to receive no less than fifty stripes.' " [38]

Of Sunday laws in England in this century, we read :—

A. D. 876.   " Alfred the Great was the first who united the Saxon heptarchy, and it was not the least part of his care to make a law that, among other festivals, this day more especially might be solemnly kept, because it was the day whereon our Saviour Christ overcame the devil ; meaning Sunday, which is the weekly memorial of our Lord's resurrection, whereby. he overcame death, and him who had the power of death, that is the devil. And whereas, before, the single punishment for sacrilege committed on any other day was to restore the value of the thing stolen, and withal lose one hand, he added that if any person was found guilty of this crime done on the Lord's day, he should be doubly punished." [39]

Nineteen years later, the pope and his council still further strengthened the sacred day. The council of Friburgh in Germany, A. D. 895, under Pope Formosus, decreed that the Lord's day, men " were to spend in prayers, and devote wholly to the service of God, who otherwise might be provoked to anger." [40] The work of establishing Sunday sacredness in England was carried steadily forward :—

" King Athelston, . . . in the year 928, made a law that there should be no marketing or civil pleadings on the Lord's

---

[38] Dialogues, etc., pp. 261, 262.   [39] Id., pp. 284, 285.   [40] Id., p. 274.

day, under the penalty of forfeiting the commodity, besides a fine of thirty shillings for each offense." [41]

In a convocation of the English clergy about this time, it was decreed that all sorts of traffic and the holding of courts, etc., on Sunday should cease. "And whoever transgressed in any of these instances, if a freeman, he was to pay twelve oræ; if a servant, be severely whipped." We are further informed that—

"About the year 943, Otho, archbishop of Canterbury, had it decreed that above all things the Lord's day should be kept with all imaginable caution, according to the canon and ancient practice." [42]

A. D. 967. King Edgar "commanded that the festival should be kept from three of the clock in the afternoon on Saturday, till day-break on Monday." [43]

"King Ethelred the younger, son of Edgar, coming to the crown about the year 1009, called a general council of all the English clergy, under Elfeagus, archbishop of Canterbury, and Wolstan, archbishop of York. And there it was required that all persons in a more zealous manner should observe the Sunday, and what belonged to it." [44]

Nor did the Sunday festival fail to gain a footing in Norway. Heylyn tells us of the piety of a Norwegian king by the name of Olaus, A. D. 1028:—

"For being taken up one Sunday in some serious thoughts, and having in his hand a small walking stick, he took his knife and whittled it, as men do sometimes, when their minds are troubled or intent on business. And when it had been told him, as by way of jest, how he had trespassed therein against the Sabbath, he gathered the small chips together, put them upon his hand, and set fire unto them, that so, saith Crantzius, he might revenge that on himself what unawares he had committed against God's commandment." [45]

---

[41] Dialogues, etc., p. 285.   [42] Id., p. 286.   [43] Id.
[44] Id., p. 286.   [45] Hist. Sab., part 2, chap. 5, sec. 2.

In Spain also the work went forward. A council was held at Coy, A. D. 1050, under Ferdinand, king of Castile, in the days of Pope Leo IX., where it was decreed that the Lord's day "was to be entirely consecrated to hearing of mass." [46]

To strengthen the sacredness of this venerable day in the minds of the people, the doctors of the church were not wanting. Heylyn makes the following statement :—

"It was delivered of the souls in purgatory by Petrus Damiani, who lived A. D. 1056, that every Lord's day they were manumitted from their pains, and fluttered up and down the lake Avernus in the shape of birds." [47]

At the same time, another argument of a similar kind was brought forward to render the observance still more strict. Morer informs us respecting that class who in this age were most zealous advocates of Sunday observance :—

"Yet still the others went on in their way; and to induce their proselytes to spend the day with greater exactness and care, they brought in the old argument of compassion and charity to the damned in hell, who during the day have some respite from their torments, and the ease and liberty they have is more or less according to the zeal and degrees of keeping it well." [48]

If, therefore, they would strictly observe this sacred festival, their friends in hell would reap the benefit, in a respite from their torments on that day ! In a council at Rome, A. D. 1078, Pope Gregory VII. decreed that as the Sabbath had been long regarded as a fast-day, those

---

[46] Dialogues, etc., p. 274.   [47] Hist. Sab., part 2, chap. 5, sec. 2.

[48] Dialogues, etc., p. 68.

who desired to be Christians should on that day abstain from eating meat.[49] In the eastern division of the Catholic church, in the eleventh century, the Sabbath was still regarded as a festival, equal in sacredness with Sunday. Heylyn contrasts with this the action of the western division of that church :—

"But it was otherwise of old in the church of Rome, where they did labor and fast. . . . And this, with little opposition or interruption, save that which had been made in the city of Rome in the beginning of the seventh century, and was soon crushed by Gregory, then bishop there, as before we noted. And howsoever Urban, of that name the second, did consecrate it to the weekly service of the blessed virgin, and instituted in the council held at Clermont, A. D. 1095, that our lady's office should be said upon it, and that upon that day all Christian folks should worship her with their best devotion." [50]

It would seem that this was a crowning indignity to the Most High. The memorial of the great Creator was set apart as a festival on which to worship Mary, under the title of "Mother of God"! In the middle of the twelfth century, the king of England was admonished not to suffer men to work upon Sunday. Henry II. entered on the government about the year 1155.

"Of him it is reported that he had an apparition at Cardiff (. . . in South Wales), which from St. Peter charged him that upon Sundays, throughout his dominions, there should be no buying or selling, and no servile work done." [51]

The sacredness of Sunday was not yet sufficiently established, because a divine warrant for its observance was still unprovided. The manner in which this urgent

---

[49] Binius, vol. 3, p. 1285, ed. 1606.   [50] Hist. Sab., part 2, chap. 5, sec. 13,
[51] Morer, p. 288; Heylyn, part 2, chap. 7, sec. 6,

necessity was met is related by Roger Hoveden, a historian of high repute, who lived at the very time when this much-needed precept was furnished by the pope. Hoveden informs us that Eustace, the abbot of Flaye in Normandy, came into England in the year 1200, to preach the word of the Lord, and that his preaching was attended by many wonderful miracles. He was very earnest in behalf of Sunday. Thus Hoveden says :—

" At London also, and many other places throughout England, he effected by his preaching, that from that time forward people did not dare to hold market of things exposed for sale on the Lord's day." [52]

But Hoveden tells us that " the enemy of mankind raised against this man of God the ministers of iniquity," and it seems that, having no commandment for Sunday, he was in a strait place. The historian continues :—

" However, the said abbot, on being censured by the ministers of Satan, was unwilling any longer to molest the prelates of England by his preaching, but returned to Normandy, unto his place whence he came." [53]

But Eustace, though repulsed, had no thought of abandoning the contest. He had no commandment from the Lord when he came into England the first time. But one year's sojourn on the continent was sufficient to provide what he lacked. Hoveden tells us how he returned the following year with the needed precept :—

" In the same year [1201], Eustace, abbot of Flaye, returned to England, and preaching therein the word of the Lord from city to city, and from place to place, forbade any person to hold

---

[52] Roger de Hoveden's Annals, Bohn's ed., vol. 2, p. 487.   [53] Id.

a market of goods on sale upon the Lord's day. For he said that the commandment under-written, as to the observance of the Lord's day, had come down from heaven:—

"THE HOLY COMMANDMENT AS TO THE LORD'S DAY,

Which came from heaven to Jerusalem, and was found upon the altar of Saint Simeon, in Golgotha, where Christ was crucified for the sins of the world. The Lord sent down this epistle, which was found upon the altar of Saint Simeon, and after looking upon which three days and three nights, some men fell upon the earth, imploring mercy of God. And after the third hour, the patriarch arose, and Acharias, the archbishop, and they opened the scroll, and received the holy epistle from God. And when they had taken the same, they found this writing therein:—

"'I am the Lord who commanded you to observe the holy day of the Lord, and ye have not kept it, and have not repented of your sins, as I have said in my gospel, "Heaven and earth shall pass away, but my words shall not pass away." Whereas, I caused to be preached unto you repentance and amendment of life, you did not believe me, I have sent against you the pagans, who have shed your blood on the earth; and yet you have not believed; and because you did not keep the Lord's day holy, for a few days you suffered hunger, but soon I gave you fullness, and after that you did still worse again. Once more, it is my will, that no one, from the ninth hour on Saturday until sunrise on Monday, shall do any work except that which is good.

"'And if any person shall do so, he shall with penance make amends for the same. And if you do not pay obedience to this command, verily I say unto you, and I swear unto you, by my seat, and by my throne, and by the cherubim who watch my holy seat, that I will give you my commands by no other epistle, but I will open the heavens, and for rain I will rain upon you stones, and wood, and hot water in the night, that no one may take precautions against the same, and that so I may destroy all wicked men.

"'This do I say unto you; for the Lord's holy day, you shall die the death; and for the other festivals of my saints which you have not kept: I will send unto you beasts that have the heads of lions, the hair of women, the tails of camels, and they shall be so ravenous that they shall devour your flesh, and you shall long to flee away to the tombs of the dead, and to hide yourselves for fear of the beasts; and I will take away the light of the sun from before your eyes, and will send darkness upon you, that not seeing, you may slay one another, and that I may remove from you my face, and may not show mercy upon you. For I will burn the bodies and the hearts of you, and of all those who do not keep as holy the day of the Lord.

" 'Hear ye my voice, that so ye may not perish in the land, for the holy day of the Lord. Depart from evil, and show repentance for your sins. For, if you do not do so, even as Sodom and Gomorrah shall you perish. Now, know ye, that you are saved by the prayers of my most holy mother, Mary, and of my most holy angels, who pray for you daily. I have given unto you wheat and wine in abundance, and for the same ye have not obeyed me. For the widows and orphans cry unto you daily, and unto them you show no mercy. The pagans show mercy, but you show none at all. The trees which bear fruit, I will cause to be dried up for your sins; the rivers and the fountains shall not give water.

" 'I gave unto you a law in Mount Sinai, which you have not kept. I gave you a law with mine own hands, which you have not observed. For you I was born into the world, and my festive day ye knew not. Being wicked men, ye have not kept the Lord's day of my resurrection. By my right hand I swear unto you, that if you do not observe the Lord's day, and the festivals of my saints, I will send unto you the pagan nations, that they may slay you. And still do you attend to the business of others, and take no consideration of this? For this will I send against you still worse beasts, who shall devour the breasts of your women. I will curse those who on the Lord's day have wrought evil.

" 'Those who act unjustly towards their brethren, will I curse. Those who judge unrighteously the poor and the orphans upon the earth, will I curse. For me you forsake, and you follow the prince of this world. Give heed to my voice, and you shall have the blessing of mercy. But you cease not from your bad works, nor from the works of the devil. Because you are guilty of perjuries and adulteries, therefore the nations shall surround you, and shall, like beasts, devour you.' " [54]

That such a document was actually brought into England at this time, and in the manner here described, is so amply attested as to leave no doubt.[55] Matthew Paris, like Hoveden, was actually a contemporary of Eustace. Hoveden properly belongs to the twelfth century, for he died shortly after the arrival of Eustace with his roll. But Matthew Paris belongs to the thirteenth, as he was but young at the time this roll (A. D. 1201) was brought into England. Both have a high reputation for truthfulness. In speaking of the writers of that century, Mosheim bears the following testimony to the credibility of Matthew Paris :—

"Among the historians, the *first place* is due to Matthew Paris, a writer of the *highest merit*, both in point of *knowledge* and *prudence*." [56]

And Dr. Murdock says of him :—

"He is accounted the best historian of the Middle Ages,—learned, independent, honest, and judicious."[57]

Matthew Paris relates the return of the abbot Eustachius (as he spells the name) from Normandy,

---

[54] Hoveden, vol. 2, pp. 526–528.

[55] See Matthew Paris's Historia Major, pp. 200, 201, ed. 1640; Binius's Councils, ad ann. 1201, vol. 3, pp. 1448, 1449; Wilkins's Concilia Magnæ Britaniæ et Hibernæ, vol. 1, pp. 510, 511, London, 1737; Sir David Dalrymple's Historical Memorials, pp. 7, 8, ed. 1769; Heylyn's History of the Sabbath, part 2, chap. 7, sec. 5; Morer's Lord's Day, pp. 288–290; Hessey's Sunday, pp. 90, 321; Gilfillan's Sabbath, p. 399.

[56] Maclaine's Mosheim, cent. 13, part 2, chap. 1, sec. 5.

[57] Murdock's Mosheim, cent. 13, part 2, chap. 1, sec. 5, note 19.

and gives us a copy of the roll which he brought, and an account of its fall from heaven, as related by the abbot himself. He also tells us how the abbot came by it, tracing the history of the roll from the point when the patriarch gathered courage to take it into his hands, till the time when our abbot was commissioned to bring it into England. Thus he says :—

" But when the patriarch and clergy of all the holy land had diligently examined the contents of this epistle, it was decreed in a general deliberation that the epistle should be sent to the judgment of the Roman pontiff, seeing that whatever he decreed to be done, would please all. And when at length the epistle had come to the knowledge of the lord pope, immediately he ordained heralds, who, being sent through different parts of the world, preached everywhere the doctrine of this epistle, the Lord working with them and confirming their words by signs following. Among whom the abbot of Flay, Eustachius by name, a devout and learned man, having entered the kingdom of England, did there shine with many miracles." [58]

Now we know what the abbot was about during the year that he was absent from England. He could not establish first-day sacredness by his first mission to England, for he had no divine warrant in its behalf. He therefore retired from the mission long enough to make known the necessities of the case to the "lord

[58] Matthew Paris's Historia Major, p. 201. His words are: " Cum autem Patriarcha et clerus omnis Terræ sanctæ, hunc epistolæ tenorem diligenter examinassent; communi omnium deliberatione decretum est, ut epistola ad judicium Romani Pontificis transmitteretur; quatenus, quicquid ipse agendum decrevit, placæt universis. Cumque tandem epistola ad domini Papæ notitiam pervenisset, continuo prædicatores ordinavit; qui per diversas mundi partes profecti, prædicaverunt ubique epistolæ tenerem; Domino cooperante et sermonem corum confirmante, sequentibus signis. Inter quos Abbos de Flai nomine Eustachius, vir religiosus et literali scientia eruditis, regnum Angliæ aggressus: multis ibidem miraculis corruscavit."—*Library of Harvard College.*

pope." But when he came the second time, he brought the divine mandate for Sunday, and with it the commission of the pope, authorizing him to proclaim that mandate to the people, and informing them that it was sent to His Holiness from Jerusalem by those who saw it fall from heaven. Had Eustace framed this document himself, and then forged a commission from the pope, a few months would have discovered the imposture. But their genuineness was never questioned, as is shown by the preservation of this roll by the best historians of that time. We therefore trace the responsibility for this roll directly to the pope of Rome. The statement of the pope that he received it from the hands of those who saw it fall from heaven, is the guaranty given by His Holiness to the people that the roll came from God. The historians then living, who record this transaction, were able to satisfy themselves that .Eustace brought the roll from the pope; and they believed the pope's statement that he had received it from heaven. It was Innocent III. who filled the office of pope at this time, of whom Bower speaks thus :—

"Innocent was perfectly well qualified to raise the papal power and authority to the highest pitch, and we shall see him improving, with great address, every opportunity that offered to compass that end." [59]

Another eminent authority makes this statement :—

"The external circumstances of his time also furthered Innocent's views, and enabled him to make his pontificate the most marked in the annals of Rome; the culminating point of the temporal as well as the spiritual supremacy of the Roman See." [60]

---

[59] History of the Popes, vol. 2, p. 535.
[60] M'Clintock and Strong's Cyclopedia, vol. 4, p. 590.

"His pontificate may be fairly considered to have been the period of the highest power of the Roman See."[61]

The dense darkness of the Dark Ages still covered the earth, when that pontiff who raised the papacy to its highest elevation occupied the papal throne. Two facts worthy of much thought should here be named in connection :—

1. The first act of papal usurpation was by an edict in behalf of Sunday.[62]

2. The utmost height of papal usurpation was marked by the pope's act of furnishing a divine precept for Sunday observance.

The mission of Eustace was attested by miracles which are worthy of perusal by those who believe in first-day sacredness because their fathers thus believed. Here they may learn what was done six centuries since, to fix these ideas in the minds of their fathers. Eustace came to York, in the North of England, and, meeting an honorable reception,—

"Preached the word of the Lord, and on the breaking of the Lord's day and the other festivals, and imposed upon the people penance, and gave absolution upon condition that in future they would pay due reverence to the Lord's day and the other festivals of the saints, doing therein no servile work."[63]

"Upon this, the people who were dutiful to God at his preaching, vowed before God that, for the future, on the Lord's day, they would neither buy nor sell anything, unless, perchance, victuals and drink to wayfarers."[64]

The abbot also made provision for the collection of alms for the benefit of the poor, and forbade the use of

[61] Id., vol. 4, p. 592.   [62] See page 274 of this work.
[63] Hoveden, vol. 2, p. 528.   [64] Hoveden, vol. 2, p. 528.

the churches for the sale of goods, and for the pleading
of causes.   Upón this, the king interfered as follows :—

" Accordingly, through these and other warnings of this holy
man, the enemy of mankind being rendered envious, he put it
into the heart of the king and of the princes of darkness to command that all who should observe the before-stated doctrines, and
more especially all those who had discountenanced the markets on
the Lord s day, should be brought before the king's court of justice, to make satisfaction as to the observance of the Lord's day." [65]

The markets on the Lord's day, it seems, were held
in the churches, and Eustace was attempting to suppress
these when he forbade the sale of goods in the churches.
And now, to confirm the authority of the roll, and to
neutralize the opposition of the king, some very extraordinary prodigies were reported.   The roll forbade labor
"from the ninth hour (that is 3 P. M.) on Saturday until
sunrise on Monday."   Now read what happened to the
disobedient :—

" One Saturday, a certain carpenter of Beverly, who, after
the ninth hour of the day, was, contrary to the wholesome advice
of his wife, making a wooden wedge, fell to the earth, being
struck with paralysis.   A woman also, a weaver, who, after the
ninth hour on Saturday, in her anxiety to finish a part of the
web, persisted in so doing, fell to the ground, struck with paralysis, and lost her voice.   At Rafferton also, a vill belonging to
Master Roger Arundel, a man made for himself a loaf and baked
it under the ashes after the ninth hour on Saturday, and ate
thereof, and put part of it by till the morning, but when he broke
it on the Lord's day blood started forth therefrom : and he who
saw it bore witness, and his testimony is true.

" At Wakefield, also, one Saturday, while a miller was, after
the ninth hour, attending to grinding his corn, there suddenly
came forth, instead of flour, such a torrent of blood, that the ves-

sel placed beneath was nearly filled with blood, and the mill-wheel stood immovable, in spite of the strong rush of the water; and those who beheld it wondered thereat, saying, ' Spare us, O Lord, spare thy people ! '

" Also in Lincolnshire a woman had prepared some dough, and taking it to the oven after the ninth hour on Saturday, she placed it in the oven, which was then at a very great heat; but when she took it out, she found it raw, on which she again put it into the oven, which was very hot; and both on the next day and on Monday, when she supposed that she would find the loaves baked, she found raw dough.

" In the same county also, when a certain woman had pre-pared her dough, intending to carry it to the oven, her husband said to her, ' It is Saturday, and is now past the ninth hour, put it one side till Monday ; ' on which the woman, obeying her hus-band, did as he commanded; and so, having covered over the dough with a linen cloth, on coming the next day to look at the dough, to see whether it had not, in rising, through the yeast that was in it, gone over the sides of the vessel, she found there the loaves ready made by the Divine Will, and well baked, without any fire of the material of this world. This was a change wrought by the right hand of Him on high." [66]

The historian laments that these miracles were lost upon the people, and that they feared the king more than they feared God, and so " like a dog to his vomit, returned to the holding of markets on the Lord's day." [67] Such was the first attempt in England after the appari-tion of St. Peter, A. D. 1155, to supply divine authority for Sunday observance. " It shows," as Morer quaintly observes, " how industrious men were in those times to have this great day solemnly observed." [63] And Gilfillan, who has occasion to mention the story of the roll from heaven, has not one word of condemnation for the pious

---

[66] Hoveden, vol. 2, pp. 529, 530.　　[67] Id.　　[68] Dialogues, etc., p. 290.

fraud in behalf of Sunday, but he simply speaks of our abbot as " This ardent person." [69]

Two years after the arrival of Eustace in England with his roll, A. D. 1203, a council was held in Scotland concerning the introduction and establishment of the Lord's day in that kingdom.[70] The roll that had fallen from heaven to supply the lack of scriptural testimony in behalf of this day, was admirably adapted to the business of this council, though Dr. Heylyn informs us that the Scotch were so ready to comply with the pope's wishes that the packet from the court of heaven and the accompanying miracles were not needed.[71] Yet Morer asserts that the packet was actually produced on this occasion :—

" To that end it was again produced and read in a council of Scotland, held under [pope] Innocent III., . . . A. D. 1203, in the reign of King William, who . . . passed it into a law that Saturday from twelve at noon ought to be accounted holy, and that no man shall deal in such worldly business as on feast-days were forbidden. As also that at the tolling of a bell, the people were to be employed in holy actions, going to sermons and the like, and to continue thus until Monday morning, a penalty being laid on those who did the contrary. About the year 1214, which was eleven years after, it was again enacted, in a parliament at Scone, by Alexander III., king of the Scots, that none should fish in any waters from Saturday after evening prayer till sunrise on Monday, which was afterward confirmed by King James I.[72]

The sacredness of this papal Lord's day seems to have been more easily established by taking in with it a

---

[69] Gilfillan's Sabbath, p. 399.

[70] Binius's Councils, vol. 3, pp. 1448, 1449 ; Heylyn, part 2, chap. 7, sec. 7.

[71] Heylyn, part 2, chap. 7, sec. 7.   [72] Dialogues, etc., pp. 290, 291.

part of the ancient Sabbath. The work of establishing this institution was everywhere carried steadily forward. Of England we read :—

"In the year 1237, Henry III. being king, and Edmund de Abendon archbishop of Canterbury, a constitution was made, requiring every minister to forbid his parishioners the frequenting of markets on the Lord's day, and leaving the church, where they ought to meet and spend the day in prayer and hearing the word of God. And this on pain of excommunication." [73]

Of France we are informed :—

"The council of Lyons sat about the year 1244, and it restrained the people from their ordinary work on the Lord's day and other festivals, on pain of ecclesiastical censures."

A. D. 1282. The council of Angeirs in France "forbid millers by water or otherwise to grind their corn from Saturday evening till Sunday evening." [74]

Nor were the Spaniards backward in this work :—

A. D. 1322. This year "a synod was called at Valladolid in Castile, and then was ratified what was formerly required, that 'none should follow husbandry, or exercise himself in any mechanical employment, on the Lord's day or other holy days, but where it was a work of necessity or charity, of which the minister of the parish was to be judge.' " [75]

The rulers of the church and realm of England were diligent in establishing the sacredness of this day. Yet the following statutes show that they were not aware of any Bible authority for enforcing its observance :—

A. D. 1358. "Istippe, archbishop of Canterbury, with very great concern and zeal, expresses himself thus: 'We have it from the relation of very credible persons, that in divers places within our province, a very naughty, nay, damnable custom has

---

[73] Dialogues, etc., p. 291.   [74] Id., p. 275.   [75] Id.

prevailed, to hold fairs and markets on the Lord's day. . . .
Wherefore, by virtue of canonical obedience, we strictly charge
and command your brotherhood, that if you find your people
faulty in the premises, you forthwith admonish or cause them to
be admonished to refrain going to markets or fairs on the Lord's
day. . . . And as for such who are obstinate, and speak or act
against you in this particular, you must endeavor to restrain
them by ecclesiastical censures, and by all lawful means put a
stop to these extravagances.'

"Nor was the civil power silent; for much about that time,
King Edward made an act that wool should not be shown at the
staple on Sundays and other solemn feasts in the year.   In the
reign of King Henry VI., Dr. Stafford being archbishop of Canterbury, A. D. 1444, it was decreed that fairs and markets should
no more be kept in churches and church-yards on the Lord's
day, or other festivals, except in time of harvest." [76]

Observe that fairs and markets were held in the
churches in England on Sundays as late as 1444! And
even later than this such fairs were allowed in harvest
time.   On the European continent the sacredness of
Sunday was persistently urged.   The council of Bourges
urges its observance as follows :—

A. D. 1532. "The Lord's day and other festivals were instituted for this purpose, that faithful Christians, abstaining from
external work, might more freely, and with greater piety, devote
themselves to God's worship." [77]

They did not seem to be aware of the fact, however,
that when the fear of God is taught by the precepts of
men, such worship is vain.[78]   The council of Rheims,
which sat the next year, made this decree :—

A. D. 1533. "Let the people assemble at their parish
churches on the Lord's day and other holidays, and be present at

---

[76] Dialogues, etc., pp. 293, 294.   [77] Id., p. 279.
[78] Isa. 29:13; Matt. 15:9.

mass, sermons, and vespers. Let no man on these days give himself to plays or dances, especially during service." And the historian adds: "In the same year another synod at Tours ordered the Lord's day and other holidays to be reverently observed under pain of excommunication." [79]

A council which assembled the following year thus frankly confessed the divine origin of the Sabbath, and the human origin of that festival which has supplanted it :—

A. D. 1584. "Let all Christians remember that the seventh day was consecrated by God, and hath been received and observed, not only by the Jews, but by all others who pretend to worship God; though we Christians have changed their Sabbath into the Lord's day. A day therefore to be kept, by forbearing all worldly business, suits, contracts, carriages, etc., and by sanctifying the rest of mind and body, in the contemplation of God and things divine, we are to do nothing but works of charity, say prayers, and sing psalms." [80]

We have thus traced Sunday observance in the Catholic church down to a period subsequent to the Reformation. That it is an ordinance of man which has usurped the place of the Bible Sabbath is most distinctly confessed by the council last quoted. Yet they endeavor to make amends for their violation of the Sabbath by spending Sunday in charity, prayers, and psalms,—a course too often adopted at the present time to excuse the violation of the fourth commandment. Who can read this long list of Sunday laws, not from the "one Lawgiver who is able to save and to destroy," but from popes, emperors, and councils, without adopting the sentiment of Neander : "The festival of Sunday, like all other festivals, was always only a human ordinance " ?

---

[79] Morer, p. 280.　　　　[80] Id., pp. 281, 282.

CHAPTER XXI.

TRACES OF THE SABBATH DURING THE DARK AGES.

The Dark Ages defined—Difficulty of tracing the people of God during this period—The Sabbath effectually suppressed in the Catholic
church at the close of the fifth century—Sabbath-keepers in Rome
about A. D. 600—The Culdees of Great Britain—Columba probably a
Sabbath-keeper—The Waldenses—Their antiquity—Their wide extent
—Their peculiarities—Sabbatarian character of a part of this people—
Important facts respecting the Waldenses and the Romanists—Other
bodies of Sabbatarians—The Cathari—The Arnoldistæ—The Passaginians—The Petrobrusians—Gregory VII., about A. D. 1074, condemns the Sabbath-keepers—The Sabbath in Constantinople in the
eleventh century—A portion of the Anabaptists—Sabbatarians in
Abyssinia and Ethiopia—The Armenians of the East Indies—The
Sabbath retained through the Dark Ages by those who were not in
the communion of the Romish church.

WITH the accession of the Roman bishop to
supremacy began the Dark Ages;[1] and as he
increased in strength, the gloom of darkness
settled with increasing intensity upon the world. The
highest elevation of the papal power marks the latest
point in the Dark Ages before the first gray dawn of
twilight.[2] That power was providentially weakened
preparatory to the Reformation of the sixteenth century,
when the light of advancing day began to manifestly dis-
sipate the gross darkness which covered the earth. The
difficulty of tracing the true people of God through this

---

[1] Mr. Croly says: "With the title of 'Universal Bishop,' the power of the
papacy and the Dark Ages alike began."—*Croly on the Apocalypse*, p. 173.

[2] M'Clintock and Strong's Cyclopedia, vol. 4, p. 591.

period is well set forth in the following language of Benedict :—

"As scarcely any fragment of their history remains, all we know of them is from accounts of their enemies, which were always uttered in the style of censure and complaint; and without which we should not have known that millions of them ever existed. It was the settled policy of Rome to obliterate every vestige of opposition to her doctrines and decrees, everything heretical, whether persons or writings, by which the faithful would be liable to be contaminated and led astray. In conformity to this, their fixed determination, all books and records of their opposers were hunted up, and committed to the flames. Before the art of printing was discovered in the fifteenth century, all books were made with the pen ; the copies, of course, were so few that their concealment was much more difficult than it would be now ; and if a few of them escaped the vigilance of the inquisitors, they would soon be worn out and gone. None of them could be admitted and preserved in the public libraries of the Catholics, from the ravages of time, and of the hands of barbarians with which all parts of Europe were at different periods overwhelmed." [3]

The first five centuries of the Christian era accomplished the suppression of the Sabbath in those churches which were under the special control of the Roman pontiff. Thenceforward we must look for the observers of the Sabbath outside the communion of the church of Rome. It was predicted that the Roman power should cast down the truth to the ground.[4] The Scriptures set forth the law of God as his truth.[5] The Dark Ages were the result of this work of the great apostasy. So dense and all-pervading was the darkness, that God's pure truth was more or less obscured, even with the true people of God in their places of retirement.

---

[3] History of the Baptist Denomination, p. 50, ed. 1849.
[4] Dan. 8: 12.   [5] Ps. 119: 142, 151.

About the year 600, as we have seen, there was in the city of Rome itself a class of Sabbath-keeping Christians who were very strict in the observance of the fourth commandment. It has been said of them that they joined with this a strict abstinence from labor on Sunday. But Dr. Twisse, a learned first-day writer, who has particularly examined the record respecting them, asserts that this Sunday observance pertained to " other persons different from the former." [6] These Sabbath-keepers were not Romanists, and the pope denounced them in strong language.

The Christians of Great Britain, before the mission of Augustine to that country, A. D. 596, were not in subjection to the bishop of Rome, but were in an eminent degree Bible Christians. They are thus described :—

" The Scottish church, when it first meets the eye of civilization, is not Romish, nor even prelatical. When the monk Augustine, with his forty missionaries, in the time of the Saxon Heptarchy, came over to Britain under the auspices of Gregory, the bishop of Rome, to convert the barbarian Saxons, he found the northern part of the island already well-nigh filled with Christians and Christian institutions. These Christians were the Culdees, whose chief seat was the little island of Hi, or Iona, on the western coast of Scotland. An Irish presbyter, Columba, feeling himself stirred with missionary zeal, and doubtless knowing the wretched condition of the savage Scots and Picts, in the year 565 took with him twelve other missionaries, and passed over to Scotland. They fixed their settlement on the little island just named, and from that point became the missionaries of all Scotland, and even penetrated into England. [7]

" The people in the South of England, converted by Augustine

---

[6] See chap. 20 of this work.

[7] M'Clintock and Strong's Cyclopedia, vol. 2, pp. 600, 601; D'Aubigné's History of the Reformation, book 17.

and his assistants, and those in the North who had been won by Culdee labor, soon met, as Christian conquest advanced from both sides ; and when they came together, it was soon seen that Roman and Culdee Christianity very decidedly differed in a great many respects. The Culdees, for the most part, had a simple and primitive form of Christianity ; while Rome presented a vast accumulation of superstitions, and was arrayed in her well-known pomp. [8]

" The Culdee went to Iona, that in quiet, with meditation, study, and prayer, he might fit himself for going out into the world as a missionary. Indeed, Iona was a great missionary institute, where preachers were trained who evangelized the rude tribes of Scotland in a very short time. To have done such a work as this in less than half a century implies apostolic activity, purity, and success.[9]

" After the success of Augustine and his monks in England, the Culdees had shut themselves up within the limits of Scotland, and had resisted for centuries all the efforts of Rome to win them over. At last, however, they were overthrown by their own rulers." [10]

There is strong incidental evidence that Columba, the leading minister of his time among the Culdees, was an observer of the ancient Sabbath of the Bible. On this point I quote two standard authors of the Roman Catholics. They certainly have no motive to put such words as I here quote, fraudulently into the mouth of Columba; for they claim him as a saint, and they are no friends of the Bible Sabbath. Nor can we see how Columba could have used these words with satisfaction, as he evidently did, when dying, had he all his life long been a violator of the ancient rest-day of the Lord. Here are the words of Dr. Alvan Butler :—

---

[8] M'Clintock and Strong's Cyclopedia, vol. 2, p. 601.
[9] Id.   [10] Id.

"Having continued his labors in Scotland thirty-four years, he clearly and openly foretold his death, and on Saturday, the ninth of June, said to his disciple Diermit: 'This day is called the Sabbath, that is, the day of rest, and such will it truly be to me; for it will put an end to my labors.'" [11]

Another distinguished Catholic author gives us his dying words thus:—

"To-day is Saturday, the day which the Holy Scriptures call the Sabbath, or rest. And it will truly be my day of rest, for it shall be the last of my laborious life." [12]

These words show, 1. That Columba believed that Saturday was the true Bible Sabbath; 2. That he did not believe the Sabbath had been changed to Sunday; 3. That this confession of faith respecting the Bible Sabbath was made with evident satisfaction, though in view of immediate death. Did any first-day man ever recur with pleasure on his death-bed to the fact that Saturday is the Bible Sabbath?

But Gilfillan quotes these words of Columba as spoken in behalf of Sunday! In giving a list of eminent men who have asserted the change of the Sabbath, or who have called Sunday the Sabbath, and have taught that it should be observed as a day of sacred rest, he brings in Columba thus :—

"The testimony of Columba is specially interesting, as it expresses the feelings of the heart at a moment which tests the sincerity of faith, and the value of a creed: 'This day,' he said to his servant, 'in the sacred volume is called the Sabbath, that is, rest; and will indeed be a Sabbath to me, for it is to me the last

---

[11] Butler's Lives of the Fathers, Martyrs, and Principal Saints, article, St. Columba, A. D. 597.

[12] The Monks of the West, vol. 2, p. 104.

day of this toilsome life, the day on which I am to rest (sabbatize), after all my labors and troubles, for on this coming sacred night of the Lord (*Dominica nocte*), at the midnight hour, I shall, as the Scriptures speak, go the way of my fathers.' " [13]

But this day which Columba said " will indeed be a Sabbath to me," was not Sunday, but Saturday.

Among the dissenters from the Romish church in the period of the Dark Ages, the first place, perhaps, is due to the Waldenses, both for their antiquity and the wide extent of their influence and doctrine. Benedict quotes from their enemies respecting the antiquity of their origin :—

" We have already observed from Claudius Seyssel, the popish archbishop, that one Leo was charged with originating the Waldensian heresy in the valleys, in the days of Constantine the Great. When those severe measures emanated from the Emperor Honorious against re-baptizers, the Baptists left the seat of opulence and power, and sought retreats in the country, and in the valleys of Piedmont ; which last place in particular became their retreat from imperial oppression." [14]

Dean Waddington quotes the following from Rainer Saccho, a popish writer, who had the best means of information respecting them :—

" There is no sect so dangerous as the Leonists, for three reasons : First, it is the most ancient, some say as old as Sylvester [pope in Constantine's time], others as the apostles themselves. Secondly, it is very generally disseminated ; there is no country where it has not gained some footing. Thirdly, while other sects are profane and blasphemous, this retains the utmost show of piety ; they live justly before men, and believe nothing respecting God which is not good." [15]

---

[13] Gilfillan's Sabbath, p. 389.　　　[14] Id., pp. 32, 33.
[15] Waddington's History of the Church, part 4, chap. 1.

Mr. Jones gives Saccho's own opinion as follows :—

"Their enemies confirm their great antiquity. Reinerius Saccho, an inquisitor, and one of their most cruel persecutors, who lived only eighty years after Waldo [A. D. 1160], admits that the Waldenses flourished five hundred years before that preacher. Gretser, the Jesuit, who also wrote against the Waldenses, and had examined the subject fully, not only admits their great antiquity, but declares his firm belief that the Toulousians and Albigenses, condemned in the years 1177 and 1178, were no other than the Waldenses." [16]

Jortin dates their withdrawal into the wilderness of the Alps as follows :—

"A. D. 601. In the seventh century, Christianity was propagated in China by the Nestorians; and the Valdenses, who abhorred the papal usurpations, are supposed to have settled themselves in the valleys of Piedmont. Monkery flourished prodigiously, and the monks and popes were in the firmest union." [17]

President Edwards says :—

"Some of the popish writers themselves own that this people never submitted to the church of Rome. One of the popish writers, speaking of the Waldenses, says, The heresy of the Waldenses is the oldest heresy in the world. It is supposed that they first betook themselves to this place among the mountains, to hide themselves from the severity of the heathen persecutions which existed before Constantine the Great. And thus the woman fled into the wilderness from the face of the serpent. Rev. 12 : 6, 14. 'And to the woman were given two wings of a great eagle, that she might fly into the wilderness, into her place, where she is nourished for a time, and times, and half a time, from the face of the serpent.' The people being settled there, their posterity continued [there] from age to age; and being, as it were, by natural walls, as well as by God's grace, separated from

---

[16] Jones's History of the Church, vol. 2, chap. 5, sec. 1.
[17] Jortin's Eccl. Hist., vol. 2, sec. 38.

the rest of the world, they never partook of the overflowing corruption." [18]

Benedict makes other quotations relative to their origin :—

" Theodore Belvedre, a popish monk, says that the heresy had always been in the valleys.   In the preface to the French Bible, the translators say that they [the Waldenses] have always had the full enjoyment of the heavenly truth contained in the Holy Scriptures ever since they were enriched with the same by the apostles, having in fair MSS. preserved the entire Bible in their native tongue from generation to generation." [19]

Of the extent to which they spread in the countries of Europe, Benedict thus speaks :—

" In the thirteenth century, from the accounts of Catholic historians, all of whom speak of the Waldenses in terms of complaint and reproach, they had founded individual churches, or were spread out in colonies in Italy, Spain, Germany, the Netherlands, Bohemia, Poland, Lithuania, Albania, Lombardy, Milan, Romagna, Vicenza, Florence, Veleponetine, Constantinople, Philadelphia, Sclavonia, Bulgaria, Diognitia, Livonia Sarmatia, Croatia, Dalmatia, Briton, and Piedmont." [20]

And Dr. Edgar gives the words of an old historian as follows :—

" The Waldensians, says Popliner, spread, not only through France, but also through nearly all the European coasts, and appeared in Gaul, Spain, England, Scotland, Italy, Germany, Bohemia, Saxony, Poland, and Lithuania." [21]

According to the testimony of their enemies, they were to some extent divided among themselves,   Dr.

---

[18] Edward's Hist. of Redemption, period 3, part 4, sec. 2.
[19] Hist. Baptist Denomination, p. 33.   [20] Id., p. 31.
[21] Variations of Popery, p. 52.

Allix quotes an old Romish writer, who says of that portion of them who were called Cathari :—

"They are also divided amongst themselves ; so what some of them say is again denied by others." [22]

And Crosby makes a similar statement :—

"There were several sects of Waldenses, or Albigenses, like as there are of Dissenters in England. Some of these did deny all baptism, others only the baptism of infants. That many of them were of this latter opinion, is affirmed in several histories of this people, as well ancient as modern." [23]

Some of their enemies affirm that they reject the Old Testament; but others, with much greater truthfulness, bear a very different testimony.[24] Thus a Romish inquisitor, as quoted by Allix, bears testimony concerning those in Bohemia :—

"They can say a great part of the Old and New Testaments by heart. They despise the decretals, and the sayings and expositions of holy men, and only cleave to the text of Scripture. . . . [They say] that the doctrine of Christ and the apostles is sufficient to salvation, without any church statutes and ordinances. That the traditions of the church are no better than the traditions of the Pharisees ; and that greater stress is laid on the observation of human traditions than on the keeping of the law of God. Why do you transgress the law of God by your traditions ? . . . They contemn all approved ecclesiastical customs which they do

---

[22] Eccl. Hist. of the Ancient Churches of Piedmont, p. 167.

[23] History of the English Baptists, vol. 1, pref. p. 35.

[24] Mr. Jones, in his "Church History,". vol. 1, chap. 3, in a note at the end of the chapter, explains this charge as follows: "But this calumny is easily accounted for. The advocates of popery, to support their usurpations and innovations in the kingdom of Christ, were driven to the Old Testament for authority, adducing the kingdom of David for their example. And when their adversaries rebutted the argument, insisting that the parallel did not hold, for that the kingdom of Christ, which is not of this world, is a very different state of things from the kingdom of David, their opponents accused them of giving up the divine authority of the Old Testament."

not read of in the gospel, as the observation of Candlemas, Palm Sunday, the reconciliation of penitents, the adoration of the cross on Good Friday. They despise the feast of Easter, and all other festivals of Christ and the saints, because of their being multiplied to that vast number, and say that one day is as good as another, and work upon holy days, where they can do it without being taken notice of." [25]

Dr. Allix quotes a Waldensian document of A. D. 1100, entitled the " Noble Lesson," and remarks :—

" The author, upon supposal that the world was drawing to an end, exhorts his brethren to prayer, to watchfulness, to a renouncing of all worldly goods. * * *

" He sets down all the judgments of God in the Old Testament as the effects of a just and good God ; and in particular the decalogue as a law given by the Lord of the whole world. He repeats the several articles of the law, not forgetting that which respects idols." [26]

Their religious views are further stated by Allix :—

" They declare themselves to be the apostles' successors, to have apostolical authority, and the keys of binding and loosing. They hold the church of Rome to be the whore of Babylon, and that all that obey her are damned, especially the clergy that are subject to her since the time of Pope Sylvester. . . . They hold that none of the ordinances of the church that have been introduced since Christ's ascension ought to be observed, as being of no worth ; the feasts, fasts, orders, blessings, offices of the church, and the like, they utterly reject." [27]

A considerable part of the people called Waldenses bore the significant designation of *Sabbati*, or *Sabbatati*, or *Insabbatati*. Mr. Jones alludes to this fact in these words :—

" Because they would not observe saints' days, they were

---

[25] Eccl. Hist. Ancient Churches of Piedmont, pp. 231, 236, 237.
[26] Id., pp. 175–177.   [27] Id , p. 209.

falsely supposed to neglect the Sabbath also, and called *Insabba-tati* or *Insabbathists.*" [28]

Mr. Benedict makes the following statement :—

" We find that the Waldenses were sometimes called *Insab-bathos*, that is, regardless of Sabbaths.   Mr. Milner supposes this name was given to them because they observed not the Romish festivals, and rested from their ordinary occupations only on Sundays.   A Sabbatarian would suppose that it was because they met for worship on the seventh day, and did not regard the first-day Sabbath." [29]

Mr. Robinson gives the statements of three classes of writers respecting the meaning of these names which were borne by the Waldenses.   But he rejects them all, alleging that these persons were led to their conclusions by the apparent meaning of the words, and not by the facts.   Here are his words :—

" Some of these Christians were called *Sabbati*, *Sabbatati*, *Insabbatati*, and more frequently *Inzabbatati*.   Led astray by sound without attending to facts, one says they were so named from the Hebrew word Sabbath, because they kept the Saturday for the Lord's day.   Another says they were so called because they rejected all the festivals or Sabbaths in the low Latin sense of the word, which the Catholic church religiously observed.   A third says, and many with various alterations and additions have said after him, they were called so from *sabot* or *zabot*, a shoe, because they distinguished themselves from other people by wear-ing shoes marked on the upper part with some peculiarity.   Is it likely that people who could not descend from their mountains without hazarding their lives through the furious zeal of the inquis-itors, should tempt danger by affixing a visible mark on their shoes ?   Besides, the shoe of the peasants happens to be famous

---

[28] Hist. Church, chap. 5, sec. 1.
[29] General History of the Baptist Denomination, vol. 2, p. 413, ed. 1813.

in this country; it was of a different fashion, and was called abarca." [30]

Mr. Robinson rejects these three statements, and then gives his own judgment, that they were so called because they lived in the mountains. These four views cover all that has been advanced relative to the meaning of these names. But Robinson's own explanation is purely fanciful, and seems to have been adopted by no other writer. He offers, however, conclusive reasons for rejecting the statement that they took their name from their shoes. There remain, therefore, only the first and second of these four statements, which are that they were called by these names because they kept the Saturday for the Lord's day, and because they did not keep the sabbath of the papists. These two statements do not conflict. In fact, if one of them be true, it almost certainly follows that the other one must be true also. There would be in such facts something worthy to give a distinguishing name to the true people of God, surrounded by the great apostasy; and the natural and obvious interpretation of the names would disclose the most striking characteristic of the people who bore them.

Jones and Benedict agree with Robinson in rejecting the idea that the Waldenses received these names from their shoes. Mr. Jones held, on the contrary, that they were given them because they did not keep the Romish festivals.[31] Mr. Benedict favors the view that it was because they kept the seventh day.[32] But let us now see who they are that make these statements respecting the

---

[30] Ecclesiastical Researches, chap. 10, pp. 303, 304.

[31] Jones's History of the Church, vol. 2, chap. 5, sec. 1.

[32] General History of the Baptist Denomination, vol. 2, p. 413.

observance of the Sabbath by the Waldenses, that Robinson alludes to in this place. He quotes out of Gretser the words of the historian Goldastus as follows :—

" Insabbatati [they were called] not because they were circumcised, but because they kept the Jewish Sabbath." [33]

Goldastus was " a learned historian and jurist, born near Bischofszell, in Switzerland, in 1576." He died in 1635.[34] He was a Calvinist writer of note.[35] He certainly had no desire to favor the cause of the seventh day. Gretser objects to his statement on the ground that the Waldenses exterminated every festival; but this was the most natural thing in the world for men who had God's own rest-day in their keeping. Gretser still further objects, that the Waldenses denied the whole Old Testament; but this charge is an utter misrepresentation, as we have already shown in the present chapter.

Robinson also quotes on this point the testimony of Archbishop Usher. Though that prelate held that the Waldenses derived these names from their shoes, he frankly acknowledges that MANY understood that they were given to them because they worshiped on the Jewish Sabbath. This testimony is valuable in that it shows that many early writers asserted the observance of " the Saturday for the Lord's day " by the people who were called Sabbatati.[36]

---

[33] Circumcisi forsan illi fuerint, qui aliis Insabbatati, non quod circumciderentur, inquit Calvinista [Goldastus] sed quod in Sabbato judaizarent.—*Eccl. Researches*, chap. 10, p. 303.

[34] Thomas's Dictionary of Biography and Mythology, article, Goldast.

[35] D'Aubigné's Reformation in the time of Calvin, vol. 3, p. 456.

[36] Nec quod in Sabbato colendo Judaizarent, ut MULTI PUTABANT, sed a zapata.—*Eccl. Researches*, chap. 10, p. 304; *Usher's De Christianar. Eccl. success. et stat. cap.* 7.

In consequence of the persecutions which they suffered, and also because of their own missionary zeal, the
people called Waldenses were widely scattered over
Europe. They bore, however, various names in different ages and in different countries. We have decisive
testimony that some of these bodies observed the seventh
day. Others observed Sunday. Eneas Sylvius says
that those in Bohemia hold "that we are to cease from
working on no day except the Lord's day." [37] This statement, let it be observed, relates only to Bohemia. But
it has been asserted that the Waldenses were so
distinct from the church of Rome they could not have
received the Sunday Lord's day from thence, and must,
therefore, have received it from the apostles! But a
few words from D'Aubigné will suffice to show that this
statement is founded in error. He describes an interview between Œcolampadius and two Waldensian pastors who had been sent by their brethren from the borders of France and Piedmont to open communication
with the reformers. It was at Bâle, in 1530. Many
things which they said pleased Œcolampadius, but some
things he disapproved. D'Aubigné makes this statement :—

" The barbes [the Waldensian pastors] were at first a little
confused at seeing that the elders had to learn of their juniors ;
however, they were humble and sincere men, and the Bâle
doctor having questioned them on the sacraments, they confessed
that through weakness and fear *they had their children baptized by Romish priests,* and that *they even communicated with
them, and sometimes attended mass.* This unexpected avowal
startled the meek Œcolampadius." [38]

---

[37] Jones's Church History, vol. 2, chap. 5, sec. 2.
[38] Reformation in the Time of Calvin, vol. 3, p. 249.

When the deputation returned word to the Waldenses that the reformers demanded of them "a strict reform," D'Aubigné says that it was "supported by some, and rejected by others." He also informs us that the demand that the Waldenses should "separate entirely from Rome" "caused divisions among them." [39]

This is a very remarkable statement. The light of many of these ancient witnesses was almost ready to go out in darkness when God raised up the reformers. They had suffered that woman Jezebel to teach among them, and to seduce the servants of God. They had even come to practice infant baptism, and the priests of Rome administered the rite! And in addition to all this, they sometimes joined with them in the service of mass! If a portion of the Waldenses in Southern Europe at the time of the Reformation had exchanged believers' baptism for the baptism of children by Romish priests, it is not difficult to see how they could also accept Sunday as a rest-day from the same source in place of the hallowed rest-day of the Lord. All had not done this, but some certainly were guilty.

D'Aubigné makes a very interesting statement respecting the French Waldenses in the fifteenth century. His language implies that they had a different Sabbath from the Catholics. He tells us some of the stories which the priests circulated against the Waldenses. These are his words:—

"Picardy in the North and Dauphiny in the South were the two provinces of France best prepared [at the opening of the Protestant Reformation] to receive the gospel. During the fifteenth century, many Picardins, as the story ran, went to *Vau-*

---

[39] Reformation in the Time of Calvin, pp. 250, 251.

dery. Seated round the fire during the long nights, simple Catholics used to tell one another how the *Vaudois* [Waldenses] met in horrible assembly in solitary places, where they found tables spread with numerous and dainty viands. These poor Christians loved, indeed, to meet together from districts often very remote. They went to the rendezvous by night, and along by-roads. The most learned of them used to recite some passages of scripture, after which they conversed together, and prayed. But such humble conventicles were ridiculously travestied. 'Do you know what they do to get there,' said the people, ' so that the officers may not stop them? The devil has given them a certain ointment, and when they want to go to *Vaudery*, they smear a little stick with it. As soon as they get astride it, they are carried up through the air, and arrive at *their Sabbath* without meeting anybody. In the midst of them sits a goat with a monkey's tail: this is Satan, who receives their adoration.' . . . These stupid stories were not peculiar to the people: they were circulated particularly by the monks. It was thus that the inquisitor Jean de Broussart spoke in 1460 from a pulpit erected in the great square at Arras. An immense multitude surrounded him; a scaffold was erected in front of the pulpit, and a number of men and women, kneeling, and wearing caps with the figure of the devil painted on them, awaited their punishment. Perhaps the faith of these poor people was mingled with error. But be that as it may, they were all burnt alive after the sermon." [40]

It seems that these Waldenses had a Sabbath peculiar to themselves. And D'Aubigné himself alludes to something peculiar in their faith which he cannot confess as the truth, and does not choose to denounce as error. He says, "Perhaps the faith of these poor people was mingled with error." To speak of the observance of the seventh day as the Sabbath of the Lord by New-Testament Christians, subjects a conscientious first-day his-

---

[40] Reformation in the Time of Calvin, vol. 1, p. 349; D'Aubigné cites as his authority, " *Histoire des Protestants de Picardie,*" by L. Rossier, p. 2.

tórian to this very dilemma.   We have a further account
of the Waldenses in France, just before the commencement of the Reformation of the sixteenth century :—

" Louis XII., king of France, being informed by the enemies
of the Waldenses inhabiting a part of the province of Provence,
that several heinous crimes were laid to their account, sent the
Master of Requests, and a certain doctor of the Sorbonne, who
was the confessor to his Majesty, to make inquiry into this matter.   On their return, they reported that they had visited all
the parishes where they dwelt, had inspected their places of worship, but that they had found there no images, nor signs of the
ornaments belonging to the mass, nor any of the ceremonies of
the Romish church ; much less could they discover any traces of
those crimes with which they were charged.   On the contrary,
they kept the Sabbath-day, observed the ordinance of baptism according to the primitive church, instructed their children in the
articles of the Christian faith and the commandments of God.
The king having heard the report of his commissioners, said with
an oath that they were better men than himself or his people." [41]

We further read concerning the Vaudois, or Waldenses, as follows :—

" The respectable French historian, De Thou, says that the
Vaudois keep the commandments of the decalogue, and allow
among them of no wickedness, detesting perjuries, imprecations,
quarrels, seditions, etc." [42]

It may be proper to add, that in 1686 the Waldenses were all driven out of the valleys of Piedmont, and
that those who returned and settled in those valleys three
years afterward, and from whom the present race of
Waldenses is descended, fought their way back, sword in
hand, pursuing in all respects a course entirely different
from that of the ancient Waldenses.[43]

---

[41] Jones's Church History, vol. 2, chap. 5, sec. 4.
[42] Hist. of the Vaudois, by Bresse, p. 126.   [43] Benedict's Hist. Bapt., p. 41.

Another class of witnesses to the truth during the Dark Ages bore the name of Cathari, that is, Puritans. Jones speaks of them as follows :—

" They were a plain, unassuming, harmless, and industrious race of Christians, patiently bearing the cross after Christ, and, both in their doctrines and manners, condemning the whole system of idolatry and superstition which reigned in the church of Rome, placing true religion in the faith, hope, and obedience of the gospel, maintaining a supreme regard to the authority of God in his word, and regulating their sentiments and practices by that divine standard. Even in the twelfth century their numbers abounded in the neighborhood of Cologne, in Flanders, the South of France, Savoy and Milan. 'They were increased,' says Egbert, 'to great multitudes, throughout all countries.' " [44]

That the Cathari did retain and observe the ancient Sabbath, is certified by their Romish adversaries. Dr. Allix quotes a Roman Catholic author of the twelfth century concerning three sorts of heretics,—the Cathari, the Passagii, and the Arnoldistæ. Allix says of this Romish writer that,—

" He lays it down also as one of their opinions, 'that the law of Moses is to be kept according to the letter, and that the keeping of the Sabbath, circumcision, and other legal observances, ought to take place. They hold also that Christ, the Son of God, is not equal with the Father, and that the Father, Son, and Holy Ghost, these three persons, are not one God and one substance; and as a surplus to these their errors,· they judge and condemn all the doctors of the church, and universally the whole Roman church. Now since they endeavor to defend this their error, by testimonies drawn from the New Testament and prophets, I shall, with [the] assistance of the grace of Christ, stop their mouths, as David did Goliath's, with their own sword.' " [45]

---

[44] Hist. Church, chap. 4, sec. 3.
[45] Eccl. Hist. of the Ancient Churches of Piedmont, pp. 168, 169, Boston

27

Dr. Allix quotes another Romish author to the same effect :—

"Alanus attributes to the Cathari almost the very same opinions [as those just enumerated] in his first book against heretics, which he wrote about the year 1192." [46]

Mr. Elliott mentions an incident concerning the Cathari, which is in harmony with what these historians assert respecting their observance of the seventh day. He says :—

"In this year [A. D. 1163] certain heretics of the sect of the Cathari, coming from the parts of Flanders to Cologne, took up their abode secretly in a barn near the city. But, as *on the Lord's day* they did not go to church, they were seized by the neighbors, and detected. On their being brought before the Catholic church, when, after long examination respecting their sect, they would be convinced by no evidence however convincing, but most pertinaciously persisted in their doctrine and resolution, they were cast out from the church, and delivered into the hands of laics. These, leading them without the city, committed them to the flames, being four men and one little girl." [47]

These statements were made respecting three classes of Christian people who lived during the Dark Ages,— the Cathari, or Puritans, the Arnoldistæ, and the Passaginians. Their views are presented in the uncandid language of their enemies. But the testimony of ancient Catholic historians is decisive that they were observers of the seventh day. The charge that they observed circumcision also, will be noticed presently. Mr. Robinson understands that the Passaginians were that portion of

---

Public Library. The author, Rev. Peter Allix, D. D., was a French Protestant, born in 1641, and was distinguished for piety and erudition.—*Lempriere's Universal Biography.*

[46] Id., p. 170.   [47] Horæ Apocalypticæ, vol. 2, p. 291.

the Waldenses who lived in the passes of the mountains. He says :—

" It is very credible that the name Passageros, or Passagini, . . . was given to such of them as lived in or near the passes or passages of the mountains, and who subsisted in part by guiding travelers or by traveling themselves for trade." [48]

Mr. Elliott says of the *name* Passagini :—

" The explanation of the term as meaning *Pilgrims*, in both the spiritual and missionary sense of the word, would be but the translation of their recognized Greek appellation, εκδημοι, and a title as distinctive as beautiful." [49]

Mosheim gives the following account of them :—

" In Lombardy, which was the principal residence of the Italian heretics, there sprung up a singular sect, known, for what reason I cannot tell, by the denomination of Passaginians, and also by that of the circumcised. Like the other sects already mentioned, they had the utmost aversion to the dominion and discipline of the church of Rome ; but they were at the same time distinguished by two religious tenets which were peculiar to themselves. The first was a notion that the observance of the law of Moses in everything except the offering of sacrifices, was obligatory upon Christians ; in consequence of which they circumcised their followers, abstained from those meats, the use of which was prohibited under the Mosaic economy, and celebrated the Jewish Sabbath. The second tenet that distinguished this sect was advanced in opposition to the doctrine of three persons in the divine nature." [50]

Mr. Benedict speaks of them as follows :—

" The account of their practicing circumcision is undoubtedly a slanderous story, forged by their enemies, and probably arose in this way : because they observed the seventh day they were

---

[48] Eccl. Researches, chap. 10, pp. 305, 306.
[49] Horæ Apocalypticæ, vol. 2, p. 342.
[50] Eccl. Hist. cent. 12, part 2, chap. 5, sec. 14.

called, by way of derision, Jews, as the Sabbatarians are frequently at this day ; and if they were Jews, it followed, of course, that they either did, or ought to, circumcise their followers. This was probably the reasoning of their enemies ; but that they actually practiced the bloody rite is altogether improbable." [51]

An eminent church historian, Michael Geddes, thus testifies :—

" This [act] of fixing something that is justly abominable to all mankind upon her adversaries, has been the constant practice of the church of Rome." [52]

Dr. Allix states the same fact, which needs to be kept in mind whenever we read of the people of God in the records of the Dark Ages :—

" I must desire the reader to consider that it is no great sin with the church of Rome to spread lies concerning those that are enemies of that faith." [53]

" There is nothing more common with the Romish party than to make use of the most horrid calumnies to blacken and expose those who have renounced her communion." [54]

Of the origin of the Petrobrusians, we have the following account by Mr. Jones :—

" But the Cathari, or Puritans, were not the only sect which, during the twelfth century, appeared in opposition to the superstition of the church of Rome. About the year 1110, in the south of France, in the provinces of Languedoc and Provence, appeared Peter de Bruys, preaching the gospel of the kingdom of heaven, and exerting the most laudable efforts to reform the abuses, and remove the superstition which disfigured the beautiful simplicity of the gospel worship. His labors were crowned with

---

[51] General Hist. Baptist Denomination, vol. 2, p. 414, ed. 1813.

[52] Acts and Decrees of the Synod of Diamper, p. 158, London, 1694.

[53] Eccl. Hist. of the Ancient Churches of Piedmont, p. 224.

[54] Id., p. 225.

abundant success. He converted a great number of disciples to the faith of Christ, and after a most indefatigable ministry of twenty years' continuance, he was burned at St. Giles, a city of Languedoc in France, A. D. 1130, by an enraged populace, instigated by the clergy, who apprehended their traffic to be in danger from this new and intrepid reformer." [55]

That this body of French Christians, who, in the very midnight of the Dark Ages, witnessed for the truth in opposition to the Romish church, were observers of the ancient Sabbath, is expressly certified by Dr. Francis White, Lord Bishop of Ely. He was appointed by the king of England to write against the Sabbath in opposition to Brabourne, who had appealed to the king in its behalf. To show that Sabbatic observance is contrary to the doctrine of the Catholic church,—a weighty argument with an Episcopalian,—he enumerates various classes of heretics who had been condemned by the Catholic church for keeping holy the seventh day. Among these heretics he places the Petrobrusians :—

" In St. Bernard's days, it was condemned in the Petrobruysans." [56]

We have seen that, according to Catholic writers, the Cathari held to the observance of the seventh day. Dr. Allix confirms the statement of Dr. White, that the Petrobrusians observed the ancient Sabbath, by stating that the doctrines of these two bodies greatly resembled each other. These are his words :—

" Petrus Cluniacensis has handled five questions against the Petrobrusians, which bear a great resemblance with the belief of the Cathari of Italy." [57]

---

[55] Hist. of the Church, chap. 4, sec. 3.
[56] Treatise of the Sabbath-day, p. 8.
[57] Eccl. Hist. of the Ancient Churches of Piedmont, p. 162.

The Sabbath-keepers in the eleventh century were of sufficient importance to call down upon themselves the anathema of the pope.   Dr. Heylyn says that—

"Gregory, of that name the seventh [about A. D. 1074] condemned those who taught that it was not lawful to do work on the day of the Sabbath." [58]

This act of the pope corroborates the testimonies we have adduced in proof of the existence of Sabbath-keepers in the Dark Ages.   Gregory the Seventh was one of the greatest men that ever filled the papal chair.   Whatever class he anathematized was of some consequence.   Gregory wasted nothing on trifles.[59]

In the eleventh century, there were Sabbath-keepers also in Constantinople and its vicinity.   The pope, in A. D. 1054, sent three legates to the emperor of the East, and to the patriarch of Constantinople, for the purpose of re-uniting the Greek and Latin churches.   Cardinal Humbert was the head of this legation.   The legates, on their arrival, set themselves to the work of refuting those doctrines which distinguish the church of Constantinople from that of Rome.   After they had attended to the questions which separated the two churches, they found it also necessary to discuss the question of the Sabbath.   For one of the most learned men of the East had put forth a treatise, in which he maintained that ministers should be allowed to marry; that the Sabbath should be kept holy; and that leavened bread should be

---

[58] Hist. of the Sabbath, part 2, chap. 5, sec. 1.

[59] Bower says of Gregory : "He was a man of most extraordinary parts, of an unbounded ambition, of a haughty and imperious temper, of resolution and courage incapable of yielding to the greatest difficulties, *perfectly acquainted with the state of the Western churches*, as well as with the different interests of the Christian princes."—*History of the Popes*, vol. 2, p. 378.

used in the supper,—all of which the church of Rome held to be deadly heresies. We quote from Mr. Bower a concise statement of the treatment which this Sabbatarian writer received :—

" Humbert likewise answered a piece that had been published by a monk of the monastery of Studium, [near Constantinople,] named Nicetas, who was deemed *one of the most learned men at the time in the East.* In that piece the monk undertook to prove that leavened bread only should be used in the eucharist, *that the Sabbath ought to be kept holy,* and that priests should be allowed to marry. But the emperor, who wanted by all means to gain the pope, for the reasons mentioned above, was, or rather pretended to be, so fully convinced with the arguments of the legate, confuting those alleged by Nicetas, that he obliged the monk publicly to recant, and anathematize *all who held the opinion* that he had endeavored to establish, with respect to unleavened bread, the Sabbath, and the marriage of the priests.

" At the same time Nicetas, in compliance with the command of the emperor, anathematized all who should question the primacy of the Roman church with respect to all other Christian churches, or should presume to censure her ever orthodox faith. The monk having thus retracted all he had written against the Holy See, his book was burnt by the emperor's order, and he absolved by the legates, from the censures he had incurred." [60]

This record shows that, in the dense darkness of the eleventh century, " one of the most learned men at that time in the East " wrote a book to prove that " the Sabbath ought to be kept holy," and in opposition to the papal doctrine of the celibacy of the clergy. It also shows how the church of Rome casts down the truth of God by means of the sword of emperors and kings. Though Nicetas retracted, under fear of the emperor and the pope, it

---

[60] History of the Popes, vol. 2, p. 358.

appears that there were others who held the same opinions; for he was " obliged " to anathematize all such, and there is no evidence that any of these persons turned from the truth because of the fall of their leader.   Indeed, if there had not been a considerable body of these Sabbatarians, the papal legate would never have deemed it worthy of his dignity to write a reply to Nicetas.

The Anabaptists are often referred to in the records of the Dark Ages.   The term signifies re-baptizers, and was applied to them because they denied the validity of infant baptism.   The designation is not accurate, however, because those persons whom they baptized, they considered as never having been baptized before, although they had been sprinkled, or even immersed in infancy. This people have been overwhelmed in obloquy in consequence of the fanatical insurrection which broke out in their name in the time of Luther.   Of those engaged in this insurrection, Buck says :—

" The first insurgents groaned under severe oppressions, and took up arms in defense of their civil liberties; and of these commotions the Anabaptists seem rather to have availed themselves, than to have been the prime movers.   That a great part were Anabaptists seems indisputable; at the same time it appears from history that a great part also were Roman Catholics, and a still greater part of those who had scarcely any religious principles at all." [61]

This matter is placed in the true light by Stebbing :—

" The overthrow of civil society, and fatal injuries to religion, were threatened by those who called themselves Anabaptists. But large numbers appear to have disputed the validity of infant baptism who had nothing else in common with them, yet who for

---

[61] Theological Dictionary, art., Anabaptists.

that one circumstance were overwhelmed with the obloquy, and the punishment richly due to a fanaticism equally fraudulent and licentious." [62]

The ancient Sabbath was retained and observed by a portion of the Anabaptists, or, to use a more proper term, Baptists. Dr. Francis White thus testifies :—

" They which maintain the Saturday Sabbath to be in force, comply with some Anabaptists." [63]

In harmony with this statement of Dr. White, is the testimony of a French writer of the sixteenth century. He names all the classes of men who have borne the name of Anabaptists. And of one of them he writes as follows :—

" Some have endured great torments, because they would not keep Sundays and festival days, in despite of Antichrist : seeing they were days appointed by Antichrist, they would not hold forth any thing which is like unto him. Others observe these days, but it is out of charity." [64]

Thus it is seen that within the limits of the old Roman Empire, and in the midst of those countries that submitted to the rule of the pope, God reserved unto himself a people who did not bow the knee to Baal; and among these the Bible Sabbath was observed from age to age.

We are now to search for the Sabbath among those who were never subjected to the Roman pontiff. In Central Africa, from the first part of the Christian era, —possibly from the time of the conversion of the Ethi-

---

[62] Hist. Church, vol. 1, pp. 183, 184.

[63] Treatise of the Sabbath-day, p. 132. He cites the History of the Anabaptists, lib. 6, p. 153.

[64] The Rise, Spring, and Foundation of the Anabaptists or Rebaptized of our Times, by Guy de Brez, A. D. 1565.

opian officer of great authority,[65] but very certainly
as early as A. D. 330,[66]—have existed the churches of
Abyssinia and Ethiopia. About the time of the accessions
of the Roman bishop to supremacy, they were lost sight
of by the nations of Europe. "Encompassed on all sides,"
says Gibbon, " by the enemies of their religion, the Ethi-
opians slept near a thousand years, forgetful of the world,
by whom they were forgotten."[67] In the latter part of
the fifteenth century, they were again brought to the
knowledge of the world by the discovery of Portuguese
navigators. Undoubtedly they have been greatly affected by the dense darkness of pagan and Mohammedan
errors with which they are encompassed; and in many respects they have lost the pure and spiritual religion of
our divine Redeemer. A modern traveler says of them :
" They have divers errors, and many ancient truths."[68]
Michæl Geddes says of them :—

" The Abyssinians do hold the Scriptures to be the perfect
rule of the Christian faith ; insomuch that they deny it to be in
the power of a general council to oblige people to believe anything
as an article of faith without an express warrant from thence."[69]

They practice circumcision, but for other reasons than
that of a religious duty.[70] Geddes further states their
views :—

" Transubstantiation, and the adoration of the consecrated
bread in the sacrament, were what the Abyssinians abhorred.

---

[65] Acts 8 : 26–40.

[66] M'Clintock and Strong's Cyclopedia, vol. 1, p. 40.

[67] Dec. and Fall, chap. 47.

[68] Maxson's Hist. Sab., p. 33, ed. 1844.

[69] Church History of Ethiopia, p. 31.

[70] Id., p. 96 ; Gibbon, chap. 15, note 25 ; chap. 47, note 160. M'Clintock
and Strong's Cyclopedia, vol. 1, p. 40.

. . . They deny purgatory, and know nothing of confirmation and extreme unction; they condemn graven images; they keep both Saturday and Sunday." [71]

Their views of the Sabbath are stated by the ambassador of the king of Ethiopia, at the court of Lisbon, in the following words, explaining their abstinence from all labor on that day :—

" Because God, after he had finished the creation of the world, rested thereon ; which day, as God would have it called the holy of holies, so the not celebrating thereof with great honor and devotion seems to be plainly contrary to God's will and precept, who will suffer heaven and earth to pass away sooner than his word ; and that, especially, since Christ came not to destroy the law, but to fulfill it. It is not, therefore, in imitation of the Jews, but in obedience to Christ and his holy apostles, that we observe that day." [72]

The ambassador states their reasons for first-day observance in these words :—

" We do observe the Lord's day after the manner of all other Christians in memory of Christ's resurrection." [73]

He had no Scripture to offer in support of this festival, and evidently rested its observance upon tradition. This account was given by the ambassador in 1534. In the early part of the next century, the emperor of Abyssinia was induced to submit to the pope in these words :—

" I confess that the pope is the vicar of Christ, the successor of St. Peter, and the sovereign of the world. To him I swear true obedience, and at his feet I offer my person and kingdom." [74] No sooner had the Roman

---

[71] Church History of Ethiopia, pp. 34, 35 ; Purchas's Pilgrimage, book 2, chap. 5.

[72] Church History of Ethiopia, pp. 87, 88. [73] Id. [74] Gibbon, chap. 47.

bishop thus brought the emperor to submit to him, than that potentate was compelled to gratify the popish hatred of the Sabbath by an edict forbidding its further observance. In the words of Geddes, he " set forth a proclamation prohibiting all his subjects, upon severe penalties, to observe Saturday any longer; " [75] or, as Gibbon expresses it, " The Abyssinians were enjoined to work and to play on the Sabbath." But the tyranny of the Romanists, after a terrible struggle, caused their overthrow and banishment, and the restoration of the ancient faith. The churches resounded with a song of triumph, "'that the sheep of Ethiopia were now delivered from the hyænas of the West;' and the gates of that solitary realm were forever shut against the arts, the science, and the fanaticism of Europe." [76]

We have proved in a former chapter that the Sabbath was extensively observed, as late as the middle of the fifth century, in the so-called Catholic church, especially in that portion most intimately connected with the Abyssinians; and that from various causes, Sunday obtained certain Sabbatic honors, in consequence of which the two days were called sisters. We have also shown in another chapter that the effectual suppression of the Sabbath in Europe is mainly due to papal influence. And so for a thousand years we have been tracing its history in the records of those men which the church of Rome has sought to kill.

These facts are strikingly corroborated by the case of the Abyssinians. In consequence of their location in the interior of Africa, the Abyssinians ceased to be

---

[75] Church History of Ethiopia, pp. 311, 312; Gobat's Abyssinia, pp. 83, 93.
[76] Gibbon, chap. 47.

known to the rest of Christendom about the fifth century. At this time, the Sabbath and the Sunday in the Catholic church were counted sisters. One thousand years later, these African churches were visited, and though surrounded by the thick darkness of pagan and Mohammedan superstition, and somewhat affected thereby, they were to be found, at the end of this period, holding the Sabbath and first-day substantially as they were held by the Catholic church when it lost sight of them. The Catholics of Europe, on the contrary, had in the meantime trampled the ancient Sabbath in the dust. Why was this great contrast?—Simply because the pope ruled in Europe; while central Africa, whatever else it may have suffered, was not cursed with his presence nor his influence. But so soon as the pope learned of the existence of the Abyssinian churches, he sought to gain control of them, and when he had gained it, one of his first acts was to suppress the Sabbath! In the end, the Abyssinians regained their independence, and thenceforward till the present time have held fast the Sabbath of the Lord.

The Armenians of the East Indies are peculiarly worthy of our attention. J. W. Massie, M. R. I. A., says of the East Indian Christians :—

"Remote from the busy haunts of commerce, or the populous seats of manufacturing industry, they may be regarded as the Eastern Piedmontese, the Vallois of Hindoostan, the witnesses prophesying in sackcloth through revolving centuries, though indeed their bodies lay as dead in the streets of the city which they had once peopled." [77]

Geddes says of those in Malabar :—

" The three great doctrines of popery, the pope's supremacy, transubstantiation, the adoration of images, were never believed nor practiced at any time in this ancient apostolical church. . . . I think one may venture to say that before the time of the late Reformation, there was no church that we know of, no, not that of the Vaudois, . . . that had so few errors in doctrine as the church of Malabar." He adds concerning those churches that " were never within the bounds of the Roman Empire," " It is in those churches that we are to meet with the least of the leaven of popery." [78]

Mr. Massie further describes these Christians :—

" The creed which these representatives of an ancient line of Christians cherished was not in conformity with papal decrees, and has with difficulty been squared with the thirty-nine articles of the Anglican episcopacy. Separated from the Western world for a thousand years, they were naturally ignorant of many novelties introduced by the councils and decrees of the Lateran ; and *their conformity with the faith and practice of the first ages* laid them open to the unpardonable guilt of heresy and schism, as estimated by the church of Rome. ' We are Christians, and not idolaters,' was their expressive reply when required to do homage to the image of the Virgin Mary. . . . La Croze states them at fifteen hundred churches, and as many towns and villages. They refused to recognize the pope, and declared they had never heard of him ; they asserted the purity and primitive truth of their faith since they came, and their bishops had for thirteen hundred years been sent from the place where the followers of Jesus were first called Christians." [79]

The Sabbatarian character of these Christians is hinted by Mr. Yeates. He says that Saturday " among them is a festival day, *agreeable to the ancient practice of the church.*" [80]

---

[78] Acts and Decrees of the Synod of Diamper, preface.
[79] Continental India, vol. 2, pp. 116, 117.
[80] East Indian Church History, pp. 133, 134.

"The ancient practice of the church," as we have seen, was to hallow the seventh day in memory of the Creator's rest. This practice has been suppressed wherever the great apostasy had power to do it. But the Christians of the East Indies, like those of Abyssinia, have lived sufficiently remote from Rome to be preserved in some degree from its blasting influence. The fact is further hinted by the same writer in the following language:—

"The inquisition was set up at Goa in the Indies, at the instance of Francis Xaverius [a famous Romish saint], who signified by letters to Pope John III., Nov. 10, 1545, 'That THE JEWISH WICKEDNESS spreads more and more in the parts of the East Indies subject to the kingdom of Portugal, and therefore he earnestly besought the said king, that to cure so great an evil he would take care to send the office of the inquisition into those countries.'" [81]

"The Jewish wickedness" was doubtless the observance of Saturday as "a festival day agreeable to the ancient practice of the church," of which this author had just spoken. The history of the past, as we have seen, shows the hatred of the papal church toward the Sabbath. And the struggle of that church to suppress the Sabbath in Abyssinia, and to subject that people to the pope, which at this very point of time was just commencing, shows that the Jesuits would not willingly tolerate Sabbatic observance in the East Indies, even though united with the observance of Sunday also.

It appears, therefore, that this Jesuit missionary desired the pope and the king of Portugal to establish the inquisition in that part of the Indies subject to Portugal, in order to root out the Sabbath from those ancient

[81] Id., pp. 139, 140,

churches. The inquisition was established in answer to this prayer, and Xavier was subsequently canonized as a saint! Nothing can more clearly show the malignity of the Roman pontiff toward the Sabbath of the Lord; and nothing more clearly illustrates the kind of men that he canonizes as saints.

Since the time of Xavier, the East Indies have fallen under British rule. A distinguished clergyman of the church of England, some years since visited the British empire in India, for the purpose of acquainting himself with these churches. He gave the following deeply interesting sketch of these ancient Christians, and in it particularly marks their Sabbatarian character :—

"The history of the Armenian church is very interesting. Of all the Christians in Central Asia, they have preserved themselves most free from Mahometan and papal corruptions. The pope assailed them for a time with great violence, but with little effect. The churches in lesser Armenia, indeed, consented to an union, which did not long continue ; but those in Persian Armenia maintained their independence; and they retain their ancient Scriptures, doctrines, and worship, to this day. ' It is marvelous,' says an intelligent traveler who was much among them, ' how the Armenian Christians have preserved their faith, equally against the vexatious oppression of the Mahometans, their sovereigns, and against the persuasions of the Romish church, which for more than two centuries has endeavored, by missionaries, priests, and monks, to attach them to her communion. It is impossible to describe the artifices and expenses of the court of Rome to effect this object, but all in vain.'

"The Bible was translated into the Armenian language in the fifth century, under very auspicious circumstances, the history of which has come down to us. It has been allowed by competent judges of the language, to be a most faithful translation. La Cruze calls it the ' Queen of Versions.' This Bible has ever remained in the possession of the Armenian people ; and many illustrious instances of genuine and enlightened piety occur in their history. . . . The Armenians in Hindoostan are our own subjects. They acknowledge our government in India, as they do that of the Sophi in Persia; and they are entitled to our regard. They have preserved the Bible in its purity; and their doctrines are, as far as the author knows, the doctrines of the Bible. Besides, they maintain the solemn observance of Christian worship throughout our empire, ON THE SEVENTH DAY, and they have as many spires pointing to heaven among the Hindoos as we ourselves. Are such a people, then, entitled to no acknowledgment on our part, as fellow-Christians? Are they forever to be ranked by us with Jews, Mahometans, and Hindoos?" [82]

It has been said, however, that Buchanan might have intended Sunday by the term "seventh day." This is a very unreasonable interpretation of his words. Episcopalian clergymen are not accustomed to call Sunday the seventh day. We have, however, testimony which cannot with candor be explained away. It is that of Purchas, written in the seventeenth century. The author speaks of several sects of the Eastern Christians "continuing from ancient times," as Syrians, Jacobites, Nestorians, Maronites, and Armenians. Of the Syrians, or Surians, as he variously spells the name, who, from his relation, appear to be identical with the Armenians, he says:—

"They keep Saturday holy, nor esteem Saturday fast lawful but on Easter even. They have solemn service on Saturdays, eat flesh, and feast it bravely like the Jews." [83]

This author speaks of these Christians disrespectfully,

---

[82] Buchanan's Christian Researches in Asia, pp. 159, 160.

[83] Purchas, his Pilgrimmes, part 2, book 8, chap. 6, sec. 5, p. 1269, London, 1625. The "Encyclopedia Britannica," vol. 8, p. 695, eighth ed., speaks of Purchas as "an Englishman admirably skilled in language and human and divine arts, a very great philosopher, historian, and theologian."

28

but he uses the uncandid statements of their adversaries, which, indeed, are no worse than those often made in these days concerning those who hallow the Bible Sabbath. These facts clearly attest the continued observance of the Sabbath during the whole period of the Dark Ages. The church of Rome was indeed able to exterminate the Sabbath from its own communion, but it was retained by the true people of God, who were measureably hidden from the papacy in the wilds of Central Europe; while those African and East Indian churches, that were never within the limits of the pope's dominion, have steadfastly retained the Sabbath to the present day.

CHAPTER XXII.

POSITION OF THE REFORMERS CONCERNING THE SABBATH AND FIRST-DAY.

The Reformation arose in the Catholic church—The Sabbath had been crushed out of that church, and innumerable festivals established in its stead—Sunday as observed by Luther, Melancthon, Zwingle, Beza, Bucer, Cranmer, and Tyndale—The position of Calvin stated at length and illustrated—Knox agreed with Calvin—Sunday in Scotland, A. D. 1601—How we should view the Reformers.

ROM the bosom of the Catholic church itself, arose the great Reformation of the sixteenth century. The Sabbath had long been extirpated from that church; and instead of that merciful institution ordained by the divine Lawgiver for the rest and refreshment of mankind, and that man might acknowledge God as his Creator, the papacy had ordained innumerable festivals, which, as a terrible burden, crushed the people to the earth. These festivals are thus enumerated by Dr. Heylyn :—

" These holy days as they were named particularly in Pope Gregory's decretal, so was a perfect list made of them in the Synod of Lyons, A. D. 1244, which being celebrated with a great concourse of people from all parts of Christendom, the canons and decrees thereof began forthwith to find a general admittance. The holy days allowed of there, were these that follow ; viz., the feast of Christ's nativity, St. Stephen, St. John the evangelist, the Innocents, St. Sylvester, the circumcision of our Lord, the Epiphany, Easter, together with the week precedent, and the week succeeding, the three days in rogation week, the day of

Christ's ascension, Whitsunday, with the two days after, St. John the Baptist, the feasts of all the twelve apostles, all the festivities of our Lady, St. Lawrence, ALL THE LORD'S DAYS IN THE YEAR, St. Michael the Archangel, All Saints, St. Martin's, the wakes, or dedication of particular churches, together with the feasts of such topical or local saints which some particular people had been pleased to honor with a day particular amongst themselves.   On these and every one of them, the people were restrained as before was said from many several kinds of work, on pain of ecclesiastical censures to be laid on them which did offend, unless on some emergent causes, either of charity or necessity, they were dispensed with for so doing. . . .   Peter de Aliaco, Cardinal of Cambray, in a discourse by him exhibited to the council of Constance [A. D. 1416], made public suit unto the fathers there assembled, that there might [be] a stop in that kind hereafter; as also that excepting Sundays and the greater festivals it might be lawful for the people, after the end of divine service, to attend their business; the poor especially, as having little time enough on the working days to get their living. But these were only the expressions of well-wishing men. The popes were otherwise resolved, and did not only keep the holy days which they found established in the same state in which they found them, but added others daily as they saw occasion. . . . Thus stood it as before I said, both for the doctrine and the practice, till men began to look into the errors and abuses in the Roman church with a more serious eye than before they did." [1]

Such was the state of things when the reformers began their labors. That they should give up these festivals and return to the observance of the ancient Sabbath, would be expecting too much of men educated in the bosom of the Romish church. Indeed, it ought not to surprise us that, while they were constrained to strike down the authority of these festivals, they should nevertheless retain the most important of them in their

---

[1] Hist. Sab., part 2, chap. 6, secs. 3, 5.

observance. The reformers spoke on this matter as follows : The Confession of the Swiss churches declares that—

"The observance of the Lord's day is founded not on any commandment of God, but on the authority of the church ; and, That the church may alter the day at pleasure." [2]

We further learn that,—

"In the Augsburg Confession, which was drawn up by Melancthon [and approved by Luther], to the question, 'What ought we to think of the Lord's day?' it is answered that the Lord's day, Easter, Whitsuntide, and other such holy days, ought to be kept because they are appointed by the church, that all things may be done in order ; but that the observance of them is not to be thought necessary to salvation, nor the violation of them, if it be done without offense to others, to be regarded as a sin." [3]

Zwingle declared "that it was lawful on the Lord's day, after divine service, for any man to pursue his labors." [4]   Beza taught that "no cessation of work on the Lord's day is required of Christians." [5]   Bucer goes further yet, "and doth not only call it a superstition, but an apostasy from Christ to think that working on the Lord's day, in itself considered, is a sinful thing." [6] And Cranmer, in his Catechism, published in 1548, says :—

"We now keep no more the Sabbath on Saturday as the Jews do ; but we observe the Sunday, and certain other days as the magistrates do judge convenient, whom in this thing we ought to obey." [7]

Tyndale said :—

---

[2] Cox's Sabbath Laws, etc., p. 287.
[3] Id.   [4] Id., p. 287.   [5] Id., p. 286.   [6] Id.   [7] Id., p. 289.

" As for the Sabbath, we be lords over the Sabbath, and may yet change it into Monday, or into any other day as we see need, or may make every tenth day holy day only if we see cause why." [8]

It is plain that both Cranmer and Tyndale believed that the ancient Sabbath was abolished, and that Sunday was only a human ordinance which it was in the power of the magistrates and the church lawfully to change whenever they saw cause for so doing. And Dr. Hessey gives the opinion of Zwingle respecting the present power of each individual church to transfer the so-called Lord's day to another day, whenever necessity urges, as, for example, in harvest time. Thus Zwingle says :—

" If we would have the Lord's day so bound to time that it shall be wickedness to transfer it to another time, in which resting from our labors equally as in that, we may hear the word of God, if necessity haply shall so require, this day so solicitously observed, would obtrude on us as a ceremony. For we are no way bound to time, but time ought so to serve us, that it is lawful, and permitted to each church, when necessity urges (as is usual to be done in harvest time), to transfer the solemnity and rest of the Lord's day, or Sabbath, to some other day." [9]

Zwingle could not, therefore, have considered Sunday as a divinely appointed memorial of the resurrection, or, indeed, as anything but a church festival.

John Calvin said, respecting the origin of the Sunday festival :—

" However, the ancients have not without sufficient reason substituted what *we* call the Lord's day in the room of the Sabbath. For since the resurrection of the Lord is the end and consummation of that true rest, which was adumbrated by the ancient Sabbath; the same day which put an end to the shadows,

---

[8] Tyndale's Answer to More, book 1, chap. 25.   [9] Hessey, p. 352.

admonishes Christians not to adhere to a shadowy ceremony. Yet I do not lay so much stress on the septenary number that I would oblige the church to an invariable adherence to it; nor will I condemn those churches which have other solemn days for their assemblies, provided they keep at a distance from superstition." [10]

It is worthy of notice that Calvin does not assign to Christ and his disciples the establishment of Sunday in the place of the Sabbath. He says this was done by the "ancients," [11] or as another translates it, "the old fathers." Nor does he say "the day which *John* called the Lord's day," but "the day which *we* call the Lord's day." And what is worthy of particular notice, he did not insist that the day which should be appropriated to worship should be one day in every seven; for he was not tied to "the septenary number." The day might come once in six days, or once in eight. And this proves conclusively that he did not regard Sunday as a divine institution in the proper sense of the word; for if he had, he would most assuredly have felt that the festival must be septenary, that is, weekly, and that he must urge "the church to an invariable adherence to it." But Calvin does not leave the matter here. He condemns as " FALSE PROPHETS " those who attempt to enforce the Sunday festival by means of the fourth commandment; and, to do this, they say that the ceremonial part, which requires the observance of the definite seventh day, is abolished, while the moral part, which simply commands

---

[10] Calvin's Institutes of the Christian Religion, book 2, chap. 8, sec. 34, translated by John Allen.

[11] Quanquam non sine delectu Dominicum quem vocamus diem veteres in locum Sabbathi subrogarunt.

the observance of one day in seven, still remains in force.   Here are his words :—

"Thus vanish all the dreams of false prophets, who in past ages have infected the people with a Jewish notion, affirming that nothing but the ceremonial part of the commandment, which, according to them, is the appointment of the seventh day, has been abrogated, but that the moral part of it, that is, the observance of one day in seven, still remains. But this is only changing the day in contempt of the Jews, while they retain the same opinion of the holiness of a day." [12]

Yet these very "dreams of false prophets," to use the words of Calvin, constitute the foundation of the modern doctrine of the change of the Sabbath; for whatever may be said of first-day sacredness in the New Testament, the fourth commandment can only be made to recognize that day by means of this very doctrine of one day in seven which Calvin so sharply denounces. Another important fact is that Calvin's commentaries on the New Testament cover all the books from which quotations are made in behalf of Sunday, except the book of the Revelation. What does Calvin say concerning the change of the Sabbath in the record of Christ's resurrection? [13]—Not one word. He does not even hint at any sacredness in the day, nor any commemoration of the day. Does he say that the meeting "after eight days" was upon Sunday?—He does not say what day it was. [14] What does he say of Sunday in treating of the day of Pentecost? [15]—Nothing. He does not so much as say that this festival was on the first day of the week.

---

[12] Calvin's Institutes, book 2, chap. 8, sec. 34.

[13] Calvin's Harmony of the Evangelists on Matt. 28; Mark 16; Luke 24.

[14] Calvin's Commentary on John 20.   [15] Id., on Acts 2:1.

What does he say of the breaking of bread at Troas?—
He thinks it took place upon the ancient Sabbath. He
says :—

> "Either he doth mean the first day of the week, which was
> next day after the Sabbath, or else some certain Sabbath. Which
> latter thing may seem to me more probable; for this cause,
> because *that day was more fit for an assembly, according to
> custom.*" [16]

He says, however, that this place might "very well"
be translated "the morrow after the Sabbath;" but he
adheres to his own translation, "one day of the Sabbaths," and not "first day of the week." He says
further :—

> "For to what end is there mentioned of the Sabbath, save
> only that he may note the opportunity and choice of the time?
> Also, it is a likely matter that Paul waited for the Sabbath, that
> the day before his departure he might the more easily gather all
> the disciples into one place." [17]

> "Therefore I think thus, that they had appointed a solemn
> day for the celebrating of the holy supper of the Lord among
> themselves, which might be commodious for them all." [18]

This shows conclusively that Calvin believed the Sabbath, and not the first day of the week, to have been the
day for meetings in the apostolic church. But what does
he say of the laying by in store on the first day of the
week?—That Paul's precept relates, not to the first day
of the week, but to the Sabbath! And he marks the
Sabbath as the day on which the sacred assemblies were
held, and the communion celebrated, and says that on
account of these things this was the most convenient day
for collecting their contribution. Thus he writes :—

---

[16] Calvin's Commentary on Acts 20 : 7.   [17] Id.   [18] Id., on Acts 20 : 7.

" *On one of the Sabbaths.* The end is this : that they may
have their alms ready in time. He therefore exhorts them not,
to wait till he came, as anything that is done suddenly, and in a
bustle, is not done well, but to contribute on the Sabbath what
might seem good, and according as every one's ability might enable ; that is, on the day on which they held their sacred assem-
-blies." [19]

" For he has an eye, first of all, to convenience, and farther,
that the sacred assembly, in which the communion of saints is
celebrated, might be an additional spur to them. Nor am I inclined to admit the view taken by Chrysostom, that the term *Sabbath* is employed here to mean the *Lord's day* (Rev. 1 : 10) ; for
the probability is, that the apostles, at the beginning, retained
the day that was already in use, but that afterwards, constrained
by the superstition of the Jews, they set aside that day, and substituted another. Now the *Lord's day* was made choice of chiefly
because our Lord's resurrection put an end to the shadows of the
law. Hence the day itself puts us in mind of our Christian liberty." [20]

These words are very remarkable. They show, first,
that by the Sabbath-day Calvin means, not the first day,
but the seventh ; secondly, that in his judgment, as late
as the time of this epistle, and of the meeting at Troas
[A. D. 60], the Sabbath was the day for the sacred assemblies of the Christians, and for the celebration of the
communion ; thirdly, " but that AFTERWARDS, constrained
by THE SUPERSTITION OF THE JEWS, they set aside that day,
and substituted another."

Calvin did not, therefore, believe that Christ changed
the Sabbath to Sunday to commemorate his resurrection ;
for he says that the resurrection abolished the Sabbath, [21]
and yet he believes that the Sabbath was the sacred day

---

[19] Calvin's Commentary on 1 Cor. 16 : 2.   [20] Id.

[21] Calvin's Institutes, book 2, chap. 8, sec. 34.

of the Christians to the entire exclusion of Sunday, as late as the year 60. Nor could he believe that the apostles set apart Sunday to commemorate the resurrection of Christ; for he thinks that they did not make choice of that day till after the year 60, and even then they did it merely because constrained so to do by the superstition of the Jews! Dr. Hessey illustrates Calvin's ideas of Sunday observance by the following incident:—

"Knox was the intimate friend of Calvin—visited Calvin, and, it is said, on one occasion found him enjoying the recreation of bowls on Sunday." [22]

Without doubt, Calvin was acting in exact harmony with his ideas of the nature of the Sunday festival. But the famous case of Michael Servetus furnishes us a still more pointed illustration of his views of the sacredness of that day. Servetus was arrested in Geneva on the personal application of John Calvin to the magistrates of that city. Such is the statement of Theodore Beza, the life-long friend of Calvin. [23] Beza's translator adds to this fact the following remarkable statement:—

"Promptness induced him to have this heresiarch arrested on a Sunday." [24]

The same fact is stated by Robinson:—

"While he waited for a boat to cross the lake in his way to Zurich, by some means Calvin got intelligence of his arrival; and although it was on a Sunday, yet he prevailed upon the chief syndic to arrest and imprison him. On that day, by the laws of

---

[22] Hessey's Bampton Lectures on Sunday, p. 201, ed. 1866. In the notes appended, p. 366, he says : "At Geneva a tradition exists, that when John Knox visited Calvin on a Sunday, he found his austere coadjutor bowling on a green." Dr. Hessey evidently credited this tradition.

[23] Beza's Life of Calvin, Sibson's Translation, p. 55, ed. 1836.

[24] Id., p. 115.

Geneva no person could be arrested except for a capital crime; but this difficulty was easily removed, for John Calvin pretended that Servetus was a heretic, and that heresy was a capital crime." [25]

" The doctor was arrested and imprisoned on Sunday, the thirteenth of August [A. D. 1553]. That very day he was brought into court." [26]

Calvin's own words respecting the arrest are these :—

" I will not deny but that he was made prisoner upon my application." [27]

The warmest friends of first-day sacredness will not deny that the least sinful part of this transaction was that it occurred on Sunday. Nevertheless, the fact that Calvin caused the arrest of Servetus on that day shows that he had no conviction that the day possessed any inherent sacredness.

John Barclay, [28] a learned man of Scotch descent, and a moderate Roman Catholic, who was born soon after the death of Calvin, and whose early life was spent in Eastern France, not very remote from Geneva, published the statement that Calvin and his friends at Geneva—

" Debated whether the reformed, for the purpose of estranging themselves more completely from the Romish church, should not adopt Thursday as the Christian Sabbath."

Another reason assigned by Calvin for this proposed change was,—

" That it would be a proper instance of Christian liberty." [29]

This statement has been credited by many learned

---

[25] Eccl. Researches, chap. 10, p. 338.

[26] Id., p. 339.   [27] Beza's Life of Calvin, p. 168.

[28] M'Clintock and Strong's Cyclopedia, vol. 1, p. 663.

[29] Hessey, p. 341, gives a clue to the title of Barclay's work. It was Parænesis ad Sectarios hujus temporis, lib. 1, cap. 13, p. 160, Rome, 1617.

Protestants,[30] some of whom must be acknowledged as men of candor and judgment. But Dr. Twisee [31] discredits Barclay, because he did not name the individuals with whom Calvin consulted, and produce them as witnesses; and because King James I. of England at one time suspected Barclay of treachery toward him. But no such crime was ever proved, nor does it appear that the king continued always to hold him in that light.[32] His veracity has never been impeached. The statement of Barclay may possibly be incorrect, but it is not inconsistent with Calvin's doctrine that the church is not tied to a festival that should come once in *seven* days, even as Tyndale said that they could change the Sabbath into Monday or could "make every tenth day holy day, only if we see cause why;" and it is in perfect

---

[30] See Heylyn's History of the Sabbath, part 2, chap. 6, sec. 8; Morer's Lord's Day, pp. 216, 217, 228; An Inquiry into the Origin of Septenary Institutions, p. 55; The Modern Sabbath Examined, p. 26, Whitaker, Treacher, and Arnot, London, 1832; Cox's Sabbath Literature, vol. 1, pp. 165, 166; Hessey, pp. 141, 142, 198, 341, and the authors there cited.

[31] Morality of the Fourth Commandment, pp. 32, 36, 39, 40.

[32] In fact, the story told by Twisse that Barclay's statements in regard to Calvin are not to be credited because he was treacherous toward King James I., who for that reason would not promote him at his court, appears to be wholly unfounded. The Encyclopedia Britannica, vol. 4, p. 439, eighth edition, assigns a very different reason. It says: "In those days a pension bestowed upon a Scottish papist would have been numbered among the national grievances." That is to say, public opinion would not then tolerate the promotion of a Romanist. But this writer believes that the king secretly favored Barclay, as will appear from this remark on page 440: "Although it does not appear that he obtained any regular provision from the king, we may perhaps suppose that he at least received occasional gratuities." This writer knew nothing of Barclay as a detected spy at the king's court. Of his standing as a man, he says, on p. 441: "If there had been any remarkable blemish in the morals of Barclay, some of his numerous adversaries would have pointed it out." M'Clintock and Strong's Cyclopedia, vol. 1, p. 663, says that he "would doubtless have succeeded at court had he not been a Romanist." See also Knight's Cyclopedia of Biography, article, Barclay.

harmony with Calvin's idea of Sunday sacredness as shown in his acts already noticed. Like the other reformers, Calvin is not always consistent with himself in his statements. Nevertheless, we have his judgment concerning the several texts which are used to prove the change of the Sabbath, and also respecting the theory that the commandment may be used to enforce, not the seventh day; but one day in seven, and it is fatal to the modern first-day doctrine.

John Knox, the great Scottish reformer, was the intimate friend of Calvin, with whom he lived at Geneva during a portion of his exile from Scotland. Though the foundation of the Presbyterian church of Scotland was laid by Knox, or rather by Calvin, for Knox carried out Calvin's system, and though that church is now very strict in the observance of Sunday as the Sabbath, yet Knox himself was of Calvin's mind as to the obligation of that day. The original Confession of Faith of that church was drawn up by Knox in A. D. 1560.[33] In that document, Knox states the duties of the first table of the law as follows :—

" To have one God, to worship and honor him; to call upon him in all our troubles; to reverence his holy name; to hear his word; to believe the same; to communicate with his holy sacraments, are the works of the first table." [34]

It is plain that Knox believed the Sabbath commandment to have been stricken out of the first table. Dr. Hessey, after speaking of certain references to Sunday in a subsequent work of his, makes this statement

---

[33] Cox's Sabbath Laws, etc., p. 123; M'Clintock and Strong's Cyclopedia, vol. 5, pp. 137–140.

[34] Quoted in Hessey's Bampton Lectures, p. 200.

respecting the present doctrine of the Sabbath in the Presbyterian church :—

"On the whole, whatever the language held at present in Scotland may be, it is certainly not owing to the great man whom the Scotch regard as the apostle of the Reformation in their country." [35]

That church now holds Sunday to be the divinely authorized memorial of the resurrection of Christ, enforced by the authority of the fourth commandment. But not thus was it held by Calvin and Knox. A British writer states the condition of things with respect to Sunday in Scotland about the year 1601 :—

"At the commencement of the seventeenth century, tailors, shoemakers, and bakers in Aberdeen were accustomed to work till eight or nine every Sunday morning. While violation of the prescribed ritual observances was punished by fine, the exclusive consecration of the Sunday which subsequently prevailed was then unknown. Indeed, there were regular 'play Sundays' in Scotland till the end of the sixteenth century." [36]

But the Presbyterian church, after Knox's time, effected an entire change with respect to Sunday observance. The same writer says :—

"The Presbyterian Kirk introduced into Scotland the Judaical observance of the Sabbath [Sunday], retaining with some inconsistency the Sunday festival of the Catholic church, while rejecting all the other feasts which its authority had consecrated." [37]

Dr. Hessey shows the method of doing this as follows :—

"Of course some difficulties had to be got over. The Sabbath was the seventh day, Sunday was the first day of the week. But

---

[35] Hessey's Bampton Lectures, p. 201.
[36] Westminster Review, July, 1858, p. 37.   [37] Id.

an ingenious theory that one day in seven was the essence of the fourth commandment, speedily reconciled them to this." [38]

The circumstances under which this new doctrine was framed, the name of its author, and the date of its publication will be given in their place. That the body of the reformers should have failed to recognize the authority of the fourth commandment, and that they did not turn men from the Romish festivals to the Sabbath of the Lord, is a matter of regret rather than of surprise. The impropriety of making them the standard of divine truth is forcibly set forth in the following language :—

" Luther and Calvin reformed many abuses, especially in the discipline of the church, and also some gross corruptions in doctrine ; but they left other things of far greater moment just as they found them. . . . It was great merit in them to go as far as they did, and it is not they, but we, who are to blame if their authority induce us to go no farther. We should rather imitate them in the boldness and spirit with which they called in question and rectified so many long-established errors ; and availing ourselves of their labors, make further progress than they were able to do. Little reason have we to allege their name, authority, and example, when they did a great deal and we do nothing at all. In this we are not imitating them, but those who opposed and counteracted them, willing to keep things as they were." [39]

---

[38] Hessey, p. 203.

[39] Dr. Priestly, as quoted in Cox's Sabbath Laws, p. 260.

CHAPTER XXIII.

LUTHER AND CARLSTADT.

The case of Carlstadt worthy of notice—His difficulty with Luther respecting the epistle of James—His boldness in standing with Luther against the pope—What Carlstadt did during Luther's captivity—How far he came under fanaticism—Who acted with Carlstadt in the removal of images from the churches, the suppression of masses, and the abolition of the law of celibacy—Luther on returning restóred the mass, and suppressed the simple ordinance of the supper—Carlstadt submitted to Luther's correction—After two years, Carlstadt felt constrained to oppose Luther respecting the supper—The grounds of their difference respecting the Reformation—Luther said Christ's flesh and blood were literally present IN the bread and wine—Carlstadt said they were simply represented by them—The controversy which followed—Carlstadt refuted by banishment—His cruel treatment in exile —He was not connected with the disorderly conduct of the Anabaptists—Why Carlstadt has been so harshly judged—D'Aubigné's estimate of this controversy—Carlstadt's labors in Switzerland—Luther writes against him—Luther and Carlstadt reconciled—D'Aubigné's estimate of Carlstadt as a scholar and a Christian—Carlstadt a Sabbatarian—Wherein Luther benefited Carlstadt—Wherein Luther might have been benefited by Carlstadt.

T is worthy of notice that at least one of the reformers of considerable prominence—Carlstadt—was a Sabbatarian. It is impossible to read the records of the Reformation without the conviction that Carlstadt was desirous of a more thorough work of reformation than was Luther; and that while Luther was disposed to tolerate certain abuses lest the Reformation should be endangered, Carlstadt was, at all hazards, for a complete return to the Holy Scriptures.

The Sabbatarian principles of Carlstadt, his intimate connection with Luther, his prominence in the early history of the Reformation, and the important bearing of Luther's decision concerning the Sabbath upon the entire history of the Protestant church, render the former worthy of notice in the history of the Sabbath. We shall give his record in the exact words of the best historians, none of whom were in sympathy with his observance of the seventh day. The manner in which they state his faults shows that they were not partial toward him. Shortly after Luther began to preach against the merit of good works, his deep interest in the work of delivering men from popish thralldom led him to deny the inspiration of some portions of those scriptures which were quoted against him. Dr. Sears thus states the case :—

" Luther was so zealous to maintain the doctrine of justification by faith, that he was prepared even to call in question the authority of some portions of Scripture, which seemed to him not to be reconcilable with it. To the epistle of James, especially, his expressions indicate the strongest repugnance." [1]

Before Luther's captivity in the castle of Wartburg, a dispute had arisen between himself and Carlstadt on this very subject. It is recorded of Carlstadt that in the year 1520—

" He published a treatise ' Concerning the Canon of Scripture,' which, although defaced by bitter attacks on Luther, was nevertheless an able work, setting forth the great principle of Protestantism, viz., the paramount authority of Scripture. He also at this time contended for the authority of the epistle of St. James, against Luther. On the publication of the bull of Leo X. against the reformers, Carlstadt showed a real and honest courage in standing firm with Luther. His work on ' Papal Sanctity '

---

[1] Life of Luther by Barnas Sears, D. D., larger ed., pp. 400, 401.

(1520) attacks the infallibility of the pope on the basis of the Bible." [2]

Luther, as is well known, while returning from the Diet of Worms, was seized by the agents of the Elector of Saxony, and hidden from his enemies in Wartburg castle. We read of Carlstadt at this time as follows :—

"In 1521, during Luther's confinement in the Wartburg, Carlstadt had almost sole control of the reform movement at Wittemburg, and was supreme in the university. He attacked monachism and celibacy in a treatise 'Concerning Celibacy, Monachism, and Widowhood.' His next point of assault was the Mass; and a riot of students and young citizens against the Mass soon followed. On Christmas, 1521, he gave the sacrament in both kinds to the laity, and in German; and in January, 1522, he married. His headlong zeal led him to do whatever he came to believe right, at once and arbitrarily. But he soon outran Luther, and one of his great mistakes was in putting the Old Testament on the same footing as the New. On Jan. 24, 1522, Carlstadt obtained the adoption of a new church constitution at Wittemburg, which is of interest only as the first Protestant organization of the Reformation." [3]

There were present at this time in Wittemberg certain fanatical teachers, who, from the town whence they came, were called "the prophets of Zwickau." They brought Carlstadt for a time so far under their influence, that he concluded academical degrees to be sinful, and that, as the inspiration of the Spirit was sufficient, there was no need of human learning. He therefore advised the students of the university to return to their homes.[4] That institution was in danger of dissolution. Such was Carlstadt's course in Luther's

---

[2] M'Clintock and Strong's Cyclopedia, vol. 2, p. 123.   [3] Id.

[4] D'Aubigné's History of the Reformation, book 9.

absence.   With the exception of this last movement, his
acts were in themselves right.

The changes made at Wittemberg during Luther's
absence are, whether timely or not, generally set down
to Carlstadt's account, and said to have been made by
him on his individual responsibility, and in a fanatical
manner.   But this was quite otherwise.   Dr. Maclaine
thus states the case :—

" The reader may perhaps imagine, from Dr. Mosheim's
account of this matter, that Carlstadt introduced these changes
merely by his own authority ; but this was far from being the
case ; the suppression of private masses, the removal of images
out of the churches, the abolition of the law which imposed celibacy
upon the clergy ; which are the changes hinted at by our historian
as rash and perilous, were effected by Carlstadt, in conjunction
with Bugenhagius, Melancthon, Jonas Amsdorf, and others, and
were confirmed by the authority of the Elector of Saxony ; so
that there is some reason to apprehend that one of the principal
causes of Luther's displeasure at these changes, was their being
introduced in his absence ; unless we suppose that he had not so
far shaken off the fetters of superstition, as to be sensible of the
absurdity and the pernicious consequences of the use of images." [5]

Carlstadt had given the cup to the laity, of which
they had long been deprived by Rome.   He had set
aside the worship of the consecrated bread.   Dr. Sears
rehearses this work of Carlstadt, and then tells us what
Luther did concerning it on his return :—

" He [Carlstadt] had so far restored the sacrament of the
Lord's supper as to distribute the wine as well as the bread to the
laity.   Luther, ' in order not to offend weak consciences,' insisted
on distributing the bread only, and prevailed.   He [Carlstadt]

---

[5] Mosheim's Church History, book 4, cent. 16, sec. 3, part 2, paragraph 22,
note.

rejected the practice of elevating and adoring the host. Luther allowed it, and introduced it again." [6]

The position of Carlstadt was at this time very trying. He had not received "many things taught by the new teachers" from Zwickau; but he had publicly taught some of their fanatical ideas relative to the influence of the Spirit of God superseding the necessity of study. But in the suppression of the idolatrous services of the Romanists, he was essentially right. He had the pain to see much of this set up again. Moreover, the Elector would not allow him either to preach or write upon the points wherein he differed from Luther. D'Aubigné states his course as follows :—

"Nevertheless, he sacrificed his self-love for the sake of peace, restrained his desire to vindicate his doctrine, was reconciled, at least in appearance, to his colleague [Luther], and soon after resumed his studies in the university." [7]

As Luther taught some doctrines which Carlstadt could not approve, he felt at last that he must speak. Dr. Sears thus writes :—

"After Carlstadt had been compelled to keep silence, from 1522 to 1524, and to submit to the superior power and authority of Luther, he could contain himself no longer. He therefore left Wittemberg, and established a press at Jena, through which he could, in a series of publications, give vent to his convictions, so long pent up." [8]

The principles at the foundation of their ideas of the Reformation were these : Carlstadt insisted on rejecting everything in the Catholic church not authorized in the

---

[6] Life of Luther, p. 401.

[7] D'Aubigné's History of the Reformation, book 9, p. 282, Porter and Coates's one-volume edition.

[8] Life of Luther, pp. 402, 403.

Bible; Luther was determined to retain everything not expressly forbidden. Dr. Sears here states their primary differences :—

" Carlstadt maintained that 'we should not, in things pertaining to God, regard what the multitude say or think, but look simply to the word of God.   Others,' he adds, 'say that, on account of the weak, we should not *hasten* to keep the commands of God; but wait till they become wise and strong.'   In regard to the ceremonies introduced into the church, he judged as the Swiss reformers did, that all were to be rejected which had not a warrant in the Bible.   'It is sufficiently against the Scriptures if you can find no ground for it in them.'

" Luther asserted, on the contrary, 'Whatever is not against the Scriptures is for the Scriptures, and the Scriptures for it. Though Christ hath not commanded adoring of the host, so neither hath he forbidden it.'   'Not so,' said Carlstadt; 'we are bound to the Bible, and no one may decide after the thoughts of his own heart.' " [9]

It is of interest to know what was the subject which caused the controversy between them, and what was the position of each.   Dr. Maclaine states the occasion of the conflict which now arose :—

" This difference of opinion between Carlstadt and Luther concerning the eucharist, was the true cause of the violent rupture between those two eminent men, and it tended very little to the honor of the latter; for, however the explication which the former gave of the words of the institution of the Lord's supper, may appear forced, yet the sentiments he entertained of that ordinance as a commemoration of Christ's death, and not as a celebration of his bodily presence, in consequence of a consubstantiation with the bread and wine, are infinitely more rational than the doctrine of Luther, which is loaded with some of the most palpable absurdities of transubstantiation; and if it be supposed

---

[9] Life of Luther, pp. 401, 402.

that Carlstadt strained the rule of interpretation too far, when he alleged that Christ pronounced the pronoun this (in the words, *This is my body*), pointing to his body, and not to the bread, what shall we think of Luther's explaining the nonsensical doctrine of consubstantiation by the similitude of a red-hot iron, in which two elements are united, as the body of Christ is with the bread of the eucharist?"[10]

Dr. Sears also states the occasion of this conflict in 1524:—

"The most important difference between him and Luther, and that which most embittered the latter against him, related to the Lord's supper. He opposed not only transubstantiation, but consubstantiation, the real presence, and the elevation and adoration of the host. Luther rejected the first, asserted the second and third, and allowed the other two. In regard to the real presence, he says: 'In the sacrament is the real body of Christ and the real blood of Christ, so that even the unworthy and ungodly partake of it; and "partake of it corporally," too, and not spiritually, as Carlstadt will have it.'"[11]

That Luther was the one chiefly in error in this controversy will be acknowledged by nearly every one at the present day. D'Aubigné cannot refrain from censuring him:—

"When once the question of the supper was raised, Luther threw away the proper element of the Reformation, and took his stand for *himself* and *his church* in an *exclusive Lutheranism.*"[12]

The controversy is thus characterized by Dr. Sears:—

"A furious controversy ensued. Both parties exceeded the bounds of Christian propriety and moderation. Carlstadt was now in the vicinity of the Anabaptist tumults, excited by Munt-

---

[10] Mosheim's History of the Church, book 4, cent. 16, sec. 3, part 2, paragraph 22, note.

[11] Life of Luther, p. 402.

[12] D'Aubigné's History of the Reformation, book 10, p. 312.

zer. He sympathized with them in some things, but disapproved of their disorders. Luther made the most of this." [13]

It is evident that in this contest Luther did not gain any decisive advantage, even in the estimation of his friends. The Elector of Saxony interfered, and banished Carlstadt! D'Aubigné relates this event as follows :—

" He issued orders to deprive Carlstadt of his appointments, and banished him, not only from Orlamund, but from the States of the electorate."

" Luther had nothing to do with this sternness on the part of the prince; it was foreign to his disposition,—and this he afterward proved." [14]

Carlstadt, for maintaining the doctrine now held by almost all Protestants concerning the supper, and for denying Luther's doctrine that Christ is personally present in the bread, was rendered a homeless wanderer for years. His banishment was in 1524. What followed is thus described :—

" From this date until 1534 he wandered through Germany, pursued by the persecuting opinions of both Lutherans and papists, and at times reduced to great straits by indigence and unpopularity. But, although he always found sympathy and hospitality among the Anabaptists, yet he is evidently clear of the charge of complicity with Muntzer's rebellion. Yet he was forbidden to write, his life was sometimes in danger, and he exhibits the melancholy spectacle of a man great and right in many respects, but whose rashness, ambition, and insincere zeal, together with many fanatical opinions, had put him under the well-founded but immoderate censure of both friends and foes." [15]

Such language seems quite unwarranted by the facts.

---

[13] Life of Luther, p. 403.
[14] D'Aubigné's History of the Reformation, book 10, pp. 314, 3
[15] M'Clintock and Strong's Cyclopedia, vol. 2, p. 123.

There was no justice in this persecution of Carlstadt. He did, for a brief time, hold some fanatical ideas, but he did not afterward maintain them. The same writer speaks further in the same strain :—

"It cannot be denied that in many respects he was apparently in advance of Luther, but his error lay in his haste to subvert and abolish the external forms and pomps before the hearts of the people, and doubtless his own, were prepared by an internal change. Biographies of him are numerous, and the Reformation no doubt owes him much of good, for which he has not the credit, as it was overshadowed by the mischief he produced."[16]

Important truth relative to the services of Carlstadt is here stated, but it is connected with intimations of evil which have no sufficient foundation in fact. Dr. Sears speaks thus of the bitter language concerning him :—

"For three centuries, Carlstadt's moral character has been treated somewhat as Luther's would have been, if only Catholic testimony had been heard. The party interested has been both witness and judge. What if we were to judge of Zwingle's Christian character by Luther's representations? The truth is, Carlstadt hardly showed a worse spirit, or employed more abusive terms toward Luther, than Luther did toward him. Carlstadt knew that in many things the truth was on his side; and yet, in these, no less than in others, he was crushed by the civil power, which was on the side of Luther."[17]

D'Aubigné speaks thus of the contest between these two men :—

"Each turns against the error which, to his mind, seems most noxious, and in assailing it, goes—it may be—beyond the truth. But this being admitted, it is still true that both are right in the

---

[16] M'Clintock and Strong's Cyclopedia, vol. 2, p. 123.
[17] Life of Luther, p. 400.

prevailing turn of their thoughts, and though ranking in different hosts, the two great teachers are nevertheless found under the same standard—that of Jesus Christ, who alone is TRUTH in the full import of that word." [18]

D'Aubigné says of them after Carlstadt had been banished :—

"It is impossible not to feel a pain at contemplating these two men, once friends, and both worthy of our esteem, thus angrily opposed." [19]

Some time after Carlstadt's banishment from Saxony, he visited Switzerland. D'Aubigné speaks of the result of his labors in that country, and what Luther did toward him :—

"His instructions soon attracted an attention nearly equal to that which had been excited by the earliest theses put forth by Luther. Switzerland seemed almost gained over to his doctrine. Bucer and Capito also appeared to adopt his views.

"Then it was that Luther's indignation rose to its height; and he put forth one of the most powerful, but also most OUTRA-GEOUS, of his controversial writings,—his book 'Against the Celestial Prophets.' " [20]

Dr. Sears also mentions the labors of Carlstadt in Switzerland, and speaks of Luther's uncandid book :—

"The work which he wrote against him, he entitled, 'The Book against the Celestial Prophets.' This was uncandid; for the controversy related chiefly to the sacrament of the supper. In the south of Germany and in Switzerland, Carlstadt found more adherents than Luther. Banished as an Anabaptist, he was received as a Zwinglian." [21]

Dr. Maclaine relates an incident which followed, that

---

[18] D'Aubigné's History of the Reformation, book 10, p. 312.

[19] Id., book 10, p. 315.   [20] Id.

[21] Life of Luther, p. 403.

is worthy of the better nature of these two illustrious men :—

" Carlstadt, after his banishment from Saxony, composed a treatise against enthusiasm in general, and against the extravagant tenets and the violent proceedings of the Anabaptists in particular. This treatise was even addressed to Luther, who was so affected by it, that, repenting of his unworthy treatment of Carlstadt, he pleaded his cause, and obtained from the Elector a permission for him to return into Saxony." [22]

" After this reconciliation with Luther, he composed a treatise on the eucharist, which breathes the most amiable spirit of moderation and humility ; and having perused the writings of Zwingle, where he saw his own sentiments on that subject maintained with the greatest perspicuity and force of evidence, he repaired the second time to Zurich, and thence to Basil, where he was admitted to the offices of pastor and professor of divinity, and where, after having lived in the exemplary and constant practice of every Christian virtue, he died, amidst the warmest effusions of piety and resignation, on the 25th of December, 1541." [23]

Of Carlstadt's scholarship, and of his conscientiousness, D'Aubigné speaks thus :—

" ' He was well acquainted,' says Dr. Scheur, ' with Latin, Greek, and Hebrew ; ' and Luther acknowledged him to be his superior in learning. Endowed with great powers of mind, he sacrificed to his convictions fame, station, country, and even his bread." [24]

His Sabbatarian character is attested by Dr. White, Lord Bishop of Ely :—

" The same [the observance of the seventh day] likewise being revived in Luther's time by Carolastadius, Sternebergius,

---

[22] Mosheim's Church History, book 4, cent. 16, sec. 3, part 2, par. 22, note.

[23] Id. Very nearly the same statement is made by Du Pin, tome 13, chap. 2, sec. 20, p. 103, A. D. 1703.

[24] Hist. Ref., book 10, p. 315.

and by some sectaries among the Anabaptists, hath both then and ever since been censured as Jewish and heretical." [25]

Dr. Sears alludes to Carlstadt's observance of the seventh day, but as is quite usual with first-day historians in such cases, he does it in such a manner as to leave the fact sufficiently obscure as to be passed over without notice by the general reader. He writes thus :—

" Carlstadt differed essentially from Luther in regard to the use to be made of the Old Testament. With him, the law of Moses was still binding. Luther, on the contrary, had a strong aversion to what he calls a legal and Judaizing religion. Carlstadt held to the divine authority of the Sabbath from the Old Testament ; Luther believed Christians were free to observe any day as a Sabbath, provided they be uniform in observing it." [26]

We have, however, Luther's own statement respecting Carlstadt's views of the Sabbath. It is from his book, " Against the Celestial Prophets : "—

" Indeed, if Carlstadt were to write further about the Sabbath, Sunday would have to give way, and the Sabbath—that is to say, Saturday—must be kept holy ; he would truly make us Jews in all things, and we should come to be circumcised ; for that is true, and cannot be denied, that he who deems it necessary to keep one law of Moses, and keeps it as a law of Moses, must deem all necessary, and keep them all." [27]

The various historians who treat of the difficulty between Luther and Carlstadt, speak freely of the motives of each. But of such matters it is best to speak but little ; the day of Judgment will show the hearts of men, and we must wait till then. We may, however, freely speak of their acts, and may with propriety name the

---

[25] Treatise of the Sabbath Day, p. 8.   [26] Life of Luther, p. 402.
[27] Quoted in the Life of Martin Luther in Pictures, p. 147, J. W. Moore, 195 Chestnut street, Philadelphia.

things wherein each would have benefited the other. Carlstadt's errors at Wittemberg were not because he rejected Luther's help, but because he was deprived of it by Luther's captivity. Luther's errors in those things wherein Carlstadt was right, were because he saw it best to reject Carlstadt's doctrine.

1. Carlstadt's error in the removal of the images, the suppression of masses, the abolition of monastic vows, or vows of celibacy, and in giving the wine as well as the bread in the supper, and in performing the service in German, instead of Latin, if it was an error, was one of time rather than doctrine. Had Luther been with him, probably all would have been deferred for some months, or perhaps some years.

2. Carlstadt would probably have been saved by Luther's presence from coming under the influence of the Zwickau prophets. As it was, he did for a brief season accept, not their teachings in general, but their doctrine that the inspiration of the Holy Spirit in believers renders human learning vain and worthless. But in both these things, Carlstadt submitted to Luther's correction. Had Luther regarded Carlstadt, he would have been benefited in the following particulars :—

1. In his zeal for the doctrine of justification by faith, he would have been saved from the denial of the inspiration of the epistle of James, and would not have called it a " strawy or chaffy epistle." [28]

2. Instead of exchanging transubstantiation—which is the Romish doctrine that the bread and wine of the supper become Christ's literal flesh and blood — for

---

[28] M'Clintock and Strong, vol. 2, p. 123; Dr. A. Clarke's Commentary, preface to James.

consubstantiation, the doctrine which he fastened upon the Lutheran church,—that Christ's flesh and blood are actually present *in* the bread and wine,—he would have given to that church the doctrine that the bread and wine simply represent the body and blood of Christ, and are used in commemoration of his sacrifice for our sins.

3. Instead of holding fast everything in the Romish church not expressly forbidden in the Bible, he would have laid all aside which had not the actual sanction of that holy book.

4. Instead of the Catholic festival of Sunday, he would have observed and transmitted to the Protestant church the ancient Sabbath of the Lord.

Carlstadt needed Luther's help, and he accepted it. Did not Luther also need that of Carlstadt? Is it not time that Carlstadt should be vindicated from the great obloquy thrown upon him by the prevailing party? And would not this have been done long since had not Carlstadt been a decided Sabbatarian?

CHAPTER XXIV.

SABBATH-KEEPERS IN THE SIXTEENTH CENTURY.

The judgment of the martyr Frith—The Reformation brings Sabbath-keepers to light in various countries—In Transylvania—In Bohemia—In Russia—In Germany—In Holland—In France—In England.

OHN FRITH, an English reformer of considerable note, and a martyr, was converted by the labors of Tyndale about 1525, and assisted him in the translation of the Bible. He was burned at Smithfield, July 4, 1533. He is spoken of in the highest terms by the historians of the English Reformation.[1] His views respecting the Sabbath and first-day are thus stated by himself:—

"The Jews have the word of God for their Saturday, sith [since] it is the seventh day, and they were commanded to keep the seventh day solemn. And we have not the word of God for us, but rather against us; for we keep not the seventh day, as the Jews do, but the first, which is not commanded by God's law."[2]

When the Reformation had lifted the vail of darkness that covered the nations of Europe, Sabbath-keepers were found in Transylvania, Bohemia, Russia, Germany, Holland, France, and England. It was not the Refor-

---

[1] M'Clintock and Strong, vol. 3, p. 679; D'Aubigné's History of the Reformation, book 18, pp. 672, 689, 706, 707; book 20, pp. 765, 766; Fox's Acts and Monuments, book 8, pp. 524–527.

[2] Frith's works, p. 69, quoted in Hessey, p. 198.

mation which gave existence to these Sabbatarians, for
the leaders of the Reformation, as a body, were not
friendly to such views. On the contrary, these observers
of the Sabbath appear to be remnants of the ancient
Sabbath-keeping churches that had witnessed for the
truth during the Dark Ages.

Transylvania, a country which now constitutes one
of the eastern divisions of the Austrian empire, was, in
the sixteenth century, an independent principality.
About the middle of that century, the country was
under the rule of Sigismund. The historian of the
Baptists, Robinson, gives the following interesting record
of events in that age and country :—

" The prince received his first religious impressions under his
chaplain, Alexius, who was a Lutheran. On his removal, he
chose Francis Davidis to succeed him, and by him was further
informed of the principles of the Reformation. Davidis was a
native of that extremely populous and well-fortified town which is
called Coloswar by the natives, Clausenberg by the Germans, and
by others, Claudiopolis. He was a man of learning, address, and
piety, and reasoned in this part of his life more justly on the
principles of the Reformation than many of his contemporaries.
In 1563 his highness invited several learned foreigners to come
into Transylvania for the purpose of helping forward the Reformation.[3]

" Several other foreigners, who had been persecuted elsewhere,
sought refuge in this country, where persecution for religion was
unknown. These refugees were Unitarian Baptists, and through
their indefatigable industry and address, the prince, the greatest
part of the senate, a great number of ministers, and a multitude
of the people went heartily into their plan of reformation.[4]

" In the end the Baptists became by far the most numerous
party, and were put in possession of a printing-office and an

---

[3] Eccl. Researches, chap. 16, p. 630.   [4] Id.

academy, and the cathedral was given to them for a place of worship. They obtained these without any violence, and while they formed their own churches according to the convictions of their members, they persecuted nobody, but allowed the same liberty to others, and great numbers of Catholics, Lutherans, and Calvinists resided in perfect freedom." [5]

Mr. Robinson further informs us that Davidis took extreme Unitarian ground with respect to the worship of Christ, which seems to have been the only serious error that can be laid to his charge. Davidis was a Unitarian Baptist minister, intrusted by his brethren with the superintendency of the churches in Transylvania. His influence in that country at one period was very great. His views of the Sabbath are thus stated :—

"He supposed the Jewish Sabbath not abrogated, and he therefore kept holy the seventh day. He believed also the doctrine of the millennium, and like an honest man, what he believed he taught. He was considered by the Transylvanian churches as an apostle, and had grown gray in their service; but the Catholics, the Lutherans, and the Calvinists thought him a Turk, a blasphemer, and an atheist, and his Polish Baptist brethren said he was half a Jew. Had he been a whole Jew, he ought not to have been imprisoned for his speculations.[6]

"By what means the Supreme Searcher of hearts only knows, but by some methods till then unknown in Transylvania, the old man was arrested, and by the senate condemned to die. He was imprisoned in the castle, and Providence, by putting a period to his life there, saved his persecutors from the disgrace of a public execution."[7]

Mr. Robinson says that "many have been blamed" for the death of Davidis, "but perhaps the secret springs of this event may never be known till the Judge of the

---

[5] Eccl. Researches, chap. 16, p. 631. [6] Id., p. 636.
[7] Id., pp. 636, 637.

30

world maketh inquisition for blood." There were many Sabbatarians in Transylvania at this time, for Mr. Robinson enumerates many persons of distinction who were of the same views with Davidis : the ambassador Bequessius, general of the army; the princess, sister of prince John; the privy counselor, Chaquius, and the two Quendi; general Andrassi, and many others of high rank; Somer, the rector of the academy at Claudiopolis; Matthias Glirius, Adam Neusner, and Christian Francken, a professor in the academy at Claudiopolis.

"These," says Robinson, "were all of the same sentiments as Davidis, as were many more of different ranks, who, after his death in prison, defended his opinion against Socinus. Palæologus was of the same mind; he had fled into Moravia, but was caught by the emperor, at the request of Pope Gregory XIV., and carried to Rome, where he was burnt for a heretick. He was an old man, and was terrified at first into a recantation, but he recollected himself, and submitted to his fate like a Christian." [8]

These persons must have been Sabbatarians. Mosheim, after saying that Davidis "left behind him disciples and friends who strenuously maintained his sentiments," adds :—

"The most eminent of these were Jacob Palæologus, of the isle of Chio, who was burned at Rome in 1585; Christian Francken, who had disputed in person with Socinus; and John Somer, who was master of the academy of Clausenberg. This little sect is branded by the Socinian writers with the ignominious appellation of SEMI-JUDAIZERS." [9]

We have a further record of Sabbatarians in Transylvania to the effect that in the time of Davidis,—

---

[8] Eccl. Researches, chap. 16, p. 640.

[9] Mosheim's Hist. Church, book 4, cent. 16, sec. 3, part 2, chap. 4, par. 23.

" John Gerendi [was] head of the Sabbatarians, a people who did not keep Sunday, but Saturday, and whose disciples took the name of Genoldists." [10]

Sabbath-keepers, also, were found in Bohemia, a country of Central Europe, at the time of the Reformation. We are dependent upon those who despised their faith and practice for a knowledge of their existence. Erasmus speaks of them as follows :—

" Now we hear that among the Bohemians a new kind of Jews has arisen called Sabbatarians, who observe the Sabbath with so much superstition, that if on that day anything falls into their eyes, they will not remove it; as if the Lord's day would not suffice for them instead of the Sabbath, which to the apostles also was sacred; or as if Christ had not sufficiently expressed how much should be allowed upon the Sabbath." [11]

We need say nothing relative to the alleged superstition of these Sabbath-keepers. The statement sufficiently refutes itself, and indicates the bitter prejudice of those who speak of them thus. But that Sabbath-keepers were found at this time in Bohemia admits of no doubt. They were of some importance, and they must also have published their views to the world; for Cox tells us that—

" Hospinian, of Zurich, in his treatise ' Concerning the Feasts of the Jews and of the Gentiles,' chapter 3 (Tiguri, 1592), replies to the arguments of these Sabbatarians." [12]

---

[10] Lamy's History of Socinianism, p. 60.

[11] " Nunc audimus apud Bohemos exoriri novum Judæorum genus, Sabbatarios appellant, qui tanta superstitione servant Sabbatum, ut si quid eo die inciderit in oculum, nolint eximere: quasi non sufficiat eis pro Sabbato Dies Dominicus, qui Apostolis etiam erat sacer, aut quasi Christus non satis expresserit quantum tribuen dum sit Sabbato." De Amabili Ecclesiæ Concordia; Opera, tome 5, p. 506, Lugd. Bat. 1704; quoted in Cox's Sabbath Literature, vol. 2, pp. 201, 202; Hessey, p. 374.

[12] Cox, vol. 2, p. 202.

The existence of this body of Sabbatarians in Bohemia at the time of the Reformation is strong presumptive proof that the Waldenses of Bohemia, noticed in the preceding chapter, though claimed as observers of Sunday, were actually observers of the ancient Sabbath.

In Russia, the observers of the seventh day are numerous at the present time. Their existence can be traced back nearly to the year 1400. They are, therefore, at least one hundred years older than the work of Luther. The first writer that I quote speaks of them as "having left the Christian faith." But even in our time, it is very common for people to speak of those who turn from the first day to the seventh, that they have renounced Christ for Moses.[13] He also speaks of them as holding to circumcision. Even Carlstadt was charged with this by Luther as a necessary deduction from the fact that he observed the day enjoined in the fourth commandment. Such being a common method of characterizing Sabbath-keepers in our time, and such also having been the case in past ages,—for when men lack argument, they use opprobrious terms,—the historian, who makes up his record of these people from the statements of the popular party, will certainly represent them as rejecting Christ and the gospel, and accepting instead Moses and the ceremonial law. I give the statements of the historians as they are, and the reader must judge. Robert Pinkerton gives the following account of them :—

---

[13] Such statements respecting the observers of the seventh day are very common. Even those who first commenced to keep the Sabbath in Newport were said to "have left Christ and gone to Moses in the observation of days, and times, and seasons, and such like."—*Seventh-day Baptist Memorial*, vol. 1, p. 32. The pastor of the first-day Baptist church of Newport said to them: "I do judge you have and still do deny Christ."—*Id.*, p. 37.

" *Seleznevtschini.* This sect are, in modern time, precisely what the Strigolniks originally were. They are Jews in principle; maintain the divine obligation of circumcision; observe the Jewish Sabbath, and the ceremonial law. There are many of them about Tula, on the river Kuma, and in other provinces, and they are very numerous in Poland and Turkey, where, having left the Christian faith, they have joined the seed of Abraham, according to the flesh, in rejecting the Messiah and the gospel." [14]

The ancient Russian name of this people was *Strigolniks.* Dr. Murdock says of them :—

" It is common to date the origin of sectarians in the Russian church, about the middle of the seventeenth century, in the time of the patriarch Nikon. But according to the Russian annals, there existed schismatics in the Russian church two hundred years before the days of Nikon ; and the disturbances which took place in his time only proved the means of augmenting their numbers, and of bringing them forward into public view. The earliest of these schismatics first appeared in Novogorod, early in the fifteenth century, under the name of *Strigolniks.*

" A Jew named Horie preached a mixture of Judaism and Christianity ; and proselyted two priests, Denis and Alexie, who gained a vast number of followers. This sect was so numerous that a national council was called, toward the close of the fifteenth century, to oppose it. Soon afterwards one Karp, an excommunicated deacon, joined the *Strigolniks,* and accused the higher clergy of selling the office of priesthood, and of so far corrupting the church, that the Holy Ghost was withdrawn from it. He was a very successful propagator of this sect." [15]

It is very customary with historians to speak of Sabbath-keeping Christians in one of the following ways : 1. To name their observance of the seventh day distinctly, but to represent them as turning from Christ to

---

[14] The Present State of the Greek Church in Russia, Appendix, p. 273, New York, 1815.

[15] Murdock's Mosheim, book 4, cent. 17, sec. 2, part 1, chap. 2, note 12.

Moses and the ceremonial law; or, 2. To speak of their Sabbatarian principles in so vague a manner that the reader will not be likely to suspect them of being Sabbath-keepers. Pinkerton speaks of these Russian Sabbath-keepers after the first of these methods; Murdock, after the second. It is plain that Murdock did not regard these people as rejecting Christ, and it is certain from Pinkerton that the two writers are speaking of the same people.

What was the origin of these Russian Sabbath-keepers? Certainly it was not from the Reformation of the sixteenth century; for they were in existence at least one century before that event. We have seen that the Waldenses, during the Dark Ages, were dispersed through many of the countries of Europe. And so, also, were the people called Cathari, if, indeed, the two were not one people. In particular, we note the fact that they were scattered through Poland, Lithuania, Sclavonia, Bulgaria, Livonia, Albania, and Sarmatia.[16] These countries are now parts of the Russian empire. Sabbath-keepers were numerous in Russia before the time of Luther. The Sabbath of the Lord was certainly retained by many of the ancient Waldenses and Cathari, as we have seen. In fact, the very things said of the Russian Sabbath-keepers, that they held to circumcision and the ceremonial law, were also said of the Cathari, and of that branch of the Waldenses called Passaginians.[17]

Is there any reasonable doubt that in these ancient Christians we have the ancestors of the Russian Sabbath-keepers of the fifteenth century?

Mr. Maxson makes the following statement :—

---

[16] See chapter 21 of this work.   [17] Id.

"We find that Sabbath-keepers appear in Germany late in the fifteenth, or early in the sixteenth century, according to 'Ross's Picture of all Religions.' By this we are to understand that their numbers were such as to lead to organization, and attract attention. A number of these formed a church and emigrated to America, in the early settlement of this country."[18]

Mr. Utter says of Sabbath-keepers in Germany and in Holland :—

"Early in the sixteenth century there are traces of Sabbath-keepers in Germany. The Old Dutch Martyrology gives an account of a Baptist minister named Stephen Benedict, somewhat famous for baptizing during a severe persecution in Holland, who is supposed by good authorities to have kept the seventh day as the Sabbath. One of the persons baptized by him was Barbary von Thiers, wife of Hans Borzen, who was executed on the 16th of September, 1529. At her trial she declared her rejection of the idolatrous sacrament of the priest, and also the Mass."[19]

We give her declaration of faith respecting Sundays and holy days :—

"God has commanded us to rest on the seventh day. Beyond this she did not go: but with the help and grace of God she would persevere therein, and in death abide thereby; for it is the true faith, and the right way in Christ."[20]

Another martyr, Christina Tolingerin, is mentioned thus :—

"Concerning holy days and Sundays, she said: 'In six days the Lord made the world, on the seventh day he rested. The other holy days have been instituted by popes, cardinals, and archbishops.' "[21]

---

[18] Maxson's Hist. Sab., p. 41.

[19] Manual of the Seventh-day Baptists, p. 16.

[20] Martyrology of the Churches of Christ, commonly called Baptists, during the era of the Reformation. From the Dutch of T. J. Van Braght, London, 1850, vol. 1, pp. 113, 114.   [21] Id. p. 113.

There were at this time Sabbath-keepers in France :—

"In France also there were Christians of this class, among whom were M. de la Roque, who wrote in defense of the Sabbath against Bossuet, Catholic bishop of Meaux." [22]

M. de la Roque is referred to by Dr. Wall in his famous History of Infant Baptism "as a learned man in other points," but in great error for asserting that "the primitive church did not baptize infants." [23] It is worthy of notice that Sabbath-keepers are always observers of scriptural baptism—the burial of penitent believers in the watery grave.   No people retaining infant baptism, or the sprinkling of believers, have observed the seventh day. [24]

The origin of the Sabbatarians of England cannot now be definitely ascertained.   Their observance of believers' baptism, and the keeping of the seventh day as the Sabbath of the Lord, strongly attest their descent from the persecuted heretics of the Dark Ages, rather than from the reformers of the sixteenth century, who retained infant baptism and the festival of Sunday. That these heretics had long been numerous in England, is thus certified by Crosby :—

"For in the time of William the Conqueror [A. D. 1070] and his son William Rufus, it appears that the Waldenses and their disciples out of France, Germany, and Holland had their frequent recourse, and did abound in England. . . . The Beringarian, or

---

[22] Manual of the S. D. Baptists, p. 16.

[23] Wall's History of Infant Baptism, vol. 2, p. 379, Oxford, 1835.

[24] I know of no exception to this statement. If there be any, it must be found in the cases of those observing both seventh and first days. Even here, there is certainly no such thing as sprinkling for baptism, but possibly there may be the baptism of young children.

Waldensian, heresy, as the chronologer calls it, had, about A. D. 1080, generally corrupted all France, Italy, and England." [25]

Mr. Maxson says of the English Sabbatarians :—

"In England we find Sabbath-keepers very early. Dr. Chambers says : 'They arose in England in the sixteenth century,' from which we understand that they then became a distinct denomination in that kingdom." [26]

Mr. Benedict speaks of the origin of English Sabbatarians as follows :—

"At what time the Seventh-day Baptists began to form churches in this kingdom does not appear; but probably it was at an early period ; and although their churches have never been numerous, yet there have been among them almost for two hundred years past, some very eminent men." [27]

[25] Hist. English Baptists, vol. 2, pref., pp. 43, 44.

[26] Maxson's Hist. Sab., p. 42.

[27] Gen. Hist. Bapt. Denom., vol. 2, p. 414, ed. 1813.

CHAPTER XXV.

HOW AND WHEN SUNDAY APPROPRIATED THE FOURTH COMMANDMENT.

The light of the Reformation destroyed many of the best Sunday arguments of the preceding Dark Ages—The controversy between the
Presbyterians and Episcopalians of England brings Sunday sacredness
to the test—The former discover the means of enforcing the observance of Sunday by the fourth commandment—How this can be done
—Effects of this extraordinary discovery—History of the Sunday
festival concluded.

HE light of the Reformation necessarily dissi-
pated into thin air many of the most substantial arguments by which the Sunday festival
had been built up during the Dark Ages. The roll that
fell from heaven, the apparition of St. Peter, the relief
of souls in purgatory, and even of the damned in hell,
and many prodigies of fearful portent,—none of these,
nor all of them combined, were likely longer to sustain
the sacredness of the venerable day. True it was that
when these were swept away, there remained, to sustain
the festival of Sunday, the canons of councils, the edicts
of kings and emperors, the decrees of the holy doctors
of the church, and, greatest of all, the imperious mandates
of the Roman pontiff. Yet these could be adduced also
in behalf of the innumerable festivals ordained by the
same great apostate church. Such authority would
answer for the Episcopalian, who devoutly accepts of all

these festivals, because commanded so to do by the church; but for those who acknowledge the Bible as the only rule of faith, the case was different. In the latter part of the sixteenth century, the Presbyterians and Episcopalians of England were involved in such a controversy as brought this matter to an issue. The Episcopalians required men to observe all the festivals of the church; the Presbyterians observed Sunday, and rejected all the rest. The Episcopalians showed the inconsistency of this discrimination, inasmuch as the same church authority had ordained them all. As the Presbyterians rejected the authority of the church, they would not keep Sunday upon that ground, especially as it would involve the observance also of all the other festivals. They had to choose, therefore, between the giving up of Sunday entirely, and the defense of its observance by the Bible. There was, indeed, another and a nobler choice that they might have made, viz., to adopt the Sabbath of the Lord; but it was too humiliating for them to unite with those who retained that ancient and sacred institution. The issue of this struggle is thus related by a distinguished German theologian, Hengstenberg :—

" The opinion that the Sabbath was transferred to the Sunday was first broached in its perfect form, and with all its consequences, in the controversy which was carried on in England between the Episcopalians and Presbyterians. The Presbyterians, who carried to extremes the principle that every institution of the church must have its foundation in the Scriptures, and would not allow that God had given, in this respect, greater liberty to the church of the New Testament, which his Spirit had brought to maturity, than to that of the Old, charged the Episcopalians with popish leaven, and superstition, and subjection to the ordinances of men, because they retained the Christian feasts. The Episcopalians, on the other hand, as a proof that greater liberty was granted to the New-Testament church in such matters as these, appealed to the fact that even the observance of the Sunday was only an arrangement of the church. The Presbyterians were now in a position which compelled them either to give up the observance of the Sunday, or to maintain that a divine appointment from God separated it from the other festivals. The first they could not do, for their Christian experience was too deep for them not to know how greatly the weakness of human nature stands in need of regularly returning periods, devoted to the service of God. They therefore decided upon the latter." [1]

Thus much for the occasion of that wonderful discovery by which the Scriptures are made to sustain the divine appointment of Sunday as the Christian Sabbath. The date of the discovery, the name of the discoverer, and the manner in which he contrived to enforce the first day of the week by the authority of the fourth commandment, are thus set forth by a candid first-day historian, Lyman Coleman:—

"The true doctrine of the Christian Sabbath was first promulgated by an English dissenter, the Rev. Nicholas Bound, D. D., of Norton, in the county of Suffolk. About the year 1595, he published a famous book, entitled, 'Sabbathum Veteris et Novi Testamenti,' or the True Doctrine of the Sabbath. In this book he maintained 'that the seventh part of our time ought to be devoted to God—that Christians are bound to rest on the Lord's day as much as the Jews were on the Mosaic Sabbath, the commandment about rest being moral and perpetual; and that it was not lawful for persons to follow their studies or worldly business on that day, nor to use such pleasures and recreations as are permitted on other days.' This book spread with wonderful rapidity. The doctrine which it propounded called forth from many hearts a ready response, and the result was a most pleasing

---

[1] Hengstenberg's Lord's Day, p. 66.

reformation in many parts of the kingdom. 'It is almost incredible,' says Fuller, 'how taking this doctrine was, partly because
of its 'own purity, and partly for the eminent piety of such persons as maintained it; so that the Lord's day, especially in corporations, began to be precisely kept; people becoming a law
unto themselves, forbearing such sports as yet by statute permitted; yea, many rejoicing at their own restraint herein.' The
law of the Sabbath was indeed a religious principle, after which
the Christian church had, for centuries, been darkly groping.
Pious men of every age had felt the necessity of divine authority
for sanctifying the day. Their conscience had been in advance
of their reason. Practically they had kept the Sabbath better
than their principles required.

"Public sentiment, however, was still unsettled in regard to
this new doctrine respecting the Sabbath, though a few at first
violently opposed it. 'Learned men were much divided in their
judgments about these Sabbatarian doctrines; some embraced
them as ancient truths consonant to Scripture, long disused and
neglected, now seasonably revived for the increase of piety.
Others conceived them grounded on a wrong bottom; but because
they tended to the manifest advance of religion, it was a pity to
oppose them; seeing none have just reason to complain, being
deceived unto their own good. But a third sort flatly fell out
with these propositions, as galling men's necks with a *Jewish
yoke* against the liberty of Christians; that Christ, as Lord
of the Sabbath, had removed the rigor thereof, and allowed
men lawful recreations; *that this doctrine put an unequal
lustre on the Sunday,* on set purpose to eclipse all other
holy days, to the derogation of the authority of the church; that
this strict observance was set up out of faction, to be a character
of difference to brand all for libertines who did not entertain it.'
No open opposition, however, was at first manifested against the
sentiments of Dr. Bound. No reply was attempted for several
years, and 'not so much as a feather of a quill in print did wag
against him.'

"His work was soon followed by several other treatises in
defense of the same sentiments. 'All the Puritans fell in with
this doctrine, and distinguished themselves by spending that part

of sacred time in public, family, and private devotion.' Even Dr. Heylyn certified the triumphant spread of those Puritanical sentiments respecting the Sabbath. . . .

" ' This doctrine,' he says, ' carrying such a fair show of piety, at least in the opinion of the common people, and such as did not examine the true grounds of it, induced many to embrace and defend it; and in a very little time it became the most bewitching error and the most popular infatuation that ever was embraced by the people of England.' " [2]

Dr. Bound was not absolutely the inventor of the seventh-part-of-time theory; but he may be said rather to have gathered up and combined the scattered hints of his predecessors, and to have added to these something of his own production. His grounds for asserting Sunday to be the Sabbath of the fourth commandment are these :—

" That which is natural, namely, that every seventh day should be kept holy unto the Lord, that still remaineth: that which is positive, namely, that day which was the seventh day from the creation, should be the Sabbath, or day of rest, that is now changed in the church of God." [3]

He says that the meaning of the declaration, " The seventh day is the Sabbath of the Lord thy God," is this :—

" There must be one [day] of seven and not [one] of eight. [4]

But the special key to the whole theory is in the statement that the seventh day in the commandment was " *genus*," that is to say, it was a kind of seventh day

---

[2] Coleman's Ancient Christianity Exemplified, chap. 26, sec. 2; Heylyn's Hist. Sab., part 2, chap. 8, sec. 7; Neal's Hist. Puritans, part 1, chap. 8.

[3] Sabbathum Veteris et Novi Testamenti; or, the True Doctrine of the Sabbath, by Nicholas Bound, D. D., sec. ed., London, 1606, p. 51.

[4] Id., p. 66.

which comprehended several species of seventh days, at least two. Thus he says :—

"So he maketh the seventh day to be *genus* in this commandment, and to be perpetual : and in it, by virtue of the commandment, to comprehend these two species or kinds : the Sabbath of the Jews and of the Gentiles, of the law and of the gospel : so that both of them were comprehended in the commandment, even as *genus* comprehendeth both his species." [5]

He enforces the first day by the fourth commandment as follows :—

"So that we have not in the gospel a new commandment for the Sabbath, diverse from that that was in the law ; but there is a diverse time appointed ; namely, not the seventh day from the creation, but the day of Christ's resurrection, and the seventh from that : both of them at several times being comprehended in the fourth commandment." [6]

He means to say that the fourth commandment enforces the seventh day from the creation to the resurrection of Christ, and that since that time it enforces a different seventh day, namely, the seventh from Christ's resurrection. Such is the perverse ingenuity by which men can evade the law of God, and yet make it appear that they are faithfully observing it.

Such was the origin of the seventh-part-of-time theory, by which the seventh day is dropped out of the fourth commandment, and one day in seven slipped into its place,—a doctrine most opportunely framed at the very period when nothing else could save the venerable day of the sun. With the aid of this theory, the Sunday of "pope and pagan" was able coolly to wrap itself in the fourth commandment, and then, in the character of a

---

[5] True Doctrine of the Sabbath, p. 71.　　　[6] Id., p. 72.

divine institution, to challenge obedience from all Bible
Christians. 'It could now cast away the other frauds on
which its very existence had depended, and support its
authority by this one alone. In the time of Constantine
it ascended the throne of the Roman empire, and during
the whole period of the Dark Ages it maintained its
supremacy from the chair of St. Peter; but now it had
ascended the throne of the Most High. And thus a day
which God " commanded not nor spake it, neither came
it into" his " mind," was enjoined upon mankind with all
the authority of his holy law. The immediate effect of
Dr. Bound's work upon the existing controversy is thus
described by an Episcopalian eye-witness, Dr. Heylyn :—

" For by inculcating to the people these new Sabbath speculations [concerning Sunday], teaching that that day only 'was
of God's appointment, and all the rest observed in the church of
England, a remnant of the will-worship in the church of Rome;'
the other holy days in this church established, were so shrewdly
shaken that till this day they are not well recovered of the blow
then given. Nor came this on the by or besides their purpose,
but as a thing that specially was intended from the first beginning." [7]

In a former chapter we called attention to the fact
that Sunday can be maintained as a divine institution
only by adopting the rule of faith acknowledged in the
church of Rome, which is the Bible, with the traditions
of the church added thereto. We have seen that in the
sixteenth century the Presbyterians of England were
brought to decide between giving up Sunday as a church
festival, and maintaining it as a divine institution by the

---

[7] Hist. Sab., part 2, chap. 8, sec. 8.

Bible.   They chose the latter course.   Yet while apparently avoiding the charge of observing a Catholic festival, by claiming to prove the Sunday institution out of the Bible, the utterly unsatisfactory nature of the several inferences adduced from the Scriptures in support of that day compelled them to resort to the traditions of the church, and to add these to their so-called Biblical evidences in its behalf.   It would be no worse to keep Sunday while frankly acknowledging it to be a festival of the Catholic church, not commanded in the Bible, than it is to profess that you observe it as a Biblical institution, and then prove it to be such by adopting the rule of faith of the Romanists.   Joaunes Perrone, an eminent Italian Catholic theologian, in an important doctrinal work entitled "Theological Lessons," makes a very impressive statement respecting the acknowledgment of tradition by Protestant Sunday-keepers.   In his chapter "Concerning the Necessity and Existence of Tradition," he lays down the proposition that it is necessary to admit doctrines which we can prove only from tradition, and cannot sustain from the Holy Scriptures.   Then he says :—

"It is not possible, indeed, if traditions of such character are rejected, that several doctrines, which the Protestants held with us since they withdrew from the Catholic church, could, in any possible manner, be established.   The fact is placed beyond a venture of a doubt, for they themselves hold with us the validity of baptism administered by heretics or infidels, the validity also of infant baptism, the true form of baptism [sprinkling]; they held, too, that the law of abstaining from blood and anything strangled is not in force; also concerning the substitution of the

31

Lord's day for the Sabbath; besides those things which I have mentioned before, and not a few others." [8]

Dr. Bound's theory of the seventh part of time has found general acceptance in all those churches which sprung from the church of Rome. Most forcibly did old Cotton Mather observe :—

" The reforming churches, flying from Rome, carried, some of them more, some of them less, all of them something, of Rome with them." [9]

One sacred treasure which they all drew from the venerable mother of harlots is the ancient festival of the sun. She had crushed out of her communion the Sabbath of the Lord, and having adopted the venerable day of the sun, had transformed it into the Lord's day of the Christian church. The reformed, flying from her communion, and carrying with them this ancient festival, now found themselves able to justify its observance as being indeed the veritable Sabbath of the Lord! As the seamless coat of Jesus, the Lord of the Sabbath, was torn from him before he was nailed to the cross, so has the fourth commandment been torn from the rest-day of the Lord, around which it was placed by the great Law-giver, and given to this papal Lord's day; and this

---

[8] Prælectiones Theologicæ, vol. 1, part 2, sec. 2, cap. 1, p. 194. "Propositio. Præter sacram Scripturam admitti necessario debent Traditiones divinæ dogmaticæ ab illa prorsus distinctæ."

" Non posse praeterea, rejectis ejusmodi traditionibus, plura dogmata, quæ nobiscum retinuerunt protestantes cum ab Ecclesia catholica recesserunt, ullo modo adstruis, res est citra omnis dubitationis aleam posita. Etenim ipsi nobiscum retinuerunt valorem baptismi ab haereticis aut infidelibus administrati, valorem item paedobaptismi, germanam baptismi formam, cessationem legis de abstinentia a sanguine et suffocato, de die dominico Sabbatis suffecto, praeter ea quæ superius commemoravimus aliaque haud pauca."

[9] Backus's Hist. of the Baptists in New England, p. 63, ed. 1777.

Barabbas, the robber, thus arrayed in the stolen fourth commandment, has from that time to the present day, and with astonishing success, challenged the obedience of the world as the divinely appointed Sabbath of the most high God. Here we close the history of the Sunday festival, now fully transformed into the *Christian Sabbath*. A rapid survey of the history of English and American Sabbath-keepers will conclude this work.

CHAPTER XXVI.

ENGLISH SABBATH-KEEPERS.

English Sabbatarians in the sixteenth century—Their doctrines—John
Trask for these doctrines pilloried, whipped, and imprisoned—He recants—Character of Mrs. Trask—Her crime—Her indomitable courage
—She suffers fifteen years' imprisonment, and dies in prison—Principles of the Traskites—Brabourne writes in behalf of the seventh day
—Appeals to King Charles I. to restore the ancient Sabbath—The
king employs Dr. White to write against Brabourne, and Dr. Heylyn
to write the history of the Sabbath—The king intimidates Brabourne,
and he recants—He returns again to the Sabbath—Philip Tandy—
James Ockford writes "The Doctrine of the Fourth Commandment"
—His book burned—Edward Stennett—Wm. Sellers—Cruel Treatment of Francis Bampfield—Thomas Bampfield—Martyrdom of John
James—How the Sabbath cause was prostrated in England.

CHAMBERS speaks thus of Sabbath-keepers in
the sixteenth century :—

"In the reign of Elizabeth, it occurred to many
conscientious and independent thinkers (as it had previously done
to some Protestants in Bohemia) that the fourth commandment
required of them the observance, not of the first, but of the specified *seventh* day of the week, and a strict bodily rest, as a service
then due to God; while others, though convinced that the day
had been altered by divine authority, took up the same opinion as to the scriptural obligation to refrain from work. The
former class became numerous enough to make a considerable
figure for more than a century in England, under the title of
' Sabbatarians '—a word now exchanged for the less ambiguous
appellation of ' Seventh-day Baptists.' " [1]

---

[1] Chambers's Cyclopedia, article, Sabbath, vol. 8, p. 402, London, 1867.

Gilfillan quotes an English writer of the year 1584, John Stockwood, who says that there was then—

" A great diversity of opinion among the vulgar people and simple sort, concerning the Sabbath-day and the right use of the same."

And Gilfillan states one of the grounds of controversy thus :—

" Some maintaining the unchanged and unchangeable obligation of the seventh-day Sabbath." [2]

In 1607 an English first-day writer, John Sprint, gave the views of the Sabbath-keepers of that time, which in truth have been substantially the same in all ages :—

" They allege reasons drawn, 1. From the precedence of the Sabbath before the law, and before the fall ; the laws of which nature are immutable. 2. From the perpetuity of the moral law. 3. And from the large extent thereof appertaining to [the Sabbath above] all [the other precepts]. 4. . . . . And of the cause of [this precept of] the law which maketh it perpetual, which is the memorial and meditation of the works of God, which belong unto the Christians as well as to the Jews." [3]

John Trask began to speak and write in favor of the seventh day as the Sabbath of the Lord about the time that King James I. and the archbishop of Canterbury published the famous " Book of Sports for Sunday," in 1618. His field of labor was London, and being a very zealous man, he was soon called to account by the persecuting authority of the church of England. He took high ground as to the sufficiency of the Scriptures to direct in all religious services, and that the civil authorities

---

[2] Gilfillan's Sabbath, p. 60.

[3] Observation of the Christian Sabbath, p. 2.

ought not to constrain men's consciences in matters of religion. He was brought before the infamous Star Chamber, where a long discussion was held respecting the Sabbath. It was on this occasion that bishop Andrews first brought forward that now famous first-day argument, that the early martyrs were tested by the question, "Hast thou kept the Lord's day?"[4]

Gilfillan, quoting the words of contemporary writers, says of Trask's trial that,—

"For 'making of conventicles and factions, by that means which may tend to sedition and commotion, and for scandalizing the king, the bishops, and the clergy,' 'he was censured in the Star Chamber to be set upon the pillory at Westminster, and from thence to be whipped to the fleet, there to remain a prisoner.'"[5]

This cruel sentence was carried into execution, and finally broke his spirit. After enduring the misery of his prison for one year, he recanted his doctrine.[6] The case of his wife is worthy of particular mention. Pagitt gives her character thus :—

"She was a woman endued with many particular virtues, well worthy the imitation of all good Christians, had not error in other things, especially a spirit of strange unparalleled opinionativeness and obstinacy in her private conceits, spoiled her."[7]

Pagitt says that she was a school-teacher of superior excellence. She was particularly careful in her dealings with the poor. He gives her reasons thus :—

"This she professed to do out of conscience, as believing she must one day come to be judged for all things done in the flesh.

---

[4] See the fifteenth chapter of this work.
[5] Gilfillan's Sabbath, p. 88. [6] Id.
[7] Pagitt's Heresiography, p. 209, London, 1661.

Therefore she resolved to go by *the safest rule*, rather against than for her private interest." [8]

Pagitt gives her crime in the following words :—

" At last for teaching only five days in the week, and resting upon Saturday, *it being known upon what account she did it*, she was carried to the new prison in Maiden Lane, a place then appointed for the restraint of several other persons of different opinions from the church of England." [9]

Observe the crime : it was not what she did, for a first-day person might have done the same, but because she did it to obey the fourth commandment. Her motive exposed her to the vengeance of the authorities. She was a woman of indomitable courage, and would not purchase her liberty by renouncing the Lord's Sabbath. During her long imprisonment, Pagitt says that some one wrote to her thus :—

" Your constant suffering would be praiseworthy, were it for truth ; but being for error, your recantation will be both more acceptable to God, and laudable before men." [10]

But her faith and patience held out till she was released by death.

" Mrs. Trask lay fifteen or sixteen years a prisoner for her opinion about the Saturday Sabbath ; in all which time she would receive no relief from anybody, notwithstanding she wanted much, alleging that it was written, ' It is more blessed to give than to receive.' Neither would she borrow, because it was written, ' Thou shalt lend to many nations, and shalt not borrow.' So she deemed it a dishonor to her Head, Christ, either to beg or borrow. Her diet for the most part during her imprisonment, that is, till a little before her death, was bread and water, roots and herbs ; no flesh nor wine, nor brewed drink. All her means

---

[8] Pagitt's Heresiography, p. 209.   [9] Id., p. 210.   [10] Id., p. 164.

was an annuity of forty shillings a year; what she lacked more to live upon she had of such prisoners as did employ her sometimes to do business for them." [11]

Pagitt, who was the contemporary of Trask, thus states the principles of the Sabbatarians of that time, whom he calls Traskites :—

"The positions concerning the Sabbath by them maintained, were these :—

"1. That the fourth commandment of the decalogue, 'Remember the Sabbath-day to keep it holy' [Ex. 20], is a divine precept, simply and entirely moral, containing nothing legally ceremonial in whole or in part, and therefore the weekly observation thereof ought to be perpetual, and to continue in force and virtue to the world's end.

"2. That the Saturday, or seventh day in every week, ought to be an everlasting holy day in the Christian church, and the religious observation of this day obligeth Christians under the gospel, as it did the Jews before the coming of Christ.

"3. That the Sunday, or Lord's day, is an ordinary working day, and it is superstition and will-worship to make the same the Sabbath of the fourth commandment." [12]

It was for this noble confession of faith that Mrs. Trask was shut up in prison till the day of her death. For the same, Mr. Trask was compelled to stand in the pillory, and was whipped from thence to the fleet, and then shut up in a wretched prison, from which he escaped by recantation after enduring its miseries for more than a year. [13]

Mr. Utter mentions the next Sabbatarian minister as follows :—

---

[11] Pagitt's Heresiography, pp. 196, 197.   [12] Id., p. 161.
[13] Manual of the Seventh-day Baptists, pp. 17, 18; Heylyn's Hist. of the Sab., part 2, chap. 8, sec. 10 ; Gilfillan's Sabbath, pp. 88, 89 ; Cox's Sabbath Literature, vol. 1, pp. 152, 153.

" Theophilus Brabourne, a learned minister of the gospel in the established church, wrote a book, which was printed at London in 1628, wherein he argued 'that the Lord's day is not the Sabbath-day by divine institution,' but 'that the seventh-day Sabbath is now in force.' Mr. Brabourne published another book in 1632, entitled 'A Defense of that most Ancient and Sacred Ordinance of God's, the Sabbath-day.' " [14]

Brabourne dedicated his book to King Charles I., requesting him to use his royal authority for the restoration of the ancient Sabbath. But those who put their trust in princes are sure to be disappointed. Dr. F. White, Bishop of Ely, thus states the occasion of his own work against the Sabbath :—

" Now because this Brabourne's treatise of the Sabbath was dedicated to his Royal Majesty, and the principles upon which he grounded all his arguments (being commonly preached, printed, and believed throughout the kingdom), might have poisoned and infected many people either with this Sabbatarian error, or with some other of like quality ; it was the king, our gracious master, his will and pleasure, that a treatise should be set forth, to prevent further mischief, and to settle his good subjects (who have long time been distracted about Sabbatarian questions) in the old and good way of the ancient and orthodoxal Catholic church. Now that which his sacred Majesty commanded, I have by your Grace's direction [Archbishop Laud] obediently performed." [15]

The king not only wished by this appointment to overthrow those who kept the day enjoined in the commandment, but also those who, by means of Dr. Bound's new theory, pretended that Sunday was that day. He therefore joined Dr. Heylyn with Bishop White in this work :—

---

[14] Manual of the S. D. Baptists, p. 18.

[15] Dr. Francis White's Treatise of the Sabbath-day, quoted in Cox's Sab. Lit., vol. 1, p. 167.

" Which burden being held of too great weight for any one to undergo, and the necessity of the work requiring a quick dispatch, it was held fit to divide the employment betwixt two. The argumentative and scholastical part was referred to the right learned Dr. White, then Bishop of Ely, who had given good proof of his ability in polemical matters in several books and disputations against the papists. The practical and historical [was to be written] by Heylyn of Westminster, who had gained some reputation for his studies in the ancient writers." [16]

The works of White and Heylyn were published simultaneously in 1635. Dr. White, in addressing himself to those who enforce Sunday observance by the fourth commandment, speaks thus of Brabourne's arguments, that not Sunday, but the ancient seventh day, is there enjoined :—

" Maintaining your own principles, that the fourth commandment is purely and simply moral and of the law of nature, it will be impossible for you, either in English or Latin, to solve Theophilus Brabourne's objections." [17]

But the king had something besides argument for Brabourne. He was brought before Archbishop Laud and the court of High Commission, and, moved by the fate of Mrs. Trask, he submitted for the time to the authority of the church of England, but sometime afterward wrote other books in behalf of the seventh day.[18] Dr. White's book has this pithy notice of the indefinite-time theory :—

" Because an indefinite time must either bind to all moments

---

[16] Heylyn's Cyprianus Anglicus, quoted in Cox, vol. 1, p. 173.

[17] Treatise of the Sabbath-day, p. 110.

[18] Hessey's Bampton Lectures, pp. 373, 374 ; Cox's Sab. Lit., vol. 2, p. 6; A. H. Lewis's Sabbath and Sunday, pp. 178–184. This work contains much valuable information respecting English and American Sabbatarians.

of time, as a debt, when the day of payment is not expressly dated, is liable to payment every moment; or else it binds to no time at all." [19]

Mr. Utter, after the statement of Brabourne's case, continues thus :—

"About this time, Philip Tandy began to promulgate in the northern part of England the same doctrine concerning the Sabbath. He was educated in the established church, of which he became a minister. Having changed his views respecting the mode of baptism and the day of the Sabbath, he abandoned that church, and 'became a mark for many shots.' He held several public disputes about his peculiar sentiments, and did much to propagate them. James Ockford was another early advocate in England of the claims of the seventh day as the Sabbath. He appears to have been well acquainted with the discussions in which Trask and Brabourne had been engaged. Being dissatisfied with the pretended conviction of Brabourne, he wrote a book in defense of Sabbatarian views, entitled 'The doctrine of the fourth commandment.' This book, published about the year 1642, was burnt by order of the authorities in the established church." [20]

The famous Stennett family furnished, for four generations, a succession of able Sabbatarian ministers. Mr. Edward Stennett, the first of these, was born about the beginning of the seventeenth century. His work, entitled "The Royal Law Contended For," was first published at London in 1658. "He was an able and devoted minister, but dissenting from the established church, he was deprived of the means of support." "He suffered much of the persecution which the Dissenters were exposed to at that time, and more especially for his faithful adherence to the cause of the Sabbath. For this

[19] Treatise of the Sabbath-day, p. 73.
[20] Manual of the S. D. Baptists, pp. 19, 20.

truth he experienced tribulation, not only from those in power, by whom he was kept a long time in prison, but also much distress from unfriendly, dissenting brethren, who strove to destroy his influence and ruin his cause." In 1664 he published a work entitled " The seventh Day is the Sabbath of the Lord." [21] In 1671 Wm. Sellers wrote a work in behalf of the seventh day, in reply to Dr. Owen. Cox states its object in these words :—

" In opposition to the opinion *that some one day in seven* is all that the fourth commandment requires to be set apart, the writer maintains the obligation of the Saturday Sabbath on the ground that ' God himself directly in the letter of the text calls the seventh day the Sabbath-day, giving both the names to one and the self-same day, as all men know that ever read the commandments.' " [22]

One of the most eminent Sabbatarian ministers of the last half of the seventeenth century was Francis Bampfield. He was originally a clergyman of the church of England. The Baptist historian, Crosby, speaks of him thus :—

" But being utterly unsatisfied in his conscience with the conditions of conformity, he took his leave of his sorrowful and weeping congregation in . . . 1662, and was quickly after imprisoned for worshiping God in his own family. So soon was his unshaken loyalty to the king forgotten, . . . that he was more frequently imprisoned and exposed to greater hardships for his nonconformity than most other dissenters." [23]

Of his imprisonment, Neal says :—

" After the act of uniformity, he continued preaching as he had opportunity in private, till he was imprisoned for five days and nights, with twenty-five of his hearers, in one room, . . . where

---

[21] Cox, vol. 1, p. 268 ; vol. 2, p. 10.   [22] Id., vol. 2, p. 35.
[23] Hist. English Baptists, vol. 1, pp. 365, 366.

they spent their time in religious exercises; but after some time he was released. Soon after, he was apprehended again, and lay nine years in Dorchester jail, though he was a person of unshaken loyalty to the king." [24]

During his imprisonment, he preached almost every day, and gathered a church even under his confinement. And when he was at liberty, he ceased not to preach in the name of Jesus. After his release, he went to London, where he preached with much success.[25] Neal says of his labors in that city :—

"When he resided in London, he formed a church on the principles of the Sabbatarian Baptists, at Pinner's hall, of which principles he was a zealous asserter. He was a celebrated preacher, and a man of serious piety." [26]

On Feb. 17, 1682, he was arrested while preaching, and on March 28 was sentenced to forfeit all his goods and to be imprisoned in Newgate for life. In consequence of the hardships which he suffered in that prison, he died, Feb. 16, 1683.[27] "Bampfield," says Wood, "dying in the said prison of Newgate, . . . aged seventy years, his body was . . . followed with a very great company of factious and schismatical people to his grave." [28] Crosby says of him :—

"All that knew him will acknowledge that he was a man of great piety. And he would in all probability have preserved the same character, with respect to his learning and judgment, had it not been for his opinion in two points; viz., that infants ought

[24] Hist. Puritans, part 2, chap. 10.

[25] Crosby's Hist. Eng. Baptists vol. 1, pp. 7, 366, 36

[26] Hist. Puritans, part 2, chap. 10.

[27] Calamy's Ejected Ministers, vol. 2, pp. 258, 259; Lewis's Sabbath and Sunday, pp. 188–193.

[28] Wood's Athenæ Oxonienses, vol. 4, p. 128.

not to be baptized, and that the Jewish Sabbath ought still to be kept." [29]

Mr. Bampfield published two works in behalf of the seventh day as the Sabbath, one in 1672, the other in 1677. In the first of these he thus sets forth the doctrine of the Sabbath :—

" The law of the seventh-day Sabbath was given before the law was proclaimed at Sinai, even from the creation, given to Adam, . . . and in him to all the world.[30] . . . The Lord Christ's obedience unto this *fourth word* in observing in his life-time the seventh day as a weekly Sabbath-day, . . . and no other day of the week as such, is a part of that perfect righteousness which every sound believer doth apply to himself in order to his being justified in the sight of God ; and every such person is to conform unto Christ in all the acts of his obedience to the ten words." [31]

His brother, Mr. Thomas Bampfield, who had been speaker in one of Cromwell's parliaments, wrote also in behalf of seventh-day observance, and was imprisoned for his religious principles in Ilchester jail.[32] About the time of Mr. Bampfield's first imprisonment, severe persecution arose against the Sabbath-keepers in London. Crosby thus bears testimony :—

" It was about this time [A. D. 1661] that a congregation of Baptists, holding the seventh day as a Sabbath, being assembled at their meeting-house in Bull-stake alley, the doors being open, about three o'clock P. M. [Oct. 19], whilst Mr. John James was preaching, one Justice Chard, with Mr. Wood, an headborough, came into the meeting-place. Wood commanded him in the

---

[29] Crosby, vol. 1, p. 367.　　　[30] Ex. 16:23; Gen. 2:3.

[31] Judgment for the Observation of the Jewish or Seventh-day Sabbath, pp. 6–8, 1672.

[32] Calamy, vol. 2, p. 260.

king's name to be silent and come down, having spoken treason against the king. But Mr. James, taking little or no notice thereof, proceeded in his work. The headborough came nearer to him in the middle of the meeting-place, and commanded him again in the king's name to come down or else he would pull him down; whereupon the disturbance grew so great that he could not proceed." [33]

The officer, having pulled him down from the pulpit, led him away to the court under a strong guard. Mr. Utter continues this narrative as follows:—

"Mr. James was himself examined and committed to Newgate, on the testimony of several profligate witnesses, who accused him of speaking treasonable words against the king. His trial took place about a month afterward, at which he conducted himself in such a manner as to create much sympathy. He was, however, sentenced to be hanged, drawn, and quartered.[34] This awful sentence did not dismay him in the least. He calmly said, 'Blessed be God; whom man condemneth, God justifieth.' While he lay in prison, under sentence of death, many persons of distinction visited him, who were greatly affected by his piety and resignation, and offered to exert themselves to secure his pardon. But he seems to have had little hope of their success. Mrs. James, by advice of her friends, twice presented petitions to the king [Charles II.], setting forth the innocence of her husband, the character of the witnesses against him, and entreating His Majesty to grant a pardon. In both instances she was repulsed with scoffs and ridicule. At the scaffold, on the day of his execution, Mr. James addressed the assembly in a very noble and affecting manner. Having finished his address, and kneeling down, he thanked God for covenant mercies, and for conscious innocence; he prayed for the witnesses against him, for the executioner, for the people of God, for the removal of divisions, for the coming of Christ, for the spectators, and for himself, that

---

[33] Crosby, vol. 2, pp. 165–171.

[34] When asked what he had to say why sentence should not be pronounced, he said he would leave with them these scriptures: Jer. 26:14, 15; Ps. 116:15.

he might enjoy a sense of God's favor and presence, and an entrance into glory.   When he had ended, the executioner said, ' The Lord receive your soul;' to which Mr. James replied, ' I thank thee.'   A friend observing to him, ' This is a happy day,' he answered, ' I bless God it is.'   Then having thanked the sheriff for his courtesy, he said, ' Father, into thy hands I commit my spirit.' . . . After he was dead, his heart was taken out and burned, his quarters were affixed to the gates of the city, and his head was set up in White chapel on a pole opposite to the alley in which his meeting-house stood." [35]

Such was the experience of English Sabbath-keepers in the seventeenth century.   It cost something to obey the fourth commandment in such times as those.   The laws of England during that century were very oppressive to all Dissenters, and bore exceedingly hard upon the Sabbath-keepers.   But God raised up able men, eminent for piety, to defend this truth during those troublous times, and, if need be, to seal their testimony with their blood.   In the seventeenth century, eleven churches of Sabbatarians flourished in England, while many scattered Sabbath-keepers were to be found in various parts of that kingdom.   Now, but three of these churches are in existence; and only remnants, even of these, remain.

To what cause shall we assign this painful fact?   It is not because their adversaries were able to confute their doctrine; for the controversial works on both sides still remain, and speak for themselves.   It is not that they lacked men of piety and of learning; for God gave them these, especially in the seventeenth century.   Nor is it that fanaticism sprang up and disgraced the cause; for there is no record of anything of this kind.   They were cruelly persecuted, but the period of their persecu-

---

[35] Manual, etc., pp. 21–23.

tion was that of their greatest prosperity. Like Moses' bush, they stood unconsumed in the burning fire. The prostration of the Sabbath cause in England is due to none of these things.

The Sabbath was wounded in the house of its own friends. They took upon themselves the responsibility, after a time, of making the Sabbath of no practical importance, and of treating its violation as no very serious transgression of the law of God. Doubtless they hoped to win men to Christ and his truth by this course; but, instead of this, they simply lowered the standard of divine truth into the dust. The Sabbath-keeping ministers assumed the pastoral care of first-day churches, in some cases as their sole charge; in others, they did this in connection with the oversight of Sabbatarian churches. The result need surprise no one; as these Sabbath-keeping ministers and churches said to all men, in thus acting, that the fourth commandment might be broken with impunity, the people took them at their word. Mr. Crosby, a first-day historian, sets this matter in a clear light: —

"If the seventh day ought to be observed as the Christian Sabbath, then all congregations that observe the first day as such must be Sabbath-breakers. . . . I must leave those gentlemen on the contrary side to their own sentiments; and to vindicate the practice of becoming pastors to a people whom in their conscience they must believe to be breakers of the Sabbath." [36]

Doubtless there have been noble exceptions to this course; but the body of English Sabbatarians for many years have failed to discharge faithfully the high trust committed to them.

[36] Crosby's Hist. Eng. Bapt., vol. 3, pp. 138, 139.

CHAPTER XXVII.

THE SABBATH IN AMERICA.

The first Sabbath-keeping church in America—Names of its members—
Origin of the second—Organization of the Seventh-day Baptist
General Conference—Statistics of the denomination at that time—
Nature of its organization—Present statistics—Educational facili-
ties—Missionary work—The American Sabbath Tract Society—Responsibility for the light of the Sabbath—The German S. D. Baptists of Pennsylvania—Reference to Sabbath-keepers in Hungary—
In Siberia—The Seventh-day Adventists—Their origin—Labors of
Joseph Bates—Of James White—The Publishing Association—Systematic Benevolence—The work of the preachers mainly in new
fields—Organization of the S. D. Adventists—Statistics—Peculiarities of their faith—Their object—The S. D. Adventists of Switzerland—Why the Sabbath is of priceless value to mankind—The
nations of the saved observe the Sabbath in the new earth.

T Newport, R. I., originated the first Sabbatarian church in America.   The first Sabbath-
keeper in America was Stephen Mumford,
who left London three years after the martyrdom of
John James, and forty-four years after the landing of
the Pilgrim Fathers at Plymouth.   Mr. Mumford, it appears, came as a missionary from the English Sabbath-
keepers.[1]   Mr. Isaac Backus, the historian of the early
New England Baptists, makes the following record : —

"Stephen Mumford came over from London in 1664, and
brought the opinion with him that the whole of the ten com-

---

[1] "When the London Seventh-day Baptists, in 1664, sent Stephen Mumford
to America, and in 1675 sent Eld. William Gibson, they did as much, in proportion to their ability, as had been done by any society for propagating the gospel
in foreign parts."—*Seventh-day Baptist Memorial*, vol. 1, p. 43.

mandments, as they were delivered from Mount Sinai, were moral and immutable; and that it was the anti-Christian power which thought to change times and laws, that changed the Sabbath from the seventh to the first day of the week. Several members of the first church in Newport embraced this sentiment, and yet continued with the church for some years, until two men and their wives, who had so done, turned back to the keeping of the first day again." [2]

Mr. Mumford, on his arrival, went earnestly to work to convert men to the observance of the fourth commandment, as we infer from the following record :—

"Stephen Mumford, the first Sabbath-keeper in America, came from London in 1664. Taçy Hubbard commenced keeping the Sabbath March 11, 1665; Samuel Hubbard commenced April 1, 1665; Rachel Langworthy, January 15, 1666; Roger Baxter, April 15, 1666; and William Hiscox, April 28, 1666. These were the first Sabbath-keepers in America. A controversy, lasting several years, sprung up between them and members of the church. They desired to retain their connection with the church, but were at last compelled to withdraw, that they might peaceably enjoy and keep God's holy day." [3] [Baxter is Baster in the "S. D. B. Memorial."]

Though Mr. Mumford faithfully taught the truth, he seems to have cherished the ideas of the English Sabbatarians, that it was possible for first-day and seventh-day observers to walk together in church fellowship. Had the first-day people been of the same mind, the light of the Sabbath would have been extinguished within a few years, as the history of English Sabbath-keepers clearly proves. But, in the providence of God, the danger was averted by the opposition which these commandment-keepers had to encounter.

[2] Church History of New England from 1783 to 1796, chap. 11, sec. 10.

[3] History of the S. D. Baptist General Conference, by James Bailey, pp. 237. 238.

Besides the persons above enumerated, four others embraced the Sabbath in 1666, but in 1668 they renounced it. These four were also members of the First-day Baptist church of Newport. Though the Sabbath-keepers who retained their integrity thought that they might lawfully commune with the members of the church who were fully persuaded to observe the first day, yet they felt otherwise with respect to those who had clearly seen the Sabbath, and had for a time observed it, and then apostatized from it. These persons "both wrote and spoke against it, which so grieved them that they could not sit down to the table of the Lord with them, nor with the church because of them." But as they were members of a first-day church, and had "no power to deal with them as of themselves without the help of the church" they "found themselves barred as to proceeding with them, as being but private brethren. So they concluded not to bring the case to the church to judge of the fact, viz., in turning from the observation of the seventh day, being contrary-minded as to that." They therefore sent to the London Sabbath-keepers for advice, and in the meantime refrained from communing with the church.

Dr. Edward Stennet wrote them in behalf of the London Sabbath-keepers: "If the church will hold communion with these apostates from the truth, you ought then to desire to be fairly dismissed from the church; which if the church refuse, you ought to withdraw yourselves." [4] They decided, however, not to leave the church. But they told "the church publicly that they

---

[4] S. D. Baptist Memorial, vol. 1, pp. 27, 28, 29.

could not have comfortable communion with those four persons that had sinned." And thus for several months they walked with little or no offense from the church; after which the leading or ministering brethren began to declare themselves concerning the ten precepts." Mr. Tory "declared the law to be done away." Mr. Luker and Mr. Clarke "made it their work to preach the non-observation of the law, day after day." But the Sabbath-keepers replied that "the ten precepts were still as holy, just, good, and spiritual as ever." Mr. Tory, "with some unpleasant words, said that 'their tune was only the fourth precept,' to which they answered that 'the whole ten precepts were of equal force with them, and that they did not plead for one without the other.' And they for several years went on with the church in a halvish kind of fellowship." [5]

Mr. Bailey thus states the result : —

"At the time of their change of sentiment and practice, [respecting the Bible Sabbath], they had no intention of establishing a church with this distinctive feature. God, evidently, had a different mission for them, and brought them to it through the severe trial of persecution. They were forced to leave the fellowship of the Baptist church, or abandon the Sabbath of the Lord their God." [6]

"These left the Baptist church on December 7, 1671." [7]

"On the 23d of December, just sixteen days after withdrawing from the Baptist church, they covenanted together in a church organization." [8]

Such was the origin of the first Sabbath-keeping

---

[5] Records of the First Baptist Church in Newport, quoted in the S. D. Baptist Memorial, vol. 1, pp. 28–39.

[6] Bailey's History, pp. 9, 10.   [7] Id., p. 237.   [8] Id., p. 238.

church in America.[9]   The second of these churches owes
its origin to this circumstance : About the year 1700,
Edmund Dunham, of Piscataway, N. J., reproved a person for laboring on Sunday.   He was asked for his authority from the Scriptures.   On searching for this, he
became satisfied that the seventh day is the only weekly
Sabbath in the Bible, and began to observe it.

" Soon after, others followed his example, and in 1707 a
Seventh-day Baptist church was organized, with seventeen mem-
bers.   Edmund Dunham was chosen pastor, and sent to Rhode
Island to receive ordination." [10]

The S. D. Baptist General Conference was organized
in 1802.   At its first annual session, it included in its
organization eight churches, nine ordained ministers,
and 1130 members.[11]   The Conference was organized
with only advisory powers, the individual churches retaining the matters of discipline and church government
in their own hands.[12]   The Conference now embraces
some eighty churches, and about eight thousand
members.   These churches are found in most of the
Northern and Western States, and are divided into five
associations, which, however, have no legislative nor dis-
ciplinary power over the churches which compose them.
There are, belonging to the denomination, five acade-
mies, one college, "and a university with academic,
collegiate, mechanical, and theological departments in
operation." [13]   The S. D. Baptist Missionary Society
sustains several home missionaries, who labor principally
on the western and southern borders of the denomina-

---

[9] Manual of the S. D. Baptists, pp. 39, 40; Backus, chap. 11, sec. 10.
[10] History S. D. Baptist General Conference, pp. 15, 238.   [11] Id., pp. 46–55.
[12] Id., pp. 57, 58, 62, 74, 82.   [13] Sabbath and Sunday, p. 232.

tion. They have within a few years past met with a good degree of success in this work. It has also a missionary station at Shanghai, China, and a small church there of faithful Christians.

The American Sabbath Tract Society is the publishing agency of that denomination. Its headquarters are at Alfred Center, N. Y. It publishes the *Sabbath Recorder,* the organ of the S. D. Baptists, and it also publishes a series of valuable works relating to the Sabbath and the law of God.

During the two hundred years which have elapsed since the organization of the first Sabbatarian church in America, God has raised up among this people men of eminent talent and moral worth. He has also, in providential ways, called attention to the sacred trust which he so long since confided to the S. D. Baptists, and which they have been so slow to realize in its immense importance.

Among those converted to the Sabbath through the agency of this people, the name of J. W. Morton is particularly worthy of honorable mention. He was sent in 1847 a missionary to the island of Hayti by the Reformed Presbyterians. Here he came in contact with Sabbatarian publications, and after a serious examination, became satisfied that the seventh day is the Sabbath of the Lord. As an honest man, what he saw to be truth he immediately obeyed, and returning home to be tried for his heresy, was summarily expelled from the Reformed Presbyterian church, without being suffered to state the reasons which had governed his conduct. He has given to the world a valuable work entitled, " Vindication of the True Sabbath," in which his experience is related, and his reasons for observing the seventh day set forth with great force and clearness.

. The S. D. Baptists do not lack men of education and of talent, and they have ample means in their possession with which to sustain the cause of God. If in time past they have not fully realized that they were debtors to all mankind because of the great truth which God committed to their trust, there is reason to believe that they are now, to some extent, awakening to this vast indebtedness.[14]

There is also in the State of Pennsylvania a small body of German S. D. Baptists, found in the counties of Lancaster, York, Franklin, and Bedford, and in the central and western parts of the State. They originated in 1728 from the teaching of Conrad Beissel, a native of Germany. They practice trine immersion, and the washing of feet, and observe open communion. They encourage celibacy, but make it obligatory upon none. Even those who have chosen this manner of life are at liberty to marry if at any time they choose so to do. They established and successfully maintained a Sabbath-school at Ephrata, their head-quarters, forty years before Robert Raikes had introduced the system of Sunday-schools. This people have suffered much persecution because of their observance of the seventh day, the laws of Pennsylvania being particularly oppressive toward Sabbatarians.[15] The German S. D. Baptists do not belong to the S. D. Baptist General Conference.

---

[14] Much interesting matter pertaining to the Seventh-day Baptists of America may be found in Utter's Manual of the S. D. Baptists; Bailey's History of the S. D. Baptist General Conference; Lewis's Sabbath and Sunday; and in the S. D. Baptist Memorial.

[15] Rupp's History of all the Religious Denominations in the United States, pp. 109–123, second edition; Bailey's History General Conference, pp. 255–258.

We have already noticed the fact that Sabbath-keepers are numerous in Russia, in Poland, and in Turkey. We find the following statement concerning Sab-keepers in Hungary : —

"A congregation of seventh-day Christians in Hungary, being refused tolerance by the laws, has embraced Judaism, in order to be allowed to exist in connection with one of the 'received religions.' " [16]

The probability is that as the laws of the Austrian empire bear very heavily upon all religious bodies not belonging to some one of the tolerated sects or orders, these "seventh-day Christians," on "being refused tolerance" in their own name, secured the privilege of observing the seventh day by allowing their doctrine to be classed by the civil authorities under the head of Judaism, and so bringing themselves under the tolerance accorded to the "received religions." We do not say that this was right, even as a technicality, but it is evidently the extent of what they did. There is no reason to believe that they abjured Christ. We also learn that there are Sabbath-keepers in the North of Asia : —

"There is a sect of Greek Christians in Siberia who keep the Jewish Sabbath (Saturday). Such sects already exist in the United States, in Germany, and we believe in England." [17]

The Sabbath was first introduced to the attention of the Adventist people at Washington, N. H. A faithful Seventh-day Baptist sister, Mrs. Rachel D. Preston,[18]

---

[16] New York *Independent*, March 18, 1869.

[17] *Semi-Weekly Tribune*, May 4, 1869.

[18] This sister was born at Vernon, Vt. Her maiden name was Rachel D. Harris. At the age of seventeen she was converted, and soon after joined the Methodist church. After her marriage, she removed with her husband to Central

from the State of New York, having removed to this place, brought with her the Sabbath of the Lòrd. Here she became interested in the doctrine of the glorious advent of the Saviour at hand. Being instructed in this subject by the Adventist people, she in turn instructed them in the commandments of God, and as early as 1844 nearly the entire church in that place, consisting of about forty persons, became observers of the Sabbath of the Lord. The oldest body of Sabbath-keepers among Seventh-day Adventists is therefore at Washington, N. H. Its present number is small, for it has been thinned by emigration and by the ravages of death; but there still remains a small company to bear witness to this ancient truth of the Bible.

From this place, several Adventist ministers received the Sabbath truth during the year 1844. One of these was Elder T. M. Preble, who has the honor of first bringing this great truth before the Adventists through the medium of the press. His essay was dated Feb. 13, 1845. He presented briefly the claims of the Bible Sabbath, and showed that it was not changed by the Saviour, but by the great apostasy. He then said : —

"Thus we see Dan. 7 : 25 fulfilled, the little horn changing 'times and laws.' Therefore it appears to me that all who keep

New York. There, at the age of twenty-eight, she became an observer of the Bible Sabbath. The Methodist minister, her pastor, did what he could to turn her from the Sabbath, but finally told her she might keep it if she would not leave them. But she was faithful to her convictions of duty, and united with the Seventh-day Baptist church of Verona, Oneida Co., N. Y. Her first husband bore the name of Oaks ; her second, that of Preston. She and her daughter, Delight Oaks, were members of the first Verona church at the time of their removal to Washington, N. H. The mother died Feb. 1, 1868 ; the daughter, several years earlier.

the first day for the Sabbath, are Pope's Sunday-keepers and God's Sabbath-breakers." [19]

Within a few months, many persons began to observe the Sabbath as the result of the light thus shed on their pathway. Elder J. B. Cook, a man of decided talent as a preacher and a writer, was one of these early converts to the Sabbath. Elders Preble and Cook were at this time in the full vigor of their mental powers, and were possessed of talent and a reputation for piety which gave them great influence among the Adventists in behalf of the Sabbath. These men were called in the providence of God to fill an important place in the work of Sabbath reform.

But both of them, while preaching and writing in its behalf, committed the fatal error of making it of no practical importance. They had apparently the same fellowship for those who rejected the Sabbath that they had for those who observed it. Such a course of action produced a natural result. After two or three years of this kind of Sabbath observance, each of these men apostatized from it, and thenceforward used what influence they possessed in warring against the fourth commandment. The larger part of those who embraced the Sabbath from their labors were not sufficiently impressed with its importance to become settled and grounded in its weighty evidences, and after a brief period they also turned back from its observance. But enough had been done to excite bitter opposition toward the Sabbath on the part of many Adventists, and to

---

[19] Eld. Preble's article appeared in the *Hope of Israel* of Feb. 28, 1845, published at Portland, Maine. This article was reprinted in the *Advent Review* of Aug. 23, 1870. The article, as rewritten by Eld. Preble and published in tract form, was also printed in the *Review* of Dec. 21, 1869.

bring out the ingenious and plausible arguments by which men attempt to prove that God has abolished his own sacred law.

Such was the fruit of their course, and such the condition of things at the time of their defection. But the result of their plan of action taught the Advent Sabbath-keepers a lesson of value, which they have never forgotten. They learned that the fourth commandment must be treated as a part of the moral law, if men are ever to be led to its sacred observance.

Elder Preble's first article in behalf of the Sabbath was the means of calling the attention of our venerable brother, Joseph Bates, to this divine institution. He soon became convinced of its obligation, and at once began to observe it. He had acted quite a prominent part in the Advent movement of 1843–44, and now, with self-sacrificing zeal, he took hold of the despised Sabbath truth to set it before his fellow-men. He did not do it in the half-way manner of Elders Preble and Cook, but as a man thoroughly in earnest, and fully alive to the importance of his subject.

The subject of the heavenly Sanctuary began about this time to interest many Adventists, and especially Elder Bates. He was one of the first to see that the central object of that Sanctuary is the ark of God. He also called attention to the proclamation of the third angel relative to God's commandments. He girded on the armor to lay it down only when his work should be accomplished. He has been instrumental in leading many to the observance of the commandments of God and the faith of Jesus, and few who have received the Sabbath from his teaching have apostatized from it.[20]

---

[20] He fell asleep March 19, 1872, in the eightieth year of his age.

It was but a few months after Elder Bates, that our esteemed and efficient brother, Elder James White, also embraced the Sabbath. He had labored with much success in the great Advent movement, and he now entered heartily into the work of Sabbath reform. Uniting with Elder Bates in the proclamation of the doctrine of the advent and the Sabbath as connected together in the Sanctuary and the message of the third angel, he has, with the blessing of God, accomplished great results in behalf of the Sabbath.

The publishing interests of the Seventh-day Adventists originated through his instrumentality. He began the work of publishing in 1849, without resources, and with very few friends, but with much toil, self-sacrifice, and anxious care; and with the blessing of God upon his efforts, he has been the means of establishing an efficient office of publication, and of disseminating many important works throughout our country, and, to some extent, to other nations also. The publication of the *Advent Review and Sabbath Herald*, the organ of the Seventh-day Adventists, was commenced by him in 1850. For most of the years of its existence, he has served as one of its editors; and for all its earlier years, he was both sole editor and publisher. During this time he has also labored with energy as a minister of the gospel of Christ.

The wants of the cause demanding an enlargement of capital and more extensive operations, to this end an Association was incorporated in the city of Battle Creek, Michigan, May 3, 1861, under the name of the Seventh-day Adventist Publishing Association. This Association owns three commodious publishing houses, with engine, power presses, and all the fixtures necessary for doing an extensive business. There are about fifty persons constantly employed in this work of publication. The Association has a capital of about $70,000.[1] Under God, it owes its prosperity to the prudent management and untiring energy of Elder James White.

The *Advent Review* has at the present time (Nov., 1873) a circulation of about 5,000 copies. The *Youth's Instructor*, a monthly paper designed for the children of Sabbath-keeping Adventists, began to be issued in 1852, and has now attained a circulation of nearly 5,000 copies.[1]

The *Advent Tidende*, a Danish monthly, with a circulation of 800, is published for the benefit of those who speak the Danish and Norwegian tongues, of whom a considerable number have embraced the Sabbath.[1]

The Seventh-day Adventists have taken a strong interest in the subject of hygiene and the laws of health, and have established a Health Institute at Battle Creek, Mich., which publishes the *Health Reformer*, a monthly journal, magazine form, circulating nearly 5,000 copies.[1]

Numerous publications on prophecy, the signs of the times, the coming of Christ, the Sabbath, the law of God, the sanctuary, etc., have been issued within the past twenty years, and have had an extensive circulation, amounting, in the aggregate, to many millions of pages.

The ordinary financial wants of the cause are sustained by a method of collecting means known as Systematic Benevolence. By this system, it is designed that each friend of the cause shall pay a certain sum weekly proportioned to the property which he possesses;

---

[1] For statistics of 1886, see Appendix.

but there is no compulsion in this matter. In this manner the burden is borne by all, so that it rests heavily upon none; and the means needed for the work flows with a steady stream into the treasury of the several churches, and finally into that of the State Conferences. A settlement is instituted each year at the State Conferences, in which the labors, receipts, and expenditures of each minister are carefully considered. Thus none are allowed to waste means, and none who are recognized as called to the ministry are allowed to suffer.

The churches sustain their meetings for the most part without the aid of preaching. They raise means to sustain the servants of Christ, but bid them mainly devote their time and strength to save those who have not the light of these important truths shining upon their pathway. So they go out everywhere, preaching the word of God, as his providence guides their feet. During the summer months, the work in new fields is carried forward principally by means of large tents, which enable the preacher to provide a suitable place of worship wherever he may think it desirable to labor.

The Seventh-day Adventists have thirteen State Conferences, which assemble annually in their respective States. These bear the names of Maine, Vermont, New England, New York and Pennsylvania, Ohio, Michigan, Indiana, Illinois, Wisconsin, Minnesota, Iowa, Missouri and Kansas, and California.[1] These Conferences are designed to meet the local wants of the cause. There is also a General Conference, which assembles yearly, composed of delegates from the State Conferences. This Conference takes the general oversight of the work in all

---

[1] For statistics of 1886, see Appendix.

the State Conferences, supplying the more destitute with laborers as far as possible, and uniting the whole strength of the body for the accomplishment of the work. It also takes the charge of missionary labor in those States which have no organized Conferences.

There are about fifty ministers who devote their whole time to the work of the gospel. There is also a considerable number who preach a portion of the time, and devote the remainder to secular labor. There are about 6,000 members in the several Conference organizations; but such is the scattered condition of this people (for they are found in all the Northern States and in several of the Southern), that a very large portion have no connection with its organization. They are to be found in single families, scattered all the way from Maine to California and Oregon. The *Review* and the *Instructor* constitute, in a great number of cases, the only preachers of their faith.

Those subjects which more especially interest this people, are the fulfillment of prophecy, the second personal advent of the Saviour as an event now near at hand, immortality through Christ alone, a change of heart through the operation of the Holy Spirit, the observance of the Sabbath of the fourth commandment, the divinity and mediatorial work of Christ, and the development of a holy character by obedience to the perfect and holy law of God. [21]

They are very strict with regard to the ordinance of baptism, believing not only that it requires men to be buried in the watery grave, but that even such baptism

---

[21] For a further knowledge of their views, see their weekly paper, the *Advent Review and Sabbath Herald*, published at Battle Creek, Michigan, at $2.00 per year, and the list of publications advertised at the close of this volume.

is faulty if administered to those who are breaking one of the ten commandments. They also believe that our Lord's direction in John 13 should be observed in connection with the supper.

They teach that the gifts of the Spirit which are set forth in 1 Cor. 12 and Eph. 4, were designed to remain in the church till the end of time. They believe that these were lost in consequence of the same apostasy that changed the Sabbath. They also believe that in the final restoration of the commandments by the work of the third angel, the gifts of the Spirit of God are restored with them. So the remnant of the church, or the last generation of its members, is said to "keep the commandments of God, and have the testimony of Jesus Christ."[22] And the angel of God explains this by saying, "The testimony of Jesus is the spirit of prophecy."[23] The spirit of prophecy, therefore, has a distinct place assigned to it in the final work of Sabbath reform. Such are their views of this portion of scripture; and their history from the beginning has been marked by the influence of this sacred gift.

In the face of strong opposition, the people known as Seventh-day Adventists have arisen to bear their testimony for the Sabbath of the Lord. They have had perils from open foes and from false brethren; but they have thus far overcome the difficulties of the way, and from each have gathered strength for the conflict before them. They have a definite work which they hope to accomplish: it is to make ready a people prepared for the advent of the Lord.

Honorable mention should be made of the Seventh-

---

[22] Rev. 12 : 17 ; 14 : 12.   [23] Rev. 19 : 10.

day Adventists of Switzerland. They first learned these precious truths from Elder M. B. Czechowski, who a few years since instructed them in the commandments of God and the faith of Jesus. Since his labors with them ceased, God has given them strength to stand with firmness for his truth, and has added to their numbers. They have a heart to obey the truth, and to sacrifice for its advancement. They number about sixty persons. There are also a few individuals of this faith in Italy, Germany, and Denmark.

The observance of the Sabbath is sometimes advocated on the ground that man needs a day of rest, and will grow prematurely old if he labors seven days in each week, which is doubtless true ; and it has also been advocated on the ground that God will bless in basket and store those who hallow his Sabbath, which may be true in many cases ; but the Bible does not urge motives of this kind in respect to this sacred institution. Without doubt there are great incidental advantages in the observance of the Sabbath. But these are not what God sets before us as the reasons for its observance. The true reason is infinitely higher than all considerations of this kind, and should constrain men to obey, even were it certain that it would cost them all that is dear in the present life.

The Sabbath has been advocated on the ground that it secures to men a day for divine worship, in which, by common consent, they may appear before God. This is a very important consideration, and yet the Bible says little concerning it. It is one of the incidental blessings of the Sabbath, and not the chief reason for its observance. The Sabbath was ordained to commemorate the creation of the heavens and the earth.

The importance of the Sabbath as a memorial of creation is that it keeps ever present the true reason why worship is due to God; for the worship of God is based upon the fact that he is the Creator, and that all other beings were created by him. The Sabbath, therefore, lies at the very foundation of divine worship, for it teaches this great truth in the most impressive manner, and no other institution does this. The true ground of divine worship, not of that on the seventh day merely, but of all worship, is found in the distinction between the Creator and his creatures. This great fact can never become obsolete, and must never be forgotten. To keep it in man's mind, God gave to him the Sabbath. He received it in his innocency, and notwithstanding the perversity of his professed people, God has preserved this sacred institution through the entire period of man's fallen state.

The four and twenty elders, in the very act of worshiping Him who sits upon the throne, state the reason why worship is due to God : —

"Thou art worthy, O Lord, to receive glory and honor and power; for thou hast created all things, and for thy pleasure they are and were created." [24]

This great truth is therefore worthy to be remembered even in the glorified state. And we shall presently learn that what God gave to man in Paradise, to keep this great truth before his mind, shall be honored by him in Paradise restored.

The future is given to us in the prophetic Scriptures. From them we learn that our earth is reserved unto

---

[24] Rev. 4 : 10, 11.

fire, and that from its ashes shall spring new heavens and earth, and ages of endless date.[25]   Over this glorified inheritance the second Adam, the Lord of the Sabbath, shall bear rule, and under his gracious protection the nations of them which are saved shall inherit the land forever.[26]   When the glory of the Lord shall thus fill the earth as the waters cover the sea, the Sabbath of the Most High is again and for the last time brought to view : —

"For as the new heavens and the new earth, which I will make, shall remain before me, saith the Lord, so shall your seed and your name remain.   And it shall come to pass, that from one new moon to another, and from one Sabbath to another, shall all flesh come to worship before, me saith the Lord." [27]

---

[25] 2 Pet. 3 ; Isa. 65 ; Rev. 21 ; 22.   Milton thus states this doctrine : —

> "The world shall burn, and from her ashes spring
> New heaven and earth, wherein the just shall dwell,
> And after all their tribulations long
> See golden days, fruitful of golden deeds,
> With joy and love triumphing, and fair truth."
>
> —*Paradise Lost*, book 3, lines 334–338.

> "So shall the world go on,
> To good malignant, to bad men benign,
> Under her own weight groaning, till the day
> Appear of respiration to the just,
> And vengeance to the wicked, at return
> Of Him so lately promised to thy aid,
> The woman's Seed obscurely then foretold,
> Now ampler known thy Saviour and thy Lord,
> Last in the clouds from heaven to be revealed
> In glory of the Father, to dissolve
> Satan with his perverted world, then raise
> From the conflagrant mass, purged and refined,
> New heavens, new earth, ages of endless date
> Founded in righteousness and peace and love,
> To bring forth fruits, joy and eternal bliss."
>
> —*Id.*, book 12, lines 537–551.

[26] Dan. 7 : 9, 10, 13, 14, 17–27 ; Ps. 2 : 7–9 ; 37 : 9–11, 18–22, 34 ; Mal. 4 : 1–3.   [27] Isa. 66 : 22, 23.

Does not Paul refer to these very facts set forth by Isaiah when he says, " There remaineth therefore a rest [Greek, *Sabbatismos*, literally " A KEEPING OF THE SAB- BATH "] to the people of God" ?[28] The reason for this monthly gathering to the New Jerusalem of all the host of the redeemed from every part of the new earth, may be found in the language of the Apocalypse : —

" And he showed me a pure river of water of life, clear as crystal, proceeding out of the throne of God and of the Lamb. In the midst of the street of it, and on either side of the river was there the tree of life, which bare twelve manner of fruits, and yielded her fruit every month ; and the leaves of the tree were for the healing [literally, the service] [29] of the nations."[30]

The gathering of the nations that are saved to the presence of the Creator, from the whole face of the new earth, on each successive Sabbath, attests the sacredness of the Sabbath even in that holy state, and sets the seal of the Most High to the perpetuity of this ancient institution.

---

[28] Heb. 4 : 9. The margin renders it " a keeping of a Sabbath." Liddell and Scott define *Sabbatismos* "a keeping of the Sabbath." They give no other defini- tion, but derive it from the verb *Sabbatizo*, which they define by these words only, "to keep the Sabbath." Schrevelius defines *Sabbatismos* by this one phrase, " ob- servance of the Sabbath." He also derives it from *Sabbatizo*. *Sabbatismos* is therefore the noun in Greek which signifies the *act of Sabbath-keeping*, while *Sab- batizo*, from which it is derived, is the verb which expresses that act.

[29] See the Lexicons of Liddell and Scott, Schrevelius, and Greenfield.

[30] Rev. 22 : 1, 2.

APPENDIX.

IN presenting this, the third edition of the "History of the Sabbath," to the public, it falls to the lot of the publishers to announce the sad fact that the eminent and devoted author of the foregoing work has been called to rest from his earthly labors.

JOHN NEVINS ANDREWS was born in Poland, Cumberland Co., Maine, on the 22d day of July, 1828. Though young in years, he was an active participant in the great Advent movement of 1843–44, to which he alludes on page 508. At the same time that Elder James White and wife commenced the observance of the seventh day as the Sabbath, he also adopted the same views and practice. Being a very thorough Bible student, and endowed with a discerning mind and quick understanding, he immediately perceived, not only the position of commanding importance which the Sabbath occupies in the Scriptures, abstractly considered, but also its vital relation to the fulfillment of prophecy in the last days as connected with the subjects of the sanctuary and the third message of Revelation 14. From that time to the close of his labors, his pen was ever busy in defense of these doctrines; and many times his opponents have had reason to quail before the crushing blows of his logic, and the friends of the truth to rejoice in the clear presentation of the views so dear to them. His numerous works, in review of opponents, and in behalf of the subjects of the fulfillment of prophecy, the second coming of Christ, the sanctuary, messages, law, and Sabbath, have perhaps contributed more than any other human agency to the rapid spread of their views. Meanwhile he was a constant contributor to the periodicals of the denomination, and a welcome preacher in all parts of the field. He served for many years on the General Conference Committee, and, for a time, as Editor of the *Review and Herald.* He was connected with that paper almost from the time of the commencement of its publication. He was either editor or associate editor from 1855 until the time of his death.

He has left, however, as his greatest work, the "History of the Sabbath," to which, for a period of ten years, he devoted the most thorough and conscientious research. Previous to the commencement of his investigations, about the year 1854, but little had been done in this direction as relating to the seventh-day Sabbath; and the testimony then accessible was of the most meager and unsatisfactory kind. With his work, a new mine was opened, and a new interest was created in the subject. For more than twenty years the testimony of this volume has been before the world. A consuming desire to break down its evidence has gnawed at the vitals of many of the opponents of the Sabbath; but how to do it has been with them the perplexing question; for facts are things which the mass of people still regard with a good degree of respect. And some men in public places have thrown over their names a lasting stain, by attempting simply to sneer it out of existence. The fossil remains of the historical forgeries in behalf of first-day observance, so fully exposed in this work, are still handed out by some who would fain appear to their fellow-men as theological teachers, but who are either themselves ignorant of the facts in the case, or presume upon the ignorance of their hearers. But the light is shining; and there are many who will not close their eyes thereto.

Reference is made on page 514 to the Seventh-day Adventists of Switzerland. After the publication of what is there said of them, in 1873, the interest in this work so increased among them that it was determined to open a mission in that country ; and Elder Andrews was appointed to take charge of it, sailing for his new field, Sept. 15, 1874. He soon made himself proficient in the French and German languages, and in July, 1876, commenced the publication of a monthly French journal, *Les Signes des Temps*, at Basel, Switzerland. To the interests of this paper, and the work in the European field, he assiduously devoted himself till his decease, Oct. 21, 1883. The number of believers in the whole European field reported to the General Conference in 1885, was 826.

In 1885 a large building for the publishing work and for meeting purposes, was erected 'at Basel, at a cost of $25,000. From this office are issued the French journal *Les Signes des Temps*, now 16 pages, semi-monthly; the *Herold der Wahrheit*, German, 16 pages, monthly; *L'Ultimo Messagio*, Italian, .16 pages, quarterly; and *Adevarulu Present*, in the Roumanian language, 16 pages, quarterly.

At Christiana, Norway, a publishing house, with meeting hall above, was erected in 1885, at a cost of $11,000. From this office are issued four monthly journals, two devoted to the religious views of Seventh-day Adventists, in the Danish and Swedish languages; and two devoted to health and temperance in the same languages.

An office of publication is also established at Great Grimsby, England, from which is issued an 8-page semi-monthly journal, called *The Present Truth*, devoted to the teaching of Sabbath views to the people of England, Scotland, Ireland, and Wales. Eight laborers are now engaged in that field, publishing the paper, holding meetings in tents and in halls, doing ship-missionary work, holding Bible-readings, etc. A laborer has also gone to Russia, where numbers are embracing the doctrine of the Sabbath.

Early in 1885 a mission to Australia was planned, and in May of that year, a company, under the supervision of Elder S. N. Haskell, departed for that distant field, and began active operations. As the result, at the time of this writing, July, 1886, a church of upwards of one hundred members has been established in Melbourne, some fifty in New Zealand have adopted the same views, and a 16-page monthly journal, called the *Bible Echo and Signs of the Times*, published in the city of Melbourne, has already reached its seventh number.

Returning to the home field, we have to record a rapid growth in the cause of Sabbath reform since the last edition of this work was issued, in 1873, as compared with the statistics of that date, given on pages 509-512. The capital of the Publishing Association, at Battle Creek, Mich., has increased from $70,000 to $250,000; the number of hands employed has grown from 50 to 115; additions to the buildings have more than doubled the room, giving now an aggregate of upwards of 30,000 square feet of floor space, devoted to the various branches of the work. The circulation of the *Review* has nearly doubled; the *Instructor* has become a weekly, with a circulation of nearly 13,000; the *Tidende* (Danish) circulates 2,400 copies semi-monthly; the *Good Health* (formerly *Health Reformer*) issues about 6,000 copies monthly; in 1874 a journal in the Swedish language, *Sanningens Harold*, was started, which has now reached a circulation of about 3,000; in 1878 the publication of a paper in the German language, called *Stimme der Wahrheit* (Voice of Truth) was commenced as a monthly, and now, as a semi-monthly, has a subscription list of between two and three thousand. In 1886 an 8-page semi-monthly journal, called the *Gospel Sickle*, designed for a certain branch of the missionary work, was commenced, and now circulates about 12,000 copies at each issue.

Of bound books, tracts, and pamphlets, the central office in Michigan issued in 1885, 27,800,000 pages, and the sales during the same period amounted to $61,785.78. The whole number of pages issued from this office alone since its establishment is 353,104,698.

In June, 1874, Elder James White commenced the publication of the *Signs of the Times* in Oakland, California. In April, 1875, a publishing house was established, and incorporated under the laws of the State. The special object of this incorporation was the publication of this paper, which has been issued weekly since that time. The business name of this institution is the "Pacific Press," and its capital stock is now (1886) $100,000. Its facilities have been increased as the work increased, and for business purposes it has an aggregate of over 25,000 square feet of floor space, and employs over one hundred hands in its various departments. The *Signs of the Times* was, from its beginning, intended for a missionary or "pioneer" paper, and is the organ of the International Tract and Missionary Society. In 1884 it was enlarged to a 16-page paper. The average circulation for the year ending Jan. 1, 1886, was 21,000 copies weekly.

In January, 1886, the *Signs* Office commenced the publication of the *American Sentinel* (monthly), designed to defend the principles of the American Constitution, guaranteeing the right of any one to observe the seventh day, and to labor the other six days,—a right which, by certain misguided parties, is now seriously threatened. The *Sentinel* has already (September, 1886) a circulation of about 12,000 copies each issue.

This office also publishes the *Pacific Health Journal and Temperance Advocate*, a 32-page bi-monthly journal, devoted to the cause of health and temperance.

Besides publishing these papers, the *Signs* Office has printed 13,183,000 pages of bound books, pamphlets, and tracts during the past year.

Something has also been done by this people in the direction of education. Battle Creek College was established in 1875. A new building has been erected the past year, increasing its capacity to five hundred students. The property is valued at $75,000. A college was started at Healdsburg, California, in 1882, with a property valuation of $50,000 and a capacity for some 300 students. In October, 1884, an Academy was dedicated at South Lancaster, Mass., with a property valuation of $40,000, and a capacity for 200 students. Besides these there are a number of local and church schools in various parts of the field. All the educational institutions are patronized to the full extent of their facilities to accommodate students.

On page 510 mention is made of the Health Institute established at Battle Creek in 1866. A large building was opened for patients in 1878. In 1884 another large addition was made to the building to accommodate the growing demand for larger capacity. It now has accommodations for 400 patients, and is largely patronized. Hundreds have received their first knowledge of Sabbath truth at this institution, and many have embraced it. At St. Helena, Cal., there is another health institution, called the Rural Health Retreat, conducted on the same general principles, and beginning to have a large patronage.

Tent-meetings are resorted to more and more extensively as a means of bringing Sabbath truth to the attention of the people. Some one hundred and twenty-five meetings of this kind are held each year. General gatherings of the people are accomplished by means of camp-meetings, of which fifty were held in

1885, securing an aggregate attendance of not less than 125,000 persons.

The method of raising means formerly known as "Systematic Benevolence," has been reduced to a more clearly defined and better understood system of tithing, by which one-tenth of every one's personal income is set apart to the support of the ministry. The amount of funds from this source was, in 1885, $122,641.69.

There are now twenty-four State Conferences in the United States, and four in foreign countries, making twenty-eight in all. Churches have increased to 741, and the membership to about 25,000. One hundred and eighty-six ministers, and one hundred and fifty-one licentiates, are laboring with voice and pen to promulgate the work of Sabbath reform, besides a large number who are going out from the schools and other organizations to act as canvassers for books and periodicals, colporters, Bible-readers, etc. Upwards of 15,000,000 pages of books, and about 12,000,000 copies of periodicals were circulated the past year, the distribution reaching every civilized country on the globe.

The claims of another important branch of religious work have not been entirely overlooked, namely, the organization and maintenance of Sabbath-schools. In the denomination there are now twenty-five State Sabbath-school Associations, and the aggregate membership is not far from 20,500.

Much of this growth is due to the organization known as the Tract and Missionary Society; and so important a place has this filled in the work, that it is entitled to more extended mention. The general organization takes the name of "The International Tract and Missionary Society." To the President of this Society we are indebted for the following sketch of the origin and progress of this branch of the work :—

The history of the Tract and Missionary societies among Seventh-day Adventists can be told in a few words, and yet very much might be related respecting the extent and results of their operations, which are seen in all parts of the world.

The origin of our Tract societies was very remarkable. In the summer of 1865, one of our sisters living in Lancaster, Mass., proposed to another sister, both in feeble health, that they should have a season of prayer for God to bless their efforts in extending a knowledge of the Sabbath reform. At that time they only had in contemplation one season of prayer; but they experienced so much of the blessing of God that they decided to meet the following Wednesday. The fruit apparent from the feeble efforts which they put forth, and the fact that much of the Spirit of God attended these seasons of prayer, led them to meet regularly at 3 P. M. on Wednesday of every week. Their number soon embraced all the sisters observing the Sabbath in the place. At this time the entire number of Sabbath-keepers in the immediate vicinity was but eight. Although no series of sermons has ever been given here, general meetings have been held from time to time, and the church now numbers one hundred and fifty. These weekly prayer-meetings continued for four years, when a Vigilant Missionary Society was organized. Those engaged in the work in Lancaster also secured the co-operation of friends in different parts of the country, who labored, by correspondence and the distribution of reading matter, to awaken an interest wherever they could find openings. In the summer of 1869, Elder James White learned of their efforts, and as it was customary for him to encourage every such enterprise, he made to this Society the first donation of publications which they ever received. It consisted of over a bushel of tracts and pamphlets for free distribution. The following year, in November, 1870, the friends of the cause organized the first Conference Tract Society among the Seventh-day Adventists at New Ipswich, New Hampshire. This organization included four of the New England States. Its object was to encourage all, old and young, to engage in missionary labor, by visiting and praying with families, and sending out reading matter, etc. Their efforts were not confined to any one section of the country, nor to their acquaintances; but wherever they could secure addresses of individuals, they sent reading matter, with letters calling attention to the same.

From this commencement, State organizations were effected in New York, Ohio, Michigan, and finally in all Seventh-day Adventist Conferences in America. A correspondence was opened with lonely Sabbath-keepers both in Europe and America, and through them publications were distributed in all parts of the world. Each Conference Tract Society has its regular officers, consisting of a president, vice-president, secretary, who also acts as treasurer, and a board of directors, corresponding in number to the districts into which the Conference is divided, each one having charge of the district in which he lives.

Every lawful means has been taken to bring the light of the Sabbath reform before the people, including the sale of denominational books by agents, the work of the colporter in visiting families, holding Bible-readings, and distributing reading matter, besides the mailing of publications and other labor performed by members of the Society. The work has opened up in Europe, even among believers who have never seen those of like faith, and through correspondence they have been led to engage in missionary work in the localities where they live. In every place where missions are now permanently established, with the exception of Basel, Switzerland, the interest was first awakened by this means.

In 1874, the International Tract and Missionary Society was organized. This Society embraces all of the State organizations, and is designed to take the general oversight of the work done by them to fill openings for labor where there are no Conference organizations, and to seek the co-operation of other societies in the distribution of literature which treats on the Sabbath reform and the speedy coming of our Lord.

To enumerate the openings and the special providences which have been over the work, would require a volume as large as this book. There is no civilized nation on the globe where reading matter, accompanied with correspondence, has not been sent. And in South America, the islands of the Atlantic and Pacific oceans, and in different parts of Europe, there are scores who observe the Sabbath as the result of this effort, who have never seen one of like faith from America. Those who embrace the truth are at once made use of as instruments to give it to others. During the past year (1885), statistics show that more has been accomplished by the Tract and Missionary societies than ever before, in the same length of time.

City missions have been opened, or missionary operations entered upon, in all the larger cities of the United States; and in many others there are individuals, not observers of the seventh day, who co-operate with us in placing the literature of the Sabbath reform before the people.

With very few exceptions, the vessels that leave New York City, Liverpool, Boston, Providence, Savannah, New Orleans, San Francisco, Portland (Oregon), Chicago, and Baltimore take with them our publications, and exchange reading matter with the vessels they meet on the ocean. Packages are left at the ports to which they sail.

In addition to what is sent by mail, twenty-six barrels of publications were freighted from South Lancaster, Mass., to various missions established by other religious bodies, who use the publications the same as they are used by Seventh-day Adventists. So thorough has been this work that there is not a town, in some of the territories, to which publications have not been sent, and there are counties in different parts of the country, where the Sabbath reform has never been preached, in which the address of every family has been taken, and in connection with proper correspondence, publications have been sent to them from six weeks to three months.

The literature used in this work is exclusively that published by Seventh-day Adventists, and their periodicals are printed not only in English, but in the Swedish, Danish, German, French, Italian, and Roumanian languages. Each one of these periodicals is taken by individuals and societies in clubs of from five up to thirty-five hundred copies, and are re-mailed or otherwise distributed by those receiving them. There is scarcely a State or Territory in the United States in which we have no Conference organized where there are not persons who have received the Sabbath by publications thus sent. Many of them have never seen a preacher or received a visit from any Seventh-day Adventist.

Sea-captains have been known to embrace the truth, and it is reported that in some cases entire ships' crews have commenced the observance of the Sabbath. They received the light in the ports which they entered, by having publications placed on board their vessels. Bible-readings are held on board vessels by our colporters at different ports.

There seems to be a power with the truth that gives success to the feeblest effort when put forth in the right direction. There are twenty-five Conference Tract Societies in America; one in England, whose operations extend over Scotland, Ireland, and Wales; one which embraces the three Scandinavian countries; and one established at Basel, Switzerland, which extends its operations through all Central Europe.

The statistics of our Tract Society for the year ending Oct. 1, 1885, show over 10,000 members. The reading matter distributed since the organization of the Society amounts to over 184,240,000 pages. We have placed over eight thousand volumes of bound books in the principal libraries of this country. This has been at an expense of over $6,000. As one of the results of these moves, individuals in different parts of the country are daily becoming interested in the Sabbath reform. The number of believers who observe the Bible Sabbath, and who are looking for the second coming of Christ, cannot be estimated. In 1884, at one of our Southern camp-meetings, it was learned that there were believers in a portion of the State where none of our ministers had ever been. Upon visiting the place, there were found over sixty keeping the Sabbath in a few counties. Thus it is in many localities; and these results may be traced directly to the tract and missionary work.

It may be proper to add that Seventh-day Adventists understand certain prophecies to foreshadow a great crisis in this country and in the world, touching the Sabbath question, as we draw near the end of all things,—a crisis which will cause those who adhere to the Sabbath, to do so in the face of opposition, legal enactment, and civil penalties, such as those have had to meet, who, in the worst ages of the world, have adhered to the true religion in preference to the false. They are equally confident that the beginnings of this revolution are already seen. The wide-spread agitation for a better Sunday observance, the introduction of this question into the field of politics, the linking of it with the temperance and other great reforms, the operations of the National Reform Association, whose object is to

secure such an amendment to the Constitution of the United
States that under it the most rigid enactments for Sunday keeping can be strictly enforced, and meanwhile the exposure of the
scriptural bankruptcy of the Sunday institution by those who
are keeping the seventh day,—all these things are rapidly drawing the line between the friends and foes of the Sabbath, throw-
ing the latter in some instances into a position of bitter hostility
to the seventh day, or rather to those who observe it.   In some
States attempts are beginning to be made to enforce such laws
as they have against Sunday labor, and in other States to secure
laws more strict than now exist, and to abolish every exemption
clause that now stands in favor of those who observe the seventh day.   Such an exemption clause was lately stricken from
the statute book in Arkansas.   Accordingly in October, 1885,
five members of a church in Washington county were indicted
by the grand jury for violating the law of that State which pro-
hibits Sunday labor.   These were quiet, unostentatious believers,
and their labor was such that it would be impossible for any one
who wished to keep the first day to be disturbed by it.   Yet
these persons were brought to trial at the term of the court that
convened at Fayetteville, Ark., Nov. 2, 1885.   The trial excited
great interest.   A verdict of guilty was rendered, and a sentence
of fine or imprisonment pronounced.   By stipulation one case
was made a test case, and appeal taken thereupon to the Supreme Court of the State.   The decision of the lower court was
confirmed, and now several other persons are in jail, serving out
fines for the same offense.

In Tennessee the same scenes have been enacted.   Appeal
was taken to the Supreme Court of that State, and the decision
of the lower court was sustained.   The sentence was a fine of
$20 and costs, or imprisonment at 25 cents a day till the whole
sum was covered.

In Georgia, Sabbath-keepers have been imprisoned, and in
Pennsylvania fined, for quietly pursuing their labor on the first
day of the week, after having conscientiously kept the seventh
day.   These things seem to be the beginning of the very devel-
opments which S. D. Adventists have long expected in fulfillment of prophecy, and serve to confirm them in the correctness

34

of their position, and in the expectation of other events soon to follow.

Cherishing, as they do, a firm belief that the close of human probation is at hand, and that this dispensation is soon to close in the personal revelation of the Son of God in the clouds of heaven, they have an incentive to earnestness and activity such as no people have ever had. Hence they constantly seek to carry forward their work on broader plans, and to enlarge continually their field of operations, in order that, so far as in their power, the world may be warned of events which they believe to be now impending, and be admonished in regard to the moral duties which God requires at their hands.

INDEX TO AUTHORS QUOTED.

INDEX OF SCRIPTURES.

INDEX OF SUBJECTS.

3 Messages of Revelation 14

J. N. Andrews account of Revelation, Chapter 14, in which we find the 3 angel's message, which is being heralded around the world.

The Sanctuary and 2300 Days

J. N. Andrews's pamphlet reflects his later study of this doctrine.

Other Titles from TEACH Services, Inc.

J. N. Andrews: Flame for the Lord

The biography of J. N. Andrews, a young man who became an Adventist, itinerant preacher, and clarified doctrine on the Sabbath for the new church.

The Judgment

J. N. Andrew's classic study on The Judgment, outlining its events and their order explains Christian beliefs from scriptures.

Meek and Mighty The Man Moses

A compilation of Ellen G. White's writings on the life of Moses from *The Signs of the Times* and *Patriarchs and Prophets*.

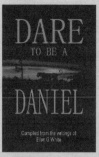

Dare to be a Daniel

A compilation of Ellen G. White's writings from *The Youth's Instructor* and other sources on the life of Daniel.

Other Titles from TEACH Services, Inc.

The Youth's Instructor Articles

A compilation of about 470 of Ellen G. White's articles that were originally published (1852–1914) in magazine form. Facsimile.

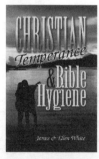

Christian Temperance & Bible Hygiene

This collection of writings by James and Ellen G. White will both inspire and instruct you in temperance and hygiene from a Biblical point of view.